CIVIL PROCEDURE

Constitution, Statutes, Rules, and Supplemental Materials—2022

CIVIL PROCEDURE

Constitution, Statutes, Rules, and Supplemental Materials—2022

Allan Ides

Loyola Law School
Christopher N. May Professor of Law

Christopher N. May

Loyola Law School
Professor Emeritus of Law

Simona Grossi

Loyola Law School
Professor of Law
Theodore A. Bruinsma Fellow

To contact Customer Service, e-mail customer.service@aspenpublishing.com, call 1-800-950-5259, or mail correspondence to:

Aspen Publishing
Attn: Order Department
PO Box 990
Frederick, MD 21705

Printed in the United States of America.

1 2 3 4 5 6 7 8 9 0

ISBN 978-1-5438-5824-2

About Aspen Publishing

Aspen Publishing is a leading provider of educational content and digital learning solutions to law schools in the U.S. and around the world. Aspen provides best-in-class solutions for legal education through authoritative textbooks, written by renowned authors, and breakthrough products such as Connected eBooks, Connected Quizzing, and PracticePerfect.

The Aspen Casebook Series (famously known among law faculty and students as the "red and black" casebooks) encompasses hundreds of highly regarded textbooks in more than eighty disciplines, from large enrollment courses, such as Torts and Contracts to emerging electives such as Sustainability and the Law of Policing. Study aids such as the *Examples & Explanations* and the *Emanuel Law Outlines* series, both highly popular collections, help law students master complex subject matter.

Major products, programs, and initiatives include:

- **Connected eBooks** are enhanced digital textbooks and study aids that come with a suite of online content and learning tools designed to maximize student success. Designed in collaboration with hundreds of faculty and students, the Connected eBook is a significant leap forward in the legal education learning tools available to students.

- **Connected Quizzing** is an easy-to-use formative assessment tool that tests law students' understanding and provides timely feedback to improve learning outcomes. Delivered through CasebookConnect.com, the learning platform already used by students to access their Aspen casebooks, Connected Quizzing is simple to implement and integrates seamlessly with law school course curricula.

- **PracticePerfect** is a visually engaging, interactive study aid to explain commonly encountered legal doctrines through easy-to-understand animated videos, illustrative examples, and numerous practice questions. Developed by a team of experts, PracticePerfect is the ideal study companion for today's law students.

- The **Aspen Learning Library** enables law schools to provide their students with access to the most popular study aids on the market across all of their courses. Available through an annual subscription, the online library consists of study aids in e-book, audio, and video formats with full text search, note-taking, and highlighting capabilities.

- Aspen's **Digital Bookshelf** is an institutional-level online education bookshelf, consolidating everything students and professors need to ensure success. This program ensures that every student has access to affordable course materials from day one.

- **Leading Edge** is a community centered on thinking differently about legal education and putting those thoughts into actionable strategies. At the core of the program is the Leading Edge Conference, an annual gathering of legal education thought leaders looking to pool ideas and identify promising directions of exploration.

CONTENTS

PART I. CONSTITUTION, STATUTES, AND RULES   1

Selected Provisions of the Constitution of the
United States of America   3

Selected Code Provisions   9

Federal Rules of Civil Procedure   55

Federal Rules of Appellate Procedure   165

PART II. SUPPLEMENTAL MATERIALS   219

     I.   Pleadings and Related Motions   221

     II.   Personal Jurisdiction   223

     III.   Service of Process and Notice   251

     IV.   Subject Matter Jurisdiction   257

     V.   Venue, Transfer, and *Forum Non Conveniens*   261

     VIII.   Joinder of Claims and Parties   263

     IX.   Class Actions   283

     XII.   Appellate Review   285

     XIII.   The Binding Effect of a Final Judgment   299

PART I

CONSTITUTION, STATUTES, AND RULES

SELECTED PROVISIONS OF THE CONSTITUTION OF THE UNITED STATES OF AMERICA

Article I

Section 8. The Congress shall have Power To lay and collect Taxes, Duties, Imposts and Excises, to pay the Debts and provide for the common Defence and general Welfare of the United States; but all Duties, Imposts and Excises shall be uniform throughout the United States;

To borrow Money on the credit of the United States;

To regulate Commerce with foreign Nations, and among the several States, and with the Indian Tribes;

To establish an uniform Rule of Naturalization, and uniform Laws on the subject of Bankruptcies throughout the United States;

…

To promote the Progress of Science and useful Arts, by securing for limited Times to Authors and Inventors the exclusive Right to their respective Writings and Discoveries;

To constitute Tribunals inferior to the supreme Court;

To define and punish Piracies and Felonies committed on the high Seas, and Offences against the Law of Nations;

To declare War, grant Letters of Marque and Reprisal, and make Rules concerning Captures on Land and Water;

To raise and support Armies, but no Appropriation of Money to that Use shall be for a longer Term than two Years;

To provide and maintain a Navy;

To make Rules for the Government and Regulation of the land and naval Forces;

To provide for calling forth the Militia to execute the Laws of the Union, suppress Insurrections and repel Invasions;

…

To exercise exclusive Legislation in all Cases whatsoever, over such District (not exceeding ten Miles square) as may, by Cession of particular States, and the Acceptance of Congress, become the Seat of the Government of the United States, and to exercise like Authority over all Places purchased by the Consent of the Legislature of the State in which the Same shall be, for the Erection of Forts, Magazines, Arsenals, dock-Yards, and other needful Buildings;—And

To make all Laws which shall be necessary and proper for carrying into Execution the foregoing Powers, and all other Powers vested by this Constitution in the Government of the United States, or in any Department or Officer thereof....

Article III

Section 1. The judicial Power of the United States, shall be vested in one supreme Court, and in such inferior Courts as the Congress may from time to time ordain and establish. The Judges, both of the supreme and inferior Courts, shall hold their Offices during good Behaviour, and shall, at stated Times, receive for their Services, a Compensation, which shall not be diminished during their Continuance in Office.

Section 2. The judicial Power shall extend to all Cases, in Law and Equity, arising under this Constitution, the Laws of the United States, and Treaties made, or which shall be made, under their Authority;—to all Cases affecting Ambassadors, other public Ministers and Consuls;—to all Cases of admiralty and maritime Jurisdiction;—to Controversies to which the United States shall be a Party;—to Controversies between two or more States;—between a State and Citizens of another State;—between Citizens of different States;—between Citizens of the same State claiming Lands under Grants of different States, and between a State, or the Citizens thereof, and foreign States, Citizens or Subjects.

In all Cases affecting Ambassadors, other public Ministers and Consuls, and those in which a State shall be Party, the supreme Court shall have original Jurisdiction. In all the other Cases before mentioned, the supreme Court shall have appellate Jurisdiction, both as to Law and Fact, with such Exceptions, and under such Regulations as the Congress shall make.

The Trial of all Crimes, except in Cases of Impeachment, shall be by Jury; and such Trial shall be held in the State where the said Crimes shall have been committed; but when not committed within any State, the Trial shall be at such Place or Places as the Congress may by Law have directed.

Section 3. Treason against the United States, shall consist only in levying War against them, or in adhering to their Enemies, giving them Aid and Comfort. No Person shall be convicted of Treason unless on the Testimony of two Witnesses to the same overt Act, or on Confession in open Court.

The Congress shall have Power to declare the Punishment of Treason, but no Attainder of Treason shall work Corruption of Blood, or Forfeiture except during the Life of the Person attainted.

Article IV

Section 1. Full Faith and Credit shall be given in each State to the public Acts, Records, and judicial Proceedings of every other State. And the Congress may by general Laws prescribe the Manner in which such Acts, Records, and Proceedings shall be proved, and the Effect thereof.

Section 2. The Citizens of each State shall be entitled to all Privileges and Immunities of Citizens in the several States....

Article V

The Congress, whenever two thirds of both Houses shall deem it necessary, shall propose Amendments to this Constitution, or, on the Application of the Legislatures of two thirds of the several States, shall call a Convention for proposing Amendments, which, in either Case, shall be valid to all Intents and Purposes, as Part of this Constitution, when ratified by the Legislatures of three fourths of the several States, or by Conventions in three fourths thereof, as the one or the other Mode of Ratification may be proposed by the Congress; Provided that no Amendment which may be made prior to the Year One thousand eight hundred and eight shall in any Manner affect the first and fourth Clauses in the Ninth Section of the first Article; and that no State, without its Consent, shall be deprived of its equal Suffrage in the Senate.

Article VI

All Debts contracted and Engagements entered into, before the Adoption of this Constitution, shall be as valid against the United States under this Constitution, as under the Confederation.

This Constitution, and the Laws of the United States which shall be made in Pursuance thereof; and all Treaties made, or which shall be made, under the Authority of the United States, shall be the supreme Law of the Land; and the Judges in every State shall be bound thereby, any Thing in the Constitution or Laws of any State to the Contrary notwithstanding.

The Senators and Representatives before mentioned, and the Members of the several State Legislatures, and all executive and judicial Officers, both of the United States and of the several States, shall be bound by Oath or Affirmation, to support this Constitution; but no religious Test shall ever be required as a Qualification to any Office or public Trust under the United States.

Amendment I

Congress shall make no law respecting an establishment of religion, or prohibiting the free exercise thereof; or abridging the freedom of speech, or of the press; or the right of the people peaceably to assemble, and to petition the government for a redress of grievances.

Amendment IV

The right of the people to be secure in their persons, houses, papers, and effects, against unreasonable searches and seizures, shall not be violated, and no warrants shall issue, but upon probable cause, supported by oath or affirmation, and particularly describing the place to be searched, and the persons or things to be seized.

Amendment V

No person shall be held to answer for a capital, or otherwise infamous crime, unless on a presentment or indictment of a grand jury, except in cases arising in the land or naval forces, or in the militia, when in actual service in time of war or public danger; nor shall any person be subject for the same offense to be twice put in jeopardy of life or limb; nor shall be compelled in any criminal case to be a witness against himself, nor be deprived of life, liberty, or property, without due process of law; nor shall private property be taken for public use, without just compensation.

Amendment VII

In suits at common law, where the value in controversy shall exceed twenty dollars, the right of trial by jury shall be preserved, and no fact tried by a jury, shall be otherwise reexamined in any court of the United States, than according to the rules of the common law.

Amendment IX

The enumeration in the Constitution, of certain rights, shall not be construed to deny or disparage others retained by the people.

Amendment X

The powers not delegated to the United States by the Constitution, nor prohibited by it to the states, are reserved to the states respectively, or to the people.

Amendment XI

The judicial power of the United States shall not be construed to extend to any suit in law or equity, commenced or prosecuted against one of the United States by citizens of another state, or by citizens or subjects of any foreign state.

Amendment XIV

Section 1. All persons born or naturalized in the United States, and subject to the jurisdiction thereof, are citizens of the United States and of the state wherein they reside. No state shall make or enforce any law which shall abridge the privileges or immunities of citizens of the United States; nor shall any state deprive any person of life, liberty, or property, without due process of law; nor deny to any person within its jurisdiction the equal protection of the laws....

Section 5. The Congress shall have power to enforce, by appropriate legislation, the provisions of this article.

...

SELECTED CODE PROVISIONS

(28 U.S.C.)

Procedural

§1253. Direct Appeals from Decisions of Three-Judge Courts

Except as otherwise provided by law, any party may appeal to the Supreme Court from an order granting or denying, after notice and hearing, an interlocutory or permanent injunction in any civil action, suit or proceeding required by any Act of Congress to be heard and determined by a district court of three judges.

§1254. Courts of Appeals; Certiorari; Certified Questions

Cases in the courts of appeals may be reviewed by the Supreme Court by the following methods:

(1) By writ of certiorari granted upon the petition of any party to any civil or criminal case, before or after rendition of judgment or decree;

(2) By certification at any time by a court of appeals of any question of law in any civil or criminal case as to which instructions are desired, and upon such certification the Supreme Court may give binding instructions or require the entire record to be sent up for decision of the entire matter in controversy.

§1257. State Courts; Certiorari

(a) Final judgments or decrees rendered by the highest court of a State in which a decision could be had, may be reviewed by the Supreme Court by writ of certiorari where the validity of a treaty or statute of the United States is drawn in question or where the validity of a statute of any State is drawn in question on the ground of its being repugnant to the Constitution, treaties, or laws of the United States, or where any title, right, privilege, or immunity is specially set up or claimed under the Constitution or the treaties or statutes of, or any commission held or authority exercised under, the United States.

(b) For the purposes of this section, the term "highest court of a State" includes the District of Columbia Court of Appeals.

§1291. Final Decisions of District Courts

The courts of appeals (other than the United States Court of Appeals for the Federal Circuit) shall have jurisdiction of appeals from all final decisions of the district courts of the United States, the United States District Court for the District of the Canal Zone, the District Court of Guam, and the District Court of the Virgin Islands, except where a direct review may be had in the Supreme Court. The jurisdiction of the United States Court of Appeals for the Federal Circuit shall be limited to the jurisdiction described in sections 1292(c) and (d) and 1295 of this title.

§1292. Interlocutory Decisions

(a) Except as provided in subsections (c) and (d) of this section, the courts of appeals shall have jurisdiction of appeals from:

(1) Interlocutory orders of the district courts of the United States, the United States District Court for the District of the Canal Zone, the District Court of Guam, and the District Court of the Virgin Islands, or of the judges thereof, granting, continuing, modifying, refusing or dissolving injunctions, or refusing to dissolve or modify injunctions, except where a direct review may be had in the Supreme Court;

(2) Interlocutory orders appointing receivers, or refusing orders to wind up receiverships or to take steps to accomplish the purposes thereof, such as directing sales or other disposals of property;

(3) Interlocutory decrees of such district courts or the judges thereof determining the rights and liabilities of the parties to admiralty cases in which appeals from final decrees are allowed.

(b) When a district judge, in making in a civil action an order not otherwise appealable under this section, shall be of the opinion that such order involves a controlling question of law as to which there is substantial ground for difference of opinion and that an immediate appeal from the order may materially advance the ultimate termination of the litigation, he shall so state in writing in such order. The Court of Appeals which would have jurisdiction of an appeal of such action may thereupon, in its discretion, permit an appeal to be taken from such order, if application is made to it within ten days after the entry of the order: *Provided, however,* That application for an appeal hereunder shall not stay proceedings in the district court unless the district judge or the Court of Appeals or a judge thereof shall so order.

(c) The United States Court of Appeals for the Federal Circuit shall have exclusive jurisdiction—

(1) of an appeal from an interlocutory order or decree described in subsection (a) or (b) of this section in any case over which the court would have jurisdiction of an appeal under section 1295 of this title; and

(2) of an appeal from a judgment in a civil action for patent infringement which would otherwise be appealable to the United States Court of Appeals for the Federal Circuit and is final except for an accounting.

(d)

(1) When the chief judge of the Court of International Trade issues an order under the provisions of section 256(b) of this title, or when any judge of the Court of International Trade, in issuing any other interlocutory order, includes in the order a statement that a controlling question of law is involved with respect to which there is a substantial ground for difference of opinion and that an immediate appeal from that order may materially advance the ultimate termination of the litigation, the United States Court of Appeals for the Federal Circuit may, in its discretion, permit an appeal to be taken from such order, if application is made to that Court within ten days after the entry of such order.

(2) When the chief judge of the United States Court of Federal Claims issues an order under section 798(b) of this title, or when any judge of the United States Claims Court [United States Court of Federal Claims], in issuing an interlocutory order, includes in the order a statement that a controlling question of law is involved with respect to which there is a substantial ground for difference of opinion and that an immediate appeal from that order may materially advance the ultimate termination of the litigation, the United States Court of Appeals for the Federal Circuit may, in its discretion, permit an appeal to be taken from such order, if application is made to that Court within ten days after the entry of such order.

(3) Neither the application for nor the granting of an appeal under this subsection shall stay proceedings in the Court of International Trade or in the Claims Court [Court of Federal Claims], as the case may be, unless a stay is ordered by a judge of the Court of International Trade or of the Claims Court [Court of Federal Claims] or by the United States Court of Appeals for the Federal Circuit or a judge of that court.

(4)

(A) The United States Court of Appeals for the Federal Circuit shall have exclusive jurisdiction of an appeal from an interlocutory order of a district court of the United States, the District Court of Guam, the District Court of the Virgin Islands, or the District Court for the Northern Mariana Islands, granting or denying, in whole or in part, a motion to transfer an action to the United States Claims Court [United States Court of Federal Claims] under section 1631 of this title.

(B) When a motion to transfer an action to the Claims Court [Court of Federal Claims] is filed in a district court, no further proceedings shall be taken in the district court until 60 days after the court has ruled upon the motion. If an appeal is taken from the district court's grant or denial of the motion, proceedings shall be further stayed until the appeal has been decided by the Court of Appeals for the Federal Circuit. The stay of proceedings in the district court shall not bar the granting of preliminary or injunctive relief, where appropriate and where expedition is reasonably necessary. However, during the period in which proceedings are stayed as provided in this subparagraph, no transfer to the Claims Court [Court of Federal Claims] pursuant to the motion shall be carried out.

(e) The Supreme Court may prescribe rules, in accordance with section 2072 of this title, to provide for an appeal of an interlocutory decision to the courts of appeals that is not otherwise provided for under subsection (a), (b), (c), or (d).

§1295. Jurisdiction of the United States Court of Appeals for the Federal Circuit

(a) The United States Court of Appeals for the Federal Circuit shall have exclusive jurisdiction—

(1) of an appeal from a final decision of a district court of the United States, the United States District Court for the District of the Canal Zone, the District Court of Guam, the District Court of the Virgin Islands, or the District Court for the Northern Mariana Islands, if the jurisdiction of that court was based, in whole or in part, on section 1338 of this title except that a case involving a claim arising under any Act of Congress relating to copyrights, exclusive rights in mask works, or trademarks and no other claims under section 1338(a) shall be governed by sections 1291, 1292, and 1294 of this title;

(2) of an appeal from a final decision of a district court of the United States, the United States District Court for the District of the Canal Zone, the District Court of Guam, the District Court of the Virgin Islands, or the District Court for the Northern Mariana Islands, if the jurisdiction of that court was based, in whole or in part, on section 1346 of this title except that jurisdiction of an appeal in a case brought in a district court under section 1346(a)(1), 1346(b), 1346(e), or 1346(f) of this title or under section 1346(a)(2) when the claim is founded upon an Act of Congress or a regulation of an executive department providing for internal revenue shall be governed by sections 1291, 1292, and 1294 of this title;

(3) of an appeal from a final decision of the United States Claims Court [United States Court of Federal Claims];

(4) of an appeal from a decision of—

(A) the Board of Patent Appeals and Interferences of the United States Patent and Trademark Office with respect to patent applications and interferences, at the instance of an applicant for a patent or any party to a patent interference, and any such appeal shall waive the right of such applicant or party to proceed under section 145 or 146 of title 35;

(B) the Under Secretary of Commerce for Intellectual Property and Director of the United States Patent and Trademark Office or the Trademark Trial and Appeal Board with respect to applications for registration of marks and other proceedings as provided in section 21 of the Trademark Act of 1946 (15 U.S.C. 1071); or

(C) a district court to which a case was directed pursuant to section 145, 146, or 154(b) of title 35;

(5) of an appeal from a final decision of the United States Court of International Trade;

(6) to review the final determinations of the United States International Trade Commission relating to unfair practices in import trade, made under section 337 of the Tariff Act of 1930 (19 U.S.C. 1337);

(7) to review, by appeal on questions of law only, findings of the Secretary of Commerce under U.S. note 6 to subchapter X of chapter 98 of the Harmonized Tariff Schedule of the United States (relating to importation of instruments or apparatus);

(8) of an appeal under section 71 of the Plant Variety Protection Act (7 U.S.C. 2461);

(9) of an appeal from a final order or final decision of the Merit Systems Protection Board, pursuant to sections 7703(b)(1) and 7703(d) of title 5;

(10) of an appeal from a final decision of an agency board of contract appeals pursuant to section 8(g)(1) of the Contract Disputes Act of 1978 (41 U.S.C. 607(g)(1));

(11) of an appeal under section 211 of the Economic Stabilization Act of 1970;

(12) of an appeal under section 5 of the Emergency Petroleum Allocation Act of 1973;

(13) of an appeal under section 506(c) of the Natural Gas Policy Act of 1978; and

(14) of an appeal under section 523 of the Energy Policy and Conservation Act.

(b) The head of any executive department or agency may, with the approval of the Attorney General, refer to the Court of Appeals for the Federal Circuit for judicial review any final decision rendered by a board of contract appeals pursuant to the terms of any contract with the United States awarded by that department or agency which the head of such department or agency has concluded is not entitled to finality pursuant to the review standards specified in section 10(b) of the Contract Disputes Act of 1978 (41 U.S.C. 609(b)). The head of each executive department or agency shall make any referral under this section within one hundred and twenty days after the receipt of a copy of the final appeal decision.

(c) The Court of Appeals for the Federal Circuit shall review the matter referred in accordance with the standards specified in section 10(b) of the Contract Disputes Act of 1978. The court shall proceed with judicial review on the administrative record made before the board of contract appeals on matters so referred as in other cases pending in such court, shall determine the issue of finality of the appeal decision, and shall, if appropriate, render judgment thereon, or remand the matter to any administrative or executive body or official with such direction as it may deem proper and just.

§1330.　Actions Against Foreign States

(a) The district courts shall have original jurisdiction without regard to amount in controversy of any nonjury civil action against a foreign state as defined in section 1603(a) of this title as to any claim for relief in personam with respect to which the foreign state is not entitled to immunity either under sections 1605-1607 of this title or under any applicable international agreement.

(b) Personal jurisdiction over a foreign state shall exist as to every claim for relief over which the district courts have jurisdiction under subsection (a) where service has been made under section 1608 of this title.

(c) For purposes of subsection (b), an appearance by a foreign state does not confer personal jurisdiction with respect to any claim for relief not arising out of any transaction or occurrence enumerated in sections 1605-1607 of this title.

§1331.　Federal Question

The district courts shall have original jurisdiction of all civil actions arising under the Constitution, laws, or treaties of the United States.

§1332.　Diversity of Citizenship; Amount in Controversy; Costs

(a) The district courts shall have original jurisdiction of all civil actions where the matter in controversy exceeds the sum or value of $75,000, exclusive of interest and costs, and is between—

(1) citizens of different States;

(2) citizens of a State and citizens or subjects of a foreign state, except that the district courts shall not have original jurisdiction under this subsection of an action between citizens of a State and citizens or subjects of a foreign state who are lawfully admitted for permanent residence in the United States and are domiciled in the same State;

(3) citizens of different States and in which citizens or subjects of a foreign state are additional parties; and

(4) a foreign state, defined in section 1603(a) of this title, as plaintiff and citizens of a State or of different States.

(b) Except when express provision therefor is otherwise made in a statute of the United States, where the plaintiff who files the case originally in the Federal courts is finally adjudged to be entitled to recover less than the sum or value of $75,000, computed without regard to any setoff or counterclaim to which the defendant may be adjudged to be entitled, and exclusive of interest and costs, the district court may deny costs to the plaintiff and, in addition, may impose costs on the plaintiff.

(c) For the purposes of this section and section 1441 of this title—

(1) a corporation shall be deemed to be a citizen of every State and foreign state by which it has been incorporated and of the State or foreign state where it has its principal place of business, except that in any direct action against the insurer of a policy or contract of liability insurance, whether incorporated or unincorporated, to which action the insured is not joined as a party-defendant, such insurer shall be deemed a citizen of—

(A) every State and foreign state of which the insured is a citizen;

(B) every State and foreign state by which the insurer has been incorporated; and

(C) the State or foreign state where the insurer has its principal place of business; and

(2) the legal representative of the estate of a decedent shall be deemed to be a citizen only of the same State as the decedent, and the legal representative of an infant or incompetent shall be deemed to be a citizen only of the same State as the infant or incompetent.

(d)

(1) In this subsection—

(A) the term "class" means all of the class members in a class action;

(B) the term "class action" means any civil action filed under rule 23 of the Federal Rules of Civil Procedure or similar State statute or rule of judicial procedure authorizing an action to be brought by 1 or more representative persons as a class action;

(C) the term "class certification order" means an order issued by a court approving the treatment of some or all aspects of a civil action as a class action; and

(D) the term "class members" means the persons (named or unnamed) who fall within the definition of the proposed or certified class in a class action.

(2) The district courts shall have original jurisdiction of any civil action in which the matter in controversy exceeds the sum or value of $5,000,000, exclusive of interest and costs, and is a class action in which—

(A) any member of a class of plaintiffs is a citizen of a State different from any defendant;

(B) any member of a class of plaintiffs is a foreign state or a citizen or subject of a foreign state and any defendant is a citizen of a State; or

(C) any member of a class of plaintiffs is a citizen of a State and any defendant is a foreign state or a citizen or subject of a foreign state.

(3) A district court may, in the interests of justice and looking at the totality of the circumstances, decline to exercise jurisdiction under paragraph (2) over a class action in which greater than one-third but less than two-thirds of the members of all proposed plaintiff classes in the aggregate and the primary defendants are citizens of the State in which the action was originally filed based on consideration of—

(A) whether the claims asserted involve matters of national or interstate interest;

(B) whether the claims asserted will be governed by laws of the State in which the action was originally filed or by the laws of other States;

(C) whether the class action has been pleaded in a manner that seeks to avoid Federal jurisdiction;

(D) whether the action was brought in a forum with a distinct nexus with the class members, the alleged harm, or the defendants;

(E) whether the number of citizens of the State in which the action was originally filed in all proposed plaintiff classes in the aggregate is substantially larger than the number of citizens from any other State, and the citizenship of the other members of the proposed class is dispersed among a substantial number of States; and

(F) whether, during the 3-year period preceding the filing of that class action, 1 or more other class actions asserting the same or similar claims on behalf of the same or other persons have been filed.

(4) A district court shall decline to exercise jurisdiction under paragraph (2)—

(A)

(i) over a class action in which—

(I) greater than two-thirds of the members of all proposed plaintiff classes in the aggregate are citizens of the State in which the action was originally filed;

(II) at least 1 defendant is a defendant—

(aa) from whom significant relief is sought by members of the plaintiff class;

(bb) whose alleged conduct forms a significant basis for the claims asserted by the proposed plaintiff class; and

(cc) who is a citizen of the State in which the action was originally filed; and

(III) principal injuries resulting from the alleged conduct or any related conduct of each defendant were incurred in the State in which the action was originally filed; and

(ii) during the 3-year period preceding the filing of that class action, no other class action has been filed asserting the same or similar factual allegations against any of the defendants on behalf of the same or other persons; or

(B) two-thirds or more of the members of all proposed plaintiff classes in the aggregate, and the primary defendants, are citizens of the State in which the action was originally filed.

(5) Paragraphs (2) through (4) shall not apply to any class action in which —

(A) the primary defendants are States, State officials, or other governmental entities against whom the district court may be foreclosed from ordering relief; or

(B) the number of members of all proposed plaintiff classes in the aggregate is less than 100.

(6) In any class action, the claims of the individual class members shall be aggregated to determine whether the matter in controversy exceeds the sum or value of $5,000,000, exclusive of interest and costs.

(7) Citizenship of the members of the proposed plaintiff classes shall be determined for purposes of paragraphs (2) through (6) as of the date of filing of the complaint or amended complaint, or, if the case stated by the initial pleading is not subject to Federal jurisdiction, as of the date of service by plaintiffs of an amended pleading, motion, or other paper, indicating the existence of Federal jurisdiction.

(8) This subsection shall apply to any class action before or after the entry of a class certification order by the court with respect to that action.

(9) Paragraph (2) shall not apply to any class action that solely involves a claim —

(A) concerning a covered security as defined under 16(f)(3) of the Securities Act of 1933 (15 U.S.C. 78p(f)(3)) and section 28(f)(5)(E) of the Securities Exchange Act of 1934 (15 U.S.C. 78bb(f)(5)(E));

(B) that relates to the internal affairs or governance of a corporation or other form of business enterprise and that arises under or by virtue of the laws of the State in which such corporation or business enterprise is incorporated or organized; or

(C) that relates to the rights, duties (including fiduciary duties), and obligations relating to or created by or pursuant to any security (as defined under section 2(a)(1) of the Securities Act of 1933 (15 U.S.C. 77b(a)(1)) and the regulations issued thereunder).

(10) For purposes of this subsection and section 1453, an unincorporated association shall be deemed to be a citizen of the State where it has its principal place of business and the State under whose laws it is organized.

(11)

(A) For purposes of this subsection and section 1453, a mass action shall be deemed to be a class action removable under paragraphs (2) through (10) if it otherwise meets the provisions of those paragraphs.

(B)

(i) As used in subparagraph (A), the term "mass action" means any civil action (except a civil action within the scope of section 1711(2)) in which monetary relief claims of 100 or more persons are proposed to be tried jointly on the ground that the plaintiffs' claims involve common questions of law or fact, except that jurisdiction shall exist only over those plaintiffs whose claims in a mass action satisfy the jurisdictional amount requirements under subsection (a).

(ii) As used in subparagraph (A), the term "mass action" shall not include any civil action in which—

(I) all of the claims in the action arise from an event or occurrence in the State in which the action was filed, and that allegedly resulted in injuries in that State or in States contiguous to that State;

(II) the claims are joined upon motion of a defendant;

(III) all of the claims in the action are asserted on behalf of the general public (and not on behalf of individual claimants or members of a purported class) pursuant to a State statute specifically authorizing such action; or

(IV) the claims have been consolidated or coordinated solely for pretrial proceedings.

(C)

(i) Any action(s) removed to Federal court pursuant to this subsection shall not thereafter be transferred to any other court pursuant to section 1407, or the rules promulgated thereunder, unless a majority of the plaintiffs in the action request transfer pursuant to section 1407.

(ii) This subparagraph will not apply—

(I) to cases certified pursuant to rule 23 of the Federal Rules of Civil Procedure; or

(II) if plaintiffs propose that the action proceed as a class action pursuant to rule 23 of the Federal Rules of Civil Procedure.

(D) The limitations periods on any claims asserted in a mass action that is removed to Federal court pursuant to this subsection shall be deemed tolled during the period that the action is pending in Federal court.

(e) The word "States," as used in this section, includes the Territories, the District of Columbia, and the Commonwealth of Puerto Rico.

§1333. Admiralty, Maritime and Prize Cases

The district courts shall have original jurisdiction, exclusive of the courts of the States, of:

(1) Any civil case of admiralty or maritime jurisdiction, saving to suitors in all cases all other remedies to which they are otherwise entitled.

(2) Any prize brought into the United States and all proceedings for the condemnation of property taken as prize.

§1334.   Bankruptcy Cases and Proceedings

(a) Except as provided in subsection (b) of this section, the district courts shall have original and exclusive jurisdiction of all cases under title 11.

(b) Except as provided in subsection (e)(2), and notwithstanding any Act of Congress that confers exclusive jurisdiction on a court or courts other than the district courts, the district courts shall have original but not exclusive jurisdiction of all civil proceedings arising under title 11, or arising in or related to cases under title 11.

(c)

(1) Except with respect to a case under chapter 15 of title 11, nothing in this section prevents a district court in the interest of justice, or in the interest of comity with State courts or respect for State law, from abstaining from hearing a particular proceeding arising under title 11 or arising in or related to a case under title 11.

(2) Upon timely motion of a party in a proceeding based upon a State law claim or State law cause of action, related to a case under title 11 but not arising under title 11 or arising in a case under title 11, with respect to which an action could not have been commenced in a court of the United States absent jurisdiction under this section, the district court shall abstain from hearing such proceeding if an action is commenced, and can be timely adjudicated, in a State forum of appropriate jurisdiction.

(d) Any decision to abstain or not to abstain made under subsection (c) (other than a decision not to abstain in a proceeding described in subsection (c)(2)) is not reviewable by appeal or otherwise by the court of appeals under section 158(d), 1291, or 1292 of this title or by the Supreme Court of the United States under section 1254 of this title. Subsection (c) and this subsection shall not be construed to limit the applicability of the stay provided for by section 362 of title 11, United States Code, as such section applies to an action affecting the property of the estate in bankruptcy.

(e) The district court in which a case under title 11 is commenced or is pending shall have exclusive jurisdiction—

(1) of all the property, wherever located, of the debtor as of the commencement of such case, and of property of the estate; and

(2) over all claims or causes of action that involve construction of section 327 of title 11, United States Code, or rules relating to disclosure requirements under section 327.

§1335. Interpleader

(a) The district courts shall have original jurisdiction of any civil action of interpleader or in the nature of interpleader filed by any person, firm, or corporation, association, or society having in his or its custody or possession money or property of the value of $500 or more, or having issued a note, bond, certificate, policy of insurance, or other instrument of value or amount of $500 or more, or providing for the delivery or payment or the loan of money or property of such amount or value, or being under any obligation written or unwritten to the amount of $500 or more, if

(1) Two or more adverse claimants, of diverse citizenship as defined in subsection (a) or (d) of section 1332 of this title, are claiming or may claim to be entitled to such money or property, or to any one or more of the benefits arising by virtue of any note, bond, certificate, policy or other instrument, or arising by virtue of any such obligation; and if

(2) the plaintiff has deposited such money or property or has paid the amount of or the loan or other value of such instrument or the amount due under such obligation into the registry of the court, there to abide the judgment of the court, or has given bond payable to the clerk of the court in such amount and with such surety as the court or judge may deem proper, conditioned upon the compliance by the plaintiff with the future order or judgment of the court with respect to the subject matter of the controversy.

(b) Such an action may be entertained although the titles or claims of the conflicting claimants do not have a common origin, or are not identical, but are adverse to and independent of one another.

§1338. Patents, Plant Variety Protection, Copyrights, Mask Works, Designs, Trademarks, and Unfair Competition

(a) The district courts shall have original jurisdiction of any civil action arising under any Act of Congress relating to patents, plant variety protection, copyrights and trademarks. Such jurisdiction shall be exclusive of the courts of the states in patent, plant variety protection and copyright cases.

(b) The district courts shall have original jurisdiction of any civil action asserting a claim of unfair competition when joined with a substantial and related claim under the copyright, patent, plant variety protection or trademark laws.

(c) Subsections (a) and (b) apply to exclusive rights in mask works under chapter 9 of title 17, and to exclusive rights in designs under chapter 13 of title 17, to the same extent as such subsections apply to copyrights.

§1343. Civil Rights and Elective Franchise

(a) The district courts shall have original jurisdiction of any civil action authorized by law to be commenced by any person:

(1) To recover damages for injury to his person or property, or because of the deprivation of any right or privilege of a citizen of the United States, by any act done in furtherance of any conspiracy mentioned in section 1985 of Title 42;

(2) To recover damages from any person who fails to prevent or to aid in preventing any wrongs mentioned in section 1985 of Title 42 which he had knowledge were about to occur and power to prevent;

(3) To redress the deprivation, under color of any State law, statute, ordinance, regulation, custom or usage, of any right, privilege or immunity secured by the Constitution of the United States or by any Act of Congress providing for equal rights of citizens or of all persons within the jurisdiction of the United States;

(4) To recover damages or to secure equitable or other relief under any Act of Congress providing for the protection of civil rights, including the right to vote.

(b) For purposes of this section—

(1) the District of Columbia shall be considered to be a State; and

(2) any Act of Congress applicable exclusively to the District of Columbia shall be considered to be a statute of the District of Columbia.

§1346. United States as Defendant

(a) The district courts shall have original jurisdiction, concurrent with the United States Claims Court [United States Court of Federal Claims], of:

(1) Any civil action against the United States for the recovery of any internal-revenue tax alleged to have been erroneously or illegally assessed or collected, or any penalty claimed to have been collected without authority or any sum alleged to have been excessive or in any manner wrongfully collected under the internal-revenue laws;

(2) Any other civil action or claim against the United States, not exceeding $10,000 in amount, founded either upon the Constitution, or any Act of Congress, or any regulation of an executive department, or upon any express or implied contract with the United States, or for liquidated or unliquidated damages in cases not sounding in tort, except that the district courts shall not have jurisdiction of any civil action or claim against the United States founded upon any express or implied contract with the United States or for liquidated or unliquidated damages in cases not sounding in tort which are subject to sections 8(g)(1) and 10(a)(1) of the Contract Disputes Act of 1978. For the

purpose of this paragraph, an express or implied contract with the Army and Air Force Exchange Service, Navy Exchanges, Marine Corps Exchanges, Coast Guard Exchanges, or Exchange Councils of the National Aeronautics and Space Administration shall be considered an express or implied contract with the United States.

(b)

(1) Subject to the provisions of chapter 171 of this title, the district courts, together with the United States District Court for the District of the Canal Zone and the District Court of the Virgin Islands, shall have exclusive jurisdiction of civil actions on claims against the United States, for money damages, accruing on and after January 1, 1945, for injury or loss of property, or personal injury or death caused by the negligent or wrongful act or omission of any employee of the Government while acting within the scope of his office or employment, under circumstances where the United States, if a private person, would be liable to the claimant in accordance with the law of the place where the act or omission occurred.

(2) No person convicted of a felony who is incarcerated while awaiting sentencing or while serving a sentence may bring a civil action against the United States or an agency, officer, or employee of the Government, for mental or emotional injury suffered while in custody without a prior showing of physical injury.

(c) The jurisdiction conferred by this section includes jurisdiction of any set-off, counterclaim, or other claim or demand whatever on the part of the United States against any plaintiff commencing an action under this section.

(d) The district courts shall not have jurisdiction under this section of any civil action or claim for a pension.

(e) The district courts shall have original jurisdiction of any civil action against the United States provided in section 6226, 6228(a), 7426, or 7428 (in the case of the United States district court for the District of Columbia) or section 7429 of the Internal Revenue Code of 1954.

(f) The district courts shall have exclusive original jurisdiction of civil actions under section 2409a to quiet title to an estate or interest in real property in which an interest is claimed by the United States.

(g) Subject to the provisions of chapter 179, the district courts of the United States shall have exclusive jurisdiction over any civil action commenced under section 453(2) of title 3, by a covered employee under chapter 5 of such title.

§1359. Parties Collusively Joined or Made

A district court shall not have jurisdiction of a civil action in which any party, by assignment or otherwise, has been improperly or collusively made or joined to invoke the jurisdiction of such court.

§1367.　Supplemental Jurisdiction

(a) Except as provided in subsections (b) and (c) or as expressly provided otherwise by Federal statute, in any civil action of which the district courts have original jurisdiction, the district courts shall have supplemental jurisdiction over all other claims that are so related to claims in the action within such original jurisdiction that they form part of the same case or controversy under Article III of the United States Constitution. Such supplemental jurisdiction shall include claims that involve the joinder or intervention of additional parties.

(b) In any civil action of which the district courts have original jurisdiction founded solely on section 1332 of this title, the district courts shall not have supplemental jurisdiction under subsection (a) over claims by plaintiffs against persons made parties under Rule 14, 19, 20, or 24 of the Federal Rules of Civil Procedure, or over claims by persons proposed to be joined as plaintiffs under Rule 19 of such rules, or seeking to intervene as plaintiffs under Rule 24 of such rules, when exercising supplemental jurisdiction over such claims would be inconsistent with the jurisdictional requirements of section 1332.

(c) The district courts may decline to exercise supplemental jurisdiction over a claim under subsection (a) if—

(1) the claim raises a novel or complex issue of State law,

(2) the claim substantially predominates over the claim or claims over which the district court has original jurisdiction,

(3) the district court has dismissed all claims over which it has original jurisdiction, or

(4) in exceptional circumstances, there are other compelling reasons for declining jurisdiction.

(d) The period of limitations for any claim asserted under subsection (a), and for any other claim in the same action that is voluntarily dismissed at the same time as or after the dismissal of the claim under subsection (a), shall be tolled while the claim is pending and for a period of 30 days after it is dismissed unless State law provides for a longer tolling period.

(e) As used in this section, the term "State" includes the District of Columbia, the Commonwealth of Puerto Rico, and any territory or possession of the United States.

§1369.　Multiparty, Multiforum Jurisdiction

(a) In general. The district courts shall have original jurisdiction of any civil action involving minimal diversity between adverse parties that arises from a single accident, where at least 75 natural persons have died in the accident at a discrete location, if—

(1) a defendant resides in a State and a substantial part of the accident took place in another State or other location, regardless of whether that defendant is also a resident of the State where a substantial part of the accident took place;

(2) any two defendants reside in different States, regardless of whether such defendants are also residents of the same State or States; or

(3) substantial parts of the accident took place in different States.

(b) Limitation of jurisdiction of district courts. The district court shall abstain from hearing any civil action described in subsection (a) in which—

(1) the substantial majority of all plaintiffs are citizens of a single State of which the primary defendants are also citizens; and

(2) the claims asserted will be governed primarily by the laws of that State.

(c) Special rules and definitions. For purposes of this section—

(1) minimal diversity exists between adverse parties if any party is a citizen of a State and any adverse party is a citizen of another State, a citizen or subject of a foreign state, or a foreign state as defined in section 1603(a) of this title;

(2) a corporation is deemed to be a citizen of any State, and a citizen or subject of any foreign state, in which it is incorporated or has its principal place of business, and is deemed to be a resident of any State in which it is incorporated or licensed to do business or is doing business;

(3) the term "injury" means—

(A) physical harm to a natural person; and

(B) physical damage to or destruction of tangible property, but only if physical harm described in subparagraph (A) exists;

(4) the term "accident" means a sudden accident, or a natural event culminating in an accident, that results in death incurred at a discrete location by at least 75 natural persons; and

(5) the term "State" includes the District of Columbia, the Commonwealth of Puerto Rico, and any territory or possession of the United States.

(d) Intervening parties. In any action in a district court which is or could have been brought, in whole or in part, under this section, any person with a claim arising from the accident described in subsection (a) shall be permitted to intervene as a party plaintiff in the action, even if that person could not have brought an action in a district court as an original matter.

(e) Notification of judicial panel on multidistrict litigation. A district court in which an action under this section is pending shall promptly notify the judicial panel on multidistrict litigation of the pendency of the action.

§1390. Scope

(a) Venue defined. — As used in this chapter, the term "venue" refers to the geographic specification of the proper court or courts for the litigation of a civil action that is within the subject-matter jurisdiction of the district courts in general, and does not refer to any grant or restriction of subject-matter jurisdiction providing for a civil action to be adjudicated only by the district court for a particular district or districts.

(b) Exclusion of certain cases.—Except as otherwise provided by law, this chapter shall not govern the venue of a civil action in which the district court exercises the jurisdiction conferred by section 1333, except that such civil actions may be transferred between district courts as provided in this chapter.

(c) Clarification regarding cases removed from State courts.—This chapter shall not determine the district court to which a civil action pending in a State court may be removed, but shall govern the transfer of an action so removed as between districts and divisions of the United States district courts.

§1391. Venue Generally

(a) Applicability of section.—Except as otherwise provided by law—

(1) this section shall govern the venue of all civil actions brought in district courts of the United States; and

(2) the proper venue for a civil action shall be determined without regard to whether the action is local or transitory in nature.

(b) Venue in general.—A civil action may be brought in—

(1) a judicial district in which any defendant resides, if all defendants are residents of the State in which the district is located;

(2) a judicial district in which a substantial part of the events or omissions giving rise to the claim occurred, or a substantial part of property that is the subject of the action is situated; or

(3) if there is no district in which an action may otherwise be brought as provided in this section, any judicial district in which any defendant is subject to the court's personal jurisdiction with respect to such action.

(c) Residency.—For all venue purposes—

(1) a natural person, including an alien lawfully admitted for permanent residence in the United States, shall be deemed to reside in the judicial district in which that person is domiciled;

(2) an entity with the capacity to sue and be sued in its common name under applicable law, whether or not incorporated, shall be deemed to reside, if a defendant, in any judicial district in which such defendant is subject to the court's personal jurisdiction with respect to the civil action in question and, if a plaintiff, only in the judicial district in which it maintains its principal place of business; and

(3) a defendant not resident in the United States may be sued in any judicial district, and the joinder of such a defendant shall be disregarded in determining where the action may be brought with respect to other defendants.

(d) Residency of corporations in States with multiple districts.—For purposes of venue under this chapter, in a State which has more than one judicial district and in which a defendant that is a corporation is subject to personal jurisdiction at the time an action is commenced, such corporation shall be deemed to reside in any district in that State within which its contacts would be sufficient to subject it to personal jurisdiction if that district were a separate State, and, if there is no such district, the corporation shall be deemed to reside in the district within which it has the most significant contacts.

(e) Actions where defendant is officer or employee of the United States—

(1) In general.—A civil action in which a defendant is an officer or employee of the United States or any agency thereof acting in his official capacity or under color of legal authority, or an agency of the United States, or the United States, may, except as otherwise provided by law, be brought in any judicial district in which

(A) a defendant in the action resides,

(B) a substantial part of the events or omissions giving rise to the claim occurred, or a substantial part of property that is the subject of the action is situated, or

(C) the plaintiff resides if no real property is involved in the action.

Additional persons may be joined as parties to any such action in accordance with the Federal Rules of Civil Procedure and with such other venue requirements as would be applicable if the United States or one of its officers, employees, or agencies were not a party.

(2) Service.—The summons and complaint in such an action shall be served as provided by the Federal Rules of Civil Procedure except that the delivery of the summons and complaint to the officer or agency as required by the rules may be made by certified mail beyond the territorial limits of the district in which the action is brought.

(f) Civil actions against a foreign state—A civil action against a foreign state as defined in section 1603(a) of this title may be brought—

(1) in any judicial district in which a substantial part of the events or omissions giving rise to the claim occurred, or a substantial part of property that is the subject of the action is situated;

(2) in any judicial district in which the vessel or cargo of a foreign state is situated, if the claim is asserted under section 1605(b) of this title;

(3) in any judicial district in which the agency or instrumentality is licensed to do business or is doing business, if the action is brought against an agency or instrumentality of a foreign state as defined in section 1603(b) of this title; or

(4) in the United States District Court for the District of Columbia if the action is brought against a foreign state or political subdivision thereof.

(g) Multiparty, multiforum litigation—A civil action in which jurisdiction of the district court is based upon section 1369 of this title may be brought in any district in which any defendant resides or in which a substantial part of the accident giving rise to the action took place.

§1392.   [Repealed]

§1394.   Banking Association's Action Against Comptroller of Currency

Any civil action by a national banking association to enjoin the Comptroller of the Currency, under the provisions of any Act of Congress relating to such associations, may be prosecuted in the judicial district where such association is located.

§1395.   Fine, Penalty or Forfeiture

(a) A civil proceeding for the recovery of a pecuniary fine, penalty or forfeiture may be prosecuted in the district where it accrues or the defendant is found.

(b) A civil proceeding for the forfeiture of property may be prosecuted in any district where such property is found.

(c) A civil proceeding for the forfeiture of property seized outside any judicial district may be prosecuted in any district into which the property is brought.

(d) A proceeding in admiralty for the enforcement of fines, penalties and forfeitures against a vessel may be brought in any district in which the vessel is arrested.

(e) Any proceeding for the forfeiture of a vessel or cargo entering a port of entry closed by the President in pursuance of law, or of goods and chattels coming from a State or section declared by proclamation of the President to be in insurrection, or of any vessel or vehicle conveying persons or property to or from such State or section or belonging in whole or in part to a resident thereof, may be prosecuted in any district into which the property is taken and in which the proceeding is instituted.

§1396.   Internal Revenue Taxes

Any civil action for the collection of internal revenue taxes may be brought in the district where the liability for such tax accrues, in the district of the taxpayer's residence, or in the district where the return was filed.

§1397.   Interpleader

Any civil action of interpleader or in the nature of interpleader under section 1335 of this title may be brought in the judicial district in which one or more of the claimants reside.

§1400.   Patents and Copyrights, Mask Works, and Designs

(a) Civil actions, suits, or proceedings arising under any Act of Congress relating to copyrights or exclusive rights in mask works or designs may be instituted in the district in which the defendant or his agent resides or may be found.

(b) Any civil action for patent infringement may be brought in the judicial district where the defendant resides, or where the defendant has committed acts of infringement and has a regular and established place of business.

§1402.   United States as Defendant

(a) Any civil action in a district court against the United States under subsection (a) of section 1346 of this title may be prosecuted only:

(1) Except as provided in paragraph (2), in the judicial district where the plaintiff resides;

(2) In the case of a civil action by a corporation under paragraph (1) of subsection (a) of section 1346, in the judicial district in which is located the principal place of business or principal office or agency of the corporation; or if it has no principal place of business or principal office or agency in any judicial district

(A) in the judicial district in which is located the office to which was made the return of the tax in respect of which the claim is made, or

(B) if no return was made, in the judicial district in which lies the District of Columbia. Notwithstanding the foregoing provisions of this paragraph a district court, for the convenience of the parties and witnesses, in the interest of justice, may transfer any such action to any other district or division.

(b) Any civil action on a tort claim against the United States under subsection (b) of section 1346 of this title may be prosecuted only in the judicial district where the plaintiff resides or wherein the act or omission complained of occurred.

(c) Any civil action against the United States under subsection (e) of section 1346 of this title may be prosecuted only in the judicial district where the property is situated at the time of levy, or if no levy is made, in the judicial district in which the event occurred which gave rise to the cause of action.

(d) Any civil action under section 2409a to quiet title to an estate or interest in real property in which an interest is claimed by the United States shall be brought in the district court of the district where the property is located or, if located in different districts, in any of such districts.

§1404.   Change of Venue

(a) For the convenience of parties and witnesses, in the interest of justice, a district court may transfer any civil action to any other district or division where it might have been brought or to any district or division to which all parties have consented.

(b) Upon motion, consent or stipulation of all parties, any action, suit or proceeding of a civil nature or any motion or hearing thereof, may be transferred, in the discretion of the court, from the division in which pending to any other division in the same district. Transfer of proceedings in rem brought by or on behalf of the United States may be transferred under this section without the consent of the United States where all other parties request transfer.

(c) A district court may order any civil action to be tried at any place within the division in which it is pending.

(d) Transfers from a district court of the United States to the District Court of Guam, the District Court for the Northern Mariana Islands, or the District Court of the Virgin Islands shall not be permitted under this section. As otherwise used in this section, the term "district court" includes the District Court of Guam, the District Court for the Northern Mariana Islands, and the District Court of the Virgin Islands, and the term "district" includes the territorial jurisdiction of each such court.

§1406. Cure or Waiver of Defects

(a) The district court of a district in which is filed a case laying venue in the wrong division or district shall dismiss, or if it be in the interest of justice, transfer such case to any district or division in which it could have been brought.

(b) Nothing in this chapter shall impair the jurisdiction of a district court of any matter involving a party who does not interpose timely and sufficient objection to the venue.

(c) As used in this section, the term "district court" includes the District Court of Guam, the District Court for the Northern Mariana Islands, and the District Court of the Virgin Islands, and the term "district" includes the territorial jurisdiction of each such court.

§1407. Multidistrict Litigation

(a) When civil actions involving one or more common questions of fact are pending in different districts, such actions may be transferred to any district for coordinated or consolidated pretrial proceedings. Such transfers shall be made by the judicial panel on multidistrict litigation authorized by this section upon its determination that transfers for such proceedings will be for the convenience of parties and witnesses and will promote the just and efficient conduct of such actions. Each action so transferred shall be remanded by the panel at or before the conclusion of such pretrial proceedings to the district from which it was transferred unless it shall have been previously terminated: *Provided, however,* That the panel may separate any claim, cross-claim, counter-claim, or third-party claim and remand any of such claims before the remainder of the action is remanded.

(b) Such coordinated or consolidated pretrial proceedings shall be conducted by a judge or judges to whom such actions are assigned by the judicial panel on multidistrict litigation. For this purpose, upon request of the panel, a circuit judge or a district judge may be designated and assigned temporarily for service in the transferee district by the Chief Justice of the United States or the chief judge of the circuit, as may be required, in accordance with the provisions of chapter 13 of this title. With the consent of the transferee district court, such actions may be assigned by the panel to a judge or judges of such district. The judge or judges to whom such actions are assigned, the members of the judicial panel on multidistrict litigation, and other circuit and district judges designated when needed by the panel may exercise the powers of a district judge in any district for the purpose of conducting pretrial depositions in such coordinated or consolidated pretrial proceedings.

(c) Proceedings for the transfer of an action under this section may be initiated by—

(i) the judicial panel on multidistrict litigation upon its own initiative, or

(ii) motion filed with the panel by a party in any action in which transfer for coordinated or consolidated pretrial proceedings under this section may be appropriate. A copy of such motion shall be filed in the district court in which the moving party's action is pending.

The panel shall give notice to the parties in all actions in which transfers for coordinated or consolidated pretrial proceedings are contemplated, and such notice shall specify the time and place of any hearing to determine whether such transfer shall be made. Orders of the panel to set a hearing and other orders of the panel issued prior to the order either directing or denying transfer shall be filed in the office of the clerk of the district court in which a transfer hearing is to be or has been held. The panel's order of transfer shall be based upon a record of such hearing at which material evidence may be offered by any party to an action pending in any district that would be affected by the proceedings under this section, and shall be supported by findings of fact and conclusions of law based upon such record. Orders of transfer and such other orders as the panel may make thereafter shall be filed in the office of the clerk of the district court of the transferee district and shall be effective when thus filed. The clerk of the transferee district court shall forthwith transmit a certified copy of the panel's order to transfer to the clerk of the district court from which the action is being transferred. An order denying transfer shall be filed in each district wherein there is a case pending in which the motion for transfer has been made.

(d) The judicial panel on multidistrict litigation shall consist of seven circuit and district judges designated from time to time by the Chief Justice of the United States, no two of whom shall be from the same circuit. The concurrence of four members shall be necessary to any action by the panel.

(e) No proceedings for review of any order of the panel may be permitted except by extraordinary writ pursuant to the provisions of title 28, section 1651, United States Code. Petitions for an extraordinary writ to review an order of the panel to set a transfer hearing and other orders of the panel issued prior to the order either directing or denying transfer shall be filed only in the court of appeals having jurisdiction over the district in which a hearing is to be or has been held. Petitions for an extraordinary writ to review an order to transfer or orders subsequent to transfer shall be filed only in the court of appeals having jurisdiction over the transferee district. There shall be no appeal or review of an order of the panel denying a motion to transfer for consolidated or coordinated proceedings.

(f) The panel may prescribe rules for the conduct of its business not inconsistent with Acts of Congress and the Federal Rules of Civil Procedure.

(g) Nothing in this section shall apply to any action in which the United States is a complainant arising under the antitrust laws. "Antitrust laws" as used herein include those acts referred to in the Act of October 15, 1914, as amended (38 Stat. 730; 15 U.S.C. 12), and also include the Act of June 19, 1936 (49 Stat. 1526; 15 U.S.C. 13, 13a, and 13b) and the Act of September 26, 1914, as added March 21, 1938 (52 Stat. 116, 117; 15 U.S.C. 56); but shall not include section 4A of the Act of October 15, 1914, as added July 7, 1955 (69 Stat. 282; 15 U.S.C. 15a).

(h) Notwithstanding the provisions of section 1404 or subsection (f) of this section, the judicial panel on multidistrict litigation may consolidate and transfer with or without the consent of the parties, for both pretrial purposes and for trial, any action brought under section 4C of the Clayton Act.

§1441. Removal of Civil Actions

(a) Generally. — Except as otherwise expressly provided by Act of Congress, any civil action brought in a State court of which the district courts of the United States have original jurisdiction, may be removed by the defendant or the defendants, to the district court of the United States for the district and division embracing the place where such action is pending.

(b) Removal based on diversity of citizenship. —

(1) In determining whether a civil action is removable on the basis of the jurisdiction under section 1332(a) of this title, the citizenship of defendants sued under fictitious names shall be disregarded.

(2) A civil action otherwise removable solely on the basis of the jurisdiction under section 1332(a) of this title may not be removed if any of the parties in interest properly joined and served as defendants is a citizen of the State in which such action is brought.

(c) Joinder of Federal law claims and State law claims. —

(1) If a civil action includes—

(A) a claim arising under the Constitution, laws, or treaties of the United States (within the meaning of section 1331 of this title), and

(B) a claim not within the original or supplemental jurisdiction of the district court or a claim that has been made nonremovable by statute, the entire action may be removed if the action would be removable without the inclusion of the claim described in subparagraph (B).

(2) Upon removal of an action described in paragraph (1), the district court shall sever from the action all claims described in paragraph (1)(B) and shall remand the severed claims to the State court from which the action was removed. Only defendants against whom a claim described in paragraph (1)(A) has been asserted are required to join in or consent to the removal under paragraph (1).

(d) Actions against foreign States.—Any civil action brought in a State court against a foreign state as defined in section 1603(a) of this title may be removed by the foreign state to the district court of the United States for the district and division embracing the place where such action is pending. Upon removal the action shall be tried by the court without jury. Where removal is based upon this subsection, the time limitations of section 1446(b) of this chapter may be enlarged at any time for cause shown.

(e) Multiparty, multiforum jurisdiction.—

(1) Notwithstanding the provisions of subsection (b) of this section, a defendant in a civil action in a State court may remove the action to the district court of the United States for the district and division embracing the place where the action is pending if—

(A) the action could have been brought in a United States district court under section 1369 of this title; or

(B) the defendant is a party to an action which is or could have been brought, in whole or in part, under section 1369 in a United States district court and arises from the same accident as the action in State court, even if the action to be removed could not have been brought in a district court as an original matter.

The removal of an action under this subsection shall be made in accordance with section 1446 of this title, except that a notice of removal may also be filed before trial of the action in State court within 30 days after the date on which the defendant first becomes a party to an action under section 1369 in a United States district court that arises from the same accident as the action in State court, or at a later time with leave of the district court.

(2) Whenever an action is removed under this subsection and the district court to which it is removed or transferred under section 1407(j) has made a liability determination requiring further proceedings as to damages, the district court shall remand the action to the State court from which it had been removed for the determination of damages, unless the court finds that, for the convenience of parties and witnesses and in the interest of justice, the action should be retained for the determination of damages.

(3) Any remand under paragraph (2) shall not be effective until 60 days after the district court has issued an order determining liability and has certified its intention to remand the removed action for the determination of damages. An appeal with respect to the liability determination of the district court may be taken during that 60-day period to the court of appeals with appellate jurisdiction over the district court. In the event a party files such an appeal, the remand shall not be effective until the appeal has been finally disposed of. Once the remand has become effective, the liability determination shall not be subject to further review by appeal or otherwise.

(4) Any decision under this subsection concerning remand for the determination of damages shall not be reviewable by appeal or otherwise.

(5) An action removed under this subsection shall be deemed to be an action under section 1369 and an action in which jurisdiction is based on section 1369 of this title for purposes of this section and sections 1407, 1697, and 1785 of this title.

(6) Nothing in this subsection shall restrict the authority of the district court to transfer or dismiss an action on the ground of inconvenient forum.

(f) Derivative removal jurisdiction.—The court to which a civil action is removed under this section is not precluded from hearing and determining any claim in such civil action because the State court from which such civil action is removed did not have jurisdiction over that claim.

§1442. Federal Officers or Agencies Sued or Prosecuted

(a) A civil action or criminal prosecution commenced in a State court against any of the following may be removed by them to the district court of the United States for the district and division embracing the place wherein it is pending:

(1) The United States or any agency thereof or any officer (or any person acting under that officer) of the United States or of any agency thereof, sued in an official or individual capacity for any act under color of such office or on account of any right, title or authority claimed under any Act of Congress for the apprehension or punishment of criminals or the collection of the revenue.

(2) A property holder whose title is derived from any such officer, where such action or prosecution affects the validity of any law of the United States.

(3) Any officer of the courts of the United States, for any Act under color of office or in the performance of his duties.

(4) Any officer of either House of Congress, for any act in the discharge of his official duty under an order of such House.

(b) A personal action commenced in any State court by an alien against any citizen of a State who is, or at the time the alleged action accrued was, a civil officer of the United States and is a nonresident of such State, wherein jurisdiction is obtained by the State court by personal service of process, may be removed by the defendant to the district court of the United States for the district and division in which the defendant was served with process.

§1443.   Civil Rights Cases

Any of the following civil actions or criminal prosecutions, commenced in a State court may be removed by the defendant to the district court of the United States for the district and division embracing the place wherein it is pending:

(1) Against any person who is denied or cannot enforce in the courts of such State a right under any law providing for the equal civil rights of citizens of the United States, or of all persons within the jurisdiction thereof;

(2) For any act under color of authority derived from any law providing for equal rights, or for refusing to do any act on the ground that it would be inconsistent with such law.

§1444.   Foreclosure Action Against United States

Any action brought under section 2410 of this title against the United States in any State court may be removed by the United States to the district court of the United States for the district and division in which the action is pending.

§1445.   Nonremovable Actions

(a) A civil action in any State court against a railroad or its receivers or trustees, arising under sections 1-4 and 5-10 of the Act of April 22, 1908 (45 U.S.C. 51-54, 55-60), may not be removed to any district court of the United States.

(b) A civil action in any State court against a carrier or its receivers or trustees to recover damages for delay, loss, or injury of shipments, arising under section 11706 or 14706 of title 49, may not be removed to any district court of the United States unless the matter in controversy exceeds $10,000, exclusive of interest and costs.

(c) A civil action in any State court arising under the workmen's compensation laws of such State may not be removed to any district court of the United States.

(d) A civil action in any State court arising under section 40302 of the Violence Against Women Act of 1994 may not be removed to any district court of the United States.

§1446.   Procedure for Removal of Civil Actions

(a) Generally.—A defendant or defendants desiring to remove any civil action from a State court shall file in the district court of the United States for the district and division within which such action is pending a notice of removal signed pursuant to Rule 11 of the Federal Rules of Civil Procedure and containing a short and plain statement of the grounds for removal, together with a copy of all process, pleadings, and orders served upon such defendant or defendants in such action.

(b) Requirements; generally. —

(1) The notice of removal of a civil action or proceeding shall be filed within 30 days after the receipt by the defendant, through service or otherwise, of a copy of the initial pleading setting forth the claim for relief upon which such action or proceeding is based, or within 30 days after the service of summons upon the defendant if such initial pleading has then been filed in court and is not required to be served on the defendant, whichever period is shorter.

(2)

(A) When a civil action is removed solely under section 1441(a), all defendants who have been properly joined and served must join in or consent to the removal of the action.

(B) Each defendant shall have 30 days after receipt by or service on that defendant of the initial pleading or summons described in paragraph (1) to file the notice of removal.

(C) If defendants are served at different times, and a later-served defendant files a notice of removal, any earlier-served defendant may consent to the removal even though that earlier-served defendant did not previously initiate or consent to removal.

(3) Except as provided in subsection (c), if the case stated by the initial pleading is not removable, a notice of removal may be filed within 30 days after receipt by the defendant, through service or otherwise, of a copy of an amended pleading, motion, order or other paper from which it may first be ascertained that the case is one which is or has become removable.

(c) Requirements; removal based on diversity of citizenship. —

(1) A case may not be removed under subsection (b)(3) on the basis of jurisdiction conferred by section 1332 more than 1 year after commencement of the action, unless the district court finds that the plaintiff has acted in bad faith in order to prevent a defendant from removing the action.

(2) If removal of a civil action is sought on the basis of the jurisdiction conferred by section 1332(a), the sum demanded in good faith in the initial pleading shall be deemed to be the amount in controversy, except that —

(A) the notice of removal may assert the amount in controversy if the initial pleading seeks —

(i) nonmonetary relief; or

(ii) a money judgment, but the State practice either does not permit demand for a specific sum or permits recovery of damages in excess of the amount demanded; and

(B) removal of the action is proper on the basis of an amount in controversy asserted under subparagraph (A) if the district court finds, by the preponderance of the evidence, that the amount in controversy exceeds the amount specified in section 1332(a).

(3)

(A) If the case stated by the initial pleading is not removable solely because the amount in controversy does not exceed the amount specified in section 1332(a), information relating to the amount in controversy in the record of the State proceeding, or in responses to discovery, shall be treated as an 'other paper' under subsection (b)(3).

(B) If the notice of removal is filed more than 1 year after commencement of the action and the district court finds that the plaintiff deliberately failed to disclose the actual amount in controversy to prevent removal, that finding shall be deemed bad faith under paragraph (1).

(d) Notice to adverse parties and State court.—Promptly after the filing of such notice of removal of a civil action the defendant or defendants shall give written notice thereof to all adverse parties and shall file a copy of the notice with the clerk of such State court, which shall effect the removal and the State court shall proceed no further unless and until the case is remanded.

(e) Counterclaim in 337 proceeding.—With respect to any counterclaim removed to a district court pursuant to section 337(c) of the Tariff Act of 1930, the district court shall resolve such counterclaim in the same manner as an original complaint under the Federal Rules of Civil Procedure, except that the payment of a filing fee shall not be required in such cases and the counterclaim shall relate back to the date of the original complaint in the proceeding before the International Trade Commission under section 337 of that Act.

[(f) Redesignated (e)]

(g) Where the civil action or criminal prosecution that is removable under section 1442(a) is a proceeding in which a judicial order for testimony or documents is sought or issued or sought to be enforced, the 30-day requirement of subsection (b) of this section and paragraph (1) of section 1455(b) is satisfied if the person or entity desiring to remove the proceeding files the notice of removal not later than 30 days after receiving, through service, notice of any such proceeding.

§1447. Procedure After Removal Generally

(a) In any case removed from a State court, the district court may issue all necessary orders and process to bring before it all proper parties whether served by process issued by the State court or otherwise.

(b) It may require the removing party to file with its clerk copies of all records and proceedings in such State court or may cause the same to be brought before it by writ of certiorari issued to such State court.

(c) A motion to remand the case on the basis of any defect other than lack of subject matter jurisdiction must be made within 30 days after the filing of the notice of removal under section 1446(a). If at any time before final judgment it appears that the district court lacks subject matter jurisdiction, the case shall be remanded. An order remanding the case may require payment of just costs and any actual expenses, including attorney fees, incurred as a result of the removal. A certified copy of the order of remand shall be mailed by the clerk to the clerk of the State court. The State court may thereupon proceed with such case.

(d) An order remanding a case to the State court from which it was removed is not reviewable on appeal or otherwise, except that an order remanding a case to the State court from which it was removed pursuant to section 1442 or 1443 of this title shall be reviewable by appeal or otherwise.

(e) If after removal the plaintiff seeks to join additional defendants whose joinder would destroy subject matter jurisdiction, the court may deny joinder, or permit joinder and remand the action to the State court.

§1453. Removal of Class Actions

(a) Definitions. In this section, the terms "class," "class action," "class certification order," and "class member" shall have the meanings given such terms under section 1332(d)(1).

(b) In general. A class action may be removed to a district court of the United States in accordance with section 1446 (except that the 1-year limitation under section 1446(b) shall not apply), without regard to whether any defendant is a citizen of the State in which the action is brought, except that such action may be removed by any defendant without the consent of all defendants.

(c) Review of remand orders.

(1) In general. Section 1447 shall apply to any removal of a case under this section, except that notwithstanding section 1447(d), a court of appeals may accept an appeal from an order of a district court granting or denying a motion to remand a class action to the State court from which it was removed if application is made to the court of appeals not less than 7 days after entry of the order.

(2) Time period for judgment. If the court of appeals accepts an appeal under paragraph (1), the court shall complete all action on such appeal, including rendering judgment, not later than 60 days after the date on which such appeal was filed, unless an extension is granted under paragraph (3).

(3) Extension of time period. The court of appeals may grant an extension of the 60-day period described in paragraph (2) if—

(A) all parties to the proceeding agree to such extension, for any period of time; or

(B) such extension is for good cause shown and in the interests of justice, for a period not to exceed 10 days.

(4) Denial of appeal. If a final judgment on the appeal under paragraph (1) is not issued before the end of the period described in paragraph (2), including any extension under paragraph (3), the appeal shall be denied.

(d) Exception. This section shall not apply to any class action that solely involves—

(1) a claim concerning a covered security as defined under section 16(f)(3) of the Securities Act of 1933 (15 U.S.C. 78p(f)(3)) and section 28(f)(5)(E) of the Securities Exchange Act of 1934 (15 U.S.C. 78bb(f)(5)(E));

(2) a claim that relates to the internal affairs or governance of a corporation or other form of business enterprise and arises under or by virtue of the laws of the State in which such corporation or business enterprise is incorporated or organized; or

(3) a claim that relates to the rights, duties (including fiduciary duties), and obligations relating to or created by or pursuant to any security (as defined under section 2(a)(1) of the Securities Act of 1933 (15 U.S.C. 77b(a)(1)) and the regulations issued thereunder).

§1631.   Transfer to Cure Want of Jurisdiction

Whenever a civil action is filed in a court as defined in section 610 of this title or an appeal, including a petition for review of administrative action, is noticed for or filed with such a court and that court finds that there is a want of jurisdiction, the court shall, if it is in the interest of justice, transfer such action or appeal to any other such court in which the action or appeal could have been brought at the time it was filed or noticed, and the action or appeal shall proceed as if it had been filed in or noticed for the court to which it is transferred on the date upon which it was actually filed in or noticed for the court from which it is transferred.

§1651.   Writs

(a) The Supreme Court and all courts established by Act of Congress may issue all writs necessary or appropriate in aid of their respective jurisdictions and agreeable to the usages and principles of law.

(b) An alternative writ or rule nisi may be issued by a justice or judge of a court which has jurisdiction.

§1652.   State Laws as Rules of Decision

The laws of the several states, except where the Constitution or treaties of the United States or Acts of Congress otherwise require or provide, shall be regarded as rules of decision in civil actions in the courts of the United States, in cases where they apply.

§1711.　Definitions

In this chapter:

(1) Class. The term "class" means all of the class members in a class action.

(2) Class action. The term "class action" means any civil action filed in a district court of the United States under rule 23 of the Federal Rules of Civil Procedure or any civil action that is removed to a district court of the United States that was originally filed under a State statute or rule of judicial procedure authorizing an action to be brought by 1 or more representatives as a class action.

(3) Class counsel. The term "class counsel" means the persons who serve as the attorneys for the class members in a proposed or certified class action.

(4) Class members. The term "class members" means the persons (named or unnamed) who fall within the definition of the proposed or certified class in a class action.

(5) Plaintiff class action. The term "plaintiff class action" means a class action in which class members are plaintiffs.

(6) Proposed settlement. The term "proposed settlement" means an agreement regarding a class action that is subject to court approval and that, if approved, would be binding on some or all class members.

§1712.　Coupon Settlements

(a) Contingent fees in coupon settlements. If a proposed settlement in a class action provides for a recovery of coupons to a class member, the portion of any attorney's fee award to class counsel that is attributable to the award of the coupons shall be based on the value to class members of the coupons that are redeemed.

(b) Other attorney's fee awards in coupon settlements.

(1) In general. If a proposed settlement in a class action provides for a recovery of coupons to class members, and a portion of the recovery of the coupons is not used to determine the attorney's fee to be paid to class counsel, any attorney's fee award shall be based upon the amount of time class counsel reasonably expended working on the action.

(2) Court approval. Any attorney's fee under this subsection shall be subject to approval by the court and shall include an appropriate attorney's fee, if any, for obtaining equitable relief, including an injunction, if applicable. Nothing in this subsection shall be construed to prohibit application of a lodestar with a multiplier method of determining attorney's fees.

(c) Attorney's fee awards calculated on a mixed basis in coupon settlements. If a proposed settlement in a class action provides for an award of coupons to class members and also provides for equitable relief, including injunctive relief—

(1) that portion of the attorney's fee to be paid to class counsel that is based upon a portion of the recovery of the coupons shall be calculated in accordance with subsection (a); and

(2) that portion of the attorney's fee to be paid to class counsel that is not based upon a portion of the recovery of the coupons shall be calculated in accordance with subsection (b).

(d) Settlement valuation expertise. In a class action involving the awarding of coupons, the court may, in its discretion upon the motion of a party, receive expert testimony from a witness qualified to provide information on the actual value to the class members of the coupons that are redeemed.

(e) Judicial scrutiny of coupon settlements. In a proposed settlement under which class members would be awarded coupons, the court may approve the proposed settlement only after a hearing to determine whether, and making a written finding that, the settlement is fair, reasonable, and adequate for class members. The court, in its discretion, may also require that a proposed settlement agreement provide for the distribution of a portion of the value of unclaimed coupons to 1 or more charitable or governmental organizations, as agreed to by the parties. The distribution and redemption of any proceeds under this subsection shall not be used to calculate attorneys' fees under this section.

§1713. Protection Against Loss by Class Members

The court may approve a proposed settlement under which any class member is obligated to pay sums to class counsel that would result in a net loss to the class member only if the court makes a written finding that nonmonetary benefits to the class member substantially outweigh the monetary loss.

§1714. Protection Against Discrimination Based on Geographic Location

The court may not approve a proposed settlement that provides for the payment of greater sums to some class members than to others solely on the basis that the class members to whom the greater sums are to be paid are located in closer geographic proximity to the court.

§1715. Notifications to Appropriate Federal and State Officials

(a) Definitions.

(1) Appropriate Federal official. In this section, the term "appropriate Federal official" means—

(A) the Attorney General of the United States; or

(B) in any case in which the defendant is a Federal depository institution, a State depository institution, a depository institution holding company, a foreign bank, or a nondepository institution subsidiary of the foregoing (as such terms are defined in section 3 of the Federal Deposit Insurance Act (12 U.S.C. 1813)), the person who has the primary Federal regulatory or supervisory responsibility with respect to the defendant, if some or all of the matters alleged in the class action are subject to regulation or supervision by that person.

(2) Appropriate State official. In this section, the term "appropriate State official" means the person in the State who has the primary regulatory or supervisory responsibility with respect to the defendant, or who licenses or otherwise authorizes the defendant to conduct business in the State, if some or all of the matters alleged in the class action are subject to regulation by that person. If there is no primary regulator, supervisor, or licensing authority, or the matters alleged in the class action are not subject to regulation or supervision by that person, then the appropriate State official shall be the State attorney general.

(b) In general. Not later than 10 days after a proposed settlement of a class action is filed in court, each defendant that is participating in the proposed settlement shall serve upon the appropriate State official of each State in which a class member resides and the appropriate Federal official, a notice of the proposed settlement consisting of—

(1) a copy of the complaint and any materials filed with the complaint and any amended complaints (except such materials shall not be required to be served if such materials are made electronically available through the Internet and such service includes notice of how to electronically access such material);

(2) notice of any scheduled judicial hearing in the class action;

(3) any proposed or final notification to class members of—

(A)

(i) the members' rights to request exclusion from the class action; or

(ii) if no right to request exclusion exists, a statement that no such right exists; and

(B) a proposed settlement of a class action;

(4) any proposed or final class action settlement;

(5) any settlement or other agreement contemporaneously made between class counsel and counsel for the defendants;

(6) any final judgment or notice of dismissal;

(7)

(A) if feasible, the names of class members who reside in each State and the estimated proportionate share of the claims of such members to the entire settlement to that State's appropriate State official; or

(B) if the provision of information under subparagraph (A) is not feasible, a reasonable estimate of the number of class members residing in each State and the estimated proportionate share of the claims of such members to the entire settlement; and

(8) any written judicial opinion relating to the materials described under subparagraphs (3) through (6).

(c) Depository institutions notification.

(1) Federal and other depository institutions. In any case in which the defendant is a Federal depository institution, a depository institution holding company, a foreign bank, or a non-depository institution subsidiary of the foregoing, the notice requirements of this section are satisfied by serving the notice required under subsection (b) upon the person who has the primary Federal regulatory or supervisory responsibility with respect to the defendant, if some or all of the matters alleged in the class action are subject to regulation or supervision by that person.

(2) State depository institutions. In any case in which the defendant is a State depository institution (as that term is defined in section 3 of the Federal Deposit Insurance Act (12 U.S.C. 1813)), the notice requirements of this section are satisfied by serving the notice required under subsection (b) upon the State bank supervisor (as that term is defined in section 3 of the Federal Deposit Insurance Act (12 U.S.C. 1813)) of the State in which the defendant is incorporated or chartered, if some or all of the matters alleged in the class action are subject to regulation or supervision by that person, and upon the appropriate Federal official.

(d) Final approval. An order giving final approval of a proposed settlement may not be issued earlier than 90 days after the later of the dates on which the appropriate Federal official and the appropriate State official are served with the notice required under subsection (b).

(e) Noncompliance if notice not provided.

(1) In general. A class member may refuse to comply with and may choose not to be bound by a settlement agreement or consent decree in a class action if the class member demonstrates that the notice required under subsection (b) has not been provided.

(2) Limitation. A class member may not refuse to comply with or to be bound by a settlement agreement or consent decree under paragraph (1) if the notice required under subsection (b) was directed to the appropriate Federal official and to either the State attorney general or the person that has primary regulatory, supervisory, or licensing authority over the defendant.

(3) Application of rights. The rights created by this subsection shall apply only to class members or any person acting on a class member's behalf, and shall not be construed to limit any other rights affecting a class member's participation in the settlement.

(f) Rule of construction. Nothing in this section shall be construed to expand the authority of, or impose any obligations, duties, or responsibilities upon, Federal or State officials.

§1738. State and Territorial Statutes and Judicial Proceedings; Full Faith and Credit

The Acts of legislature of any State, Territory, or Possession of the United States, or copies thereof, shall be authenticated by affixing the seal of such State, Territory or Possession thereto.

The records and judicial proceedings of any court of any such State, Territory or Possession, or copies thereof, shall be proved or admitted in other courts within the United States and its Territories and Possessions by the attestation of the clerk and seal of the court annexed, if a seal exists, together with a certificate of a judge of the court that the said attestation is in proper form.

Such Acts, records and judicial proceedings or copies thereof, so authenticated, shall have the same full faith and credit in every court within the United States and its Territories and Possessions as they have by law or usage in the courts of such State, Territory or Possession from which they are taken.

§1746. Unsworn Declarations Under Penalty of Perjury

Wherever, under any law of the United States or under any rule, regulation, order, or requirement made pursuant to law, any matter is required or permitted to be supported, evidenced, established, or proved by the sworn declaration, verification, certificate, statement, oath, or affidavit, in writing of the person making the same (other than a deposition, or an oath of office, or an oath required to be taken before a specified official other than a notary public), such matter may, with like force and effect, be supported, evidenced, established, or proved by the unsworn declaration, certificate, verification, or statement, in writing of such person which is subscribed by him, as true under penalty of perjury, and dated, in substantially the following form:

(1) If executed without the United States: "I declare (or certify, verify, or state) under penalty of perjury under the laws of the United States of America that the foregoing is true and correct.

Executed on (date).

(Signature)."

(2) If executed within the United States, its territories, possessions, or commonwealths: "I declare (or certify, verify, or state) under penalty of perjury that the foregoing is true and correct.

Executed on (date).

(Signature)."

§1782. Assistance to Foreign and International Tribunals and to Litigants Before Such Tribunals

(a) The district court of the district in which a person resides or is found may order him to give his testimony or statement or to produce a document or other thing for use in a proceeding in a foreign or international tribunal, including criminal investigations conducted before formal accusation. The order may be made pursuant to a letter rogatory issued, or request made, by a foreign or international tribunal or upon the application of any interested person and may direct that the testimony or statement be given, or the document or other thing be produced, before a person appointed by the court. By virtue of his appointment, the person appointed has power to administer any necessary oath and take the testimony or statement. The order may prescribe the practice and procedure, which may be in whole or part the practice and procedure of the foreign country or the international tribunal, for taking the testimony or statement or producing the document or other thing. To the extent that the order does not prescribe otherwise, the testimony or statement shall be taken, and the document or other thing produced, in accordance with the Federal Rules of Civil Procedure.

A person may not be compelled to give his testimony or statement or to produce a document or other thing in violation of any legally applicable privilege.

(b) This chapter does not preclude a person within the United States from voluntarily giving his testimony or statement, or producing a document or other thing, for use in a proceeding in a foreign or international tribunal before any person and in any manner acceptable to him.

§1861. Declaration of Policy

It is the policy of the United States that all litigants in Federal courts entitled to trial by jury shall have the right to grand and petit juries selected at random from a fair cross section of the community in the district or division wherein the court convenes. It is further the policy of the United States that all citizens shall have the opportunity to be considered for service on grand and petit juries in the district courts of the United States, and shall have an obligation to serve as jurors when summoned for that purpose.

§1863. Plan for Random Jury Selection

(a) Each United States district court shall devise and place into operation a written plan for random selection of grand and petit jurors that shall be designed to achieve the objectives of sections 1861 and 1862 of this title, and that shall otherwise comply with the provisions of this title. The plan shall be placed into operation after approval by a reviewing panel consisting of the members of the judicial council of the circuit and either the chief judge of the district whose plan is being reviewed or such other active district judge of that district as the chief judge of the district may designate. The panel shall examine the plan to ascertain that it complies with the provisions of this title. If the reviewing panel finds that the plan does not comply, the panel shall state the particulars in which the plan fails to comply and direct the district court to present within a reasonable time an alternative plan remedying the defect or defects. Separate plans may be adopted for each division or combination of divisions within a judicial district. The district court may modify a plan at any time and it shall modify the plan when so directed by the reviewing panel. The district court shall promptly notify the panel, the Administrative Office of the United States Courts, and the Attorney General of the United States, of the initial adoption and future modifications of the plan by filing copies therewith. Modifications of the plan made at the instance of the district court shall become effective after approval by the panel. Each district court shall submit a report on the jury selection process within its jurisdiction to the Administrative Office of the United States Courts in such form and at such times as the Judicial Conference of the United States may specify. The Judicial Conference of the United States may, from time to time, adopt rules and regulations governing the provisions and the operation of the plans formulated under this title.

(b) Among other things, such plan shall—

(1) either establish a jury commission, or authorize the clerk of the court, to manage the jury selection process. If the plan establishes a jury commission, the district court shall appoint one citizen to serve with the clerk of the court as the jury commission: *Provided, however,* That the plan for the District of Columbia may establish a jury commission consisting of three citizens. The citizen jury commissioner shall not belong to the same political party as the clerk serving with him. The clerk or the jury commission, as the case may be, shall act under the supervision and control of the chief judge of the district court or such other judge of the district court as the plan may provide. Each jury commissioner shall, during his tenure in office, reside in the judicial district or division for which he is appointed. Each citizen jury commissioner shall receive compensation to be fixed by the district court plan at a rate not to exceed $50 per day for each day necessarily employed in the performance of his duties, plus reimbursement for travel, subsistence, and other necessary expenses incurred by him in the performance of such duties. The Judicial Conference of the United States may establish standards for allowance of travel, subsistence, and other necessary expenses incurred by jury commissioners.

(2) specify whether the names of prospective jurors shall be selected from the voter registration lists or the lists of actual voters of the political subdivisions within the district or division. The plan shall prescribe some other source or sources of names in addition to voter lists where necessary to foster the policy and protect the rights secured by sections 1861 and 1862 of this title. The plan for the District of Columbia may require the names of prospective jurors to

be selected from the city directory rather than from voter lists. The plans for the districts of Puerto Rico and the Canal Zone may prescribe some other source or sources of names of prospective jurors in lieu of voter lists, the use of which shall be consistent with the policies declared and rights secured by sections 1861 and 1862 of this title. The plan for the district of Massachusetts may require the names of prospective jurors to be selected from the resident list provided for in chapter 234A, Massachusetts General Laws, or comparable authority, rather than from voter lists.

(3) specify detailed procedures to be followed by the jury commission or clerk in selecting names from the sources specified in paragraph (2) of this subsection. These procedures shall be designed to ensure the random selection of a fair cross section of the persons residing in the community in the district or division wherein the court convenes. They shall ensure that names of persons residing in each of the counties, parishes, or similar political subdivisions within the judicial district or division are placed in a master jury wheel; and shall ensure that each county, parish, or similar political subdivision within the district or division is substantially proportionally represented in the master jury wheel for that judicial district, division, or combination of divisions. For the purposes of determining proportional representation in the master jury wheel, either the number of actual voters at the last general election in each county, parish, or similar political subdivision, or the number of registered voters if registration of voters is uniformly required throughout the district or division, may be used.

(4) provide for a master jury wheel (or a device similar in purpose and function) into which the names of those randomly selected shall be placed. The plan shall fix a minimum number of names to be placed initially in the master jury wheel, which shall be at least one-half of 1 per centum of the total number of persons on the lists used as a source of names for the district or division; but if this number of names is believed to be cumbersome and unnecessary, the plan may fix a smaller number of names to be placed in the master wheel, but in no event less than one thousand. The chief judge of the district court, or such other district court judge as the plan may provide, may order additional names to be placed in the master jury wheel from time to time as necessary. The plan shall provide for periodic emptying and refilling of the master jury wheel at specified times, the interval for which shall not exceed four years.

(5)

(A) except as provided in subparagraph (B), specify those groups of persons or occupational classes whose members shall, on individual request therefor, be excused from jury service. Such groups or classes shall be excused only if the district court finds, and the plan states, that jury service by such class or group would entail undue hardship or extreme inconvenience to the members thereof, and excuse of members thereof would not be inconsistent with sections 1861 and 1862 of this title.

(B) specify that volunteer safety personnel, upon individual request, shall be excused from jury service. For purposes of this subparagraph, the term "volunteer safety personnel" means individuals serving a public agency (as defined in section 1203(6) of title I of the Omnibus Crime Control and Safe Streets Act of 1968) in an official capacity, without compensation, as firefighters or members of a rescue squad or ambulance crew.

(6) specify that the following persons are barred from jury service on the ground that they are exempt:

(A) members in active service in the Armed Forces of the United States;

(B) members of the fire or police departments of any State, the District of Columbia, any territory or possession of the United States, or any subdivision of a State, the District of Columbia, or such territory or possession;

(C) public officers in the executive, legislative, or judicial branches of the Government of the United States, or of any State, the District of Columbia, any territory or possession of the United States, or any subdivision of a State, the District of Columbia, or such territory or possession, who are actively engaged in the performance of official duties.

(7) fix the time when the names drawn from the qualified jury wheel shall be disclosed to parties and to the public. If the plan permits these names to be made public, it may nevertheless permit the chief judge of the district court, or such other district court judge as the plan may provide, to keep these names confidential in any case where the interests of justice so require.

(8) specify the procedures to be followed by the clerk or jury commission in assigning persons whose names have been drawn from the qualified jury wheel to grand and petit jury panels.

(c) The initial plan shall be devised by each district court and transmitted to the reviewing panel specified in subsection (a) of this section within one hundred and twenty days of the date of enactment of the Jury Selection and Service Act of 1968 [enacted March 27, 1968]. The panel shall approve or direct the modification of each plan so submitted within sixty days thereafter. Each plan or modification made at the direction of the panel shall become effective after approval at such time thereafter as the panel directs, in no event to exceed ninety days from the date of approval. Modifications made at the instance of the district court under subsection (a) of this section shall be effective at such time thereafter as the panel directs, in no event to exceed ninety days from the date of modification.

(d) State, local, and Federal officials having custody, possession, or control of voter registration lists, lists of actual voters, or other appropriate records shall make such lists and records available to the jury commission or clerks for inspection, reproduction, and copying at all reasonable times as the commission or clerk may deem necessary and proper for the performance of duties under this title. The district courts shall have jurisdiction upon application by the Attorney General of the United States to compel compliance with this subsection by appropriate process.

§1865.   Qualification for Jury Service

(a) The chief judge of the district court, or such other district court judge as the plan may provide, on his initiative or upon recommendation of the clerk or jury commission, or the clerk under supervision of the court if the court's jury selection plan so authorizes, shall determine solely on the basis of information provided on the juror qualification form and other competent evidence whether a person is unqualified for, or exempt, or to be excused from jury service. The clerk shall enter such determination in the space provided on the juror qualification form and in any alphabetical list of names drawn from the master jury wheel. If a person did not appear in response to a summons, such fact shall be noted on said list.

(b) In making such determination the chief judge of the district court, or such other district court judge as the plan may provide, or the clerk if the court's jury selection plan so provides, shall deem any person qualified to serve on grand and petit juries in the district court unless he—

(1) is not a citizen of the United States eighteen years old who has resided for a period of one year within the judicial district;

(2) is unable to read, write, and understands the English language with a degree of proficiency sufficient to fill out satisfactorily the juror qualification form;

(3) is unable to speak the English language;

(4) is incapable, by reason of mental or physical infirmity, to render satisfactory jury service; or

(5) has a charge pending against him for the commission of, or has been convicted in a State or Federal court of record of, a crime punishable by imprisonment for more than one year and his civil rights have not been restored.

§1870.   Challenges

In civil cases, each party shall be entitled to three peremptory challenges. Several defendants or several plaintiffs may be considered as a single party for the purposes of making challenges, or the court may allow additional peremptory challenges and permit them to be exercised separately or jointly.

All challenges for cause or favor, whether to the array or panel or to individual jurors, shall be determined by the court.

§1912.   Damages and Costs on Affirmance

Where a judgment is affirmed by the Supreme Court or a court of appeals, the court in its discretion may adjudge to the prevailing party just damages for his delay, and single or double costs.

§1920.   Taxation of Costs

A judge or clerk of any court of the United States may tax as costs the following:
(1) Fees of the clerk and marshal;
(2) Fees of the court reporter for all or any part of the stenographic transcript necessarily obtained for use in the case;
(3) Fees and disbursements for printing and witnesses;
(4) Fees for exemplification and copies of papers necessarily obtained for use in the case;
(5) Docket fees under section 1923 of this title;
(6) Compensation of court appointed experts, compensation of interpreters, and salaries, fees, expenses, and costs of special interpretation services under section 1828 of this title.
A bill of costs shall be filed in the case and, upon allowance, included in the judgment or decree.

§1927.   Counsel's Liability for Excessive Costs

Any attorney or other person admitted to conduct cases in any court of the United States or any Territory thereof who so multiplies the proceedings in any case unreasonably and vexatiously may be required by the court to satisfy personally the excess costs, expenses, and attorneys' fees reasonably incurred because of such conduct.

§1961.   Interest

(a) Interest shall be allowed on any money judgment in a civil case recovered in a district court. Execution therefor may be levied by the marshal, in any case where, by the law of the State in which such court is held, execution may be levied for interest on judgments recovered in the courts of the State. Such interest shall be calculated from the date of the entry of the judgment, at a rate equal to the weekly average 1-year constant maturity Treasury yield, as published by the Board of Governors of the Federal Reserve System, for the calendar week preceding[.] the date of the judgment. The Director of the Administrative Office of the United States Courts shall distribute notice of that rate and any changes in it to all Federal judges.
(b) Interest shall be computed daily to the date of payment except as provided in section 2516(b) of this title and section 1304(b)(1) of title 31, and shall be compounded annually.
(c)
(1) This section shall not apply in any judgment of any court with respect to any internal revenue tax case. Interest shall be allowed in such cases at the

underpayment rate or overpayment rate (whichever is appropriate) established under section 6621 of the Internal Revenue Code of 1954.

(2) Except as otherwise provided in paragraph (1) of this subsection, interest shall be allowed on all final judgments against the United States in the United States Court of Appeals for the Federal circuit, at the rate provided in subsection (a) and as provided in subsection (b).

(3) Interest shall be allowed, computed, and paid on judgments of the United States Claims Court [United States Court of Federal Claims] only as provided in paragraph (1) of this subsection or in any other provision of law.

(4) This section shall not be construed to affect the interest on any judgment of any court not specified in this section.

§2072. Rules of Procedure and Evidence; Power to Prescribe

(a) The Supreme Court shall have the power to prescribe general rules of practice and procedure and rules of evidence for cases in the United States district courts (including proceedings before magistrates thereof) and courts of appeals.

(b) Such rules shall not abridge, enlarge or modify any substantive right. All laws in conflict with such rules shall be of no further force or effect after such rules have taken effect.

(c) Such rules may define when a ruling of a district court is final for the purposes of appeal under section 1291 of this title.

§2201. Creation of Remedy

(a) In a case of actual controversy within its jurisdiction, except with respect to Federal taxes other than actions brought under section 7428 of the Internal Revenue Code of 1986, a proceeding under section 505 or 1146 of title 11, or in any civil action involving an antidumping or countervailing duty proceeding regarding a class or kind of merchandise of a free trade area country (as defined in section 516A(f)(10) of the Tariff Act of 1930), as determined by the administering authority, any court of the United States, upon the filing of an appropriate pleading, may declare the rights and other legal relations of any interested party seeking such declaration, whether or not further relief is or could be sought. Any such declaration shall have the force and effect of a final judgment or decree and shall be reviewable as such.

(b) For limitations on actions brought with respect to drug patents see section 505 or 512 of the Federal Food, Drug, and Cosmetic Act.

§2202.   Further Relief

Further necessary or proper relief based on a declaratory judgment or decree may be granted, after reasonable notice and hearing, against any adverse party whose rights have been determined by such judgment.

§2283.   Stay of State Court Proceedings

A court of the United States may not grant an injunction to stay proceedings in a State court except as expressly authorized by Act of Congress, or where necessary in aid of its jurisdiction, or to protect or effectuate its judgments.

§2284.   Three-Judge Court; When Required; Composition; Procedure

(a) A district court of three judges shall be convened when otherwise required by Act of Congress, or when an action is filed challenging the constitutionality of the apportionment of congressional districts or the apportionment of any statewide legislative body.

(b) In any action required to be heard and determined by a district court of three judges under subsection (a) of this section, the composition and procedure of the court shall be as follows:

(1) Upon the filing of a request for three judges, the judge to whom the request is presented shall, unless he determines that three judges are not required, immediately notify the chief judge of the circuit, who shall designate two other judges, at least one of whom shall be a circuit judge. The judges so designated, and the judge to whom the request was presented, shall serve as members of the court to hear and determine the action or proceeding.

(2) If the action is against a State, or officer or agency thereof, at least five days' notice of hearing of the action shall be given by registered or certified mail to the Governor and attorney general of the State.

(3) A single judge may conduct all proceedings except the trial, and enter all orders permitted by the rules of civil procedure except as provided in this subsection. He may grant a temporary restraining order on a specific finding, based on evidence submitted, that specified irreparable damage will result if the order is not granted, which order, unless previously revoked by the district judge, shall remain in force only until the hearing and determination by the district court of three judges of an application for a preliminary injunction. A single judge shall not appoint a master, or order a reference, or hear and determine any application for a preliminary or permanent injunction or motion to vacate such an injunction, or enter judgment on the merits. Any action

of a single judge may be reviewed by the full court at any time before final judgment.

§2361.   Process and Procedure

In any civil action of interpleader or in the nature of interpleader under section 1335 of this title, a district court may issue its process for all claimants and enter its order restraining them from instituting or prosecuting any proceeding in any State or United States court affecting the property, instrument or obligation involved in the interpleader action until further order of the court. Such process and order shall be returnable at such time as the court or judge thereof directs, and shall be addressed to and served by the United States marshals for the respective districts where the claimants reside or may be found.

Such district court shall hear and determine the case, and may discharge the plaintiff from further liability, make the injunction permanent, and make all appropriate orders to enforce its judgment.

§2403.   Intervention by United States or a State; Constitutional Question

(a) In any action, suit or proceeding in a court of the United States to which the United States or any agency, officer or employee thereof is not a party, wherein the constitutionality of any Act of Congress affecting the public interest is drawn in question, the court shall certify such fact to the Attorney General, and shall permit the United States to intervene for presentation of evidence, if evidence is otherwise admissible in the case, and for argument on the question of constitutionality. The United States shall, subject to the applicable provisions of law, have all the rights of a party and be subject to all liabilities of a party as to court costs to the extent necessary for a proper presentation of the facts and law relating to the question of constitutionality.

(b) In any action, suit, or proceeding in a court of the United States to which a State or any agency, officer, or employee thereof is not a party, wherein the constitutionality of any statute of that State affecting the public interest is drawn in question, the court shall certify such fact to the attorney general of the State, and shall permit the State to intervene for presentation of evidence, if evidence is otherwise admissible in the case, and for argument on the question of constitutionality. The State shall, subject to the applicable provisions of law, have all the rights of a party and be subject to all liabilities of a party as to court costs to the extent necessary for a proper presentation of the facts and law relating to the question of constitutionality.

Substantive

42 U.S.C. §1983

Every person who, under color of any statute, ordinance, regulation, custom, or usage, of any State or Territory or the District of Columbia, subjects, or causes to be subjected, any citizen of the United States or other person within the jurisdiction thereof to the deprivation of any rights, privileges, or immunities secured by the Constitution and laws, shall be liable to the party injured in an action at law, suit in equity, or other proper proceeding for redress, except that in any action brought against a judicial officer for an act or omission taken in such officer's judicial capacity, injunctive relief shall not be granted unless a declaratory decree was violated or declaratory relief was unavailable. For the purposes of this section, any Act of Congress applicable exclusively to the District of Columbia shall be considered to be a statute of the District of Columbia.

FEDERAL RULES OF CIVIL PROCEDURE

Title I.   Scope of Rules; Form of Action

Rule 1.   Scope and Purpose

These rules govern the procedure in all civil actions and proceedings in the United States district courts, except as stated in Rule 81. They should be construed, administered, and employed by the court and the parties to secure the just, speedy, and inexpensive determination of every action and proceeding.

Rule 2.   One Form of Action

There is one form of action—the civil action.

Title II.   Commencing an Action; Service of Process, Pleadings, Motions, and Orders

Rule 3.   Commencing an Action

A civil action is commenced by filing a complaint with the court.

Rule 4.   Summons

(a) Contents; Amendments.
(1) *Contents.* A summons must:
   (A) name the court and the parties;
   (B) be directed to the defendant;
   (C) state the name and address of the plaintiff's attorney or—if unrepresented—of the plaintiff;
   (D) state the time within which the defendant must appear and defend;

(E) notify the defendant that a failure to appear and defend will result in a default judgment against the defendant for the relief demanded in the complaint;

(F) be signed by the clerk; and

(G) bear the court's seal.

(2) *Amendments.* The court may permit a summons to be amended.

(b) Issuance. On or after filing the complaint, the plaintiff may present a summons to the clerk for signature and seal. If the summons is properly completed, the clerk must sign, seal, and issue it to the plaintiff for service on the defendant. A summons—or a copy of a summons that is addressed to multiple defendants—must be issued for each defendant to be served.

(c) Service.

(1) *In General.* A summons must be served with a copy of the complaint. The plaintiff is responsible for having the summons and complaint served within the time allowed by Rule 4(m) and must furnish the necessary copies to the person who makes service.

(2) *By Whom.* Any person who is at least 18 years old and not a party may serve a summons and complaint.

(3) *By a Marshal or Someone Specially Appointed.* At the plaintiff's request, the court may order that service be made by a United States marshal or deputy marshal or by a person specially appointed by the court. The court must so order if the plaintiff is authorized to proceed in forma pauperis under 28 U.S.C. §1915 or as a seaman under 28 U.S.C. §1916.

(d) Waiving Service.

(1) *Requesting a Waiver.* An individual, corporation, or association that is subject to service under Rule 4(e), (f), or (h) has a duty to avoid unnecessary expenses of serving the summons. The plaintiff may notify such a defendant that an action has been commenced and request that the defendant waive service of a summons. The notice and request must:

(A) be in writing and be addressed:

(i) to the individual defendant; or

(ii) for a defendant subject to service under Rule 4(h), to an officer, a managing or general agent, or any other agent authorized by appointment or by law to receive service of process;

(B) name the court where the complaint was filed;

(C) be accompanied by a copy of the complaint, 2 copies of the waiver form appended to this Rule 4, and a prepaid means for returning the form;

(D) inform the defendant, using the form appended to this Rule 4, of the consequences of waiving and not waiving service;

(E) state the date when the request is sent;

(F) give the defendant a reasonable time of at least 30 days after the request was sent—or at least 60 days if sent to the defendant outside any judicial district of the United States—to return the waiver; and

(G) be sent by first-class mail or other reliable means.

(2) *Failure to Waive.* If a defendant located within the United States fails, without good cause, to sign and return a waiver requested by a plaintiff located within the United States, the court must impose on the defendant:

(A) the expenses later incurred in making service; and

(B) the reasonable expenses, including attorney's fees, of any motion required to collect those service expenses.

(3) *Time to Answer After a Waiver.* A defendant who, before being served with process, timely returns a waiver need not serve an answer to the complaint until 60 days after the request was sent—or until 90 days after it was sent to the defendant outside any judicial district of the United States.

(4) *Results of Filing a Waiver.* When the plaintiff files a waiver, proof of service is not required and these rules apply as if a summons and complaint had been served at the time of filing the waiver.

(5) *Jurisdiction and Venue Not Waived.* Waiving service of a summons does not waive any objection to personal jurisdiction or to venue.

(e) **Serving an Individual Within a Judicial District of the United States.** Unless federal law provides otherwise, an individual—other than a minor, an incompetent person, or a person whose waiver has been filed—may be served in a judicial district of the United States by:

(1) following state law for serving a summons in an action brought in courts of general jurisdiction in the state where the district court is located or where service is made; or

(2) doing any of the following:

(A) delivering a copy of the summons and of the complaint to the individual personally;

(B) leaving a copy of each at the individual's dwelling or usual place of abode with someone of suitable age and discretion who resides there; or

(C) delivering a copy of each to an agent authorized by appointment or by law to receive service of process.

(f) **Serving an Individual in a Foreign Country.** Unless federal law provides otherwise, an individual—other than a minor, an incompetent person, or a person whose waiver has been filed—may be served at a place not within any judicial district of the United States:

(1) by any internationally agreed means of service that is reasonably calculated to give notice, such as those authorized by the Hague Convention on the Service Abroad of Judicial and Extrajudicial Documents;

(2) if there is no internationally agreed means, or if an international agreement allows but does not specify other means, by a method that is reasonably calculated to give notice:

    (A) as prescribed by the foreign country's law for service in that country in an action in its courts of general jurisdiction;

    (B) as the foreign authority directs in response to a letter rogatory or letter of request; or

    (C) unless prohibited by the foreign country's law, by:

        (i) delivering a copy of the summons and of the complaint to the individual personally; or

        (ii) using any form of mail that the clerk addresses and sends to the individual and that requires a signed receipt; or

(3) by other means not prohibited by international agreement, as the court orders.

    (g) Serving a Minor or an Incompetent Person. A minor or an incompetent person in a judicial district of the United States must be served by following state law for serving a summons or like process on such a defendant in an action brought in the courts of general jurisdiction of the state where service is made. A minor or an incompetent person who is not within any judicial district of the United States must be served in the manner prescribed by Rule 4(f)(2)(A), (f)(2)(B), or (f)(3).

    (h) Serving a Corporation, Partnership, or Association. Unless federal law provides otherwise or the defendant's waiver has been filed, a domestic or foreign corporation, or a partnership or other unincorporated association that is subject to suit under a common name, must be served:

(1) in a judicial district of the United States:

    (A) in the manner prescribed by Rule 4(e)(1) for serving an individual; or

    (B) by delivering a copy of the summons and of the complaint to an officer, a managing or general agent, or any other agent authorized by appointment or by law to receive service of process and — if the agent is one authorized by statute and the statute so requires — by also mailing a copy of each to the defendant; or

(2) at a place not within any judicial district of the United States, in any manner prescribed by Rule 4(f) for serving an individual, except personal delivery under (f)(2)(C)(i).

    (i) Serving the United States and Its Agencies, Corporations, Officers, or Employees.

(1) *United States.* To serve the United States, a party must:

    (A) (i) deliver a copy of the summons and of the complaint to the United States attorney for the district where the action is brought — or to an assistant

United States attorney or clerical employee whom the United States attorney designates in a writing filed with the court clerk—or

(ii) send a copy of each by registered or certified mail to the civil-process clerk at the United States attorney's office;

(B) send a copy of each by registered or certified mail to the Attorney General of the United States at Washington, D.C.; and

(C) if the action challenges an order of a nonparty agency or officer of the United States, send a copy of each by registered or certified mail to the agency or officer.

(2) *Agency; Corporation; Officer or Employee Sued in an Official Capacity.* To serve a United States agency or corporation, or a United States officer or employee sued only in an official capacity, a party must serve the United States and also send a copy of the summons and of the complaint by registered or certified mail to the agency, corporation, officer, or employee.

(3) *Officer or Employee Sued Individually.* To serve a United States officer or employee sued in an individual capacity for an act or omission occurring in connection with duties performed on the United States' behalf (whether or not the officer or employee is also sued in an official capacity), a party must serve the United States and also serve the officer or employee under Rule 4(e), (f), or (g).

(4) *Extending Time.* The court must allow a party a reasonable time to cure its failure to:

(A) serve a person required to be served under Rule 4(i)(2), if the party has served either the United States attorney or the Attorney General of the United States; or

(B) serve the United States under Rule 4(i)(3), if the party has served the United States officer or employee.

(j) Serving a Foreign, State, or Local Government.

(1) *Foreign State.* A foreign state or its political subdivision, agency, or instrumentality must be served in accordance with 28 U.S.C. §1608.

(2) *State or Local Government.* A state, a municipal corporation, or any other state-created governmental organization that is subject to suit must be served by:

(A) delivering a copy of the summons and of the complaint to its chief executive officer; or

(B) serving a copy of each in the manner prescribed by that state's law for serving a summons or like process on such a defendant.

(k) Territorial Limits of Effective Service.

(1) *In General.* Serving a summons or filing a waiver of service establishes personal jurisdiction over a defendant:

(A) who is subject to the jurisdiction of a court of general jurisdiction in the state where the district court is located;

(B) who is a party joined under Rule 14 or 19 and is served within a judicial district of the United States and not more than 100 miles from where the summons was issued;

(C) when authorized by a federal statute.

(2) *Federal Claim Outside State-Court Jurisdiction.* For a claim that arises under federal law, serving a summons or filing a waiver of service establishes personal jurisdiction over a defendant if:

(A) the defendant is not subject to jurisdiction in any state's courts of general jurisdiction; and

(B) exercising jurisdiction is consistent with the United States Constitution and laws.

(l) Proving Service.

(1) *Affidavit Required.* Unless service is waived, proof of service must be made to the court. Except for service by a United States marshal or deputy marshal, proof must be by the server's affidavit.

(2) *Service Outside the United States.* Service not within any judicial district of the United States must be proved as follows:

(A) if made under Rule 4(f)(1), as provided in the applicable treaty or convention; or

(B) if made under Rule 4(f)(2) or (f)(3), by a receipt signed by the addressee, or by other evidence satisfying the court that the summons and complaint were delivered to the addressee.

(3) *Validity of Service; Amending Proof.* Failure to prove service does not affect the validity of service. The court may permit proof of service to be amended.

(m) Time Limit for Service. If a defendant is not served within 90 days after the complaint is filed, the court—on motion or on its own after notice to the plaintiff—must dismiss the action without prejudice against that defendant or order that service be made within a specified time. But if the plaintiff shows good cause for the failure, the court must extend the time for service for an appropriate period. This subdivision (m) does not apply to service in a foreign country under Rule 4(f), 4(h)(2), or 4(j)(1).

(n) Asserting Jurisdiction over Property or Assets.

(1) *Federal Law.* The court may assert jurisdiction over property if authorized by a federal statute. Notice to claimants of the property must be given as provided in the statute or by serving a summons under this rule.

(2) *State Law.* On a showing that personal jurisdiction over a defendant cannot be obtained in the district where the action is brought by reasonable efforts to serve a summons under this rule, the court may assert jurisdiction over the defendant's assets found in the district. Jurisdiction is acquired by seizing the assets under the circumstances and in the manner provided by state law in that district.

Rule 4.   Notice of a Lawsuit and Request to Waive Service of Summons

(Caption)

To (*name the defendant or — if the defendant is a corporation, partnership, or association —name an officer or agent authorized to receive service*):

Why are you getting this?

A lawsuit has been filed against you, or the entity you represent, in this court under the number shown above. A copy of the complaint is attached.

This is not a summons, or an official notice from the court. It is a request that, to avoid expenses, you waive formal service of a summons by signing and returning the enclosed waiver. To avoid these expenses, you must return the signed waiver within (*give at least 30 days or at least 60 days if the defendant is outside any judicial district of the United States*) from the date shown below, which is the date this notice was sent. Two copies of the waiver form are enclosed, along with a stamped, self-addressed envelope or other prepaid means for returning one copy. You may keep the other copy.

What happens next?

If you return the signed waiver, I will file it with the court. The action will then proceed as if you had been served on the date the waiver is filed, but no summons will be served on you and you will have 60 days from the date this notice is sent (see the date below) to answer the complaint (or 90 days if this notice is sent to you outside any judicial district of the United States).

If you do not return the signed waiver within the time indicated, I will arrange to have the summons and complaint served on you. And I will ask the court to require you, or the entity you represent, to pay the expenses of making service.

Please read the enclosed statement about the duty to avoid unnecessary expenses.

I certify that this request is being sent to you on the date below.

Date: _____

_____
(Signature of the attorney or unrepresented party)

_____
(Printed name)

_____
(Address)

_____
(E-mail address)

_____
(Telephone number)

Rule 4.   Waiver of the Service of Summons

(Caption)

To (*name the plaintiff's attorney or the unrepresented plaintiff*):

I have received your request to waive service of a summons in this action along with a copy of the complaint, two copies of this waiver form, and a prepaid means of returning one signed copy of the form to you.

I, or the entity I represent, agree to save the expense of serving a summons and complaint in this case.

I understand that I, or the entity I represent, will keep all defenses or objections to the lawsuit, the court's jurisdiction, and the venue of the action, but that I waive any objections to the absence of a summons or of service.

I also understand that I, or the entity I represent, must file and serve an answer or a motion under Rule 12 within 60 days from _____, the date when this request was sent (or 90 days if it was sent outside the United States). If I fail to do so, a default judgment will be entered against me or the entity I represent.

Date: _____

_____

(Signature of the attorney or unrepresented party)

_____

(Printed name)

_____

(Address)

_____

(E-mail address)

_____

(Telephone number)

(Attach the following)

Duty to Avoid Unnecessary Expenses of Serving Summons

Rule 4 of the Federal Rules of Civil Procedure requires certain defendants to cooperate in saving unnecessary expenses of serving a summons and complaint. A defendant who is located in the United States and who fails to return a signed waiver of service requested by a plaintiff located in the United States will be required to pay the expenses of service, unless the defendant shows good cause for the failure.

"Good cause" does not include a belief that the lawsuit is groundless, or that it has been brought in an improper venue, or that the court has no jurisdiction over this matter or over the defendant or the defendant's property.

If the waiver is signed and returned, you can still make these and all other defenses and objections, but you cannot object to the absence of a summons or of service.

If you waive service, then you must, within the time specified on the waiver form, serve an answer or a motion under Rule 12 on the plaintiff and file a copy with the court. By signing and returning the waiver form, you are allowed more time to respond than if a summons had been served.

Rule 4.1.   Serving Other Process

(a) **In General.** Process—other than a summons under Rule 4 or a subpoena under Rule 45—must be served by a United States marshal or deputy marshal or by a person specially appointed for that purpose. It may be served anywhere within the territorial limits of the state where the district court is located and, if authorized by a federal statute, beyond those limits. Proof of service must be made under Rule 4(l).

(b) **Enforcing Orders: Committing for Civil Contempt.** An order committing a person for civil contempt of a decree or injunction issued to enforce federal law may be served and enforced in any district. Any other order in a civil-contempt proceeding may be served only in the state where the issuing court is located or elsewhere in the United States within 100 miles from where the order was issued.

Rule 5.   Serving and Filing Pleadings and Other Papers

(a) **Service: When Required.**

(1) *In General.* Unless these rules provide otherwise, each of the following papers must be served on every party:

(A) an order stating that service is required;

(B) a pleading filed after the original complaint, unless the court orders otherwise under Rule 5(c) because there are numerous defendants;

(C) a discovery paper required to be served on a party, unless the court orders otherwise;

(D) a written motion, except one that may be heard ex parte; and

(E) a written notice, appearance, demand, or offer of judgment, or any similar paper.

(2) *If a Party Fails to Appear.* No service is required on a party who is in default for failing to appear. But a pleading that asserts a new claim for relief against such a party must be served on that party under Rule 4.

(3) *Seizing Property.* If an action is begun by seizing property and no person is or need be named as a defendant, any service required before the filing of an appearance, answer, or claim must be made on the person who had custody or possession of the property when it was seized.

(b) Service: How Made.

(1) *Serving an Attorney.* If a party is represented by an attorney, service under this rule must be made on the attorney unless the court orders service on the party.

(2) *Service in General.* A paper is served under this rule by:

(A) handing it to the person;

(B) leaving it:

(i) at the person's office with a clerk or other person in charge or, if no one is in charge, in a conspicuous place in the office; or

(ii) if the person has no office or the office is closed, at the person's dwelling or usual place of abode with someone of suitable age and discretion who resides there;

(C) mailing it to the person's last known address—in which event service is complete upon mailing;

(D) leaving it with the court clerk if the person has no known address;

(E) sending it to a registered user by filing it with the court's electronic-filing system or sending it by other electronic means that the person consented to in writing—in either of which events service is complete upon filing or sending, but is not effective if the filer or sender learns that it did not reach the person to be served; or

(F) delivering it by any other means that the person consented to in writing—in which event service is complete when the person making service delivers it to the agency designated to make delivery.

(3) *Using Court Facilities.* [Abrogated (Apr. 26, 2018, eff. Dec. 1, 2018.)]

(c) Serving Numerous Defendants.

(1) *In General.* If an action involves an unusually large number of defendants, the court may, on motion or on its own, order that:

(A) defendants' pleadings and replies to them need not be served on other defendants;

(B) any crossclaim, counterclaim, avoidance, or affirmative defense in those pleadings and replies to them will be treated as denied or avoided by all other parties; and

(C) filing any such pleading and serving it on the plaintiff constitutes notice of the pleading to all parties.

(2) *Notifying Parties.* A copy of every such order must be served on the parties as the court directs.

(d) Filing.

(1) *Required Filings; Certificate of Service.*

(A) *Papers after the Complaint.* Any paper after the complaint that is required to be served must be filed no later than a reasonable time after service. But disclosures under Rule 26(a)(1) or (2) and the following discovery requests and responses must not be filed until they are used in the proceeding or the court orders filing: depositions, interrogatories, requests for documents or tangible things or to permit entry onto land, and requests for admission.

(B) *Certificate of Service.* No certificate of service is required when a paper is served by filing it with the court's electronic-filing system. When a paper that is required to be served is served by other means:

(i) if the paper is filed, a certificate of service must be filed with it or within a reasonable time after service; and

(ii) if the paper is not filed, a certificate of service need not be filed unless filing is required by court order or by local rule.

(2) *Nonelectronic Filing.* A paper not filed electronically is filed by delivering it:

(A) to the clerk; or

(B) to a judge who agrees to accept it for filing, and who must then note the filing date on the paper and promptly send it to the clerk.

(3) *Electronic Filing and Signing.*

(A) *By a Represented Person—Generally Required; Exceptions.* A person represented by an attorney must file electronically, unless nonelectronic filing is allowed by the court for good cause or is allowed or required by local rule.

(B) *By an Unrepresented Person—When Allowed or Required.* A person not represented by an attorney:

(i) may file electronically only if allowed by court order or by local rule; and

(ii) may be required to file electronically only by court order, or by a local rule that includes reasonable exceptions.

(C) *Signing.* A filing made through a person's electronic-filing account and authorized by that person, together with that person's name on a signature block, constitutes the person's signature.

(D) *Same as a Written Paper.* A paper filed electronically is a written paper for purposes of these rules.

(4) *Acceptance by the Clerk.* The clerk must not refuse to file a paper solely because it is not in the form prescribed by these rules or by a local rule or practice.

Rule 5.1. Constitutional Challenge to a Statute—Notice, Certification, and Intervention

(a) **Notice by a Party.** A party that files a pleading, written motion, or other paper drawing into question the constitutionality of a federal or state statute must promptly:

(1) file a notice of constitutional question stating the question and identifying the paper that raises it, if:

(A) a federal statute is questioned and the parties do not include the United States, one of its agencies, or one of its officers or employees in an official capacity; or

(B) a state statute is questioned and the parties do not include the state, one of its agencies, or one of its officers or employees in an official capacity; and

(2) serve the notice and paper on the Attorney General of the United States if a federal statute is questioned—or on the state attorney general if a state statute is questioned—either by certified or registered mail or by sending it to an electronic address designated by the attorney general for this purpose.

(b) Certification by the Court. The court must, under 28 U.S.C. §2403, certify to the appropriate attorney general that a statute has been questioned.

(c) Intervention; Final Decision on the Merits. Unless the court sets a later time, the attorney general may intervene within 60 days after the notice is filed or after the court certifies the challenge, whichever is earlier. Before the time to intervene expires, the court may reject the constitutional challenge, but may not enter a final judgment holding the statute unconstitutional.

(d) No Forfeiture. A party's failure to file and serve the notice, or the court's failure to certify, does not forfeit a constitutional claim or defense that is otherwise timely asserted.

Rule 5.2.   Privacy Protection for Filings Made with the Court

(a) Redacted Filings. Unless the court orders otherwise, in an electronic or paper filing with the court that contains an individual's social-security number, taxpayer-identification number, or birth date, the name of an individual known to be a minor, or a financial-account number, a party or nonparty making the filing may include only:

(1) the last four digits of the social-security number and taxpayer-identification number;

(2) the year of the individual's birth;

(3) the minor's initials; and

(4) the last four digits of the financial-account number.

(b) Exemptions from the Redaction Requirement. The redaction requirement does not apply to the following:

(1) a financial-account number that identifies the property allegedly subject to forfeiture in a forfeiture proceeding;

(2) the record of an administrative or agency proceeding;

(3) the official record of a state-court proceeding;

(4) the record of a court or tribunal, if that record was not subject to the redaction requirement when originally filed;

(5) a filing covered by Rule 5.2(c) or (d); and

(6) a pro se filing in an action brought under 28 U.S.C. §§2241, 2254, or 2255.

(c) Limitations on Remote Access to Electronic Files; Social-Security Appeals and Immigration Cases. Unless the court orders otherwise, in an action for benefits under the Social Security Act, and in an action or proceeding relating to an order of removal, to relief from removal, or to immigration benefits or detention, access to an electronic file is authorized as follows:

(1) the parties and their attorneys may have remote electronic access to any part of the case file, including the administrative record;

(2) any other person may have electronic access to the full record at the courthouse, but may have remote electronic access only to:

(A) the docket maintained by the court; and

(B) an opinion, order, judgment, or other disposition of the court, but not any other part of the case file or the administrative record.

(d) Filings Made Under Seal. The court may order that a filing be made under seal without redaction. The court may later unseal the filing or order the person who made the filing to file a redacted version for the public record.

(e) Protective Orders. For good cause, the court may by order in a case:

(1) require redaction of additional information; or

(2) limit or prohibit a nonparty's remote electronic access to a document filed with the court.

(f) Option for Additional Unredacted Filing Under Seal. A person making a redacted filing may also file an unredacted copy under seal. The court must retain the unredacted copy as part of the record.

(g) Option for Filing a Reference List. A filing that contains redacted information may be filed together with a reference list that identifies each item of redacted information and specifies an appropriate identifier that uniquely corresponds to each item listed. The list must be filed under seal and may be amended as of right. Any reference in the case to a listed identifier will be construed to refer to the corresponding item of information.

(h) Waiver of Protection of Identifiers. A person waives the protection of Rule 5.2(a) as to the person's own information by filing it without redaction and not under seal.

Rule 6. Computing and Extending Time; Time for Motion Papers

(a) **Computing Time.** The following rules apply in computing any time period specified in these rules, in any local rule or court order, or in any statute that does not specify a method of computing time.

(1) *Period Stated in Days or a Longer Unit.* When the period is stated in days or a longer unit of time:

(A) exclude the day of the event that triggers the period;

(B) count every day, including intermediate Saturdays, Sundays, and legal holidays; and

(C) include the last day of the period, but if the last day is a Saturday, Sunday, or legal holiday, the period continues to run until the end of the next day that is not a Saturday, Sunday, or legal holiday.

(2) *Period Stated in Hours.* When the period is stated in hours:

(A) begin counting immediately on the occurrence of the event that triggers the period;

(B) count every hour, including hours during intermediate Saturdays, Sundays, and legal holidays; and

(C) if the period would end on a Saturday, Sunday, or legal holiday, the period continues to run until the same time on the next day that is not a Saturday, Sunday, or legal holiday.

(3) *Inaccessibility of the Clerk's Office.* Unless the court orders otherwise, if the clerk's office is inaccessible:

(A) on the last day for filing under Rule 6(a)(1), then the time for filing is extended to the first accessible day that is not a Saturday, Sunday, or legal holiday; or

(B) during the last hour for filing under Rule 6(a)(2), then the time for filing is extended to the same time on the first accessible day that is not a Saturday, Sunday, or legal holiday.

(4) *"Last Day" Defined.* Unless a different time is set by a statute, local rule, or court order, the last day ends:

(A) for electronic filing, at midnight in the court's time zone; and

(B) for filing by other means, when the clerk's office is scheduled to close.

(5) *"Next Day" Defined.* The "next day" is determined by continuing to count forward when the period is measured after an event and backward when measured before an event.

(6) *"Legal Holiday" Defined.* "Legal holiday" means:

(A) the day set aside by statute for observing New Year's Day, Martin Luther King Jr.'s Birthday, Washington's Birthday, Memorial Day, Independence Day, Labor Day, Columbus Day, Veterans' Day, Thanksgiving Day, or Christmas Day;

(B) any day declared a holiday by the President or Congress; and

(C) for periods that are measured after an event, any other day declared a holiday by the state where the district court is located.

(b) Extending Time.

(1) *In General.* When an act may or must be done within a specified time, the court may, for good cause, extend the time:

(A) with or without motion or notice if the court acts, or if a request is made, before the original time or its extension expires; or

(B) on motion made after the time has expired if the party failed to act because of excusable neglect.

(2) *Exceptions.* A court must not extend the time to act under Rules 50(b) and (d), 52(b), 59(b), (d), and (e), and 60(b).

(c) Motions, Notices of Hearing, and Affidavits.

(1) *In General.* A written motion and notice of the hearing must be served at least 14 days before the time specified for the hearing, with the following exceptions:

(A) when the motion may be heard ex parte;

(B) when these rules set a different time; or

(C) when a court order—which a party may, for good cause, apply for ex parte—sets a different time.

(2) *Supporting Affidavit.* Any affidavit supporting a motion must be served with the motion. Except as Rule 59(c) provides otherwise, any opposing affidavit must be served at least 7 days before the hearing, unless the court permits service at another time.

(d) Additional Time After Certain Kinds of Service. When a party may or must act within a specified time after service and service is made under Rule 5(b)(2)(C) (mail), (D) (leaving with clerk), or (F) (other means consented to), 3 days are added after the period would otherwise expire under Rule 6(a).

Title III. Pleadings and Motions

Rule 7. Pleadings Allowed; Form of Motions and Other Papers

(a) Pleadings. Only these pleadings are allowed:

(1) a complaint;

(2) an answer to a complaint;

(3) an answer to a counterclaim designated as a counterclaim;

(4) an answer to a crossclaim;

(5) a third-party complaint;

(6) an answer to a third-party complaint; and

(7) if the court orders one, a reply to an answer.

(b) Motions and Other Papers.

(1) *In General.* A request for a court order must be made by motion. The motion must:

    (A) be in writing unless made during a hearing or trial;

    (B) state with particularity the grounds for seeking the order; and \

    (C) state the relief sought.

  (2) *Form.* The rules governing captions and other matters of form in pleadings apply to motions and other papers.

Rule 7.1.   Disclosure Statement

(a) Who Must File; Contents. A nongovernmental corporate party must file two copies of a disclosure statement that:

  (1) identifies any parent corporation and any publicly held corporation owning 10% or more of its stock; or

  (2) states that there is no such corporation.

(b) Time to File; Supplemental Filing. A party must:

  (1) file the disclosure statement with its first appearance, pleading, petition, motion, response, or other request addressed to the court; and

  (2) promptly file a supplemental statement if any required information changes.

Rule 8.   General Rules of Pleading

(a) Claim for Relief. A pleading that states a claim for relief must contain:

  (1) a short and plain statement of the grounds for the court's jurisdiction, unless the court already has jurisdiction and the claim needs no new jurisdictional support;

  (2) a short and plain statement of the claim showing that the pleader is entitled to relief; and

  (3) a demand for the relief sought, which may include relief in the alternative or different types of relief.

(b) Defenses; Admissions and Denials.

  (1) *In General.* In responding to a pleading, a party must:

    (A) state in short and plain terms its defenses to each claim asserted against it; and

    (B) admit or deny the allegations asserted against it by an opposing party.

  (2) *Denials—Responding to the Substance.* A denial must fairly respond to the substance of the allegation.

  (3) *General and Specific Denials.* A party that intends in good faith to deny all the allegations of a pleading—including the jurisdictional grounds—may do so by a general denial. A party that does not intend to deny all the allegations must

either specifically deny designated allegations or generally deny all except those specifically admitted.

(4) *Denying Part of an Allegation.* A party that intends in good faith to deny only part of an allegation must admit the part that is true and deny the rest.

(5) *Lacking Knowledge or Information.* A party that lacks knowledge or information sufficient to form a belief about the truth of an allegation must so state, and the statement has the effect of a denial.

(6) *Effect of Failing to Deny.* An allegation—other than one relating to the amount of damages—is admitted if a responsive pleading is required and the allegation is not denied. If a responsive pleading is not required, an allegation is considered denied or avoided.

(c) Affirmative Defenses.

(1) *In General.* In responding to a pleading, a party must affirmatively state any avoidance or affirmative defense, including:

- accord and satisfaction;
- arbitration and award;
- assumption of risk;
- contributory negligence;
- duress;
- estoppel;
- failure of consideration;
- fraud;
- illegality;
- injury by fellow servant;
- laches;
- license;
- payment;
- release;
- res judicata;
- statute of frauds;
- statute of limitations; and
- waiver.

(2) *Mistaken Designation.* If a party mistakenly designates a defense as a counterclaim, or a counterclaim as a defense, the court must, if justice requires, treat the pleading as though it were correctly designated, and may impose terms for doing so.

(d) Pleading to Be Concise and Direct; Alternative Statements; Inconsistency.

(1) *In General.* Each allegation must be simple, concise, and direct. No technical form is required.

(2) *Alternative Statements of a Claim or Defense.* A party may set out two or more statements of a claim or defense alternatively or hypothetically, either in a single count or defense or in separate ones. If a party makes alternative statements, the pleading is sufficient if any one of them is sufficient.

(3) *Inconsistent Claims or Defenses.* A party may state as many separate claims or defenses as it has, regardless of consistency.

(e) Construing Pleadings. Pleadings must be construed so as to do justice.

Rule 9.   Pleading Special Matters

(a) Capacity or Authority to Sue; Legal Existence.

(1) *In General.* Except when required to show that the court has jurisdiction, a pleading need not allege:

(A) a party's capacity to sue or be sued;

(B) a party's authority to sue or be sued in a representative capacity; or

(C) the legal existence of an organized association of persons that is made a party.

(2) *Raising Those Issues.* To raise any of those issues, a party must do so by a specific denial, which must state any supporting facts that are peculiarly within the party's knowledge.

(b) Fraud or Mistake; Conditions of Mind. In alleging fraud or mistake, a party must state with particularity the circumstances constituting fraud or mistake. Malice, intent, knowledge, and other conditions of a person's mind may be alleged generally.

(c) Conditions Precedent. In pleading conditions precedent, it suffices to allege generally that all conditions precedent have occurred or been performed. But when denying that a condition precedent has occurred or been performed, a party must do so with particularity.

(d) Official Document or Act. In pleading an official document or official act, it suffices to allege that the document was legally issued or the act legally done.

(e) Judgment. In pleading a judgment or decision of a domestic or foreign court, a judicial or quasi-judicial tribunal, or a board or officer, it suffices to plead the judgment or decision without showing jurisdiction to render it.

(f) Time and Place. An allegation of time or place is material when testing the sufficiency of a pleading.

(g) Special Damages. If an item of special damage is claimed, it must be specifically stated.

(h) Admiralty or Maritime Claim.

(1) *How Designated.* If a claim for relief is within the admiralty or maritime jurisdiction and also within the court's subject-matter jurisdiction on some other ground, the pleading may designate the claim as an admiralty or maritime claim for purposes of Rules 14(c), 38(e), and 82 and the Supplemental Rules for Admiralty or Maritime Claims and Asset Forfeiture Actions. A claim cognizable only in the admiralty or maritime jurisdiction is an admiralty or maritime claim for those purposes, whether or not so designated.

(2) *Designation for Appeal.* A case that includes an admiralty or maritime claim within this subdivision (h) is an admiralty case within 28 U.S.C. §1292(a)(3).

Rule 10.   Form of Pleadings

(a) Caption; Names of Parties. Every pleading must have a caption with the court's name, a title, a file number, and a Rule 7(a) designation. The title of the complaint must name all the parties; the title of other pleadings, after naming the first party on each side, may refer generally to other parties.

(b) Paragraphs; Separate Statements. A party must state its claims or defenses in numbered paragraphs, each limited as far as practicable to a single set of circumstances. A later pleading may refer by number to a paragraph in an earlier pleading. If doing so would promote clarity, each claim founded on a separate transaction or occurrence—and each defense other than a denial—must be stated in a separate count or defense.

(c) Adoption by Reference; Exhibits. A statement in a pleading may be adopted by reference elsewhere in the same pleading or in any other pleading or motion. A copy of a written instrument that is an exhibit to a pleading is a part of the pleading for all purposes.

Rule 11.   Signing Pleadings, Motions, and Other Papers; Representations to the Court; Sanctions

(a) Signature. Every pleading, written motion, and other paper must be signed by at least one attorney of record in the attorney's name—or by a party personally if the party is unrepresented. The paper must state the signer's address, e-mail address, and telephone number. Unless a rule or statute specifically states otherwise, a pleading need not be verified or accompanied by an affidavit. The court must strike an unsigned paper unless the omission is promptly corrected after being called to the attorney's or party's attention.

(b) **Representations to the Court.** By presenting to the court a pleading, written motion, or other paper—whether by signing, filing, submitting, or later advocating it—an attorney or unrepresented party certifies that to the best of the person's knowledge, information, and belief, formed after an inquiry reasonable under the circumstances:

(1) it is not being presented for any improper purpose, such as to harass, cause unnecessary delay, or needlessly increase the cost of litigation;

(2) the claims, defenses, and other legal contentions are warranted by existing law or by a nonfrivolous argument for extending, modifying, or reversing existing law or for establishing new law;

(3) the factual contentions have evidentiary support or, if specifically so identified, will likely have evidentiary support after a reasonable opportunity for further investigation or discovery; and

(4) the denials of factual contentions are warranted on the evidence or, if specifically so identified, are reasonably based on belief or a lack of information.

(c) **Sanctions.**

(1) *In General.* If, after notice and a reasonable opportunity to respond, the court determines that Rule 11(b) has been violated, the court may impose an appropriate sanction on any attorney, law firm, or party that violated the rule or is responsible for the violation. Absent exceptional circumstances, a law firm must be held jointly responsible for a violation committed by its partner, associate, or employee.

(2) *Motion for Sanctions.* A motion for sanctions must be made separately from any other motion and must describe the specific conduct that allegedly violates Rule 11(b). The motion must be served under Rule 5, but it must not be filed or be presented to the court if the challenged paper, claim, defense, contention, or denial is withdrawn or appropriately corrected within 21 days after service or within another time the court sets. If warranted, the court may award to the prevailing party the reasonable expenses, including attorney's fees, incurred for the motion.

(3) *On the Court's Initiative.* On its own, the court may order an attorney, law firm, or party to show cause why conduct specifically described in the order has not violated Rule 11(b).

(4) *Nature of a Sanction.* A sanction imposed under this rule must be limited to what suffices to deter repetition of the conduct or comparable conduct by others similarly situated. The sanction may include nonmonetary directives; an order to pay a penalty into court; or, if imposed on motion and warranted for

effective deterrence, an order directing payment to the movant of part or all of the reasonable attorney's fees and other expenses directly resulting from the violation.

(5) *Limitations on Monetary Sanctions.* The court must not impose a monetary sanction:

(A) against a represented party for violating Rule 11(b)(2); or

(B) on its own, unless it issued the show-cause order under Rule 11(c)(3) before voluntary dismissal or settlement of the claims made by or against the party that is, or whose attorneys are, to be sanctioned.

(6) *Requirements for an Order.* An order imposing a sanction must describe the sanctioned conduct and explain the basis for the sanction.

(d) **Inapplicability to Discovery.** This rule does not apply to disclosures and discovery requests, responses, objections, and motions under Rules 26 through 37.

Rule 12.   Defenses and Objections: When and How Presented; Motion for Judgment on the Pleadings; Consolidating Motions; Waiving Defenses; Pretrial Hearing

(a) **Time to Serve a Responsive Pleading.**

(1) *In General.* Unless another time is specified by this rule or a federal statute, the time for serving a responsive pleading is as follows:

(A) A defendant must serve an answer:

(i) within 21 days after being served with the summons and complaint; or

(ii) if it has timely waived service under Rule 4(d), within 60 days after the request for a waiver was sent, or within 90 days after it was sent to the defendant outside any judicial district of the United States.

(B) A party must serve an answer to a counterclaim or crossclaim within 21 days after being served with the pleading that states the counterclaim or crossclaim.

(C) A party must serve a reply to an answer within 21 days after being served with an order to reply, unless the order specifies a different time.

(2) *United States and Its Agencies, Officers, or Employees Sued in an Official Capacity.* The United States, a United States agency, or a United States officer or employee sued only in an official capacity must serve an answer to a complaint, counterclaim, or crossclaim within 60 days after service on the United States attorney.

(3) *United States Officers or Employees Sued in an Individual Capacity.* A United States officer or employee sued in an individual capacity for an act or omission occurring in connection with duties performed on the United States' behalf must serve an answer to a complaint, counterclaim, or crossclaim within

60 days after service on the officer or employee or service on the United States attorney, whichever is later.

    (4) *Effect of a Motion.* Unless the court sets a different time, serving a motion under this rule alters these periods as follows:

        (A) if the court denies the motion or postpones its disposition until trial, the responsive pleading must be served within 14 days after notice of the court's action; or

        (B) if the court grants a motion for a more definite statement, the responsive pleading must be served within 14 days after the more definite statement is served.

    (b) How to Present Defenses. Every defense to a claim for relief in any pleading must be asserted in the responsive pleading if one is required. But a party may assert the following defenses by motion:

    (1) lack of subject-matter jurisdiction;

    (2) lack of personal jurisdiction;

    (3) improper venue;

    (4) insufficient process;

    (5) insufficient service of process;

    (6) failure to state a claim upon which relief can be granted; and

    (7) failure to join a party under Rule 19.

A motion asserting any of these defenses must be made before pleading if a responsive pleading is allowed. If a pleading sets out a claim for relief that does not require a responsive pleading, an opposing party may assert at trial any defense to that claim. No defense or objection is waived by joining it with one or more other defenses or objections in a responsive pleading or in a motion.

    (c) Motion for Judgment on the Pleadings. After the pleadings are closed — but early enough not to delay trial — a party may move for judgment on the pleadings.

    (d) Result of Presenting Matters Outside the Pleadings. If, on a motion under Rule 12(b)(6) or 12(c), matters outside the pleadings are presented to and not excluded by the court, the motion must be treated as one for summary judgment under Rule 56. All parties must be given a reasonable opportunity to present all the material that is pertinent to the motion.

    (e) Motion for a More Definite Statement. A party may move for a more definite statement of a pleading to which a responsive pleading is allowed but which is so vague or ambiguous that the party cannot reasonably prepare a response. The motion must be made before filing a responsive pleading and must point out the defects complained of and the details desired. If the court orders a more definite statement and the order is not obeyed within 14 days after notice of the order or within the time the court sets, the court may strike the pleading or issue any other appropriate order.

(f) Motion to Strike. The court may strike from a pleading an insufficient defense or any redundant, immaterial, impertinent, or scandalous matter. The court may act:

(1) on its own; or

(2) on motion made by a party either before responding to the pleading or, if a response is not allowed, within 21 days after being served with the pleading.

(g) Joining Motions.

(1) *Right to Join.* A motion under this rule may be joined with any other motion allowed by this rule.

(2) *Limitation on Further Motions.* Except as provided in Rule 12(h)(2) or (3), a party that makes a motion under this rule must not make another motion under this rule raising a defense or objection that was available to the party but omitted from its earlier motion.

(h) Waiving and Preserving Certain Defenses.

(1) *When Some Are Waived.* A party waives any defense listed in Rule 12(b)(2)-(5) by:

(A) omitting it from a motion in the circumstances described in Rule 12(g)(2); or

(B) failing to either:

(i) make it by motion under this rule; or

(ii) include it in a responsive pleading or in an amendment allowed by Rule 15(a)(1) as a matter of course.

(2) *When to Raise Others.* Failure to state a claim upon which relief can be granted, to join a person required by Rule 19(b), or to state a legal defense to a claim may be raised:

(A) in any pleading allowed or ordered under Rule 7(a);

(B) by a motion under Rule 12(c); or

(C) at trial.

(3) *Lack of Subject-Matter Jurisdiction.* If the court determines at any time that it lacks subject-matter jurisdiction, the court must dismiss the action.

(i) Hearing Before Trial. If a party so moves, any defense listed in Rule 12(b)(1)-(7)—whether made in a pleading or by motion—and a motion under Rule 12(c) must be heard and decided before trial unless the court orders a deferral until trial.

Rule 13.   Counterclaim and Crossclaim

(a) Compulsory Counterclaim.

(1) *In General.* A pleading must state as a counterclaim any claim that—at the time of its service—the pleader has against an opposing party if the claim:

(A) arises out of the transaction or occurrence that is the subject matter of the opposing party's claim; and

(B) does not require adding another party over whom the court cannot acquire jurisdiction.

(2) *Exceptions.* The pleader need not state the claim if:

(A) when the action was commenced, the claim was the subject of another pending action; or

(B) the opposing party sued on its claim by attachment or other process that did not establish personal jurisdiction over the pleader on that claim, and the pleader does not assert any counterclaim under this rule.

(b) Permissive Counterclaim. A pleading may state as a counterclaim against an opposing party any claim that is not compulsory.

(c) Relief Sought in a Counterclaim. A counterclaim need not diminish or defeat the recovery sought by the opposing party. It may request relief that exceeds in amount or differs in kind from the relief sought by the opposing party.

(d) Counterclaim Against the United States. These rules do not expand the right to assert a counterclaim—or to claim a credit—against the United States or a United States officer or agency.

(e) Counterclaim Maturing or Acquired After Pleading. The court may permit a party to file a supplemental pleading asserting a counterclaim that matured or was acquired by the party after serving an earlier pleading.

(f) [Abrogated]

(g) Crossclaim Against a Coparty. A pleading may state as a crossclaim any claim by one party against a coparty if the claim arises out of the transaction or occurrence that is the subject matter of the original action or of a counterclaim, or if the claim relates to any property that is the subject matter of the original action. The crossclaim may include a claim that the coparty is or may be liable to the crossclaimant for all or part of a claim asserted in the action against the crossclaimant.

(h) Joining Additional Parties. Rules 19 and 20 govern the addition of a person as a party to a counterclaim or crossclaim.

(i) Separate Trials; Separate Judgments. If the court orders separate trials under Rule 42(b), it may enter judgment on a counterclaim or crossclaim under Rule 54(b) when it has jurisdiction to do so, even if the opposing party's claims have been dismissed or otherwise resolved.

Rule 14.   Third-Party Practice

(a) When a Defending Party May Bring in a Third Party.

(1) *Timing of the Summons and Complaint.* A defending party may, as third-party plaintiff, serve a summons and complaint on a nonparty who is or may be liable to it for all or part of the claim against it. But the third-party plaintiff must, by motion, obtain the court's leave if it files the third-party complaint more than 14 days after serving its original answer.

(2) *Third-Party Defendant's Claims and Defenses.* The person served with the summons and third-party complaint—the "third-party defendant":

(A) must assert any defense against the third-party plaintiff's claim under Rule 12;

(B) must assert any counterclaim against the third-party plaintiff under Rule 13(a), and may assert any counterclaim against the third-party plaintiff under Rule 13(b) or any crossclaim against another third-party defendant under Rule 13(g);

(C) may assert against the plaintiff any defense that the third-party plaintiff has to the plaintiff's claim; and

(D) may also assert against the plaintiff any claim arising out of the transaction or occurrence that is the subject matter of the plaintiff's claim against the third-party plaintiff.

(3) *Plaintiff's Claims Against a Third-Party Defendant.* The plaintiff may assert against the third-party defendant any claim arising out of the transaction or occurrence that is the subject matter of the plaintiff's claim against the third-party plaintiff. The third-party defendant must then assert any defense under Rule 12 and any counterclaim under Rule 13(a), and may assert any counterclaim under Rule 13(b) or any crossclaim under Rule 13(g).

(4) *Motion to Strike, Sever, or Try Separately.* Any party may move to strike the third-party claim, to sever it, or to try it separately.

(5) *Third-Party Defendant's Claim Against a Nonparty.* A third-party defendant may proceed under this rule against a nonparty who is or may be liable to the third-party defendant for all or part of any claim against it.

(6) *Third-Party Complaint In Rem.* If it is within the admiralty or maritime jurisdiction, a third-party complaint may be in rem. In that event, a reference in this rule to the "summons" includes the warrant of arrest, and a reference to the defendant or third-party plaintiff includes, when appropriate, a person who asserts a right under Supplemental Rule C(6)(a)(i) in the property arrested.

(b) When a Plaintiff May Bring in a Third Party. When a claim is asserted against a plaintiff, the plaintiff may bring in a third party if this rule would allow a defendant to do so.

(c) Admiralty or Maritime Claim.

(1) *Scope of Impleader.* If a plaintiff asserts an admiralty or maritime claim under Rule 9(h), the defendant or a person who asserts a right under Supplemental Rule C(6)(a)(i) may, as a third-party plaintiff, bring in a third-party defendant who may be wholly or partly liable—either to the plaintiff or to the third-party plaintiff—for remedy over, contribution, or otherwise on account of the same transaction, occurrence, or series of transactions or occurrences.

(2) *Defending Against a Demand for Judgment for the Plaintiff.* The third-party plaintiff may demand judgment in the plaintiff's favor against the third-party defendant. In that event, the third-party defendant must defend under Rule 12 against the plaintiff's claim as well as the third-party plaintiff's claim; and the action proceeds as if the plaintiff had sued both the third-party defendant and the third-party plaintiff.

Rule 15.   Amended and Supplemental Pleadings

(a) Amendments Before Trial.

(1) *Amending as a Matter of Course.* A party may amend its pleading once as a matter of course within:

(A) 21 days after serving it, or

(B) if the pleading is one to which a responsive pleading is required, 21 days after service of a responsive pleading or 21 days after service of a motion under Rule 12(b), (e), or (f), whichever is earlier.

(2) *Other Amendments.* In all other cases, a party may amend its pleading only with the opposing party's written consent or the court's leave. The court should freely give leave when justice so requires.

(3) *Time to Respond.* Unless the court orders otherwise, any required response to an amended pleading must be made within the time remaining to respond to the original pleading or within 14 days after service of the amended pleading, whichever is later.

(b) Amendments During and After Trial.

(1) *Based on an Objection at Trial.* If, at trial, a party objects that evidence is not within the issues raised in the pleadings, the court may permit the pleadings to be amended. The court should freely permit an amendment when doing so will aid in presenting the merits and the objecting party fails to satisfy the court that the evidence would prejudice that party's action or defense on the merits. The court may grant a continuance to enable the objecting party to meet the evidence.

(2) *For Issues Tried by Consent.* When an issue not raised by the pleadings is tried by the parties' express or implied consent, it must be treated in all respects as if raised in the pleadings. A party may move—at any time, even after judgment—to amend the pleadings to conform them to the evidence and to raise

an unpleaded issue. But failure to amend does not affect the result of the trial of that issue.

(c) Relation Back of Amendments.
(1) *When an Amendment Relates Back.* An amendment to a pleading relates back to the date of the original pleading when:

(A) the law that provides the applicable statute of limitations allows relation back;

(B) the amendment asserts a claim or defense that arose out of the conduct, transaction, or occurrence set out—or attempted to be set out—in the original pleading; or

(C) the amendment changes the party or the naming of the party against whom a claim is asserted, if Rule 15(c)(1)(B) is satisfied and if, within the period provided by Rule 4(m) for serving the summons and complaint, the party to be brought in by amendment:

(i) received such notice of the action that it will not be prejudiced in defending on the merits; and

(ii) knew or should have known that the action would have been brought against it, but for a mistake concerning the proper party's identity.

(2) *Notice to the United States.* When the United States or a United States officer or agency is added as a defendant by amendment, the notice requirements of Rule 15(c)(1)(C)(i) and (ii) are satisfied if, during the stated period, process was delivered or mailed to the United States attorney or the United States attorney's designee, to the Attorney General of the United States, or to the officer or agency.

(d) Supplemental Pleadings. On motion and reasonable notice, the court may, on just terms, permit a party to serve a supplemental pleading setting out any transaction, occurrence, or event that happened after the date of the pleading to be supplemented. The court may permit supplementation even though the original pleading is defective in stating a claim or defense. The court may order that the opposing party plead to the supplemental pleading within a specified time.

Rule 16.   Pretrial Conferences; Scheduling; Management

(a) Purposes of a Pretrial Conference. In any action, the court may order the attorneys and any unrepresented parties to appear for one or more pretrial conferences for such purposes as:

(1) expediting disposition of the action;

(2) establishing early and continuing control so that the case will not be protracted because of lack of management;

(3) discouraging wasteful pretrial activities;

(4) improving the quality of the trial through more thorough preparation; and

(5) facilitating settlement.

(b) Scheduling.

(1) *Scheduling Order.* Except in categories of actions exempted by local rule, the district judge—or a magistrate judge when authorized by local rule—must issue a scheduling order:

(A) after receiving the parties' report under Rule 26(f); or

(B) after consulting with the parties' attorneys and any unrepresented parties at a scheduling conference.

(2) *Time to Issue.* The judge must issue the scheduling order as soon as practicable, but unless the judge finds good cause for delay, the judge must issue it within the earlier of 90 days after any defendant has been served with the complaint or 60 days after any defendant has appeared.

(3) *Contents of the Order.*

(A) *Required Contents.* The scheduling order must limit the time to join other parties, amend the pleadings, complete discovery, and file motions.

(B) *Permitted Contents.* The scheduling order may:

(i) modify the timing of disclosures under Rules 26(a) and 26(e)(1);

(ii) modify the extent of discovery;

(iii) provide for disclosure, discovery, or preservation of electronically stored information;

(iv) include any agreements the parties reach for asserting claims of privilege or of protection as trial-preparation material after information is produced, including agreements reached under Federal Rule of Evidence 502;

(v) direct that before moving for an order relating to discovery, the movant must request a conference with the court;

(vi) set dates for pretrial conferences and for trial; and

(vii) include other appropriate matters.

(4) *Modifying a Schedule.* A schedule may be modified only for good cause and with the judge's consent.

(c) Attendance and Matters for Consideration at a Pretrial Conference.

(1) *Attendance.* A represented party must authorize at least one of its attorneys to make stipulations and admissions about all matters that can reasonably be anticipated for discussion at a pretrial conference. If appropriate, the court may require that a party or its representative be present or reasonably available by other means to consider possible settlement.

(2) *Matters for Consideration.* At any pretrial conference, the court may consider and take appropriate action on the following matters:

(A) formulating and simplifying the issues, and eliminating frivolous claims or defenses;

(B) amending the pleadings if necessary or desirable;

(C) obtaining admissions and stipulations about facts and documents to avoid unnecessary proof, and ruling in advance on the admissibility of evidence;

(D) avoiding unnecessary proof and cumulative evidence, and limiting the use of testimony under Federal Rule of Evidence 702;

(E) determining the appropriateness and timing of summary adjudication under Rule 56;

(F) controlling and scheduling discovery, including orders affecting disclosures and discovery under Rule 26 and Rules 29 through 37;

(G) identifying witnesses and documents, scheduling the filing and exchange of any pretrial briefs, and setting dates for further conferences and for trial;

(H) referring matters to a magistrate judge or a master;

(I) settling the case and using special procedures to assist in resolving the dispute when authorized by statute or local rule;

(J) determining the form and content of the pretrial order;

(K) disposing of pending motions;

(L) adopting special procedures for managing potentially difficult or protracted actions that may involve complex issues, multiple parties, difficult legal questions, or unusual proof problems;

(M) ordering a separate trial under Rule 42(b) of a claim, counterclaim, crossclaim, third-party claim, or particular issue;

(N) ordering the presentation of evidence early in the trial on a manageable issue that might, on the evidence, be the basis for a judgment as a matter of law under Rule 50(a) or a judgment on partial findings under Rule 52(c);

(O) establishing a reasonable limit on the time allowed to present evidence; and

(P) facilitating in other ways the just, speedy, and inexpensive disposition of the action.

(d) Pretrial Orders. After any conference under this rule, the court should issue an order reciting the action taken. This order controls the course of the action unless the court modifies it.

(e) Final Pretrial Conference and Orders. The court may hold a final pretrial conference to formulate a trial plan, including a plan to facilitate the admission of evidence. The conference must be held as close to the start of trial as is reasonable, and must be attended by at least one attorney who will conduct the trial for each party and by any unrepresented party. The court may modify the order issued after a final pretrial conference only to prevent manifest injustice.

(f) Sanctions.

(1) *In General.* On motion or on its own, the court may issue any just orders, including those authorized by Rule 37(b)(2)(A)(ii)-(vii), if a party or its attorney:

(A) fails to appear at a scheduling or other pretrial conference;

(B) is substantially unprepared to participate—or does not participate in good faith—in the conference; or

(C) fails to obey a scheduling or other pretrial order.

(2) *Imposing Fees and Costs.* Instead of or in addition to any other sanction, the court must order the party, its attorney, or both to pay the reasonable expenses—including attorney's fees—incurred because of any noncompliance with this rule, unless the noncompliance was substantially justified or other circumstances make an award of expenses unjust.

Title IV.   Parties

Rule 17.   Plaintiff and Defendant; Capacity; Public Officers

(a) **Real Party in Interest.**

(1) *Designation in General.* An action must be prosecuted in the name of the real party in interest. The following may sue in their own names without joining the person for whose benefit the action is brought:

(A) an executor;

(B) an administrator;

(C) a guardian;

(D) a bailee;

(E) a trustee of an express trust;

(F) a party with whom or in whose name a contract has been made for another's benefit; and

(G) a party authorized by statute.

(2) *Action in the Name of the United States for Another's Use or Benefit.* When a federal statute so provides, an action for another's use or benefit must be brought in the name of the United States.

(3) *Joinder of the Real Party in Interest.* The court may not dismiss an action for failure to prosecute in the name of the real party in interest until, after an objection, a reasonable time has been allowed for the real party in interest to ratify, join, or be substituted into the action. After ratification, joinder, or substitution, the action proceeds as if it had been originally commenced by the real party in interest.

(b) **Capacity to Sue or Be Sued.** Capacity to sue or be sued is determined as follows:

(1) for an individual who is not acting in a representative capacity, by the law of the individual's domicile;

(2) for a corporation, by the law under which it was organized; and

(3) for all other parties, by the law of the state where the court is located, except that:

(A) a partnership or other unincorporated association with no such capacity under that state's law may sue or be sued in its common name to enforce a substantive right existing under the United States Constitution or laws; and

(B) 28 U.S.C. §§754 and 959(a) govern the capacity of a receiver appointed by a United States court to sue or be sued in a United States court.

(c) Minor or Incompetent Person.

(1) *With a Representative.* The following representatives may sue or defend on behalf of a minor or an incompetent person:

(A) a general guardian;

(B) a committee;

(C) a conservator; or

(D) a like fiduciary.

(2) *Without a Representative.* A minor or an incompetent person who does not have a duly appointed representative may sue by a next friend or by a guardian ad litem. The court must appoint a guardian ad litem—or issue another appropriate order—to protect a minor or incompetent person who is unrepresented in an action.

(d) Public Officer's Title and Name. A public officer who sues or is sued in an official capacity may be designated by official title rather than by name, but the court may order that the officer's name be added.

Rule 18.   Joinder of Claims

(a) In General. A party asserting a claim, counterclaim, crossclaim, or third-party claim may join, as independent or alternative claims, as many claims as it has against an opposing party.

(b) Joinder of Contingent Claims. A party may join two claims even though one of them is contingent on the disposition of the other; but the court may grant relief only in accordance with the parties' relative substantive rights. In particular, a plaintiff may state a claim for money and a claim to set aside a conveyance that is fraudulent as to that plaintiff, without first obtaining a judgment for the money.

Rule 19.   Required Joinder of Parties

(a) Persons Required to Be Joined if Feasible.

(1) *Required Party.* A person who is subject to service of process and whose joinder will not deprive the court of subject-matter jurisdiction must be joined as a party if:

(A) in that person's absence, the court cannot accord complete relief among existing parties; or

(B) that person claims an interest relating to the subject of the action and is so situated that disposing of the action in the person's absence may:

(i) as a practical matter impair or impede the person's ability to protect the interest; or

(ii) leave an existing party subject to a substantial risk of incurring double, multiple, or otherwise inconsistent obligations because of the interest.

(2) *Joinder by Court Order.* If a person has not been joined as required, the court must order that the person be made a party. A person who refuses to join as a plaintiff may be made either a defendant or, in a proper case, an involuntary plaintiff.

(3) *Venue.* If a joined party objects to venue and the joinder would make venue improper, the court must dismiss that party.

(b) When Joinder Is Not Feasible. If a person who is required to be joined if feasible cannot be joined, the court must determine whether, in equity and good conscience, the action should proceed among the existing parties or should be dismissed. The factors for the court to consider include:

(1) the extent to which a judgment rendered in the person's absence might prejudice that person or the existing parties;

(2) the extent to which any prejudice could be lessened or avoided by:

(A) protective provisions in the judgment;

(B) shaping the relief; or

(C) other measures;

(3) whether a judgment rendered in the person's absence would be adequate; and

(4) whether the plaintiff would have an adequate remedy if the action were dismissed for nonjoinder.

(c) Pleading the Reasons for Nonjoinder. When asserting a claim for relief, a party must state:

(1) the name, if known, of any person who is required to be joined if feasible but is not joined; and

(2) the reasons for not joining that person.

(d) Exception for Class Actions. This rule is subject to Rule 23.

Rule 20.   Permissive Joinder of Parties

(a) Persons Who May Join or Be Joined.

(1) *Plaintiffs.* Persons may join in one action as plaintiffs if:

(A) they assert any right to relief jointly, severally, or in the alternative with respect to or arising out of the same transaction, occurrence, or series of transactions or occurrences; and

(B) any question of law or fact common to all plaintiffs will arise in the action.

(2) *Defendants.* Persons—as well as a vessel, cargo, or other property subject to admiralty process in rem—may be joined in one action as defendants if:

(A) any right to relief is asserted against them jointly, severally, or in the alternative with respect to or arising out of the same transaction, occurrence, or series of transactions or occurrences; and

(B) any question of law or fact common to all defendants will arise in the action.

(3) *Extent of Relief.* Neither a plaintiff nor a defendant need be interested in obtaining or defending against all the relief demanded. The court may grant judgment to one or more plaintiffs according to their rights, and against one or more defendants according to their liabilities.

(b) **Protective Measures.** The court may issue orders—including an order for separate trials—to protect a party against embarrassment, delay, expense, or other prejudice that arises from including a person against whom the party asserts no claim and who asserts no claim against the party.

Rule 21.   Misjoinder and Nonjoinder of Parties

Misjoinder of parties is not a ground for dismissing an action. On motion or on its own, the court may at any time, on just terms, add or drop a party. The court may also sever any claim against a party.

Rule 22.   Interpleader

(a) **Grounds.**

(1) *By a Plaintiff.* Persons with claims that may expose a plaintiff to double or multiple liability may be joined as defendants and required to interplead. Joinder for interpleader is proper even though:

(A) the claims of the several claimants, or the titles on which their claims depend, lack a common origin or are adverse and independent rather than identical; or

(B) the plaintiff denies liability in whole or in part to any or all of the claimants.

(2) *By a Defendant.* A defendant exposed to similar liability may seek interpleader through a crossclaim or counterclaim.

(b) Relation to Other Rules and Statutes. This rule supplements—and does not limit—the joinder of parties allowed by Rule 20. The remedy this rule provides is in addition to—and does not supersede or limit—the remedy provided by 28 U.S.C. §§1335, 1397, and 2361. An action under those statutes must be conducted under these rules.

Rule 23.   Class Actions

(a) Prerequisites. One or more members of a class may sue or be sued as representative parties on behalf of all members only if:
(1) the class is so numerous that joinder of all members is impracticable;
(2) there are questions of law or fact common to the class;
(3) the claims or defenses of the representative parties are typical of the claims or defenses of the class; and
(4) the representative parties will fairly and adequately protect the interests of the class.

(b) Types of Class Actions. A class action may be maintained if Rule 23(a) is satisfied and if:
(1) prosecuting separate actions by or against individual class members would create a risk of:
(A) inconsistent or varying adjudications with respect to individual class members that would establish incompatible standards of conduct for the party opposing the class; or
(B) adjudications with respect to individual class members that, as a practical matter, would be dispositive of the interests of the other members not parties to the individual adjudications or would substantially impair or impede their ability to protect their interests;
(2) the party opposing the class has acted or refused to act on grounds that apply generally to the class, so that final injunctive relief or corresponding declaratory relief is appropriate respecting the class as a whole; or
(3) the court finds that the questions of law or fact common to class members predominate over any questions affecting only individual members, and that a class action is superior to other available methods for fairly and efficiently adjudicating the controversy. The matters pertinent to these findings include:
(A) the class members' interests in individually controlling the prosecution or defense of separate actions;
(B) the extent and nature of any litigation concerning the controversy already begun by or against class members;
(C) the desirability or undesirability of concentrating the litigation of the claims in the particular forum; and
(D) the likely difficulties in managing a class action.

(c) **Certification Order; Notice to Class Members; Judgment; Issue Classes; Subclasses.**

(1) *Certification Order.*

(A) *Time to Issue.* At an early practicable time after a person sues or is sued as a class representative, the court must determine by order whether to certify the action as a class action.

(B) *Defining the Class; Appointing Class Counsel.* An order that certifies a class action must define the class and the class claims, issues, or defenses, and must appoint class counsel under Rule 23(g).

(C) *Altering or Amending the Order.* An order that grants or denies class certification may be altered or amended before final judgment.

(2) *Notice.*

(A) *For (b)(1) or (b)(2) Classes.* For any class certified under Rule 23(b)(1) or (b)(2), the court may direct appropriate notice to the class.

(B) *For (b)(3) Classes.* For any class certified under Rule 23(b)(3)—or upon ordering notice under Rule 23(e)(1) to a class proposed to be certified for purposes of settlement under Rule 23(b)(3)—the court must direct to class members the best notice that is practicable under the circumstances, including individual notice to all members who can be identified through reasonable effort. The notice may be by one or more of the following: United States mail, electronic means, or other appropriate means. The notice must clearly and concisely state in plain, easily understood language:

(i) the nature of the action;

(ii) the definition of the class certified;

(iii) the class claims, issues, or defenses;

(iv) that a class member may enter an appearance through an attorney if the member so desires;

(v) that the court will exclude from the class any member who requests exclusion;

(vi) the time and manner for requesting exclusion; and

(vii) the binding effect of a class judgment on members under Rule 23(c)(3).

(3) *Judgment.* Whether or not favorable to the class, the judgment in a class action must:

(A) for any class certified under Rule 23(b)(1) or (b)(2), include and describe those whom the court finds to be class members; and

(B) for any class certified under Rule 23(b)(3), include and specify or describe those to whom the Rule 23(c)(2) notice was directed, who have not requested exclusion, and whom the court finds to be class members.

(4) *Particular Issues.* When appropriate, an action may be brought or maintained as a class action with respect to particular issues.

(5) *Subclasses.* When appropriate, a class may be divided into subclasses that are each treated as a class under this rule.

(d) Conducting the Action.

(1) *In General.* In conducting an action under this rule, the court may issue orders that:

(A) determine the course of proceedings or prescribe measures to prevent undue repetition or complication in presenting evidence or argument;

(B) require—to protect class members and fairly conduct the action—giving appropriate notice to some or all class members of:

(i) any step in the action;

(ii) the proposed extent of the judgment; or

(iii) the members' opportunity to signify whether they consider the representation fair and adequate, to intervene and present claims or defenses, or to otherwise come into the action;

(C) impose conditions on the representative parties or on intervenors;

(D) require that the pleadings be amended to eliminate allegations about representation of absent persons and that the action proceed accordingly; or

(E) deal with similar procedural matters.

(2) *Combining and Amending Orders.* An order under Rule 23(d)(1) may be altered or amended from time to time and may be combined with an order under Rule 16.

(e) Settlement, Voluntary, or Compromise. The claims, issues, or defenses of a certified class—or a class proposed to be certified for purposes of settlement—may be settled, voluntarily dismissed, or compromised only with the court's approval. The following procedures apply to a proposed settlement, voluntary dismissal, or compromise:

(1) *Notice to the Class.*

(A) *Information That Parties Must Provide to the Court.* The parties must provide the court with information sufficient to enable it to determine whether to give notice of the proposal to the class.

(B) *Grounds for a Decision to Give Notice.* The court must direct notice in a reasonable manner to all class members who would be bound by the proposal if giving notice is justified by the parties' showing that the court will likely be able to:

(i) approve the proposal under Rule 23(e)(2); and

(ii) certify the class for purposes of judgment on the proposal.

(2) *Approval of the Proposal.* If the proposal would bind class members, the court may approve it only after a hearing and only on finding that it is fair, reasonable, and adequate after considering whether:

(A) the class representatives and class counsel have adequately represented the class;

(B) the proposal was negotiated at arm's length;

(C) the relief provided for the class is adequate, taking into account:

(i) the costs, risks, and delay of trial and appeal;

(ii) the effectiveness of any proposed method of distributing relief to the class, including the method of processing class-member claims;

(iii) the terms of any proposed award of attorney's fees, including timing of payment; and

(iv) any agreement required to be identified under Rule 23(e)(3); and

(D) the proposal treats class members equitably relative to each other.

(3) *Identifying Agreements.* The parties seeking approval must file a statement identifying any agreement made in connection with the proposal.

(4) *New Opportunity to Be Excluded.* If the class action was previously certified under Rule 23(b)(3), the court may refuse to approve a settlement unless it affords a new opportunity to request exclusion to individual class members who had an earlier opportunity to request exclusion but did not do so.

(5) *Class-Member Objections.*

(A) *In General.* Any class member may object to the proposal if it requires court approval under this subdivision (e). The objection must state whether it applies only to the objector, to a specific subset of the class, or to the entire class, and also state with specificity the grounds for the objection.

(B) *Court Approval Required for Payment in Connection with an Objection.* Unless approved by the court after a hearing, no payment or other consideration may be provided in connection with:

(i) forgoing or withdrawing an objection, or

(ii) forgoing, dismissing, or abandoning an appeal from a judgment approving the proposal.

(C) *Procedure for Approval After an Appeal.* If approval under Rule 23(e)(5)(B) has not been obtained before an appeal is docketed in the court of appeals, the procedure of Rule 62.1 applies while the appeal remains pending.

(f) Appeals. A court of appeals may permit an appeal from an order granting or denying class-action certification under this rule, but not from an order under Rule 23(e)(1). A party must file a petition for permission to appeal with the circuit clerk within 14 days after the order is entered, or within 45 days after the order is entered if any party is the United States, a United States agency, or a United States officer or employee sued for an act or omission occurring in connection with duties performed on the United States' behalf. An appeal does not stay proceedings in the district court unless the district judge or the court of appeals so orders.

(g) Class Council.

(1) *Appointing Class Counsel.* Unless a statute provides otherwise, a court that certifies a class must appoint class counsel. In appointing class counsel, the court:

(A) must consider:

(i) the work counsel has done in identifying or investigating potential claims in the action;

(ii) counsel's experience in handling class actions, other complex litigation, and the types of claims asserted in the action;

(iii) counsel's knowledge of the applicable law; and

(iv) the resources that counsel will commit to representing the class;

(B) may consider any other matter pertinent to counsel's ability to fairly and adequately represent the interests of the class;

(C) may order potential class counsel to provide information on any subject pertinent to the appointment and to propose terms for attorney's fees and nontaxable costs;

(D) may include in the appointing order provisions about the award of attorney's fees or nontaxable costs under Rule 23(h); and

(E) may make further orders in connection with the appointment.

(2) *Standard for Appointing Class Counsel.* When one applicant seeks appointment as class counsel, the court may appoint that applicant only if the applicant is adequate under Rule 23(g)(1) and (4). If more than one adequate applicant seeks appointment, the court must appoint the applicant best able to represent the interests of the class.

(3) *Interim Counsel.* The court may designate interim counsel to act on behalf of a putative class before determining whether to certify the action as a class action.

(4) *Duty of Class Counsel.* Class counsel must fairly and adequately represent the interests of the class.

(h) **Attorney's Fees and Nontaxable Costs.** In a certified class action, the court may award reasonable attorney's fees and nontaxable costs that are authorized by law or by the parties' agreement. The following procedures apply:

(1) A claim for an award must be made by motion under Rule 54(d)(2), subject to the provisions of this subdivision (h), at a Federal Rule Civil Procedure Rule 23.2 time the court sets. Notice of the motion must be served on all parties and, for motions by class counsel, directed to class members in a reasonable manner.

(2) A class member, or a party from whom payment is sought, may object to the motion.

(3) The court may hold a hearing and must find the facts and state its legal conclusions under Rule 52(a).

(4) The court may refer issues related to the amount of the award to a special master or a magistrate judge, as provided in Rule 54(d)(2)(D).

Rule 23.1.   Derivative Actions

(a) **Prerequisites.** This rule applies when one or more shareholders or members of a corporation or an unincorporated association bring a derivative action to enforce a right that the corporation or association may properly assert but has failed to enforce. The derivative action may not be maintained if it appears that the plaintiff does not fairly and adequately represent the interests of shareholders or members who are similarly situated in enforcing the right of the corporation or association.

(b) Pleading Requirements. The complaint must be verified and must:

(1) allege that the plaintiff was a shareholder or member at the time of the transaction complained of, or that the plaintiff's share or membership later devolved on it by operation of law;

(2) allege that the action is not a collusive one to confer jurisdiction that the court would otherwise lack; and

(3) state with particularity:

(A) any effort by the plaintiff to obtain the desired action from the directors or comparable authority and, if necessary, from the shareholders or members; and

(B) the reasons for not obtaining the action or not making the effort.

(c) Settlement, Dismissal, and Compromise. A derivative action may be settled, voluntarily dismissed, or compromised only with the court's approval. Notice of a proposed settlement, voluntary dismissal, or compromise must be given to shareholders or members in the manner that the court orders.

Rule 23.2.   Actions Relating to Unincorporated Associations

This rule applies to an action brought by or against the members of an unincorporated association as a class by naming certain members as representative parties. The action may be maintained only if it appears that those parties will fairly and adequately protect the interests of the association and its members. In conducting the action, the court may issue any appropriate orders corresponding with those in Rule 23(d), and the procedure for settlement, voluntary dismissal, or compromise must correspond with the procedure in Rule 23(e).

Rule 24.   Intervention

(a) Intervention of Right. On timely motion, the court must permit anyone to intervene who:

(1) is given an unconditional right to intervene by a federal statute; or

(2) claims an interest relating to the property or transaction that is the subject of the action, and is so situated that disposing of the action may as a practical matter impair or impede the movant's ability to protect its interest, unless existing parties adequately represent that interest.

(b) Permissive Intervention.

(1) *In General.* On timely motion, the court may permit anyone to intervene who:

(A) is given a conditional right to intervene by a federal statute; or

(B) has a claim or defense that shares with the main action a common question of law or fact.

(2) *By a Government Officer or Agency.* On timely motion, the court may permit a federal or state governmental officer or agency to intervene if a party's claim or defense is based on:

(A) a statute or executive order administered by the officer or agency; or

(B) any regulation, order, requirement, or agreement issued or made under the statute or executive order.

(3) *Delay or Prejudice.* In exercising its discretion, the court must consider whether the intervention will unduly delay or prejudice the adjudication of the original parties' rights.

(c) Notice and Pleading Required. A motion to intervene must be served on the parties as provided in Rule 5. The motion must state the grounds for intervention and be accompanied by a pleading that sets out the claim or defense for which intervention is sought.

Rule 25.   Substitution of Parties

(a) Death.

(1) *Substitution if the Claim Is Not Extinguished.* If a party dies and the claim is not extinguished, the court may order substitution of the proper party. A motion for substitution may be made by any party or by the decedent's successor or representative. If the motion is not made within 90 days after service of a statement noting the death, the action by or against the decedent must be dismissed.

(2) *Continuation Among the Remaining Parties.* After a party's death, if the right sought to be enforced survives only to or against the remaining parties, the action does not abate, but proceeds in favor of or against the remaining parties. The death should be noted on the record.

(3) *Service.* A motion to substitute, together with a notice of hearing, must be served on the parties as provided in Rule 5 and on nonparties as provided in Rule 4. A statement noting death must be served in the same manner. Service may be made in any judicial district.

(b) Incompetency. If a party becomes incompetent, the court may, on motion, permit the action to be continued by or against the party's representative. The motion must be served as provided in Rule 25(a)(3).

(c) Transfer of Interest. If an interest is transferred, the action may be continued by or against the original party unless the court, on motion, orders the transferee to be substituted in the action or joined with the original party. The motion must be served as provided in Rule 25(a)(3).

(d) Public Officers; Death or Separation from Office. An action does not abate when a public officer who is a party in an official capacity dies, resigns, or otherwise ceases to hold office while the action is pending. The officer's successor is automatically substituted as a party. Later proceedings should be in the substituted party's name, but any misnomer not affecting the parties' substantial rights must be disregarded. The court may order substitution at any time, but the absence of such an order does not affect the substitution.

Title V.   Disclosures and Discovery

Rule 26.   Duty to Disclose; General Provisions Governing Discovery

(a) Required Disclosures.
(1) *Initial Disclosure.*
    (A) *In General.* Except as exempted by Rule 26(a)(1)(B) or as otherwise stipulated or ordered by the court, a party must, without awaiting a discovery request, provide to the other parties:
        (i) the name and, if known, the address and telephone number of each individual likely to have discoverable information—along with the subjects of that information—that the disclosing party may use to support its claims or defenses, unless the use would be solely for impeachment;
        (ii) a copy—or a description by category and location—of all documents, electronically stored information, and tangible things that the disclosing party has in its possession, custody, or control and may use to support its claims or defenses, unless the use would be solely for impeachment;
        (iii) a computation of each category of damages claimed by the disclosing party—who must also make available for inspection and copying as under Rule 34 the documents or other evidentiary material, unless privileged or protected from disclosure, on which each computation is based, including materials bearing on the nature and extent of injuries suffered; and
        (iv) for inspection and copying as under Rule 34, any insurance agreement under which an insurance business may be liable to satisfy all or part of a possible judgment in the action or to indemnify or reimburse for payments made to satisfy the judgment.

(B) *Proceedings Exempt from Initial Disclosure.* The following proceedings are exempt from initial disclosure:

(i) an action for review on an administrative record;

(ii) a petition for habeas corpus or any other proceeding to challenge a criminal conviction or sentence;

(iii) an action brought without an attorney by a person in the custody of the United States, a state, or a state subdivision;

(iv) an action to enforce or quash an administrative summons or subpoena;

(v) an action by the United States to recover benefit payments;

(vi) an action by the United States to collect on a student loan guaranteed by the United States;

(vii) a proceeding ancillary to a proceeding in another court; and

(viii) an action to enforce an arbitration award.

(C) *Time for Initial Disclosures—In General.* A party must make the initial disclosures at or within 14 days after the parties' Rule 26(f) conference unless a different time is set by stipulation or court order, or unless a party objects during the conference that initial disclosures are not appropriate in this action and states the objection in the proposed discovery plan. In ruling on the objection, the court must determine what disclosures, if any, are to be made and must set the time for disclosure.

(D) *Time for Initial Disclosures—For Parties Served or Joined Later.* A party that is first served or otherwise joined after the Rule 26(f) conference must make the initial disclosures within 30 days after being served or joined, unless a different time is set by stipulation or court order.

(E) *Basis for Initial Disclosure; Unacceptable Excuses.* A party must make its initial disclosures based on the information then reasonably available to it. A party is not excused from making its disclosures because it has not fully investigated the case or because it challenges the sufficiency of another party's disclosures or because another party has not made its disclosures.

(2) **Disclosure of Expert Testimony.**

(A) *In General.* In addition to the disclosures required by Rule 26(a)(1), a party must disclose to the other parties the identity of any witness it may use at trial to present evidence under Federal Rule of Evidence 702, 703, or 705.

(B) *Witnesses Who Must Provide a Written Report.* Unless otherwise stipulated or ordered by the court, this disclosure must be accompanied by a written report—prepared and signed by the witness—if the witness is one retained or specially employed to provide expert testimony in the case or one whose duties as the party's employee regularly involve giving expert testimony. The report must contain:

(i) a complete statement of all opinions the witness will express and the basis and reasons for them;

(ii) the facts or data considered by the witness in forming them;

(iii) any exhibits that will be used to summarize or support them;

(iv) the witness's qualifications, including a list of all publications authored in the previous 10 years;

(v) a list of all other cases in which, during the previous 4 years, the witness testified as an expert at trial or by deposition; and

(vi) a statement of the compensation to be paid for the study and testimony in the case.

(C) *Witnesses Who Do Not Provide a Written Report.* Unless otherwise stipulated or ordered by the court, if the witness is not required to provide a written report, this disclosure must state:

(i) the subject matter on which the witness is expected to present evidence under Federal Rule of Evidence 702, 703, or 705; and

(ii) a summary of the facts and opinions to which the witness is expected to testify.

(D) *Time to Disclose Expert Testimony.* A party must make these disclosures at the times and in the sequence that the court orders. Absent a stipulation or a court order, the disclosures must be made:

(i) at least 90 days before the date set for trial or for the case to be ready for trial; or

(ii) if the evidence is intended solely to contradict or rebut evidence on the same subject matter identified by another party under Rule 26(a)(2)(B) or (C), within 30 days after the other party's disclosure.

(E) *Supplementing the Disclosure.* The parties must supplement these disclosures when required under Rule 26(e).

(3) **Pretrial Disclosures.**

(A) *In General.* In addition to the disclosures required by Rule 26(a)(1) and (2), a party must provide to the other parties and promptly file the following information about the evidence that it may present at trial other than solely for impeachment:

(i) the name and, if not previously provided, the address and telephone number of each witness—separately identifying those the party expects to present and those it may call if the need arises;

(ii) the designation of those witnesses whose testimony the party expects to present by deposition and, if not taken stenographically, a transcript of the pertinent parts of the deposition; and

(iii) an identification of each document or other exhibit, including summaries of other evidence—separately identifying those items the party expects to offer and those it may offer if the need arises.

(B) *Time for Pretrial Disclosures; Objections.* Unless the court orders otherwise, these disclosures must be made at least 30 days before trial. Within 14 days after they are made, unless the court sets a different time, a party may serve and promptly file a list of the following objections: any objections to the use under Rule 32(a) of a deposition designated by another party under Rule 26(a)(3)(A)(ii); and any objection, together with the grounds for it, that may be made to the admissibility of materials identified under Rule 26(a)(3)(A)(iii).

An objection not so made—except for one under Federal Rule of Evidence 402 or 403—is waived unless excused by the court for good cause.

(4) *Form of Disclosures.* Unless the court orders otherwise, all disclosures under Rule 26(a) must be in writing, signed, and served.

(b) Discovery Scope and Limits.

(1) *Scope in General.* Unless otherwise limited by court order, the scope of discovery is as follows: Parties may obtain discovery regarding any nonprivileged matter that is relevant to any party's claim or defense and proportional to the needs of the case, considering the importance of the issues at stake in the action, the amount in controversy, the parties' relative access to relevant information, the parties' resources, the importance of the discovery in resolving the issues, and whether the burden or expense of the proposed discovery outweighs its likely benefit. Information within this scope of discovery need not be admissible in evidence to be discoverable.

(2) *Limitations on Frequency and Extent.*

(A) *When Permitted.* By order, the court may alter the limits in these rules on the number of depositions and interrogatories or on the length of depositions under Rule 30. By order or local rule, the court may also limit the number of requests under Rule 36.

(B) *Specific Limitations on Electronically Stored Information.* A party need not provide discovery of electronically stored information from sources that the party identifies as not reasonably accessible because of undue burden or cost. On motion to compel discovery or for a protective order, the party from whom discovery is sought must show that the information is not reasonably accessible because of undue burden or cost. If that showing is made, the court may nonetheless order discovery from such sources if the requesting party shows good cause, considering the limitations of Rule 26(b)(2)(C). The court may specify conditions for the discovery.

(C) *When Required.* On motion or on its own, the court must limit the frequency or extent of discovery otherwise allowed by these rules or by local rule if it determines that:

(i) the discovery sought is unreasonably cumulative or duplicative, or can be obtained from some other source that is more convenient, less burdensome, or less expensive;

(ii) the party seeking discovery has had ample opportunity to obtain the information by discovery in the action; or

(iii) the proposed discovery is outside the scope permitted by Rule 26(b)(1).

(3) *Trial Preparation: Materials.*

(A) *Documents and Tangible Things.* Ordinarily, a party may not discover documents and tangible things that are prepared in anticipation of litigation or for trial by or for another party or its representative (including the other party's attorney, consultant, surety, indemnitor, insurer, or agent). But, subject to Rule 26(b)(4), those materials may be discovered if:

    (i) they are otherwise discoverable under Rule 26(b)(1); and

    (ii) the party shows that it has substantial need for the materials to prepare its case and cannot, without undue hardship, obtain their substantial equivalent by other means.

    (B) *Protection Against Disclosure.* If the court orders discovery of those materials, it must protect against disclosure of the mental impressions, conclusions, opinions, or legal theories of a party's attorney or other representative concerning the litigation.

    (C) *Previous Statement.* Any party or other person may, on request and without the required showing, obtain the person's own previous statement about the action or its subject matter. If the request is refused, the person may move for a court order, and Rule 37(a)(5) applies to the award of expenses. A previous statement is either:

    (i) a written statement that the person has signed or otherwise adopted or approved; or

    (ii) a contemporaneous stenographic, mechanical, electrical, or other recording—or a transcription of it—that recites substantially verbatim the person's oral statement.

  (4) **Trial Preparation: Experts.**

    (A) *Deposition of an Expert Who May Testify.* A party may depose any person who has been identified as an expert whose opinions may be presented at trial. If Rule 26(a)(2)(B) requires a report from the expert, the deposition may be conducted only after the report is provided.

    (B) *Trial-Preparation Protection for Draft Reports or Disclosures.* Rules 26(b)(3)(A) and (B) protect drafts of any report or disclosure required under Rule 26(a)(2), regardless of the form in which the draft is recorded.

    (C) *Trial-Preparation Protection for Communications Between a Party's Attorney and Expert Witnesses.* Rules 26(b)(3)(A) and (B) protect communications between the party's attorney and any witness required to provide a report under Rule 26(a)(2)(B), regardless of the form of the communications, except to the extent that the communications:

    (i) relate to compensation for the expert's study or testimony;

    (ii) identify facts or data that the party's attorney provided and that the expert considered in forming the opinions to be expressed; or

    (iii) identify assumptions that the party's attorney provided and that the expert relied on in forming the opinions to be expressed.

    (D) *Expert Employed Only for Trial Preparation.* Ordinarily, a party may not, by interrogatories or deposition, discover facts known or opinions held by an expert who has been retained or specially employed by another party in anticipation of litigation or to prepare for trial and who is not expected to be called as a witness at trial. But a party may do so only:

(i) as provided in Rule 35(b); or

(ii) on showing exceptional circumstances under which it is impracticable for the party to obtain facts or opinions on the same subject by other means.

(E) *Payment.* Unless manifest injustice would result, the court must require that the party seeking discovery:

(i) pay the expert a reasonable fee for time spent in responding to discovery under Rule 26(b)(4)(A) or (D); and

(ii) for discovery under (D), also pay the other party a fair portion of the fees and expenses it reasonably incurred in obtaining the expert's facts and opinions.

(5) ***Claiming Privilege or Protecting Trial-Preparation Materials.***

(A) *Information Withheld.* When a party withholds information otherwise discoverable by claiming that the information is privileged or subject to protection as trial-preparation material, the party must:

(i) Expressly make the claim; and

(ii) Describe the nature of the documents, communications, or tangible things not produced or disclosed—and do so in a manner that, without revealing information itself privileged or protected, will enable other parties to assess the claim.

(B) *Information Produced.* If information produced in discovery is subject to a claim of privilege or of protection as trial-preparation material, the party making the claim may notify any party that received the information of the claim and the basis for it. After being notified, a party must promptly return, sequester, or destroy the specified information and any copies it has; must not use or disclose the information until the claim is resolved; must take reasonable steps to retrieve the information if the party disclosed it before being notified; and may promptly present the information to the court under seal for a determination of the claim. The producing party must preserve the information until the claim is resolved.

(c) Protective Orders.

(1) ***In General.*** A party or any person from whom discovery is sought may move for a protective order in the court where the action is pending—or as an alternative on matters relating to a deposition, in the court for the district where the deposition will be taken. The motion must include a certification that the movant has in good faith conferred or attempted to confer with other affected parties in an effort to resolve the dispute without court action. The court may, for good cause, issue an order to protect a party or person from annoyance, embarrassment, oppression, or undue burden or expense, including one or more of the following:

(A) forbidding the disclosure or discovery;

(B) specifying terms, including time and place or the allocation of expenses, for the disclosure or discovery;

(C) prescribing a discovery method other than the one selected by the party seeking discovery;

(D) forbidding inquiry into certain matters, or limiting the scope of disclosure or discovery to certain matters;

(E) designating the persons who may be present while the discovery is conducted;

(F) requiring that a deposition be sealed and opened only on court order;

(G) requiring that a trade secret or other confidential research, development, or commercial information not be revealed or be revealed only in a specified way; and

(H) requiring that the parties simultaneously file specified documents or information in sealed envelopes, to be opened as the court directs.

(2) *Ordering Discovery.* If a motion for a protective order is wholly or partly denied, the court may, on just terms, order that any party or person provide or permit discovery.

(3) *Awarding Expenses.* Rule 37(a)(5) applies to the award of expenses.

(d) Timing and Sequence of Discovery.

(1) *Timing.* A party may not seek discovery from any source before the parties have conferred as required by Rule 26(f), except in a proceeding exempted from initial disclosure under Rule 26(a)(1)(B), or when authorized by these rules, by stipulation, or by court order.

(2) *Early Rule 34 Requests.*

(A) *Time to Deliver.* More than 21 days after the summons and complaint are served on a party, a request under Rule 34 may be delivered:

(i) to that party by any other party, and

(ii) by that party to any plaintiff or to any other party that has been served.

(B) *When Considered Served.* The request is considered to have been served at the first Rule 26(f) conference.

(3) *Sequence.* Unless the parties stipulate or the court orders otherwise for the parties' and witnesses' convenience and in the interests of justice:

(A) methods of discovery may be used in any sequence; and

(B) discovery by one party does not require any other party to delay its discovery.

(e) Supplementing Disclosures and Responses.

(1) *In General.* A party who has made a disclosure under Rule 26(a)—or who has responded to an interrogatory, request for production, or request for admission—must supplement or correct its disclosure or response:

(A) in a timely manner if the party learns that in some material respect the disclosure or response is incomplete or incorrect, and if the additional or corrective information has not otherwise been made known to the other parties during the discovery process or in writing; or

(B) as ordered by the court.

(2) *Expert Witness.* For an expert whose report must be disclosed under Rule 26(a)(2)(B), the party's duty to supplement extends both to information included in the report and to information given during the expert's deposition. Any additions or changes to this information must be disclosed by the time the party's pretrial disclosures under Rule 26(a)(3) are due.

(f) Conference of the Parties; Planning for Discovery.

(1) *Conference Timing.* Except in a proceeding exempted from initial disclosure under Rule 26(a)(1)(B) or when the court orders otherwise, the parties must confer as soon as practicable—and in any event at least 21 days before a scheduling conference is to be held or a scheduling order is due under Rule 16(b).

(2) *Conference Content; Parties' Responsibilities.* In conferring, the parties must consider the nature and basis of their claims and defenses and the possibilities for promptly settling or resolving the case; make or arrange for the disclosures required by Rule 26(a)(1); discuss any issues about preserving discoverable information; and develop a proposed discovery plan. The attorneys of record and all unrepresented parties that have appeared in the case are jointly responsible for arranging the conference, for attempting in good faith to agree on the proposed discovery plan, and for submitting to the court within 14 days after the conference a written report outlining the plan. The court may order the parties or attorneys to attend the conference in person.

(3) *Discovery Plan.* A discovery plan must state the parties' views and proposals on:

(A) what changes should be made in the timing, form, or requirement for disclosures under Rule 26(a), including a statement of when initial disclosures were made or will be made;

(B) the subjects on which discovery may be needed, when discovery should be completed, and whether discovery should be conducted in phases or be limited to or focused on particular issues;

(C) any issues about disclosure, discovery, or preservation of electronically stored information, including the form or forms in which it should be produced;

(D) any issues about claims of privilege or of protection as trial-preparation materials, including—if the parties agree on a procedure to assert these claims after production—whether to ask the court to include their agreement in an order under Federal Rule of Evidence 502;

(E) what changes should be made in the limitations on discovery imposed under these rules or by local rule, and what other limitations should be imposed; and

(F) any other orders that the court should issue under Rule 26(c) or under Rule 16(b) and (c).

(4) *Expedited Schedule.* If necessary to comply with its expedited schedule for Rule 16(b) conferences, a court may by local rule:

(A) require the parties' conference to occur less than 21 days before the scheduling conference is held or a scheduling order is due under Rule 16(b); and

(B) require the written report outlining the discovery plan to be filed less than 14 days after the parties' conference, or excuse the parties from submitting a written report and permit them to report orally on their discovery plan at the Rule 16(b) conference.

(g) Signing Disclosures and Discovery Requests, Responses, and Objections.

(1) *Signature Required; Effect of Signature.* Every disclosure under Rule 26(a)(1) or (a)(3) and every discovery request, response, or objection must be signed by at least one attorney of record in the attorney's own name—or by the party personally, if unrepresented—and must state the signer's address, e-mail address, and telephone number. By signing, an attorney or party certifies that to the best of the person's knowledge, information, and belief formed after a reasonable inquiry:

(A) with respect to a disclosure, it is complete and correct as of the time it is made; and

(B) with respect to a discovery request, response, or objection, it is:

(i) consistent with these rules and warranted by existing law or by a nonfrivolous argument for extending, modifying, or reversing existing law, or for establishing new law;

(ii) not interposed for any improper purpose, such as to harass, cause unnecessary delay, or needlessly increase the cost of litigation; and

(iii) neither unreasonable nor unduly burdensome or expensive, considering the needs of the case, prior discovery in the case, the amount in controversy, and the importance of the issues at stake in the action.

(2) *Failure to Sign.* Other parties have no duty to act on an unsigned disclosure, request, response, or objection until it is signed, and the court must strike it unless a signature is promptly supplied after the omission is called to the attorney's or party's attention.

(3) *Sanction for Improper Certification.* If a certification violates this rule without substantial justification, the court, on motion or on its own, must impose an appropriate sanction on the signer, the party on whose behalf the signer was acting, or both. The sanction may include an order to pay the reasonable expenses, including attorney's fees, caused by the violation.

Rule 27.   Depositions to Perpetuate Testimony

(a) Before an Action Is Filed.

(1) *Petition.* A person who wants to perpetuate testimony about any matter cognizable in a United States court may file a verified petition in the district court

for the district where any expected adverse party resides. The petition must ask for an order authorizing the petitioner to depose the named persons in order to perpetuate their testimony. The petition must be titled in the petitioner's name and must show:

(A) that the petitioner expects to be a party to an action cognizable in a United States court but cannot presently bring it or cause it to be brought;

(B) the subject matter of the expected action and the petitioner's interest;

(C) the facts that the petitioner wants to establish by the proposed testimony and the reasons to perpetuate it;

(D) the names or a description of the persons whom the petitioner expects to be adverse parties and their addresses, so far as known; and

(E) the name, address, and expected substance of the testimony of each deponent.

(2) *Notice and Service.* At least 21 days before the hearing date, the petitioner must serve each expected adverse party with a copy of the petition and a notice stating the time and place of the hearing. The notice may be served either inside or outside the district or state in the manner provided in Rule 4. If that service cannot be made with reasonable diligence on an expected adverse party, the court may order service by publication or otherwise. The court must appoint an attorney to represent persons not served in the manner provided in Rule 4 and to cross-examine the deponent if an unserved person is not otherwise represented. If any expected adverse party is a minor or is incompetent, Rule 17(c) applies.

(3) *Order and Examination.* If satisfied that perpetuating the testimony may prevent a failure or delay of justice, the court must issue an order that designates or describes the persons whose depositions may be taken, specifies the subject matter of the examinations, and states whether the depositions will be taken orally or by written interrogatories. The depositions may then be taken under these rules, and the court may issue orders like those authorized by Rules 34 and 35. A reference in these rules to the court where an action is pending means, for purposes of this rule, the court where the petition for the deposition was filed.

(4) *Using the Deposition.* A deposition to perpetuate testimony may be used under Rule 32(a) in any later-filed district-court action involving the same subject matter if the deposition either was taken under these rules or, although not so taken, would be admissible in evidence in the courts of the state where it was taken.

(b) Pending Appeal.

(1) *In General.* The court where a judgment has been rendered may, if an appeal has been taken or may still be taken, permit a party to depose witnesses to perpetuate their testimony for use in the event of further proceedings in that court.

(2) *Motion.* The party who wants to perpetuate testimony may move for leave to take the depositions, on the same notice and service as if the action were pending in the district court. The motion must show:

(A) the name, address, and expected substance of the testimony of each deponent; and

(B) the reasons for perpetuating the testimony.

(3) *Court Order.* If the court finds that perpetuating the testimony may prevent a failure or delay of justice, the court may permit the depositions to be taken and may issue orders like those authorized by Rules 34 and 35. The depositions may be taken and used as any other deposition taken in a pending district-court action.

(c) **Perpetuation by an Action.** This rule does not limit a court's power to entertain an action to perpetuate testimony.

Rule 28.   Persons Before Whom Depositions May Be Taken

(a) **Within the United States.**

(1) *In General.* Within the United States or a territory or insular possession subject to United States jurisdiction, a deposition must be taken before:

(A) an officer authorized to administer oaths either by federal law or by the law in the place of examination; or

(B) a person appointed by the court where the action is pending to administer oaths and take testimony.

(2) *Definition of "Officer."* The term "officer" in Rules 30, 31, and 32 includes a person appointed by the court under this rule or designated by the parties under Rule 29(a).

(b) **In a Foreign Country.**

(1) *In General.* A deposition may be taken in a foreign country:

(A) under an applicable treaty or convention;

(B) under a letter of request, whether or not captioned a "letter rogatory";

(C) on notice, before a person authorized to administer oaths either by federal law or by the law in the place of examination; or

(D) before a person commissioned by the court to administer any necessary oath and take testimony.

(2) *Issuing a Letter of Request or a Commission.* A letter of request, a commission, or both may be issued:

(A) on appropriate terms after an application and notice of it; and

(B) without a showing that taking the deposition in another manner is impracticable or inconvenient.

(3) *Form of a Request, Notice, or Commission.* When a letter of request or any other device is used according to a treaty or convention, it must be captioned in the form prescribed by that treaty or convention. A letter of request may be addressed "To the Appropriate Authority in [name of country]." A deposition notice or a commission must designate by name or descriptive title the person before whom the deposition is to be taken.

(4) *Letter of Request—Admitting Evidence.* Evidence obtained in response to a letter of request need not be excluded merely because it is not a verbatim transcript, because the testimony was not taken under oath, or because of any similar departure from the requirements for depositions taken within the United States.

(c) Disqualification. A deposition must not be taken before a person who is any party's relative, employee, or attorney; who is related to or employed by any party's attorney; or who is financially interested in the action.

Rule 29. Stipulations About Discovery Procedure

Unless the court orders otherwise, the parties may stipulate that:
(a) a deposition may be taken before any person, at any time or place, on any notice, and in the manner specified—in which event it may be used in the same way as any other deposition; and

(b) other procedures governing or limiting discovery be modified—but a stipulation extending the time for any form of discovery must have court approval if it would interfere with the time set for completing discovery, for hearing a motion, or for trial.

Rule 30. Depositions by Oral Examination

(a) When a Deposition May Be Taken.
(1) *Without Leave.* A party may, by oral questions, depose any person, including a party, without leave of court except as provided in Rule 30(a)(2). The deponent's attendance may be compelled by subpoena under Rule 45.
(2) *With Leave.* A party must obtain leave of court, and the court must grant leave to the extent consistent with Rule 26(b)(1) and (2):
 (A) if the parties have not stipulated to the deposition and:
   (i) the deposition would result in more than 10 depositions being taken under this rule or Rule 31 by the plaintiffs, or by the defendants, or by the third-party defendants;
   (ii) the deponent has already been deposed in the case; or
   (iii) the party seeks to take the deposition before the time specified in Rule 26(d), unless the party certifies in the notice, with supporting facts, that the deponent is expected to leave the United States and be unavailable for examination in this country after that time; or
 (B) if the deponent is confined in prison.

(b) Notice of the Deposition; Other Formal Requirements.
(1) *Notice in General.* A party who wants to depose a person by oral questions must give reasonable written notice to every other party. The notice must

state the time and place of the deposition and, if known, the deponent's name and address. If the name is unknown, the notice must provide a general description sufficient to identify the person or the particular class or group to which the person belongs.

(2) *Producing Documents.* If a subpoena duces tecum is to be served on the deponent, the materials designated for production, as set out in the subpoena, must be listed in the notice or in an attachment. The notice to a party deponent may be accompanied by a request under Rule 34 to produce documents and tangible things at the deposition.

(3) *Method of Recording.*

(A) *Method Stated in the Notice.* The party who notices the deposition must state in the notice the method for recording the testimony. Unless the court orders otherwise, testimony may be recorded by audio, audiovisual, or stenographic means. The noticing party bears the recording costs. Any party may arrange to transcribe a deposition.

(B) *Additional Method.* With prior notice to the deponent and other parties, any party may designate another method for recording the testimony in addition to that specified in the original notice. That party bears the expense of the additional record or transcript unless the court orders otherwise.

(4) *By Remote Means.* The parties may stipulate—or the court may on motion order—that a deposition be taken by telephone or other remote means. For the purpose of this rule and Rules 28(a), 37(a)(2), and 37(b)(1), the deposition takes place where the deponent answers the questions.

(5) *Officer's Duties.*

(A) *Before the Deposition.* Unless the parties stipulate otherwise, a deposition must be conducted before an officer appointed or designated under Rule 28. The officer must begin the deposition with an on-the-record statement that includes:

(i) the officer's name and business address;

(ii) the date, time, and place of the deposition;

(iii) the deponent's name;

(iv) the officer's administration of the oath or affirmation to the deponent; and

(v) the identity of all persons present.

(B) *Conducting the Deposition; Avoiding Distortion.* If the deposition is recorded nonstenographically, the officer must repeat the items in Rule 30(b)(5)(A)(i)-(iii) at the beginning of each unit of the recording medium. The deponent's and attorneys' appearance or demeanor must not be distorted through recording techniques.

(C) *After the Deposition.* At the end of a deposition, the officer must state on the record that the deposition is complete and must set out any stipulations made by the attorneys about custody of the transcript or recording and of the exhibits, or about any other pertinent matters.

(6) *Notice or Subpoena Directed to an Organization.* In its notice or subpoena, a party may name as the deponent a public or private corporation, a partnership, an association, a governmental agency, or other entity and must describe with reasonable particularity the matters for examination. The named organization must designate one or more officers, directors, or managing agents, or designate other persons who consent to testify on its behalf; and it may set out the matters on which each person designated will testify. Before or promptly after the notice or subpoena is served, the serving party and the organization must confer in good faith about the matters for examination. A subpoena must advise a nonparty organization of its duty to confer with the serving party and to designate each person who will testify. The persons designated must testify about information known or reasonably available to the organization. This paragraph (6) does not preclude a deposition by any other procedure allowed by these rules.

(c) Examination and Cross-Examination; Record of the Examination; Objections; Written Questions.

(1) *Examination and Cross-Examination.* The examination and cross-examination of a deponent proceed as they would at trial under the Federal Rules of Evidence, except Rules 103 and 615. After putting the deponent under oath or affirmation, the officer must record the testimony by the method designated under Rule 30(b)(3)(A). The testimony must be recorded by the officer personally or by a person acting in the presence and under the direction of the officer.

(2) *Objections.* An objection at the time of the examination—whether to evidence, to a party's conduct, to the officer's qualifications, to the manner of taking the deposition, or to any other aspect of the deposition—must be noted on the record, but the examination still proceeds; the testimony is taken subject to any objection. An objection must be stated concisely in a nonargumentative and nonsuggestive manner. A person may instruct a deponent not to answer only when necessary to preserve a privilege, to enforce a limitation ordered by the court, or to present a motion under Rule 30(d)(3).

(3) *Participating Through Written Questions.* Instead of participating in the oral examination, a party may serve written questions in a sealed envelope on the party noticing the deposition, who must deliver them to the officer. The officer must ask the deponent those questions and record the answers verbatim.

(d) Duration; Sanction; Motion to Terminate or Limit.

(1) *Duration.* Unless otherwise stipulated or ordered by the court, a deposition is limited to 1 day of 7 hours. The court must allow additional time consistent with Rule 26(b)(1) and (2) if needed to fairly examine the deponent or if the deponent, another person, or any other circumstance impedes or delays the examination.

(2) *Sanction.* The court may impose an appropriate sanction—including the reasonable expenses and attorney's fees incurred by any party—on a person who impedes, delays, or frustrates the fair examination of the deponent.

(3) *Motion to Terminate or Limit.*

(A) *Grounds.* At any time during a deposition, the deponent or a party may move to terminate or limit it on the ground that it is being conducted in bad faith or in a manner that unreasonably annoys, embarrasses, or oppresses the deponent or party. The motion may be filed in the court where the action is pending or the deposition is being taken. If the objecting deponent or party so demands, the deposition must be suspended for the time necessary to obtain an order.

(B) *Order.* The court may order that the deposition be terminated or may limit its scope and manner as provided in Rule 26(c). If terminated, the deposition may be resumed only by order of the court where the action is pending.

(C) *Award of Expenses.* Rule 37(a)(5) applies to the award of expenses.

(e) Review by the Witness; Changes.

(1) *Review; Statement of Changes.* On request by the deponent or a party before the deposition is completed, the deponent must be allowed 30 days after being notified by the officer that the transcript or recording is available in which:

(A) to review the transcript or recording; and

(B) if there are changes in form or substance, to sign a statement listing the changes and the reasons for making them.

(2) *Changes Indicated in the Officer's Certificate.* The officer must note in the certificate prescribed by Rule 30(f)(1) whether a review was requested and, if so, must attach any changes the deponent makes during the 30-day period.

(f) Certification and Delivery; Exhibits; Copies of the Transcript or Recording; Filing.

(1) *Certification and Delivery.* The officer must certify in writing that the witness was duly sworn and that the deposition accurately records the witness's testimony. The certificate must accompany the record of the deposition. Unless the court orders otherwise, the officer must seal the deposition in an envelope or package bearing the title of the action and marked "Deposition of [witness's name]" and must promptly send it to the attorney who arranged for the transcript or recording. The attorney must store it under conditions that will protect it against loss, destruction, tampering, or deterioration.

(2) *Documents and Tangible Things.*

(A) *Originals and Copies.* Documents and tangible things produced for inspection during a deposition must, on a party's request, be marked for identification and attached to the deposition. Any party may inspect and copy them. But if the person who produced them wants to keep the originals, the person may:

(i) offer copies to be marked, attached to the deposition, and then used as originals—after giving all parties a fair opportunity to verify the copies by comparing them with the originals; or

(ii) give all parties a fair opportunity to inspect and copy the originals after they are marked—in which event the originals may be used as if attached to the deposition.

(B) *Order Regarding the Originals.* Any party may move for an order that the originals be attached to the deposition pending final disposition of the case.

(3) *Copies of the Transcript or Recording.* Unless otherwise stipulated or ordered by the court, the officer must retain the stenographic notes of a deposition taken stenographically or a copy of the recording of a deposition taken by another method. When paid reasonable charges, the officer must furnish a copy of the transcript or recording to any party or the deponent.

(4) *Notice of Filing.* A party who files the deposition must promptly notify all other parties of the filing.

(g) **Failure to Attend a Deposition or Serve a Subpoena; Expenses.** A party who, expecting a deposition to be taken, attends in person or by an attorney may recover reasonable expenses for attending, including attorney's fees, if the noticing party failed to:

(1) attend and proceed with the deposition; or

(2) serve a subpoena on a nonparty deponent, who consequently did not attend.

Rule 31.   Depositions by Written Questions

(a) **When a Deposition May Be Taken.**

(1) *Without Leave.* A party may, by written questions, depose any person, including a party, without leave of court except as provided in Rule 31(a)(2). The deponent's attendance may be compelled by subpoena under Rule 45.

(2) *With Leave.* A party must obtain leave of court, and the court must grant leave to the extent consistent with Rule 26(b)(1) and (2):

(A) if the parties have not stipulated to the deposition and:

(i) the deposition would result in more than 10 depositions being taken under this rule or Rule 30 by the plaintiffs, or by the defendants, or by the third-party defendants;

(ii) the deponent has already been deposed in the case; or

(iii) the party seeks to take a deposition before the time specified in Rule 26(d); or

(B) if the deponent is confined in prison.

(3) *Service; Required Notice.* A party who wants to depose a person by written questions must serve them on every other party, with a notice stating, if known, the deponent's name and address. If the name is unknown, the notice must provide a general description sufficient to identify the person or the particular class or group to which the person belongs. The notice must also state the

name or descriptive title and the address of the officer before whom the deposition will be taken.

(4) *Questions Directed to an Organization.* A public or private corporation, a partnership, an association, or a governmental agency may be deposed by written questions in accordance with Rule 30(b)(6).

(5) *Questions from Other Parties.* Any questions to the deponent from other parties must be served on all parties as follows: cross-questions, within 14 days after being served with the notice and direct questions; redirect questions, within 7 days after being served with cross-questions; and recross-questions, within 7 days after being served with redirect questions. The court may, for good cause, extend or shorten these times.

(b) Delivery to the Officer; Officer's Duties. The party who noticed the deposition must deliver to the officer a copy of all the questions served and of the notice. The officer must promptly proceed in the manner provided in Rule 30(c), (e), and (f) to:

(1) take the deponent's testimony in response to the questions;

(2) prepare and certify the deposition; and

(3) send it to the party, attaching a copy of the questions and of the notice.

(c) Notice of Completion or Filing.

(1) *Completion.* The party who noticed the deposition must notify all other parties when it is completed.

(2) *Filing.* A party who files the deposition must promptly notify all other parties of the filing.

Rule 32.   Using Depositions in Court Proceedings

(a) Using Depositions.

(1) *In General.* At a hearing or trial, all or part of a deposition may be used against a party on these conditions:

(A) the party was present or represented at the taking of the deposition or had reasonable notice of it;

(B) it is used to the extent it would be admissible under the Federal Rules of Evidence if the deponent were present and testifying; and

(C) the use is allowed by Rule 32(a)(2) through (8).

(2) *Impeachment and Other Uses.* Any party may use a deposition to contradict or impeach the testimony given by the deponent as a witness, or for any other purpose allowed by the Federal Rules of Evidence.

(3) *Deposition of Party, Agent, or Designee.* An adverse party may use for any purpose the deposition of a party or anyone who, when deposed, was the party's officer, director, managing agent, or designee under Rule 30(b)(6) or 31(a)(4).

(4) *Unavailable Witness.* A party may use for any purpose the deposition of a witness, whether or not a party, if the court finds:

(A) that the witness is dead;

(B) that the witness is more than 100 miles from the place of hearing or trial or is outside the United States, unless it appears that the witness's absence was procured by the party offering the deposition;

(C) that the witness cannot attend or testify because of age, illness, infirmity, or imprisonment;

(D) that the party offering the deposition could not procure the witness's attendance by subpoena; or

(E) on motion and notice, that exceptional circumstances make it desirable — in the interest of justice and with due regard to the importance of live testimony in open court — to permit the deposition to be used.

(5) *Limitations on Use.*

(A) *Deposition Taken on Short Notice.* A deposition must not be used against a party who, having received less than 14 days' notice of the deposition, promptly moved for a protective order under Rule 26(c)(1)(B) requesting that it not be taken or be taken at a different time or place — and this motion was still pending when the deposition was taken.

(B) *Unavailable Deponent; Party Could Not Obtain an Attorney.* A deposition taken without leave of court under the unavailability provision of Rule 30(a)(2)(A)(iii) must not be used against a party who shows that, when served with the notice, it could not, despite diligent efforts, obtain an attorney to represent it at the deposition.

(6) *Using Part of a Deposition.* If a party offers in evidence only part of a deposition, an adverse party may require the offeror to introduce other parts that in fairness should be considered with the part introduced, and any party may itself introduce any other parts.

(7) *Substituting a Party.* Substituting a party under Rule 25 does not affect the right to use a deposition previously taken.

(8) *Deposition Taken in an Earlier Action.* A deposition lawfully taken and, if required, filed in any federal- or state-court action may be used in a later action involving the same subject matter between the same parties, or their representatives or successors in interest, to the same extent as if taken in the later action. A deposition previously taken may also be used as allowed by the Federal Rules of Evidence.

(b) Objections to Admissibility. Subject to Rules 28(b) and 32(d)(3), an objection may be made at a hearing or trial to the admission of any deposition testimony that would be inadmissible if the witness were present and testifying.

(c) Form of Presentation. Unless the court orders otherwise, a party must provide a transcript of any deposition testimony the party offers, but may provide the court with the testimony in nontranscript form as well. On any party's request, deposition testimony offered in a jury trial for any purpose other than impeachment must be presented in nontranscript form, if available, unless the court for good cause orders otherwise.

(d) Waiver of Objections.

(1) *To the Notice.* An objection to an error or irregularity in a deposition notice is waived unless promptly served in writing on the party giving the notice.

(2) *To the Officer's Qualification.* An objection based on disqualification of the officer before whom a deposition is to be taken is waived if not made:

(A) before the deposition begins; or

(B) promptly after the basis for disqualification becomes known or, with reasonable diligence, could have been known.

(3) *To the Taking of the Deposition.*

(A) *Objection to Competence, Relevance, or Materiality.* An objection to a deponent's competence—or to the competence, relevance, or materiality of testimony—is not waived by a failure to make the objection before or during the deposition, unless the ground for it might have been corrected at that time.

(B) *Objection to an Error or Irregularity.* An objection to an error or irregularity at an oral examination is waived if:

(i) it relates to the manner of taking the deposition, the form of a question or answer, the oath or affirmation, a party's conduct, or other matters that might have been corrected at that time; and

(ii) it is not timely made during the deposition.

(C) *Objection to a Written Question.* An objection to the form of a written question under Rule 31 is waived if not served in writing on the party submitting the question within the time for serving responsive questions or, if the question is a recross-question, within 7 days after being served with it.

(4) *To Completing and Returning the Deposition.* An objection to how the officer transcribed the testimony—or prepared, signed, certified, sealed, endorsed, sent, or otherwise dealt with the deposition—is waived unless a motion to suppress is made promptly after the error or irregularity becomes known or, with reasonable diligence, could have been known.

Rule 33.   Interrogatories to Parties

(a) In General.

(1) *Number.* Unless otherwise stipulated or ordered by the court, a party may serve on any other party no more than 25 written interrogatories, including all discrete subparts. Leave to serve additional interrogatories may be granted to the extent consistent with Rule 26(b)(1) and (2).

(2) *Scope.* An interrogatory may relate to any matter that may be inquired into under Rule 26(b). An interrogatory is not objectionable merely because it asks for an opinion or contention that relates to fact or the application of law to

fact, but the court may order that the interrogatory need not be answered until designated discovery is complete, or until a pretrial conference or some other time.

(b) Answers and Objections.

(1) *Responding Party.* The interrogatories must be answered:

(A) by the party to whom they are directed; or

(B) if that party is a public or private corporation, a partnership, an association, or a governmental agency, by any officer or agent, who must furnish the information available to the party.

(2) *Time to Respond.* The responding party must serve its answers and any objections within 30 days after being served with the interrogatories. A shorter or longer time may be stipulated to under Rule 29 or be ordered by the court.

(3) *Answering Each Interrogatory.* Each interrogatory must, to the extent it is not objected to, be answered separately and fully in writing under oath.

(4) *Objections.* The grounds for objecting to an interrogatory must be stated with specificity. Any ground not stated in a timely objection is waived unless the court, for good cause, excuses the failure.

(5) *Signature.* The person who makes the answers must sign them, and the attorney who objects must sign any objections.

(c) Use. An answer to an interrogatory may be used to the extent allowed by the Federal Rules of Evidence.

(d) Option to Produce Business Records. If the answer to an interrogatory may be determined by examining, auditing, compiling, abstracting, or summarizing a party's business records (including electronically stored information), and if the burden of deriving or ascertaining the answer will be substantially the same for either party, the responding party may answer by:

(1) specifying the records that must be reviewed, in sufficient detail to enable the interrogating party to locate and identify them as readily as the responding party could; and

(2) giving the interrogating party a reasonable opportunity to examine and audit the records and to make copies, compilations, abstracts, or summaries.

Rule 34. Producing Documents, Electronically Stored Information, and Tangible Things, or Entering onto Land, for Inspection and Other Purposes

(a) In General. A party may serve on any other party a request within the scope of Rule 26(b):

(1) to produce and permit the requesting party or its representative to inspect, copy, test, or sample the following items in the responding party's possession, custody, or control:

(A) any designated documents or electronically stored information—including writings, drawings, graphs, charts, photographs, sound recordings, images, and other data or data compilations—stored in any medium from which information can be obtained either directly or, if necessary, after translation by the responding party into a reasonably usable form; or

(B) any designated tangible things; or

(2) to permit entry onto designated land or other property possessed or controlled by the responding party, so that the requesting party may inspect, measure, survey, photograph, test, or sample the property or any designated object or operation on it.

(b) Procedure.

(1) *Contents of the Request.* The request:

(A) must describe with reasonable particularity each item or category of items to be inspected;

(B) must specify a reasonable time, place, and manner for the inspection and for performing the related acts; and

(C) may specify the form or forms in which electronically stored information is to be produced.

(2) *Responses and Objections.*

(A) *Time to Respond.* The party to whom the request is directed must respond in writing within 30 days after being served or—if the request was delivered under Rule 26(d)(2)—within 30 days after the parties' first Rule 26(f) conference. A shorter or longer time may be stipulated to under Rule 29 or be ordered by the court.

(B) *Responding to Each Item.* For each item or category, the response must either state that inspection and related activities will be permitted as requested or state with specificity the grounds for objecting to the request, including the reasons. The responding party may state that it will produce copies of documents or of electronically stored information instead of permitting inspection. The production must then be completed no later than the time for inspection specified in the request or another reasonable time specified in the response.

(C) *Objections.* An objection must state whether any responsive materials are being withheld on the basis of that objection. An objection to part of a request must specify the part and permit inspection of the rest.

(D) *Responding to a Request for Production of Electronically Stored Information.* The response may state an objection to a requested form for producing electronically stored information. If the responding party objects to a requested form—or if no form was specified in the request—the party must state the form or forms it intends to use.

(E) *Producing the Documents or Electronically Stored Information.* Unless otherwise stipulated or ordered by the court, these procedures apply to producing documents or electronically stored information:

(i) A party must produce documents as they are kept in the usual course of business or must organize and label them to correspond to the categories in the request;

(ii) If a request does not specify a form for producing electronically stored information, a party must produce it in a form or forms in which it is ordinarily maintained or in a reasonably usable form or forms; and

(iii) A party need not produce the same electronically stored information in more than one form.

(c) **Nonparties.** As provided in Rule 45, a nonparty may be compelled to produce documents and tangible things or to permit an inspection.

Rule 35.   Physical and Mental Examinations

(a) **Order for an Examination.**

(1) *In General.* The court where the action is pending may order a party whose mental or physical condition—including blood group—is in controversy to submit to a physical or mental examination by a suitably licensed or certified examiner. The court has the same authority to order a party to produce for examination a person who is in its custody or under its legal control.

(2) *Motion and Notice; Contents of the Order.* The order:

(A) may be made only on motion for good cause and on notice to all parties and the person to be examined; and

(B) must specify the time, place, manner, conditions, and scope of the examination, as well as the person or persons who will perform it.

(b) **Examiner's Report.**

(1) *Request by the Party or Person Examined.* The party who moved for the examination must, on request, deliver to the requester a copy of the examiner's report, together with like reports of all earlier examinations of the same condition. The request may be made by the party against whom the examination order was issued or by the person examined.

(2) *Contents.* The examiner's report must be in writing and must set out in detail the examiner's findings, including diagnoses, conclusions, and the results of any tests.

(3) *Request by the Moving Party.* After delivering the reports, the party who moved for the examination may request—and is entitled to receive—from the party against whom the examination order was issued like reports of all earlier or later examinations of the same condition. But those reports need not be delivered

by the party with custody or control of the person examined if the party shows that it could not obtain them.

(4) *Waiver of Privilege.* By requesting and obtaining the examiner's report, or by deposing the examiner, the party examined waives any privilege it may have—in that action or any other action involving the same controversy—concerning testimony about all examinations of the same condition.

(5) *Failure to Deliver a Report.* The court on motion may order—on just terms—that a party deliver the report of an examination. If the report is not provided, the court may exclude the examiner's testimony at trial.

(6) *Scope.* This subdivision (b) applies also to an examination made by the parties' agreement, unless the agreement states otherwise. This subdivision does not preclude obtaining an examiner's report or deposing an examiner under other rules.

Rule 36.   Requests for Admission

(a) Scope and Procedure.

(1) *Scope.* A party may serve on any other party a written request to admit, for purposes of the pending action only, the truth of any matters within the scope of Rule 26(b)(1) relating to:

(A) facts, the application of law to fact, or opinions about either; and

(B) the genuineness of any described documents.

(2) *Form; Copy of a Document.* Each matter must be separately stated. A request to admit the genuineness of a document must be accompanied by a copy of the document unless it is, or has been, otherwise furnished or made available for inspection and copying.

(3) *Time to Respond; Effect of Not Responding.* A matter is admitted unless, within 30 days after being served, the party to whom the request is directed serves on the requesting party a written answer or objection addressed to the matter and signed by the party or its attorney. A shorter or longer time for responding may be stipulated to under Rule 29 or be ordered by the court.

(4) *Answer.* If a matter is not admitted, the answer must specifically deny it or state in detail why the answering party cannot truthfully admit or deny it. A denial must fairly respond to the substance of the matter; and when good faith requires that a party qualify an answer or deny only a part of a matter, the answer must specify the part admitted and qualify or deny the rest. The answering party may assert lack of knowledge or information as a reason for failing to admit or deny only if the party states that it has made reasonable inquiry and that the information it knows or can readily obtain is insufficient to enable it to admit or deny.

(5) *Objections.* The grounds for objecting to a request must be stated. A party must not object solely on the ground that the request presents a genuine issue for trial.

(6) *Motion Regarding the Sufficiency of an Answer or Objection.* The requesting party may move to determine the sufficiency of an answer or objection. Unless the court finds an objection justified, it must order that an answer be served. On finding that an answer does not comply with this rule, the court may order either that the matter is admitted or that an amended answer be served. The court may defer its final decision until a pretrial conference or a specified time before trial. Rule 37(a)(5) applies to an award of expenses.

(b) Effect of an Admission; Withdrawing or Amending It. A matter admitted under this rule is conclusively established unless the court, on motion, permits the admission to be withdrawn or amended. Subject to Rule 16(e), the court may permit withdrawal or amendment if it would promote the presentation of the merits of the action and if the court is not persuaded that it would prejudice the requesting party in maintaining or defending the action on the merits. An admission under this rule is not an admission for any other purpose and cannot be used against the party in any other proceeding.

Rule 37.   Failure to Make Disclosures or to Cooperate in Discovery; Sanctions

(a) Motion for an Order Compelling Disclosure or Discovery.
(1) *In General.* On notice to other parties and all affected persons, a party may move for an order compelling disclosure or discovery. The motion must include a certification that the movant has in good faith conferred or attempted to confer with the person or party failing to make disclosure or discovery in an effort to obtain it without court action.

(2) *Appropriate Court.* A motion for an order to a party must be made in the court where the action is pending. A motion for an order to a nonparty must be made in the court where the discovery is or will be taken.

(3) *Specific Motions.*

(A) *To Compel Disclosure.* If a party fails to make a disclosure required by Rule 26(a), any other party may move to compel disclosure and for appropriate sanctions.

(B) *To Compel a Discovery Response.* A party seeking discovery may move for an order compelling an answer, designation, production, or inspection. This motion may be made if:

(i) a deponent fails to answer a question asked under Rule 30 or 31;

(ii) a corporation or other entity fails to make a designation under Rule 30(b)(6) or 31(a)(4);

(iii) a party fails to answer an interrogatory submitted under Rule 33; or

(iv) a party fails to produce documents or fails to respond that inspection will be permitted—or fails to permit inspection—as requested under Rule 34.

(C) *Related to a Deposition.* When taking an oral deposition, the party asking a question may complete or adjourn the examination before moving for an order.

(4) *Evasive or Incomplete Disclosure, Answer, or Response.* For purposes of this subdivision (a), an evasive or incomplete disclosure, answer, or response must be treated as a failure to disclose, answer, or respond.

(5) *Payment of Expenses; Protective Orders.*

(A) *If the Motion Is Granted (or Disclosure or Discovery Is Provided After Filing).* If the motion is granted—or if the disclosure or requested discovery is provided after the motion was filed—the court must, after giving an opportunity to be heard, require the party or deponent whose conduct necessitated the motion, the party or attorney advising that conduct, or both to pay the movant's reasonable expenses incurred in making the motion, including attorney's fees. But the court must not order this payment if:

(i) the movant filed the motion before attempting in good faith to obtain the disclosure or discovery without court action;

(ii) the opposing party's nondisclosure, response, or objection was substantially justified; or

(iii) other circumstances make an award of expenses unjust.

(B) *If the Motion Is Denied.* If the motion is denied, the court may issue any protective order authorized under Rule 26(c) and must, after giving an opportunity to be heard, require the movant, the attorney filing the motion, or both to pay the party or deponent who opposed the motion its reasonable expenses incurred in opposing the motion, including attorney's fees. But the court must not order this payment if the motion was substantially justified or other circumstances make an award of expenses unjust.

(C) *If the Motion Is Granted in Part and Denied in Part.* If the motion is granted in part and denied in part, the court may issue any protective order authorized under Rule 26(c) and may, after giving an opportunity to be heard, apportion the reasonable expenses for the motion.

(b) Failure to Comply with a Court Order.

(1) *Sanctions Sought in the District Where the Deposition Is Taken.* If the court where the discovery is taken orders a deponent to be sworn or to answer a question and the deponent fails to obey, the failure may be treated as contempt of court. If a deposition-related motion is transferred to the court where the action is pending, and that court orders a deponent to be sworn or to answer a question and the deponent fails to obey, the failure may be treated as contempt of either the court where the discovery is taken or the court where the action is pending.

(2) *Sanctions Sought in the District Where the Action Is Pending.*

(A) *For Not Obeying a Discovery Order.* If a party or a party's officer, director, or managing agent—or a witness designated under Rule 30(b)(6) or 31(a)(4)—fails to obey an order to provide or permit discovery, including an order under Rule 26(f), 35, or 37(a), the court where the action is pending may issue further just orders. They may include the following:

      (i) directing that the matters embraced in the order or other designated facts be taken as established for purposes of the action, as the prevailing party claims;

      (ii) prohibiting the disobedient party from supporting or opposing designated claims or defenses, or from introducing designated matters in evidence;

      (iii) striking pleadings in whole or in part;

      (iv) staying further proceedings until the order is obeyed;

      (v) dismissing the action or proceeding in whole or in part;

      (vi) rendering a default judgment against the disobedient party; or

      (vii) treating as contempt of court the failure to obey any order except an order to submit to a physical or mental examination.

      (B) *For Not Producing a Person for Examination.* If a party fails to comply with an order under Rule 35(a) requiring it to produce another person for examination, the court may issue any of the orders listed in Rule 37(b)(2)(A)(i)-(vi), unless the disobedient party shows that it cannot produce the other person.

      (C) *Payment of Expenses.* Instead of or in addition to the orders above, the court must order the disobedient party, the attorney advising that party, or both to pay the reasonable expenses, including attorney's fees, caused by the failure, unless the failure was substantially justified or other circumstances make an award of expenses unjust.

      (c) Failure to Disclose, to Supplement an Earlier Response, or to Admit.

      (1) *Failure to Disclose or Supplement.* If a party fails to provide information or identify a witness as required by Rule 26(a) or (e), the party is not allowed to use that information or witness to supply evidence on a motion, at a hearing, or at a trial, unless the failure was substantially justified or is harmless. In addition to or instead of this sanction, the court, on motion and after giving an opportunity to be heard:

      (A) may order payment of the reasonable expenses, including attorney's fees, caused by the failure;

      (B) may inform the jury of the party's failure; and

      (C) may impose other appropriate sanctions, including any of the orders listed in Rule 37(b)(2)(A)(i)-(vi).

      (2) *Failure to Admit.* If a party fails to admit what is requested under Rule 36 and if the requesting party later proves a document to be genuine or the matter true, the requesting party may move that the party who failed to admit pay the reasonable expenses, including attorney's fees, incurred in making that proof. The court must so order unless:

      (A) the request was held objectionable under Rule 36(a);

(B) the admission sought was of no substantial importance;

(C) the party failing to admit had a reasonable ground to believe that it might prevail on the matter; or

(D) there was other good reason for the failure to admit.

(d) Party's Failure to Attend Its Own Deposition, Serve Answers to Interrogatories, or Respond to a Request for Inspection.

(1) *In General.*

(A) *Motion; Grounds for Sanctions.* The court where the action is pending may, on motion, order sanctions if:

(i) a party or a party's officer, director, or managing agent—or a person designated under Rule 30(b)(6) or 31(a)(4)—fails, after being served with proper notice, to appear for that person's deposition; or

(ii) a party, after being properly served with interrogatories under Rule 33 or a request for inspection under Rule 34, fails to serve its answers, objections, or written response.

(B) *Certification.* A motion for sanctions for failing to answer or respond must include a certification that the movant has in good faith conferred or attempted to confer with the party failing to act in an effort to obtain the answer or response without court action.

(2) *Unacceptable Excuse for Failing to Act.* A failure described in Rule 37(d)(1)(A) is not excused on the ground that the discovery sought was objectionable, unless the party failing to act has a pending motion for a protective order under Rule 26(c).

(3) *Types of Sanctions.* Sanctions may include any of the orders listed in Rule 37(b)(2)(A)(i)-(vi). Instead of or in addition to these sanctions, the court must require the party failing to act, the attorney advising that party, or both to pay the reasonable expenses, including attorney's fees, caused by the failure, unless the failure was substantially justified or other circumstances make an award of expenses unjust.

(e) Failure to Preserve Electronically Stored Information. If electronically stored information that should have been preserved in the anticipation or conduct of litigation is lost because a party failed to take reasonable steps to preserve it, and it cannot be restored or replaced through additional discovery, the court:

(1) upon finding prejudice to another party from loss of the information, may order measures no greater than necessary to cure the prejudice; or

(2) only upon finding that the party acted with the intent to deprive another party of the information's use in the litigation may:

(A) presume that the lost information was unfavorable to the party;

(B) instruct the jury that it may or must presume the information was unfavorable to the party; or

(C) dismiss the action or enter a default judgment.

(f) Failure to Participate in Framing a Discovery Plan. If a party or its attorney fails to participate in good faith in developing and submitting a proposed discovery plan as required by Rule 26(f), the court may, after giving an opportunity to be heard, require that party or attorney to pay to any other party the reasonable expenses, including attorney's fees, caused by the failure.

Title VI.   Trials

Rule 38.   Right to a Jury Trial; Demand

(a) Right Preserved. The right of trial by jury as declared by the Seventh Amendment to the Constitution — or as provided by a federal statute — is preserved to the parties inviolate.

(b) Demand. On any issue triable of right by a jury, a party may demand a jury trial by:
(1) serving the other parties with a written demand — which may be included in a pleading — no later than 14 days after the last pleading directed to the issue is served; and
(2) filing the demand in accordance with Rule 5(d).

(c) Specifying Issues. In its demand, a party may specify the issues that it wishes to have tried by a jury; otherwise, it is considered to have demanded a jury trial on all the issues so triable. If the party has demanded a jury trial on only some issues, any other party may — within 14 days after being served with the demand or within a shorter time ordered by the court — serve a demand for a jury trial on any other or all factual issues triable by jury.

(d) Waiver; Withdrawal. A party waives a jury trial unless its demand is properly served and filed. A proper demand may be withdrawn only if the parties consent.

(e) Admiralty and Maritime Claims. These rules do not create a right to a jury trial on issues in a claim that is an admiralty or maritime claim under Rule 9(h).

Rule 39.   Trial by Jury or by the Court

(a) When a Demand Is Made. When a jury trial has been demanded under Rule 38, the action must be designated on the docket as a jury action. The trial on all issues so demanded must be by jury unless:

(1) the parties or their attorneys file a stipulation to a nonjury trial or so stipulate on the record; or

(2) the court, on motion or on its own, finds that on some or all of those issues there is no federal right to a jury trial.

(b) When No Demand Is Made. Issues on which a jury trial is not properly demanded are to be tried by the court. But the court may, on motion, order a jury trial on any issue for which a jury might have been demanded.

(c) Advisory Jury; Jury Trial by Consent. In an action not triable of right by a jury, the court, on motion or on its own:

(1) may try any issue with an advisory jury; or

(2) may, with the parties' consent, try any issue by a jury whose verdict has the same effect as if a jury trial had been a matter of right, unless the action is against the United States and a federal statute provides for a nonjury trial.

Rule 40.   Scheduling Cases for Trial

Each court must provide by rule for scheduling trials. The court must give priority to actions entitled to priority by a federal statute.

Rule 41.   Dismissal of Actions

(a) Voluntary Dismissal.

(1) *By the Plaintiff.*

(A) *Without a Court Order.* Subject to Rules 23(e), 23.1(c), 23.2, and 66 and any applicable federal statute, the plaintiff may dismiss an action without a court order by filing:

(i) a notice of dismissal before the opposing party serves either an answer or a motion for summary judgment; or

(ii) a stipulation of dismissal signed by all parties who have appeared.

(B) *Effect.* Unless the notice or stipulation states otherwise, the dismissal is without prejudice. But if the plaintiff previously dismissed any federal- or state-court action based on or including the same claim, a notice of dismissal operates as an adjudication on the merits.

(2) *By Court Order; Effect.* Except as provided in Rule 41(a)(1), an action may be dismissed at the plaintiff's request only by court order, on terms that the court considers proper. If a defendant has pleaded a counterclaim before being served with the plaintiff's motion to dismiss, the action may be dismissed over the defendant's objection only if the counterclaim can remain pending for independent adjudication. Unless the order states otherwise, a dismissal under this paragraph (2) is without prejudice.

(b) Involuntary Dismissal; Effect. If the plaintiff fails to prosecute or to comply with these rules or a court order, a defendant may move to dismiss the action or any claim against it. Unless the dismissal order states otherwise, a dismissal under this subdivision (b) and any dismissal not under this rule—except one for lack of jurisdiction, improper venue, or failure to join a party under Rule 19—operates as an adjudication on the merits.

(c) Dismissing a Counterclaim, Crossclaim, or Third-Party Claim. This rule applies to a dismissal of any counterclaim, crossclaim, or third-party claim. A claimant's voluntary dismissal under Rule 41(a)(1)(A)(i) must be made:
(1) before a responsive pleading is served; or
(2) if there is no responsive pleading, before evidence is introduced at a hearing or trial.

(d) Costs of a Previously Dismissed Action. If a plaintiff who previously dismissed an action in any court files an action based on or including the same claim against the same defendant, the court:
(1) may order the plaintiff to pay all or part of the costs of that previous action; and
(2) may stay the proceedings until the plaintiff has complied.

Rule 42. Consolidation; Separate Trials

(a) Consolidation. If actions before the court involve a common question of law or fact, the court may:
(1) join for hearing or trial any or all matters at issue in the actions;
(2) consolidate the actions; or
(3) issue any other orders to avoid unnecessary cost or delay.

(b) Separate Trials. For convenience, to avoid prejudice, or to expedite and economize, the court may order a separate trial of one or more separate issues, claims, crossclaims, counterclaims, or third-party claims. When ordering a separate trial, the court must preserve any federal right to a jury trial.

Rule 43. Taking Testimony

(a) In Open Court. At trial, the witnesses' testimony must be taken in open court unless a federal statute, the Federal Rules of Evidence, these rules, or other rules adopted by the Supreme Court provide otherwise. For good cause in compelling circumstances and with appropriate safeguards, the court may permit testimony in open court by contemporaneous transmission from a different location.

(b) Affirmation Instead of an Oath. When these rules require an oath, a solemn affirmation suffices.

(c) Evidence on a Motion. When a motion relies on facts outside the record, the court may hear the matter on affidavits or may hear it wholly or partly on oral testimony or on depositions.

(d) Interpreter. The court may appoint an interpreter of its choosing; fix reasonable compensation to be paid from funds provided by law or by one or more parties; and tax the compensation as costs.

Rule 44.   Proving an Official Record

(a) Means of Proving.
(1) *Domestic Record.* Each of the following evidences an official record—or an entry in it—that is otherwise admissible and is kept within the United States, any state, district, or commonwealth, or any territory subject to the administrative or judicial jurisdiction of the United States:
   (A) an official publication of the record; or
   (B) a copy attested by the officer with legal custody of the record—or by the officer's deputy—and accompanied by a certificate that the officer has custody. The certificate must be made under seal:
      (i) by a judge of a court of record in the district or political subdivision where the record is kept; or
      (ii) by any public officer with a seal of office and with official duties in the district or political subdivision where the record is kept.
(2) *Foreign Record.*
   (A) *In General.* Each of the following evidences a foreign official record—or an entry in it—that is otherwise admissible:
      (i) an official publication of the record; or
      (ii) the record—or a copy—that is attested by an authorized person and is accompanied either by a final certification of genuineness or by a certification under a treaty or convention to which the United States and the country where the record is located are parties.
   (B) *Final Certification of Genuineness.* A final certification must certify the genuineness of the signature and official position of the attester or of any foreign official whose certificate of genuineness relates to the attestation or is in a chain of certificates of genuineness relating to the attestation. A final certification may be made by a secretary of a United States embassy or legation; by a consul general, vice consul, or consular agent of the United States; or by a diplomatic or consular official of the foreign country assigned or accredited to the United States.

(C) *Other Means of Proof.* If all parties have had a reasonable opportunity to investigate a foreign record's authenticity and accuracy, the court may, for good cause, either:

(i) admit an attested copy without final certification; or

(ii) permit the record to be evidenced by an attested summary with or without a final certification.

(b) Lack of a Record. A written statement that a diligent search of designated records revealed no record or entry of a specified tenor is admissible as evidence that the records contain no such record or entry. For domestic records, the statement must be authenticated under Rule 44(a)(1). For foreign records, the statement must comply with (a)(2)(C)(ii).

(c) Other Proof. A party may prove an official record—or an entry or lack of an entry in it—by any other method authorized by law.

Rule 44.1.   Determining Foreign Law

A party who intends to raise an issue about a foreign country's law must give notice by a pleading or other writing. In determining foreign law, the court may consider any relevant material or source, including testimony, whether or not submitted by a party or admissible under the Federal Rules of Evidence. The court's determination must be treated as a ruling on a question of law.

Rule 45.   Subpoena

(a) In General.
(1) *Form and Contents.*
   (A) *Requirements—In General.* Every subpoena must:
   (i) state the court from which it issued;
   (ii) state the title of the action and its civil-action number;
   (iii) command each person to whom it is directed to do the following at a specified time and place: attend and testify; produce designated documents, electronically stored information, or tangible things in that person's possession, custody, or control; or permit the inspection of premises; and
   (iv) set out the text of Rule 45(d) and (e).
   (B) *Command to Attend a Deposition—Notice of the Recording Method.* A subpoena commanding attendance at a deposition must state the method for recording the testimony.
   (C) *Combining or Separating a Command to Produce or to Permit Inspection; Specifying the Form for Electronically Stored Information.* A command to produce documents, electronically stored information, or tangible

things or to permit the inspection of premises may be included in a subpoena commanding attendance at a deposition, hearing, or trial, or may be set out in a separate subpoena. A subpoena may specify the form or forms in which electronically stored information is to be produced.

(D) *Command to Produce; Included Obligations.* A command in a subpoena to produce documents, electronically stored information, or tangible things requires the responding person to permit inspection, copying, testing, or sampling of the materials.

(2) *Issuing Court.* A subpoena must issue from the court where the action is pending.

(3) *Issued by Whom.* The clerk must issue a subpoena, signed but otherwise in blank, to a party who requests it. That party must complete it before service. An attorney also may issue and sign a subpoena if the attorney is authorized to practice in the issuing court.

(4) *Notice to Other Parties Before Service.* If the subpoena commands the production of documents, electronically stored information, or tangible things or the inspection of premises before trial, then before it is served on the person to whom it is directed, a notice and a copy of the subpoena must be served on each party.

(b) Service.

(1) *By Whom and How; Tendering Fees.* Any person who is at least 18 years old and not a party may serve a subpoena. Serving a subpoena requires delivering a copy to the named person and, if the subpoena requires that person's attendance, tendering the fees for 1 day's attendance and the mileage allowed by law. Fees and mileage need not be tendered when the subpoena issues on behalf of the United States or any of its officers or agencies.

(2) *Service in the United States.* (A) subpoena may be served at any place within the United States.

(3) *Service in a Foreign Country.* 28 U.S.C. §1783 governs issuing and serving a subpoena directed to a United States national or resident who is in a foreign country.

(4) *Proof of Service.* Proving service, when necessary, requires filing with the issuing court a statement showing the date and manner of service and the names of the persons served. The statement must be certified by the server.

(c) Place of compliance.

(1) *For a Trial, Hearing, or Deposition.* A subpoena may command a person to attend a trial, hearing, or deposition only as follows:

(A) within 100 miles of where the person resides, is employed, or regularly transacts business in person; or

(B) within the state where the person resides, is employed, or regularly transacts business in person, if the person

(i) is a party or a party's officer; or

(ii) is commanded to attend a trial and would not incur substantial expense.

(2) *For Other Discovery.* A subpoena may command:

(A) production of documents, electronically stored information, or tangible things at a place within 100 miles of where the person resides, is employed, or regularly transacts business in person; and

(B) inspection of premises at the premises to be inspected.

(d) Protecting a Person Subject to a Subpoena.

(1) *Avoiding Undue Burden or Expense; Sanctions.* A party or attorney responsible for issuing and serving a subpoena must take reasonable steps to avoid imposing undue burden or expense on a person subject to the subpoena. The court for the district where compliance is required must enforce this duty and impose an appropriate sanction—which may include lost earnings and reasonable attorney's fees—on a party or attorney who fails to comply.

(2) *Command to Produce Materials or Permit Inspection.*

(A) *Appearance Not Required.* A person commanded to produce documents, electronically stored information, or tangible things, or to permit the inspection of premises, need not appear in person at the place of production or inspection unless also commanded to appear for a deposition, hearing, or trial.

(B) *Objections.* A person commanded to produce documents or tangible things or to permit inspection may serve on the party or attorney designated in the subpoena a written objection to inspecting, copying, testing or sampling any or all of the materials or to inspecting the premises—or to producing electronically stored information in the form or forms requested. The objection must be served before the earlier of the time specified for compliance or 14 days after the subpoena is served. If an objection is made, the following rules apply:

(i) At any time, on notice to the commanded person, the serving party may move the court for the district where compliance is required for an order compelling production or inspection.

(ii) These acts may be required only as directed in the order, and the order must protect a person who is neither a party nor a party's officer from significant expense resulting from compliance.

(3) *Quashing or Modifying a Subpoena.*

(A) *When Required.* On timely motion, the court for the district where compliance is required must quash or modify a subpoena that:

(i) fails to allow a reasonable time to comply;

(ii) requires a person to comply beyond the geographical limits specified in Rule 45(c);

(iii) requires disclosure of privileged or other protected matter, if no exception or waiver applies; or

(iv) subjects a person to undue burden.

(B) *When Permitted.* To protect a person subject to or affected by a subpoena, the court for the district where compliance is required may, on motion, quash or modify the subpoena if it requires;

(i) disclosing a trade secret or other confidential research, development, or commercial information; or

(ii) disclosing an unretained expert's opinion or information that does not describe specific occurrences in dispute and results from the expert's study that was not requested by a party.

(C) *Specifying Conditions as an Alternative.* In the circumstances described in Rule 45(d)(3)(B), the court may, instead of quashing or modifying a subpoena, order appearance or production under specified conditions if the serving party:

(i) shows a substantial need for the testimony or material that cannot be otherwise met without undue hardship; and

(ii) ensures that the subpoenaed person will be reasonably compensated.

(e) Duties in Responding to a Subpoena.

(1) *Producing Documents or Electronically Stored Information.* These procedures apply to producing documents or electronically stored information:

(A) *Documents.* A person responding to a subpoena to produce documents must produce them as they are kept in the ordinary course of business or must organize and label them to correspond to the categories in the demand.

(B) *Form for Producing Electronically Stored Information Not Specified.* If a subpoena does not specify a form for producing electronically stored information, the person responding must produce it in a form or forms in which it is ordinarily maintained or in a reasonably usable form or forms.

(C) *Electronically Stored Information Produced in Only One Form.* The person responding need not produce the same electronically stored information in more than one form.

(D) *Inaccessible Electronically Stored Information.* The person responding need not provide discovery of electronically stored information from sources that the person identifies as not reasonably accessible because of undue burden or cost. On motion to compel discovery or for a protective order, the person responding must show that the information is not reasonably accessible because of undue burden or cost. If that showing is made, the court may nonetheless order discovery from such sources if the requesting party shows good cause, considering the limitations of Rule 26(b)(2)(C). The court may specify conditions for the discovery.

(2) *Claiming Privilege or Protection.*

(A) *Information Withheld.* A person withholding subpoenaed information under a claim that it is privileged or subject to protection as trial-preparation material must:

(i) expressly make the claim; and

(ii) describe the nature of the withheld documents, communications, or tangible things in a manner that, without revealing information itself privileged or protected, will enable the parties to assess the claim.

(B) *Information Produced.* If information produced in response to a subpoena is subject to a claim of privilege or of protection as trial-preparation material, the person making the claim may notify any party that received the information of the claim and the basis for it. After being notified, a party must promptly return, sequester, or destroy the specified information and any copies it has; must not use or disclose the information until the claim is resolved; must take reasonable steps to retrieve the information if the party disclosed it before being notified; and may promptly present the information under seal to the court for the district where compliance is required for a determination of the claim. The person who produced the information must preserve the information until the claim is resolved.

(f) **Transferring a Subpoena-Related Motion.** When the court where compliance is required did not issue the subpoena, it may transfer a motion under this rule to the issuing court if the person subject to the subpoena consents or if the court finds exceptional circumstances. Then, if the attorney for a person subject to a subpoena is authorized to practice in the court where the motion was made, the attorney may file papers and appear on the motion as an officer of the issuing court. To enforce its order, the issuing court may transfer the order to the court where the motion was made.

(g) **Contempt.** The court for the district where compliance is required—and also, after a motion is transferred, the issuing court—may hold in contempt a person who, having been served, fails without adequate excuse to obey the subpoena.

Rule 46.   Objecting to a Ruling or Order

A formal exception to a ruling or order is unnecessary. When the ruling or order is requested or made, a party need only state the action that it wants the court to take or objects to, along with the grounds for the request or objection. Failing to object does not prejudice a party who had no opportunity to do so when the ruling or order was made.

Rule 47.   Selecting Jurors

(a) **Examining Jurors.** The court may permit the parties or their attorneys to examine prospective jurors or may itself do so. If the court examines the jurors, it must permit the parties or their attorneys to make any further inquiry it considers proper, or must itself ask any of their additional questions it considers proper.

(b) **Peremptory Challenges.** The court must allow the number of peremptory challenges provided by 28 U.S.C. §1870.

(c) **Excusing a Juror.** During trial or deliberation, the court may excuse a juror for good cause.

Rule 48.   Number of Jurors; Verdict; Polling

(a) **Number of Jurors.** A jury must begin with at least 6 and no more than 12 members, and each juror must participate in the verdict unless excused under Rule 47(c).

(b) **Verdict.** Unless the parties stipulate otherwise, the verdict must be unanimous and must be returned by a jury of at least 6 members.

(c) **Polling.** After a verdict is returned but before the jury is discharged, the court must on a party's request, or may on its own, poll the jurors individually. If the poll reveals a lack of unanimity or lack of assent by the number of jurors that the parties stipulated to, the court may direct the jury to deliberate further or may order a new trial.

Rule 49.   Special Verdict; General Verdict and Questions

(a) **Special Verdict.**
(1) *In General.* The court may require a jury to return only a special verdict in the form of a special written finding on each issue of fact. The court may do so by:
(A) submitting written questions susceptible of a categorical or other brief answer;
(B) submitting written forms of the special findings that might properly be made under the pleadings and evidence; or
(C) using any other method that the court considers appropriate.
(2) *Instructions.* The court must give the instructions and explanations necessary to enable the jury to make its findings on each submitted issue.
(3) *Issues Not Submitted.* A party waives the right to a jury trial on any issue of fact raised by the pleadings or evidence but not submitted to the jury unless, before the jury retires, the party demands its submission to the jury. If the party does not demand submission, the court may make a finding on the issue. If the

court makes no finding, it is considered to have made a finding consistent with its judgment on the special verdict.

(b) General Verdict with Answers to Written Questions.

(1) *In General.* The court may submit to the jury forms for a general verdict, together with written questions on one or more issues of fact that the jury must decide. The court must give the instructions and explanations necessary to enable the jury to render a general verdict and answer the questions in writing, and must direct the jury to do both.

(2) *Verdict and Answers Consistent.* When the general verdict and the answers are consistent, the court must approve, for entry under Rule 58, an appropriate judgment on the verdict and answers.

(3) *Answers Inconsistent with the Verdict.* When the answers are consistent with each other but one or more is inconsistent with the general verdict, the court may:

(A) approve, for entry under Rule 58, an appropriate judgment according to the answers, notwithstanding the general verdict;

(B) direct the jury to further consider its answers and verdict; or

(C) order a new trial.

(4) *Answers Inconsistent with Each Other and the Verdict.* When the answers are inconsistent with each other and one or more is also inconsistent with the general verdict, judgment must not be entered; instead, the court must direct the jury to further consider its answers and verdict, or must order a new trial.

Rule 50. Judgment as a Matter of Law in a Jury Trial; Related Motion for a New Trial; Conditional Ruling

(a) Judgment as a Matter of Law.

(1) *In General.* If a party has been fully heard on an issue during a jury trial and the court finds that a reasonable jury would not have a legally sufficient evidentiary basis to find for the party on that issue, the court may:

(A) resolve the issue against the party; and

(B) grant a motion for judgment as a matter of law against the party on a claim or defense that, under the controlling law, can be maintained or defeated only with a favorable finding on that issue.

(2) *Motion.* A motion for judgment as a matter of law may be made at any time before the case is submitted to the jury. The motion must specify the judgment sought and the law and facts that entitle the movant to the judgment.

(b) Renewing the Motion After Trial; Alternative Motion for a New Trial. If the court does not grant a motion for judgment as a matter of law made under Rule 50(a), the court is considered to have submitted the action to the jury subject to the court's later deciding the legal questions raised by the motion. No later than 28 days after the entry of judgment—or if the motion addresses a jury issue not decided by a verdict, no later than 28 days after the jury was discharged—the movant may file a renewed motion for judgment as a matter of law and may include an alternative or joint request for a new trial under Rule 59. In ruling on the renewed motion, the court may:

(1) allow judgment on the verdict, if the jury returned a verdict;

(2) order a new trial; or

(3) direct the entry of judgment as a matter of law.

(c) Granting the Renewed Motion; Conditional Ruling on a Motion for a New Trial.

(1) *In General.* If the court grants a renewed motion for judgment as a matter of law, it must also conditionally rule on any motion for a new trial by determining whether a new trial should be granted if the judgment is later vacated or reversed. The court must state the grounds for conditionally granting or denying the motion for a new trial.

(2) *Effect of a Conditional Ruling.* Conditionally granting the motion for a new trial does not affect the judgment's finality; if the judgment is reversed, the new trial must proceed unless the appellate court orders otherwise. If the motion for a new trial is conditionally denied, the appellee may assert error in that denial; if the judgment is reversed, the case must proceed as the appellate court orders.

(d) Time for a Losing Party's New-Trial Motion. Any motion for a new trial under Rule 59 by a party against whom judgment as a matter of law is rendered must be filed no later than 28 days after the entry of the judgment.

(e) Denying the Motion for Judgment as a Matter of Law; Reversal on Appeal. If the court denies the motion for judgment as a matter of law, the prevailing party may, as appellee, assert grounds entitling it to a new trial should the appellate court conclude that the trial court erred in denying the motion. If the appellate court reverses the judgment, it may order a new trial, direct the trial court to determine whether a new trial should be granted, or direct the entry of judgment.

Rule 51. Instructions to the Jury; Objections; Preserving a Claim of Error

(a) Requests.

(1) *Before or at the Close of the Evidence.* At the close of the evidence or at any earlier reasonable time that the court orders, a party may file and furnish to every other party written requests for the jury instructions it wants the court to give.

(2) *After the Close of the Evidence.* After the close of the evidence, a party may:

> (A) file requests for instructions on issues that could not reasonably have been anticipated by an earlier time that the court set for requests; and

> (B) with the court's permission, file untimely requests for instructions on any issue.

(b) Instructions. The court:

(1) must inform the parties of its proposed instructions and proposed action on the requests before instructing the jury and before final jury arguments;

(2) must give the parties an opportunity to object on the record and out of the jury's hearing before the instructions and arguments are delivered; and

(3) may instruct the jury at any time before the jury is discharged.

(c) Objections.

(1) *How to Make.* A party who objects to an instruction or the failure to give an instruction must do so on the record, stating distinctly the matter objected to and the grounds for the objection.

(2) *When to Make.* An objection is timely if:

> (A) a party objects at the opportunity provided under Rule 51(b)(2); or

> (B) a party was not informed of an instruction or action on a request before that opportunity to object, and the party objects promptly after learning that the instruction or request will be, or has been, given or refused.

(d) Assigning Error; Plain Error.

(1) *Assigning Error.* A party may assign as error:

> (A) an error in an instruction actually given, if that party properly objected; or

> (B) a failure to give an instruction, if that party properly requested it and—unless the court rejected the request in a definitive ruling on the record—also properly objected.

(2) *Plain Error.* A court may consider a plain error in the instructions that has not been preserved as required by Rule 51(d)(1) if the error affects substantial rights.

Rule 52.   Findings and Conclusions by the Court; Judgment on Partial Findings

(a) Findings and Conclusions.

(1) *In General.* In an action tried on the facts without a jury or with an advisory jury, the court must find the facts specially and state its conclusions of law separately. The findings and conclusions may be stated on the record after the

close of the evidence or may appear in an opinion or a memorandum of decision filed by the court. Judgment must be entered under Rule 58.

(2) *For an Interlocutory Injunction.* In granting or refusing an interlocutory injunction, the court must similarly state the findings and conclusions that support its action.

(3) *For a Motion.* The court is not required to state findings or conclusions when ruling on a motion under Rule 12 or 56 or, unless these rules provide otherwise, on any other motion.

(4) *Effect of a Master's Findings.* A master's findings, to the extent adopted by the court, must be considered the court's findings.

(5) *Questioning the Evidentiary Support.* A party may later question the sufficiency of the evidence supporting the findings, whether or not the party requested findings, objected to them, moved to amend them, or moved for partial findings.

(6) *Setting Aside the Findings.* Findings of fact, whether based on oral or other evidence, must not be set aside unless clearly erroneous, and the reviewing court must give due regard to the trial court's opportunity to judge the witnesses' credibility.

(b) Amended or Additional Findings. On a party's motion filed no later than 28 days after the entry of judgment, the court may amend its findings—or make additional findings—and may amend the judgment accordingly. The motion may accompany a motion for a new trial under Rule 59.

(c) Judgment on Partial Findings. If a party has been fully heard on an issue during a nonjury trial and the court finds against the party on that issue, the court may enter judgment against the party on a claim or defense that, under the controlling law, can be maintained or defeated only with a favorable finding on that issue. The court may, however, decline to render any judgment until the close of the evidence. A judgment on partial findings must be supported by findings of fact and conclusions of law as required by Rule 52(a).

Rule 53.   Masters

(a) Appointment.

(1) *Scope.* Unless a statute provides otherwise, a court may appoint a master only to:

    (A) perform duties consented to by the parties;

    (B) hold trial proceedings and make or recommend findings of fact on issues to be decided without a jury if appointment is warranted by:

        (i) some exceptional condition; or

        (ii) the need to perform an accounting or resolve a difficult computation of damages; or

(C) address pretrial and posttrial matters that cannot be effectively and timely addressed by an available district judge or magistrate judge of the district.

(2) *Disqualification.* A master must not have a relationship to the parties, attorneys, action, or court that would require disqualification of a judge under 28 U.S.C. §455, unless the parties, with the court's approval, consent to the appointment after the master discloses any potential grounds for disqualification.

(3) *Possible Expense or Delay.* In appointing a master, the court must consider the fairness of imposing the likely expenses on the parties and must protect against unreasonable expense or delay.

(b) Order Appointing a Master.

(1) *Notice.* Before appointing a master, the court must give the parties notice and an opportunity to be heard. Any party may suggest candidates for appointment.

(2) *Contents.* The appointing order must direct the master to proceed with all reasonable diligence and must state:

(A) the master's duties, including any investigation or enforcement duties, and any limits on the master's authority under Rule 53(c);

(B) the circumstances, if any, in which the master may communicate ex parte with the court or a party;

(C) the nature of the materials to be preserved and filed as the record of the master's activities;

(D) the time limits, method of filing the record, other procedures, and standards for reviewing the master's orders, findings, and recommendations; and

(E) the basis, terms, and procedure for fixing the master's compensation under Rule 53(g).

(3) *Issuing.* The court may issue the order only after:

(A) the master files an affidavit disclosing whether there is any ground for disqualification under 28 U.S.C. §455; and

(B) if a ground is disclosed, the parties, with the court's approval, waive the disqualification.

(4) *Amending.* The order may be amended at any time after notice to the parties and an opportunity to be heard.

(c) Master's Authority.

(1) *In General.* Unless the appointing order directs otherwise, a master may:

(A) regulate all proceedings;

(B) take all appropriate measures to perform the assigned duties fairly and efficiently; and

(C) if conducting an evidentiary hearing, exercise the appointing court's power to compel, take, and record evidence.

(2) **Sanctions.** The master may by order impose on a party any noncontempt sanction provided by Rule 37 or 45, and may recommend a contempt sanction against a party and sanctions against a nonparty.

(d) Master's Orders. A master who issues an order must file it and promptly serve a copy on each party. The clerk must enter the order on the docket.

(e) Master's Reports. A master must report to the court as required by the appointing order. The master must file the report and promptly serve a copy on each party, unless the court orders otherwise.

(f) Action on the Master's Order, Report, or Recommendations.

(1) *Opportunity for a Hearing; Action in General.* In acting on a master's order, report, or recommendations, the court must give the parties notice and an opportunity to be heard; may receive evidence; and may adopt or affirm, modify, wholly or partly reject or reverse, or resubmit to the master with instructions.

(2) *Time to Object or Move to Adopt or Modify.* A party may file objections to—or a motion to adopt or modify—the master's order, report, or recommendations no later than 21 days after a copy is served, unless the court sets a different time.

(3) *Reviewing Factual Findings.* The court must decide de novo all objections to findings of fact made or recommended by a master, unless the parties, with the court's approval, stipulate that:

(A) the findings will be reviewed for clear error; or

(B) the findings of a master appointed under Rule 53(a)(1)(A) or (C) will be final.

(4) *Reviewing Legal Conclusions.* The court must decide de novo all objections to conclusions of law made or recommended by a master.

(5) *Reviewing Procedural Matters.* Unless the appointing order establishes a different standard of review, the court may set aside a master's ruling on a procedural matter only for an abuse of discretion.

(g) Compensation.

(1) *Fixing Compensation.* Before or after judgment, the court must fix the master's compensation on the basis and terms stated in the appointing order, but the court may set a new basis and terms after giving notice and an opportunity to be heard.

(2) *Payment.* The compensation must be paid either:

(A) by a party or parties; or

(B) from a fund or subject matter of the action within the court's control.

(3) *Allocating Payment.* The court must allocate payment among the parties after considering the nature and amount of the controversy, the parties' means, and the extent to which any party is more responsible than other parties for the

reference to a master. An interim allocation may be amended to reflect a decision on the merits.

(h) Appointing a Magistrate Judge. A magistrate judge is subject to this rule only when the order referring a matter to the magistrate judge states that the reference is made under this rule.

Title VII.   Judgment

Rule 54.   Judgment; Costs

(a) Definition; Form. "Judgment" as used in these rules includes a decree and any order from which an appeal lies. A judgment should not include recitals of pleadings, a master's report, or a record of prior proceedings.

(b) Judgment on Multiple Claims or Involving Multiple Parties. When an action presents more than one claim for relief—whether as a claim, counter-claim, crossclaim, or third-party claim—or when multiple parties are involved, the court may direct entry of a final judgment as to one or more, but fewer than all, claims or parties only if the court expressly determines that there is no just reason for delay. Otherwise, any order or other decision, however designated, that adjudicates fewer than all the claims or the rights and liabilities of fewer than all the parties does not end the action as to any of the claims or parties and may be revised at any time before the entry of a judgment adjudicating all the claims and all the parties' rights and liabilities.

(c) Demand for Judgment; Relief to Be Granted. A default judgment must not differ in kind from, or exceed in amount, what is demanded in the pleadings. Every other final judgment should grant the relief to which each party is entitled, even if the party has not demanded that relief in its pleadings.

(d) Costs; Attorney's Fees.
(1) *Costs Other Than Attorney's Fees.* Unless a federal statute, these rules, or a court order provides otherwise, costs—other than attorney's fees—should be allowed to the prevailing party. But costs against the United States, its officers, and its agencies may be imposed only to the extent allowed by law. The clerk may tax costs on 14 days' notice. On motion served within the next 7 days, the court may review the clerk's action.
(2) *Attorney's Fees.*
(A) *Claim to Be by Motion.* A claim for attorney's fees and related non-taxable expenses must be made by motion unless the substantive law requires those fees to be proved at trial as an element of damages.

(B) *Timing and Contents of the Motion.* Unless a statute or a court order provides otherwise, the motion must:

(i) be filed no later than 14 days after the entry of judgment;

(ii) specify the judgment and the statute, rule, or other grounds entitling the movant to the award;

(iii) state the amount sought or provide a fair estimate of it; and

(iv) disclose, if the court so orders, the terms of any agreement about fees for the services for which the claim is made.

(C) *Proceedings.* Subject to Rule 23(h), the court must, on a party's request, give an opportunity for adversary submissions on the motion in accordance with Rule 43(c) or 78. The court may decide issues of liability for fees before receiving submissions on the value of services. The court must find the facts and state its conclusions of law as provided in Rule 52(a).

(D) *Special Procedures by Local Rule; Reference to a Master or a Magistrate Judge.* By local rule, the court may establish special procedures to resolve fee-related issues without extensive evidentiary hearings. Also, the court may refer issues concerning the value of services to a special master under Rule 53 without regard to the limitations of Rule 53(a)(1), and may refer a motion for attorney's fees to a magistrate judge under Rule 72(b) as if it were a dispositive pretrial matter.

(E) *Exceptions.* Subparagraphs (A)-(D) do not apply to claims for fees and expenses as sanctions for violating these rules or as sanctions under 28 U.S.C. §1927.

Rule 55.   Default; Default Judgment

(a) **Entering a Default.** When a party against whom a judgment for affirmative relief is sought has failed to plead or otherwise defend, and that failure is shown by affidavit or otherwise, the clerk must enter the party's default.

(b) **Entering a Default Judgment.**

(1) *By the Clerk.* If the plaintiff's claim is for a sum certain or a sum that can be made certain by computation, the clerk—on the plaintiff's request, with an affidavit showing the amount due—must enter judgment for that amount and costs against a defendant who has been defaulted for not appearing and who is neither a minor nor an incompetent person.

(2) *By the Court.* In all other cases, the party must apply to the court for a default judgment. A default judgment may be entered against a minor or incompetent person only if represented by a general guardian, conservator, or other like fiduciary who has appeared. If the party against whom a default judgment is sought has appeared personally or by a representative, that party or its representative must be served with written notice of the application at least 7 days before the hearing. The court may conduct hearings or make referrals—preserving any

federal statutory right to a jury trial—when, to enter or effectuate judgment, it needs to:

    (A) conduct an accounting;

    (B) determine the amount of damages;

    (C) establish the truth of any allegation by evidence; or

    (D) investigate any other matter.

(c) Setting Aside a Default or a Default Judgment. The court may set aside an entry of default for good cause, and it may set aside a final default judgment under Rule 60(b).

(d) Judgment Against the United States. A default judgment may be entered against the United States, its officers, or its agencies only if the claimant establishes a claim or right to relief by evidence that satisfies the court.

Rule 56.   Summary Judgment

(a) Motion for Summary Judgment or Partial Summary Judgment. A party may move for summary judgment, identifying each claim or defense—or the part of each claim or defense—on which summary judgment is sought. The court shall grant summary judgment if the movant shows that there is no genuine dispute as to any material fact and the movant is entitled to judgment as a matter of law. The court should state on the record the reasons for granting or denying the motion.

(b) Time to File a Motion. Unless a different time is set by local rule or the court orders otherwise, a party may file a motion for summary judgment at any time until 30 days after the close of all discovery.

(c) Procedures.

(1) *Supporting Factual Positions.* A party asserting that a fact cannot be or is genuinely disputed must support the assertion by:

    (A) citing to particular parts of materials in the record, including depositions, documents, electronically stored information, affidavits or declarations, stipulations (including those made for purposes of the motion only), admissions, interrogatory answers, or other materials; or

    (B) showing that the materials cited do not establish the absence or presence of a genuine dispute, or that an adverse party cannot produce admissible evidence to support the fact.

(2) *Objection That a Fact Is Not Supported by Admissible Evidence.* A party may object that the material cited to support or dispute a fact cannot be presented in a form that would be admissible in evidence.

(3) **Materials Not Cited.** The court need consider only the cited materials, but it may consider other materials in the record.

(4) **Affidavits or Declarations.** An affidavit or declaration used to support or oppose a motion must be made on personal knowledge, set out facts that would be admissible in evidence, and show that the affiant or declarant is competent to testify on the matters stated.

(d) When Facts Are Unavailable to the Nonmovant. If a nonmovant shows by affidavit or declaration that, for specified reasons, it cannot present facts essential to justify its opposition, the court may:

(1) defer considering the motion or deny it;

(2) allow time to obtain affidavits or declarations or to take discovery; or

(3) issue any other appropriate order.

(e) Failing to Properly Support or Address a Fact. If a party fails to properly support an assertion of fact or fails to properly address another party's assertion of fact as required by Rule 56(c), the court may:

(1) give an opportunity to properly support or address the fact;

(2) consider the fact undisputed for purposes of the motion;

(3) grant summary judgment if the motion and supporting materials— including the facts considered undisputed—show that the movant is entitled to it; or

(4) issue any other appropriate order.

(f) Judgment Independent of the Motion. After giving notice and a reasonable time to respond, the court may:

(1) grant summary judgment for a nonmovant;

(2) grant the motion on grounds not raised by a party; or

(3) consider summary judgment on its own after identifying for the parties material facts that may not be genuinely in dispute.

(g) Failing to Grant All the Requested Relief. If the court does not grant all the relief requested by the motion, it may enter an order stating any material fact—including an item of damages or other relief—that is not genuinely in dispute and treating the fact as established in the case.

(h) Affidavit or Declaration Submitted in Bad Faith. If satisfied that an affidavit or declaration under this rule is submitted in bad faith or solely for delay, the court—after notice and a reasonable time to respond—may order the submitting party to pay the other party the reasonable expenses, including attorney's fees, it incurred as a result. An offending party or attorney may also be held in contempt or subjected to other appropriate sanctions.

Rule 57. Declaratory Judgment

These rules govern the procedure for obtaining a declaratory judgment under 28 U.S.C. §2201. Rules 38 and 39 govern a demand for a jury trial. The existence of another adequate remedy does not preclude a declaratory judgment that is otherwise appropriate. The court may order a speedy hearing of a declaratory-judgment action.

Rule 58. Entering Judgment

(a) Separate Document. Every judgment and amended judgment must be set out in a separate document, but a separate document is not required for an order disposing of a motion:
   (1) for judgment under Rule 50(b);
   (2) to amend or make additional findings under Rule 52(b);
   (3) for attorney's fees under Rule 54;
   (4) for a new trial, or to alter or amend the judgment, under Rule 59; or
   (5) for relief under Rule 60.

(b) Entering Judgment.
   (1) *Without the Court's Direction.* Subject to Rule 54(b) and unless the court orders otherwise, the clerk must, without awaiting the court's direction, promptly prepare, sign, and enter the judgment when:
      (A) the jury returns a general verdict;
      (B) the court awards only costs or a sum certain; or
      (C) the court denies all relief.
   (2) *Court's Approval Required.* Subject to Rule 54(b), the court must promptly approve the form of the judgment, which the clerk must promptly enter, when:
      (A) the jury returns a special verdict or a general verdict with answers to written questions; or
      (B) the court grants other relief not described in this subdivision (b).

(c) Time of Entry. For purposes of these rules, judgment is entered at the following times:
   (1) if a separate document is not required, when the judgment is entered in the civil docket under Rule 79(a); or
   (2) if a separate document is required, when the judgment is entered in the civil docket under Rule 79(a) and the earlier of these events occurs:
      (A) it is set out in a separate document; or
      (B) 150 days have run from the entry in the civil docket.

(d) **Request for Entry.** A party may request that judgment be set out in a separate document as required by Rule 58(a).

(e) **Cost or Fee Awards.** Ordinarily, the entry of judgment may not be delayed, nor the time for appeal extended, in order to tax costs or award fees. But if a timely motion for attorney's fees is made under Rule 54(d)(2), the court may act before a notice of appeal has been filed and become effective to order that the motion have the same effect under Federal Rule of Appellate Procedure 4(a)(4) as a timely motion under Rule 59.

Rule 59.   New Trial; Altering or Amending a Judgment

(a) **In General.**
(1) *Grounds for New Trial.* The court may, on motion, grant a new trial on all or some of the issues—and to any party—as follows:
    (A) after a jury trial, for any reason for which a new trial has heretofore been granted in an action at law in federal court; or
    (B) after a nonjury trial, for any reason for which a rehearing has heretofore been granted in a suit in equity in federal court.
(2) *Further Action After a Nonjury Trial.* After a nonjury trial, the court may, on motion for a new trial, open the judgment if one has been entered, take additional testimony, amend findings of fact and conclusions of law or make new ones, and direct the entry of a new judgment.

(b) **Time to File a Motion for a New Trial.** A motion for a new trial must be filed no later than 28 days after the entry of judgment.

(c) **Time to Serve Affidavits.** When a motion for a new trial is based on affidavits, they must be filed with the motion. The opposing party has 14 days after being served to file opposing affidavits. The court may permit reply affidavits.

(d) **New Trial on the Court's Initiative or for Reasons Not in the Motion.** No later than 28 days after the entry of judgment, the court, on its own, may order a new trial for any reason that would justify granting one on a party's motion. After giving the parties notice and an opportunity to be heard, the court may grant a timely motion for a new trial for a reason not stated in the motion. In either event, the court must specify the reasons in its order.

(e) **Motion to Alter or Amend a Judgment.** A motion to alter or amend a judgment must be filed no later than 28 days after the entry of the judgment.

Rule 60.   Relief from a Judgment or Order

(a) **Corrections Based on Clerical Mistakes; Oversights and Omissions.** The court may correct a clerical mistake or a mistake arising from oversight or omission whenever one is found in a judgment, order, or other part of the record. The court may do so on motion or on its own, with or without notice. But after an appeal has been docketed in the appellate court and while it is pending, such a mistake may be corrected only with the appellate court's leave.

(b) **Grounds for Relief from a Final Judgment, Order, or Proceeding.** On motion and just terms, the court may relieve a party or its legal representative from a final judgment, order, or proceeding for the following reasons:
　(1) mistake, inadvertence, surprise, or excusable neglect;
　(2) newly discovered evidence that, with reasonable diligence, could not have been discovered in time to move for a new trial under Rule 59(b);
　(3) fraud (whether previously called intrinsic or extrinsic), misrepresentation, or misconduct by an opposing party;
　(4) the judgment is void;
　(5) the judgment has been satisfied, released or discharged; it is based on an earlier judgment that has been reversed or vacated; or applying it prospectively is no longer equitable; or
　(6) any other reason that justifies relief.

(c) **Timing and Effect of the Motion.**
　(1) *Timing.* A motion under Rule 60(b) must be made within a reasonable time—and for reasons (1), (2), and (3) no more than a year after the entry of the judgment or order or the date of the proceeding.
　(2) *Effect on Finality.* The motion does not affect the judgment's finality or suspend its operation.

(d) **Other Powers to Grant Relief.** This rule does not limit a court's power to:
　(1) entertain an independent action to relieve a party from a judgment, order, or proceeding;
　(2) grant relief under 28 U.S.C. §1655 to a defendant who was not personally notified of the action; or
　(3) set aside a judgment for fraud on the court.

(e) **Bills and Writs Abolished.** The following are abolished: bills of review, bills in the nature of bills of review, and writs of coram nobis, coram vobis, and audita querela.

Rule 61.   Harmless Error

Unless justice requires otherwise, no error in admitting or excluding evidence—or any other error by the court or a party—is ground for granting a new trial, for setting aside a verdict, or for vacating, modifying, or otherwise disturbing a judgment or order. At every stage of the proceeding, the court must disregard all errors and defects that do not affect any party's substantial rights.

Rule 62.   Stay of Proceedings to Enforce a Judgment

(a) **Automatic Stay.** Except as provided in Rule 62(c) and (d), execution on a judgment and proceedings to enforce it are stayed for 30 days after its entry, unless the court orders otherwise.

(b) **Stay by Bond or Other Security.** At any time after judgment is entered, a party may obtain a stay by providing a bond or other security. The stay takes effect when the court approves the bond or other security and remains in effect for the time specified in the bond or other security.

(c) **Stay of an Injunction, Receivership, or Patent Accounting Order.** Unless the court orders otherwise, the following are not stayed after being entered, even if an appeal is taken:
  (1) an interlocutory or final judgment in an action for an injunction or receivership; or
  (2) a judgment or order that directs an accounting in an action for patent infringement.

(d) **Injunction Pending an Appeal.** While an appeal is pending from an interlocutory order or final judgment that grants, continues, modifies, refuses, dissolves, or refuses to dissolve or modify an injunction, the court may suspend, modify, restore, or grant an injunction on terms for bond or other terms that secure the opposing party's rights. If the judgment appealed from is rendered by a statutory three-judge district court, the order must be made either:
  (1) by that court sitting in open session; or
  (2) by the assent of all its judges, as evidenced by their signatures.

(e) **Stay Without Bond on an Appeal by the United States, Its Officers, or Its Agencies.** The court must not require a bond, obligation, or other security from the appellant when granting a stay on an appeal by the United States, its officers, or its agencies or on an appeal directed by a department of the federal government.

(f) Stay in Favor of a Judgment Debtor Under State Law. If a judgment is a lien on the judgment debtor's property under the law of the state where the court is located, the judgment debtor is entitled to the same stay of execution the state court would give.

(g) Appellate Court's Power Not Limited. This rule does not limit the power of the appellate court or one of its judges or justices:

(1) to stay proceedings—or suspend, modify, restore, or grant an injunction—while an appeal is pending; or

(2) to issue an order to preserve the status quo or the effectiveness of the judgment to be entered.

(h) Stay with Multiple Claims or Parties. A court may stay the enforcement of a final judgment entered under Rule 54(b) until it enters a later judgment or judgments, and may prescribe terms necessary to secure the benefit of the stayed judgment for the party in whose favor it was entered.

Rule 62.1.   Indicative Ruling on a Motion for Relief That Is Barred by a Pending Appeal

(a) Relief Pending Appeal. If a timely motion is made for relief that the court lacks authority to grant because of an appeal that has been docketed and is pending, the court may:

(1) defer considering the motion;

(2) deny the motion; or

(3) state either that it would grant the motion if the court of appeals remands for that purpose or that the motion raises a substantial issue.

(b) Notice to the Court of Appeals. The movant must promptly notify the circuit clerk under Federal Rule of Appellate Procedure 12.1 if the district court states that it would grant the motion or that the motion raises a substantial issue.

(c) Remand. The district court may decide the motion if the court of appeals remands for that purpose.

Rule 63.   Judge's Inability to Proceed

If a judge conducting a hearing or trial is unable to proceed, any other judge may proceed upon certifying familiarity with the record and determining that the case may be completed without prejudice to the parties. In a hearing or a non-jury trial, the successor judge must, at a party's request, recall any witness whose testimony is material and disputed and who is available to testify again without undue burden. The successor judge may also recall any other witness.

Title VIII.   Provisional and Final Remedies

Rule 64.   Seizing a Person or Property

(a) **Remedies Under State Law—In General.** At the commencement of and throughout an action, every remedy is available that, under the law of the state where the court is located, provides for seizing a person or property to secure satisfaction of the potential judgment. But a federal statute governs to the extent it applies.

(b) **Specific Kinds of Remedies.** The remedies available under this rule include the following—however designated and regardless of whether state procedure requires an independent action:

- arrest;
- attachment;
- garnishment;
- replevin;
- sequestration; and
- other corresponding or equivalent remedies.

Rule 65.   Injunctions and Restraining Orders

(a) **Preliminary Injunction.**
(1) *Notice.* The court may issue a preliminary injunction only on notice to the adverse party.
(2) *Consolidating the Hearing with the Trial on the Merits.* Before or after beginning the hearing on a motion for a preliminary injunction, the court may advance the trial on the merits and consolidate it with the hearing. Even when consolidation is not ordered, evidence that is received on the motion and that would be admissible at trial becomes part of the trial record and need not be repeated at trial. But the court must preserve any party's right to a jury trial.

(b) **Temporary Restraining Order.**
(1) *Issuing Without Notice.* The court may issue a temporary restraining order without written or oral notice to the adverse party or its attorney only if:

(A) specific facts in an affidavit or a verified complaint clearly show that immediate and irreparable injury, loss, or damage will result to the movant before the adverse party can be heard in opposition; and

(B) the movant's attorney certifies in writing any efforts made to give notice and the reasons why it should not be required.

(2) *Contents; Expiration.* Every temporary restraining order issued without notice must state the date and hour it was issued; describe the injury and state why it is irreparable; state why the order was issued without notice; and be promptly filed in the clerk's office and entered in the record. The order expires at the time after entry—not to exceed 14 days—that the court sets, unless before that time the court, for good cause, extends it for a like period or the adverse party consents to a longer extension. The reasons for an extension must be entered in the record.

(3) *Expediting the Preliminary-Injunction Hearing.* If the order is issued without notice, the motion for a preliminary injunction must be set for hearing at the earliest possible time, taking precedence over all other matters except hearings on older matters of the same character. At the hearing, the party who obtained the order must proceed with the motion; if the party does not, the court must dissolve the order.

(4) *Motion to Dissolve.* On 2 days' notice to the party who obtained the order without notice—or on shorter notice set by the court—the adverse party may appear and move to dissolve or modify the order. The court must then hear and decide the motion as promptly as justice requires.

(c) **Security.** The court may issue a preliminary injunction or a temporary restraining order only if the movant gives security in an amount that the court considers proper to pay the costs and damages sustained by any party found to have been wrongfully enjoined or restrained. The United States, its officers, and its agencies are not required to give security.

(d) **Contents and Scope of Every Injunction and Restraining Order.**
(1) *Contents.* Every order granting an injunction and every restraining order must:

(A) state the reasons why it issued;

(B) state its terms specifically; and

(C) describe in reasonable detail—and not by referring to the complaint or other document—the act or acts restrained or required.

(2) *Persons Bound.* The order binds only the following who receive actual notice of it by personal service or otherwise:

(A) the parties;

(B) the parties' officers, agents, servants, employees, and attorneys; and

(C) other persons who are in active concert or participation with anyone described in Rule 65(d)(2)(A) or (B).

(e) **Other Laws Not Modified.** These rules do not modify the following:

(1) any federal statute relating to temporary restraining orders or preliminary injunctions in actions affecting employer and employee;

(2) 28 U.S.C. §2361, which relates to preliminary injunctions in actions of interpleader or in the nature of interpleader; or

(3) 28 U.S.C. §2284, which relates to actions that must be heard and decided by a three-judge district court.

(f) **Copyright Impoundment.** This rule applies to copyright-impoundment proceedings.

Rule 65.1.   Proceedings Against a Security Provider

Whenever these rules (including the Supplemental Rules for Admiralty or Maritime Claims and Asset Forfeiture Actions) require or allow a party to give security, and security is given with one or more security providers, each provider submits to the court's jurisdiction and irrevocably appoints the court clerk as its agent for receiving service of any papers that affect its liability on the security. The security provider's liability may be enforced on motion without an independent action. The motion and any notice that the court orders may be served on the court clerk, who must promptly send a copy of each to every security provider whose address is known.

Rule 66.   Receivers

These rules govern an action in which the appointment of a receiver is sought or a receiver sues or is sued. But the practice in administering an estate by a receiver or a similar court-appointed officer must accord with the historical practice in federal courts or with a local rule. An action in which a receiver has been appointed may be dismissed only by court order.

Rule 67.   Deposit into Court

(a) **Depositing Property.** If any part of the relief sought is a money judgment or the disposition of a sum of money or some other deliverable thing, a party—on notice to every other party and by leave of court—may deposit with the court all or part of the money or thing, whether or not that party claims any of it. The depositing party must deliver to the clerk a copy of the order permitting deposit.

(b) Investing and Withdrawing Funds. Money paid into court under this rule must be deposited and withdrawn in accordance with 28 U.S.C. §§2041 and 2042 and any like statute. The money must be deposited in an interest-bearing account or invested in a court-approved, interest-bearing instrument.

Rule 68. Offer of Judgment

(a) Making an Offer; Judgment on an Accepted Offer. At least 14 days before the date set for trial, a party defending against a claim may serve on an opposing party an offer to allow judgment on specified terms, with the costs then accrued. If, within 14 days after being served, the opposing party serves written notice accepting the offer, either party may then file the offer and notice of acceptance, plus proof of service. The clerk must then enter judgment.

(b) Unaccepted Offer. An unaccepted offer is considered withdrawn, but it does not preclude a later offer. Evidence of an unaccepted offer is not admissible except in a proceeding to determine costs.

(c) Offer After Liability Is Determined. When one party's liability to another has been determined but the extent of liability remains to be determined by further proceedings, the party held liable may make an offer of judgment. It must be served within a reasonable time—but at least 14 days—before the date set for a hearing to determine the extent of liability.

(d) Paying Costs After an Unaccepted Offer. If the judgment that the offeree finally obtains is not more favorable than the unaccepted offer, the offeree must pay the costs incurred after the offer was made.

Rule 69. Execution

(a) In General.

(1) *Money Judgment; Applicable Procedure.* A money judgment is enforced by a writ of execution, unless the court directs otherwise. The procedure on execution—and in proceedings supplementary to and in aid of judgment or execution—must accord with the procedure of the state where the court is located, but a federal statute governs to the extent it applies.

(2) *Obtaining Discovery.* In aid of the judgment or execution, the judgment creditor or a successor in interest whose interest appears of record may obtain discovery from any person—including the judgment debtor—as provided in these rules or by the procedure of the state where the court is located.

(b) Against Certain Public Officers. When a judgment has been entered against a revenue officer in the circumstances stated in 28 U.S.C. §2006, or against an officer of Congress in the circumstances stated in 2 U.S.C. §118, the judgment must be satisfied as those statutes provide.

Rule 70.   Enforcing a Judgment for a Specific Act

(a) **Party's Failure to Act; Ordering Another to Act.** If a judgment requires a party to convey land, to deliver a deed or other document, or to perform any other specific act and the party fails to comply within the time specified, the court may order the act to be done—at the disobedient party's expense—by another person appointed by the court. When done, the act has the same effect as if done by the party.

(b) **Vesting Title.** If the real or personal property is within the district, the court—instead of ordering a conveyance—may enter a judgment divesting any party's title and vesting it in others. That judgment has the effect of a legally executed conveyance.

(c) **Obtaining a Writ of Attachment or Sequestration.** On application by a party entitled to performance of an act, the clerk must issue a writ of attachment or sequestration against the disobedient party's property to compel obedience.

(d) **Obtaining a Writ of Execution or Assistance.** On application by a party who obtains a judgment or order for possession, the clerk must issue a writ of execution or assistance.

(e) **Holding in Contempt.** The court may also hold the disobedient party in contempt.

Rule 71.   Enforcing Relief For or Against a Nonparty

When an order grants relief for a nonparty or may be enforced against a nonparty, the procedure for enforcing the order is the same as for a party.

Title IX.   Special Proceedings

Rule 71.1.   Condemning Real or Personal Property

(a) **Applicability of Other Rules.** These rules govern proceedings to condemn real and personal property by eminent domain, except as this rule provides otherwise.

(b) **Joinder of Properties.** The plaintiff may join separate pieces of property in a single action, no matter whether they are owned by the same persons or sought for the same use.

(c) **Complaint.**

(1) *Caption.* The complaint must contain a caption as provided in Rule 10(a). The plaintiff must, however, name as defendants both the property—designated generally by kind, quantity, and location—and at least one owner of some part of or interest in the property.

(2) *Contents.* The complaint must contain a short and plain statement of the following:

(A) the authority for the taking;

(B) the uses for which the property is to be taken;

(C) a description sufficient to identify the property;

(D) the interests to be acquired; and

(E) for each piece of property, a designation of each defendant who has been joined as an owner or owner of an interest in it.

(3) *Parties.* When the action commences, the plaintiff need join as defendants only those persons who have or claim an interest in the property and whose names are then known. But before any hearing on compensation, the plaintiff must add as defendants all those persons who have or claim an interest and whose names have become known or can be found by a reasonably diligent search of the records, considering both the property's character and value and the interests to be acquired. All others may be made defendants under the designation "Unknown Owners."

(4) *Procedure.* Notice must be served on all defendants as provided in Rule 71.1(d), whether they were named as defendants when the action commenced or were added later. A defendant may answer as provided in Rule 71.1(e). The court, meanwhile, may order any distribution of a deposit that the facts warrant.

(5) *Filing; Additional Copies.* In addition to filing the complaint, the plaintiff must give the clerk at least one copy for the defendants' use and additional copies at the request of the clerk or a defendant.

(d) **Process.**

(1) *Delivering Notice to the Clerk.* On filing a complaint, the plaintiff must promptly deliver to the clerk joint or several notices directed to the named defendants. When adding defendants, the plaintiff must deliver to the clerk additional notices directed to the new defendants.

(2) *Contents of the Notice.*

(A) *Main Contents.* Each notice must name the court, the title of the action, and the defendant to whom it is directed. It must describe the property sufficiently to identify it, but need not describe any property other than that to be taken from the named defendant. The notice must also state:

(i) that the action is to condemn property;

(ii) the interest to be taken;

(iii) the authority for the taking;

(iv) the uses for which the property is to be taken;

(v) that the defendant may serve an answer on the plaintiff's attorney within 21 days after being served with the notice;

(vi) that the failure to so serve an answer constitutes consent to the taking and to the court's authority to proceed with the action and fix the compensation; and

(vii) that a defendant who does not serve an answer may file a notice of appearance.

(B) *Conclusion.* The notice must conclude with the name, telephone number, and e-mail address of the plaintiff's attorney and an address within the district in which the action is brought where the attorney may be served.

(3) **Serving the Notice.**

(A) *Personal Service.* When a defendant whose address is known resides within the United States or a territory subject to the administrative or judicial jurisdiction of the United States, personal service of the notice (without a copy of the complaint) must be made in accordance with Rule 4.

(B) *Service by Publication.*

(i) A defendant may be served by publication only when the plaintiff's attorney files a certificate stating that the attorney believes the defendant cannot be personally served, because after diligent inquiry within the state where the complaint is filed, the defendant's place of residence is still unknown or, if known, that it is beyond the territorial limits of personal service. Service is then made by publishing the notice—once a week for at least three successive weeks—in a newspaper published in the county where the property is located or, if there is no such newspaper, in a newspaper with general circulation where the property is located. Before the last publication, a copy of the notice must also be mailed to every defendant who cannot be personally served but whose place of residence is then known. Unknown owners may be served by publication in the same manner by a notice addressed to "Unknown Owners."

(ii) Service by publication is complete on the date of the last publication. The plaintiff's attorney must prove publication and mailing by a certificate, attach a printed copy of the published notice, and mark on the copy the newspaper's name and the dates of publication.

(4) **Effect of Delivery and Service.** Delivering the notice to the clerk and serving it have the same effect as serving a summons under Rule 4.

(5) **Proof of Service; Amending the Proof or Notice.** Rule 4(l) governs proof of service. The court may permit the proof or the notice to be amended.

(e) Appearance or Answer.

(1) *Notice of Appearance.* A defendant that has no objection or defense to the taking of its property may serve a notice of appearance designating the

property in which it claims an interest. The defendant must then be given notice of all later proceedings affecting the defendant.

(2) *Answer.* A defendant that has an objection or defense to the taking must serve an answer within 21 days after being served with the notice. The answer must:

(A) identify the property in which the defendant claims an interest;

(B) state the nature and extent of the interest; and

(C) state all the defendant's objections and defenses to the taking.

(3) *Waiver of Other Objections and Defenses; Evidence on Compensation.* A defendant waives all objections and defenses not stated in its answer. No other pleading or motion asserting an additional objection or defense is allowed. But at the trial on compensation, a defendant—whether or not it has previously appeared or answered—may present evidence on the amount of compensation to be paid and may share in the award.

(f) **Amending Pleadings.** Without leave of court, the plaintiff may—as often as it wants—amend the complaint at any time before the trial on compensation. But no amendment may be made if it would result in a dismissal inconsistent with Rule 71.1(i)(1) or (2). The plaintiff need not serve a copy of an amendment, but must serve notice of the filing, as provided in Rule 5(b), on every affected party who has appeared and, as provided in Rule 71.1(d), on every affected party who has not appeared. In addition, the plaintiff must give the clerk at least one copy of each amendment for the defendants' use, and additional copies at the request of the clerk or a defendant. A defendant may appear or answer in the time and manner and with the same effect as provided in Rule 71.1(e).

(g) **Substituting Parties.** If a defendant dies, becomes incompetent, or transfers an interest after being joined, the court may, on motion and notice of hearing, order that the proper party be substituted. Service of the motion and notice on a nonparty must be made as provided in Rule 71.1(d)(3).

(h) **Trial of the Issues.**

(1) *Issues Other Than Compensation; Compensation.* In an action involving eminent domain under federal law, the court tries all issues, including compensation, except when compensation must be determined:

(A) by any tribunal specially constituted by a federal statute to determine compensation; or

(B) if there is no such tribunal, by a jury when a party demands one within the time to answer or within any additional time the court sets, unless the court appoints a commission.

(2) *Appointing a Commission; Commission's Powers and Report.*

(A) *Reasons for Appointing.* If a party has demanded a jury, the court may instead appoint a three-person commission to determine compensation because of the character, location, or quantity of the property to be condemned or for other just reasons.

(B) *Alternate Commissioners.* The court may appoint up to two additional persons to serve as alternate commissioners to hear the case and replace commissioners who, before a decision is filed, the court finds unable or disqualified to perform their duties. Once the commission renders its final decision, the court must discharge any alternate who has not replaced a commissioner.

(C) *Examining the Prospective Commissioners.* Before making its appointments, the court must advise the parties of the identity and qualifications of each prospective commissioner and alternate, and may permit the parties to examine them. The parties may not suggest appointees, but for good cause may object to a prospective commissioner or alternate.

(D) *Commission's Powers and Report.* A commission has the powers of a master under Rule 53(c). Its action and report are determined by a majority. Rule 53(d), (e), and (f) apply to its action and report.

(i) Dismissal of the Action or a Defendant.
(1) *Dismissing the Action.*

(A) *By the Plaintiff.* If no compensation hearing on a piece of property has begun, and if the plaintiff has not acquired title or a lesser interest or taken possession, the plaintiff may, without a court order, dismiss the action as to that property by filing a notice of dismissal briefly describing the property.

(B) *By Stipulation.* Before a judgment is entered vesting the plaintiff with title or a lesser interest in or possession of property, the plaintiff and affected defendants may, without a court order, dismiss the action in whole or in part by filing a stipulation of dismissal. And if the parties so stipulate, the court may vacate a judgment already entered.

(C) *By Court Order.* At any time before compensation has been determined and paid, the court may, after a motion and hearing, dismiss the action as to a piece of property. But if the plaintiff has already taken title, a lesser interest, or possession as to any part of it, the court must award compensation for the title, lesser interest, or possession taken.

(2) *Dismissing a Defendant.* The court may at any time dismiss a defendant who was unnecessarily or improperly joined.

(3) *Effect.* A dismissal is without prejudice unless otherwise stated in the notice, stipulation, or court order.

(j) Deposit and Its Distribution.
(1) *Deposit.* The plaintiff must deposit with the court any money required by law as a condition to the exercise of eminent domain and may make a deposit when allowed by statute.

(2) *Distribution; Adjusting Distribution.* After a deposit, the court and attorneys must expedite the proceedings so as to distribute the deposit and to determine and pay compensation. If the compensation finally awarded to a defendant

exceeds the amount distributed to that defendant, the court must enter judgment against the plaintiff for the deficiency. If the compensation awarded to a defendant is less than the amount distributed to that defendant, the court must enter judgment against that defendant for the overpayment.

(k) Condemnation Under a State's Power of Eminent Domain. This rule governs an action involving eminent domain under state law. But if state law provides for trying an issue by jury—or for trying the issue of compensation by jury or commission or both—that law governs.

(l) Costs. Costs are not subject to Rule 54(d).

Rule 72.   Magistrate Judges: Pretrial Order

(a) Nondispositive Matters. When a pretrial matter not dispositive of a party's claim or defense is referred to a magistrate judge to hear and decide, the magistrate judge must promptly conduct the required proceedings and, when appropriate, issue a written order stating the decision. A party may serve and file objections to the order within 14 days after being served with a copy. A party may not assign as error a defect in the order not timely objected to. The district judge in the case must consider timely objections and modify or set aside any part of the order that is clearly erroneous or is contrary to law.

(b) Dispositive Motions and Prisoner Petitions.
(1) *Findings and Recommendations.* A magistrate judge must promptly conduct the required proceedings when assigned, without the parties' consent, to hear a pretrial matter dispositive of a claim or defense or a prisoner petition challenging the conditions of confinement. A record must be made of all evidentiary proceedings and may, at the magistrate judge's discretion, be made of any other proceedings. The magistrate judge must enter a recommended disposition, including, if appropriate, proposed findings of fact. The clerk must promptly mail a copy to each party.

(2) *Objections.* Within 14 days after being served with a copy of the recommended disposition, a party may serve and file specific written objections to the proposed findings and recommendations. A party may respond to another party's objections within 14 days after being served with a copy. Unless the district judge orders otherwise, the objecting party must promptly arrange for transcribing the record, or whatever portions of it the parties agree to or the magistrate judge considers sufficient.

(3) *Resolving Objections.* The district judge must determine de novo any part of the magistrate judge's disposition that has been properly objected to. The district judge may accept, reject, or modify the recommended disposition; receive further evidence; or return the matter to the magistrate judge with instructions.

Rule 73.   Magistrate Judges: Trial by Consent; Appeal

(a) Trial by Consent. When authorized under 28 U.S.C. §636(c), a magistrate judge may, if all parties consent, conduct a civil action or proceeding, including a jury or nonjury trial. A record must be made in accordance with 28 U.S.C. §636(c)(5).

(b) Consent Procedure.
(1) *In General.* When a magistrate judge has been designated to conduct civil actions or proceedings, the clerk must give the parties written notice of their opportunity to consent under 28 U.S.C. §636(c). To signify their consent, the parties must jointly or separately file a statement consenting to the referral. A district judge or magistrate judge may be informed of a party's response to the clerk's notice only if all parties have consented to the referral.

(2) *Reminding the Parties About Consenting.* A district judge, magistrate judge, or other court official may remind the parties of the magistrate judge's availability, but must also advise them that they are free to withhold consent without adverse substantive consequences.

(3) *Vacating a Referral.* On its own for good cause—or when a party shows extraordinary circumstances—the district judge may vacate a referral to a magistrate judge under this rule.

(c) Appealing a Judgment. In accordance with 28 U.S.C. §636(c)(3), an appeal from a judgment entered at a magistrate judge's direction may be taken to the court of appeals as would any other appeal from a district-court judgment.

Rule 74.   [Abrogated.]

Rule 75.   [Abrogated.]

Rule 76.   [Abrogated.]

Title X.   District Courts and Clerks: Conducting Business; Issuing Orders

Rule 77.   Conducting Business; Clerk's Authority; Notice of an Order or Judgment

(a) When Court Is Open. Every district court is considered always open for filing any paper, issuing and returning process, making a motion, or entering an order.

(b) Place for Trial and Other Proceedings. Every trial on the merits must be conducted in open court and, so far as convenient, in a regular courtroom. Any other act or proceeding may be done or conducted by a judge in chambers, without the attendance of the clerk or other court official, and anywhere inside or outside the district. But no hearing—other than one ex parte—may be conducted outside the district unless all the affected parties consent.

(c) Clerk's Office Hours; Clerk's Orders.
(1) *Hours.* The clerk's office—with a clerk or deputy on duty—must be open during business hours every day except Saturdays, Sundays, and legal holidays. But a court may, by local rule or order, require that the office be open for specified hours on Saturday or a particular legal holiday other than one listed in Rule 6(a)(46)(A).
(2) *Orders.* Subject to the court's power to suspend, alter, or rescind the clerk's action for good cause, the clerk may:
    (A) issue process;
    (B) enter a default;
    (C) enter a default judgment under Rule 55(b)(1); and
    (D) act on any other matter that does not require the court's action.

(d) Serving Notice of an Order or Judgment.
(1) *Service.* Immediately after entering an order or judgment, the clerk must serve notice of the entry, as provided in Rule 5(b), on each party who is not in default for failing to appear. The clerk must record the service on the docket. A party also may serve notice of the entry as provided in Rule 5(b).
(2) *Time to Appeal Not Affected by Lack of Notice.* Lack of notice of the entry does not affect the time for appeal or relieve—or authorize the court to relieve—a party for failing to appeal within the time allowed, except as allowed by Federal Rule of Appellate Procedure (4)(a).

Rule 78.   Hearing Motions; Submission on Briefs

(a) Providing a Regular Schedule for Oral Hearings. A court may establish regular times and places for oral hearings on motions.

(b) Providing for Submission on Briefs. By rule or order, the court may provide for submitting and determining motions on briefs, without oral hearings.

Rule 79.   Records Kept by the Clerk

(a) Civil Docket.
(1) *In General.* The clerk must keep a record known as the "civil docket" in the form and manner prescribed by the Director of the Administrative Office

of the United States Courts with the approval of the Judicial Conference of the United States. The clerk must enter each civil action in the docket. Actions must be assigned consecutive file numbers, which must be noted in the docket where the first entry of the action is made.

(2) *Items to Be Entered.* The following items must be marked with the file number and entered chronologically in the docket:

(A) papers filed with the clerk;

(B) process issued, and proofs of service or other returns showing execution; and

(C) appearances, orders, verdicts, and judgments.

(3) *Contents of Entries; Jury Trial Demanded.* Each entry must briefly show the nature of the paper filed or writ issued, the substance of each proof of service or other return, and the substance and date of entry of each order and judgment. When a jury trial has been properly demanded or ordered, the clerk must enter the word "jury" in the docket.

(b) Civil Judgments and Orders. The clerk must keep a copy of every final judgment and appealable order; of every order affecting title to or a lien on real or personal property; and of any other order that the court directs to be kept. The clerk must keep these in the form and manner prescribed by the Director of the Administrative Office of the United States Courts with the approval of the Judicial Conference of the United States.

(c) Indexes; Calendars. Under the court's direction, the clerk must:

(1) keep indexes of the docket and of the judgments and orders described in Rule 79(b); and

(2) prepare calendars of all actions ready for trial, distinguishing jury trials from nonjury trials.

(d) Other Records. The clerk must keep any other records required by the Director of the Administrative Office of the United States Courts with the approval of the Judicial Conference of the United States.

Rule 80. Stenographic Transcript as Evidence

If stenographically reported testimony at a hearing or trial is admissible in evidence at a later trial, the testimony may be proved by a transcript certified by the person who reported it.

Title XI.　General Provisions

Rule 81.　Applicability of the Rules in General; Removed Actions

(a) Applicability to Particular Proceedings.

(1) *Prize Proceedings.* These rules do not apply to prize proceedings in admiralty governed by 10 U.S.C. §§7651-7681.

(2) *Bankruptcy.* These rules apply to bankruptcy proceedings to the extent provided by the Federal Rules of Bankruptcy Procedure.

(3) *Citizenship.* These rules apply to proceedings for admission to citizenship to the extent that the practice in those proceedings is not specified in federal statutes and has previously conformed to the practice in civil actions. The provisions of 8 U.S.C. §1451 for service by publication and for answer apply in proceedings to cancel citizenship certificates.

(4) *Special Writs.* These rules apply to proceedings for habeas corpus and for quo warranto to the extent that the practice in those proceedings:

(A) is not specified in a federal statute, the Rules Governing Section 2254 Cases, or the Rules Governing Section 2255 Cases; and

(B) has previously conformed to the practice in civil actions.

(5) *Proceedings Involving a Subpoena.* These rules apply to proceedings to compel testimony or the production of documents through a subpoena issued by a United States officer or agency under a federal statute, except as otherwise provided by statute, by local rule, or by court order in the proceedings.

(6) *Other Proceedings.* These rules, to the extent applicable, govern proceedings under the following laws, except as these laws provide other procedures:

(A) 7 U.S.C. §§292, 499g(c), for reviewing an order of the Secretary of Agriculture;

(B) 9 U.S.C., relating to arbitration;

(C) 15 U.S.C. §522, for reviewing an order of the Secretary of the Interior;

(D) 15 U.S.C. §715d(c), for reviewing an order denying a certificate of clearance;

(E) 29 U.S.C. §§159, 160, for enforcing an order of the National Labor Relations Board;

(F) 33 U.S.C. §§918, 921, for enforcing or reviewing a compensation order under the Longshore and Harbor Workers' Compensation Act; and

(G) 45 U.S.C. §159, for reviewing an arbitration award in a railway-labor dispute.

(b) Scire Facias and Mandamus. The writs of scire facias and mandamus are abolished. Relief previously available through them may be obtained by appropriate action or motion under these rules.

(c) Removed Actions.

(1) *Applicability.* These rules apply to a civil action after it is removed from a state court.

(2) *Further Pleading.* After removal, repleading is unnecessary unless the court orders it. A defendant who did not answer before removal must answer or present other defenses or objections under these rules within the longest of these periods:

(A) 21 days after receiving—through service or otherwise—a copy of the initial pleading stating the claim for relief;

(B) 21 days after being served with the summons for an initial pleading on file at the time of service; or

(C) 7 days after the notice of removal is filed.

(3) *Demand for a Jury Trial.*

(A) *As Affected by State Law.* A party who, before removal, expressly demanded a jury trial in accordance with state law need not renew the demand after removal. If the state law did not require an express demand for a jury trial, a party need not make one after removal unless the court orders the parties to do so within a specified time. The court must so order at a party's request and may so order on its own. A party who fails to make a demand when so ordered waives a jury trial.

(B) *Under Rule 38.* If all necessary pleadings have been served at the time of removal, a party entitled to a jury trial under Rule 38 must be given one if the party serves a demand within 14 days after:

(i) it files a notice of removal; or

(ii) it is served with a notice of removal filed by another party.

(d) Law Applicable.

(1) *"State Law" Defined.* When these rules refer to state law, the term "law" includes the state's statutes and the state's judicial decisions.

(2) *"State" Defined.* The term "state" includes, where appropriate, the District of Columbia and any United States commonwealth or territory.

(3) *"Federal Statute" Defined in the District of Columbia.* In the United States District Court for the District of Columbia, the term "federal statute" includes any Act of Congress that applies locally to the District.

Rule 82.   Jurisdiction and Venue Unaffected

These rules do not extend or limit the jurisdiction of the district courts or the venue of actions in those courts. An admiralty or maritime claim under Rule 9(h) is governed by 28 U.S.C. §§1390.

Rule 83.   Rules by District Courts; Judge's Directives

(a) Local Rules.

(1) *In General.* After giving public notice and an opportunity for comment, a district court, acting by a majority of its district judges, may adopt and amend rules governing its practice. A local rule must be consistent with—but not duplicate—federal statutes and rules adopted under 28 U.S.C. §§2072 and 2075, and must conform to any uniform numbering system prescribed by the Judicial Conference of the United States. A local rule takes effect on the date specified by the district court and remains in effect unless amended by the court or abrogated by the judicial council of the circuit. Copies of rules and amendments must, on their adoption, be furnished to the judicial council and the Administrative Office of the United States Courts and be made available to the public.

(2) *Requirement of Form.* A local rule imposing a requirement of form must not be enforced in a way that causes a party to lose any right because of a nonwillful failure to comply.

(b) Procedure When There Is No Controlling Law. A judge may regulate practice in any manner consistent with federal law, rules adopted under 28 U.S.C. §§2072 and 2075, and the district's local rules. No sanction or other disadvantage may be imposed for noncompliance with any requirement not in federal law, federal rules, or the local rules unless the alleged violator has been furnished in the particular case with actual notice of the requirement.

Rule 84.   Forms

[Abrogated (Apr. 29, 2015, eff. Dec. 1, 2015).]

Rule 85.   Title

These rules may be cited as the Federal Rules of Civil Procedure.

Rule 86.   Effective Dates

(a) In General. These rules and any amendments take effect at the time specified by the Supreme Court, subject to 28 U.S.C. §2074. They govern:

(1) proceedings in an action commenced after their effective date; and

(2) proceedings after that date in an action then pending unless:

(A) the Supreme Court specifies otherwise; or

(B) the court determines that applying them in a particular action would be infeasible or work an injustice.

(b) December 1, 2007 Amendments. If any provision in Rules 1-5.1, 6-73, or 77-86 conflicts with another law, priority in time for the purpose of 28 U.S.C. §2072(b) is not affected by the amendments taking effect on December 1, 2007.

FEDERAL RULES OF APPELLATE PROCEDURE

Title I. Applicability of Rules

Rule 1. Scope of Rules; Definition; Title

(a) Scope of Rules.

(1) These rules govern procedure in the United States courts of appeals.

(2) When these rules provide for filing a motion or other document in the district court, the procedure must comply with the practice of the district court.

(b) Definition. In these rules, "state" includes the District of Columbia and any United States commonwealth or territory.

(c) Title. These rules are to be known as the Federal Rules of Appellate Procedure.

Rule 2. Suspension of Rules

On its own or a party's motion, a court of appeals may—to expedite its decision or for other good cause—suspend any provision of these rules in a particular case and order proceedings as it directs, except as otherwise provided in Rule 26(b).

Title II. Appeal from a Judgment or Order of a District Court

Rule 3. Appeal as of Right—How Taken

(a) Filing the Notice of Appeal.

(1) An appeal permitted by law as of right from a district court to a court of appeals may be taken only by filing a notice of appeal with the district clerk within the time allowed by Rule 4. At the time of filing, the appellant must furnish the clerk with enough copies of the notice to enable the clerk to comply with Rule 3(d).

(2) An appellant's failure to take any step other than the timely filing of a notice of appeal does not affect the validity of the appeal, but is ground only for the court of appeals to act as it considers appropriate, including dismissing the appeal.

(3) An appeal from a judgment by a magistrate judge in a civil case is taken in the same way as an appeal from any other district court judgment.

(4) An appeal by permission under 28 U.S.C. §1292(b) or an appeal in a bankruptcy case may be taken only in the manner prescribed by Rules 5 and 6, respectively.

(b) Joint or Consolidated Appeals.

(1) When two or more parties are entitled to appeal from a district-court judgment or order, and their interests make joinder practicable, they may file a joint notice of appeal. They may then proceed on appeal as a single appellant.

(2) When the parties have filed separate timely notices of appeal, the appeals may be joined or consolidated by the court of appeals.

(c) Contents of the Notice of Appeal.

(1) The notice of appeal must:

(A) specify the party or parties taking the appeal by naming each one in the caption or body of the notice, but an attorney representing more than one party may describe those parties with such terms as "all plaintiffs," "the defendants," "the plaintiffs A, B, et al.," or "all defendants except X";

(B) designate the judgment—or appealable order—from which the appeal is taken; and

(C) name the court to which the appeal is taken.

(2) A pro se notice of appeal is considered filed on behalf of the signer and the signer's spouse and minor children (if they are parties), unless the notice clearly indicates otherwise.

(3) In a class action, whether or not the class has been certified, the notice of appeal is sufficient if it names one person qualified to bring the appeal as representative of the class.

(4) The notice of appeal encompasses all orders that, for purposes of appeal, merge into the designated judgment or appealable order. It is not necessary to designate those orders in the notice of appeal.

(5) In a civil case, a notice of appeal encompasses the final judgment, whether or not that judgment is set out in a separate document under Federal Rule of Civil Procedure 58, I the notice designates:

(A) an order that adjudicates all remaining claims and the rights and liabilities of all remaining parties; or

(B) an order described in Rule 4(a)(4)(A).

(6) An appellant may designate only part of a judgment or appealable order by expressly stating that the notice of appeal is so limited. Without such an express statement, specific designations do not limit the scope of the notice of appeal.

(7) An appeal must not be dismissed for informality of form or title of the notice of appeal, for failure to name a party whose intent to appeal is otherwise

clear form the notice, or for failure to properly designate the judgment if the notice of appeal was filed after entry of the judgment and designates an order that merged into that judgment.

(8) Forms 1A and 1B in the Appendix of Forms are suggested forms of notices of appeal.

(d) Serving the Notice of Appeal.

(1) The district clerk must serve notice of the filing of a notice of appeal by sending a copy to each party's counsel of record—excluding the appellant's—or, if a party is proceeding pro se, to the party's last known address. When a defendant in a criminal case appeals, the clerk must also serve a copy of the notice of appeal on the defendant. The clerk must promptly send a copy of the notice of appeal and of the docket entries—and any later docket entries—to the clerk of the court of appeals named in the notice. The district clerk must note, on each copy, the date when the notice of appeal was filed.

(2) If an inmate confined in an institution files a notice of appeal in the manner provided by Rule 4(c), the district clerk must also note the date when the clerk docketed the notice.

(3) The district clerk's failure to serve notice does not affect the validity of the appeal. The clerk must note on the docket the names of the parties to whom the clerk sends copies, with the date of sending. Service is sufficient despite the death of a party or the party's counsel.

(e) Payment of Fees. Upon filing a notice of appeal, the appellant must pay the district clerk all required fees. The district clerk receives the appellate docket fee on behalf of the court of appeals.

Rule 3.1.   Appeal from a Judgment of a Magistrate Judge in a Civil Case (Abrogated April 24, 1998, eff. Dec. 1, 1998)

Rule 4.   Appeal as of Right—When Taken

(a) Appeal in a Civil Case.
(1) Time for Filing a Notice of Appeal.

(A) In a civil case, except as provided in Rules 4(a)(1)(B), 4(a)(4), and 4(c), the notice of appeal required by Rule 3 must be filed with the district clerk within 30 days after entry of the judgment or order appealed from.

(B) The notice of appeal may be filed by any party within 60 days after entry of the judgment or order appealed if one of the parties is:

(i) the United States;

(ii) a United States agency;

(iii) a United States officer or employee sued in an official capacity; or

(iv) a current or former United States officer or employee sued in an individual capacity for an act or omission occurring in connection with duties performed on the United States' behalf—including all instances in which the United States represents that person when the judgment or order is entered or files the appeal for that person.

(C) An appeal from an order granting or denying an application for a writ of error *coram nobis* is an appeal in a civil case for purposes of Rule 4(a).

(2) **Filing Before Entry of Judgment.** A notice of appeal filed after the court announces a decision or order—but before the entry of the judgment or order—is treated as filed on the date of and after the entry.

(3) **Multiple Appeals.** If one party timely files a notice of appeal, any other party may file a notice of appeal within 14 days after the date when the first notice was filed, or within the time otherwise prescribed by this Rule 4(a), whichever period ends later.

(4) **Effect of a Motion on a Notice of Appeal.**

(A) If a party files in the district court any of the following motions under the Federal Rules of Civil Procedure—and does so within the time allowed by those rules—the time to file an appeal runs for all parties from the entry of the order disposing of the last such remaining motion:

(i) for judgment under Rule 50(b);

(ii) to amend or make additional factual findings under Rule 52(b), whether or not granting the motion would alter the judgment;

(iii) for attorney's fees under Rule 54 if the district court extends the time to appeal under Rule 58;

(iv) to alter or amend the judgment under Rule 59;

(v) for a new trial under Rule 59; or

(vi) for relief under Rule 60 if the motion is filed no later than 28 days after the judgment is entered.

(B)(i) If a party files a notice of appeal after the court announces or enters a judgment—but before it disposes of any motion listed in Rule 4(a)(4)(A)—the notice becomes effective to appeal a judgment or order, in whole or in part, when the order disposing of the last such remaining motion is entered.

(ii) A party intending to challenge an order disposing of any motion listed in Rule 4(a)(4)(A), or a judgment's alteration or amendment upon such a motion, must file a notice of appeal, or an amended notice of appeal—in compliance with Rule 3(c)—within the time prescribed by this Rule measured from the entry of the order disposing of the last such remaining motion.

(iii) No additional fee is required to file an amended notice.

(5) **Motion for Extension of Time.**

(A) The district court may extend the time to file a notice of appeal if:

(i) a party so moves no later than 30 days after the time prescribed by this Rule 4(a) expires; and

(ii) regardless of whether its motion is filed before or during the 30 days after the time prescribed by this Rule 4(a) expires, that party shows excusable neglect or good cause.

(B) A motion filed before the expiration of the time prescribed in Rule 4(a)(1) or (3) may be ex parte unless the court requires otherwise. If the motion is filed after the expiration of the prescribed time, notice must be given to the other parties in accordance with local rules.

(C) No extension under this Rule 4(a)(5) may exceed 30 days after the prescribed time or 14 days after the date when the order granting the motion is entered, whichever is later.

(6) **Reopening the Time to File an Appeal.** The district court may reopen the time to file an appeal for a period of 14 days after the date when its order to reopen is entered, but only if all the following conditions are satisfied:

(A) the court finds that the moving party did not receive notice under Federal Rule of Civil Procedure 77(d) of the entry of the judgment or order sought to be appealed within 21 days after entry;

(B) the motion is filed within 180 days after the judgment or order is entered or within 14 days after the moving party receives notice under Federal Rule of Civil Procedure 77(d) of the entry, whichever is earlier;

(C) the court finds that the moving party was entitled to notice of the entry of the judgment or order sought to be appealed but did not receive the notice from the district court or any party within 21 days after entry; and

(D) the court finds that no party would be prejudiced.

(7) **Entry Defined.**

(A) A judgment or order is entered for purposes of this Rule 4(a):

(i) if Federal Rule of Civil Procedure 58(a) does not require a separate document, when the judgment or order is entered in the civil docket under Federal Rule of Civil Procedure 79(a); or

(ii) if Federal Rule of Civil Procedure 58(a) requires a separate document, when the judgment or order is entered in the civil docket under Federal Rule of Civil Procedure 79(a) and when the earlier of these events occurs:

- the judgment or order is set forth on a separate document, or
- 150 days have run from entry of the judgment or order in the civil docket under Federal Rule of Civil Procedure 79(a).

(B) A failure to set forth a judgment or order on a separate document when required by Federal Rule of Civil Procedure 58(a) does not affect the validity of an appeal from the judgment or order.

(b) **Appeal in a Criminal Case.**

(1) **Time for Filing a Notice of Appeal.**

(A) In a criminal case, a defendant's notice of appeal must be filed in the district court within 14 days after the later of:

(i) the entry of either the judgment or the order being appealed; or

(ii) the filing of the government's notice of appeal.

(B) When the government is entitled to appeal, its notice of appeal must be filed in the district court within 30 days after the later of:

(i) the entry of the judgment or order being appealed; or

(ii) the filing of a notice of appeal by any defendant.

(2) **Filing Before Entry of Judgment.** A notice of appeal filed after the court announces a decision, sentence, or order—but before the entry of the judgment or order—is treated as filed on the date of and after the entry.

(3) **Effect of a Motion on a Notice of Appeal.**

(A) If a defendant timely makes any of the following motions under the Federal Rules of Criminal Procedure, the notice of appeal from a judgment of conviction must be filed within 14 days after the entry of the order disposing of the last such remaining motion, or within 14 days after the entry of the judgment of conviction, whichever period ends later. This provision applies to a timely motion:

(i) for judgment of acquittal under Rule 29;

(ii) for a new trial under Rule 33, but if based on newly discovered evidence, only if the motion is made no later than 14 days after the entry of the judgment; or

(iii) for arrest of judgment under Rule 34.

(B) A notice of appeal filed after the court announces a decision, sentence, or order—but before it disposes of any of the motions referred to in Rule 4(b)(3)(A)—becomes effective upon the later of the following:

(i) the entry of the order disposing of the last such remaining motion; or

(ii) the entry of the judgment of conviction.

(C) A valid notice of appeal is effective—without amendment—to appeal from an order disposing of any of the motions referred to in Rule 4(b)(3)(A).

(4) **Motion for Extension of Time.** Upon a finding of excusable neglect or good cause, the district court may—before or after the time has expired, with or without motion and notice—extend the time to file a notice of appeal for a period not to exceed 30 days from the expiration of the time otherwise prescribed by this Rule 4(b).

(5) **Jurisdiction.** The filing of a notice of appeal under this Rule 4(b) does not divest a district court of jurisdiction to correct a sentence under Federal Rule of Criminal Procedure 35(a), nor does the filing of a motion under 35(a) affect the validity of a notice of appeal filed before entry of the order disposing of the motion. The filing of a motion under Federal Rule of Criminal Procedure 35(a) does not suspend the time for filing a notice of appeal from a judgment of conviction.

(6) **Entry Defined.** A judgment or order is entered for purposes of this Rule 4(b) when it is entered on the criminal docket.

(c) **Appeal by an Inmate Confined in an Institution.**

(1) If an institution has a system designed for legal mail, an inmate confined there must use that system to receive the benefit of this Rule (c)(1). If an inmate files

a notice of appeal in either a civil or a criminal case, the notice is timely if it is deposited in the institution's internal mail system on or before the last day for filing and:

    (A) it is accompanied by:

        (i) a declaration in compliance with 28 U.S.C. §1746—or a notarized statement—setting out the date of deposit and stating that first-class postage is being prepaid; or

        (ii) evidence (such as a postmark or date stamp) showing that the notice was so deposited and that postage was prepaid; or

    (B) the court of appeals exercises its discretion to permit the later filing of a declaration or notarized statement that satisfies Rule 4(c)(1)(A)(i).

    (2) If an inmate files the first notice of appeal in a civil case under this Rule 4(c), the 14-day period provided in Rule 4(a)(3) for another party to file a notice of appeal runs from the date when the district court dockets the first notice.

    (3) When a defendant in a criminal case files a notice of appeal under this Rule 4(c), the 30-day period for the government to file its notice of appeal runs from the entry of the judgment or order appealed from or from the district court's docketing of the defendant's notice of appeal, whichever is later.

(d) Mistaken Filing in the Court of Appeals. If a notice of appeal in either a civil or a criminal case is mistakenly filed in the court of appeals, the clerk of that court must note on the notice the date when it was received and send it to the district clerk. The notice is then considered filed in the district court on the date so noted.

Rule 5. Appeal by Permission

(a) Petition for Permission to Appeal.

    (1) To request permission to appeal when an appeal is within the court of appeals' discretion, a party must file a petition with the circuit clerk and serve it on all other parties to the district-court action.

    (2) The petition must be filed within the time specified by the statute or rule authorizing the appeal or, if no such time is specified, within the time provided by Rule 4(a) for filing a notice of appeal.

    (3) If a party cannot petition for appeal unless the district court first enters an order granting permission to do so or stating that the necessary conditions are met, the district court may amend its order, either on its own or in response to a party's motion, to include the required permission or statement. In that event, the time to petition runs from entry of the amended order.

(b) Contents of the Petition; Answer or Cross-Petition; Oral Argument.

    (1) The petition must include the following:

    (A) the facts necessary to understand the question presented;

    (B) the question itself;

    (C) the relief sought;

(D) the reasons why the appeal should be allowed and is authorized by a statute or rule; and

(E) an attached copy of:

(i) the order, decree, or judgment complained of and any related opinion or memorandum, and

(ii) any order stating the district court's permission to appeal or finding that the necessary conditions are met.

(2) A party may file an answer in opposition or a cross-petition within 10 days after the petition is served.

(3) The petition and answer will be submitted without oral argument unless the court of appeals orders otherwise.

(c) Form of Papers; Number of Copies; Length Limits. All papers must conform to Rule 32(c)(2). An original and 3 copies must be filed unless the court requires a different number by local rule or by order in a particular case. Except by the court's permission, and excluding the accompanying documents required by Rule 5(b)(1)(E):

(1) a paper produced using a computer must not exceed 5,200 words; and

(2) a handwritten or typewritten paper must not exceed 20 pages.

(d) Grant of Permission; Fees; Cost Bond; Filing the Record.

(1) Within 14 days after the entry of the order granting permission to appeal, the appellant must:

(A) pay the district clerk all required fees; and

(B) file a cost bond if required under Rule 7.

(2) A notice of appeal need not be filed. The date when the order granting permission to appeal is entered serves as the date of the notice of appeal for calculating time under these rules.

(3) The district clerk must notify the circuit clerk once the petitioner has paid the fees. Upon receiving this notice, the circuit clerk must enter the appeal on the docket. The record must be forwarded and filed in accordance with Rules 11 and 12(c).

Rule 5.1.   Appeal by Leave Under 28 U.S.C. §636(c)(5) (Abrogated April 24, 1998, eff. Dec. 1, 1998)

Rule 6.   Appeal in a Bankruptcy Case from a Final Judgment, Order, or Decree of a District Court or Bankruptcy Appellate Panel

(a) Appeal from a Judgment, Order, or Decree of a District Court Exercising Original Jurisdiction in a Bankruptcy Case. An appeal to a court of appeals from a final judgment, order, or decree of a district court exercising jurisdiction under 28 U.S.C. §1334 is taken as any other civil appeal under these rules.

(b) Appeal from a Judgment, Order, or Decree of a District Court or Bankruptcy Appellate Panel Exercising Appellate Jurisdiction in a Bankruptcy Case.

(1) **Applicability of Other Rules.** These rules apply to an appeal to a court of appeals under 28 U.S.C. §158(d)(1) from a final judgment, order, or decree of a district court or bankruptcy appellate panel exercising appellate jurisdiction under 28 U.S.C. §158(a) or (b), but with these qualifications:

(A) Rules 4(a)(4), 4(b), 9, 10, 11, 12(c), 13-20, 22-23, and 24(b) do not apply;

(B) the reference in Rule 3(c) to "Forms 1A and 1B in the Appendix of Forms" must be read as a reference to Form 5;

(C) when the appeal is from a bankruptcy appellate panel, "district court," as used in any applicable rule, means "appellate panel"; and

(D) in Rule 12.1, "district court" includes a bankruptcy court or bankruptcy appellate panel.

(2) **Additional Rules.** In addition to the rules made applicable by Rule 6(b)(1), the following rules apply:

(A) **Motion for rehearing.**

(i) If a timely motion for rehearing under Bankruptcy Rule 8015 is filed, the time to appeal for all parties runs from the entry of the order disposing of the motion. A notice of appeal filed after the district court or bankruptcy appellate panel announces or enters a judgment, order, or decree—but before disposition of the motion for rehearing—becomes effective when the order disposing of the motion for rehearing is entered.

(ii) Appellate review of the order disposing of the motion requires the party, in compliance with Rules 3(c) and 6(b)(1)(B), to amend a previously filed notice of appeal. A party intending to challenge an altered or amended judgment, order, or decree must file a notice of appeal or amended notice of appeal within the time prescribed by Rule 4—excluding Rules 4(a)(4) and 4(b) measured from the entry of the order disposing of the motion.

(iii) No additional fee is required to file an amended notice.

(B) **The record on appeal.**

(i) Within 14 days after filing the notice of appeal, the appellant must file with the clerk possessing the record assembled in accordance with Bankruptcy Rule 8006—and serve on the appellee—a statement of the issues to be presented on appeal and a designation of the record to be certified and sent to the circuit clerk.

(ii) An appellee who believes that other parts of the record are necessary must, within 14 days after being served with the appellant's designation, file with the clerk and serve on the appellant a designation of additional parts to be included.

(iii) The record on appeal consists of:

- the redesignated record as provided above;

- the proceedings in the district court or bankruptcy appellate panel; and

- a certified copy of the docket entries prepared by the clerk under Rule 3(d).

(C) **Forwarding the record.**

(i) When the record is complete, the district clerk or bankruptcy appellate panel clerk must number the documents constituting the record and send them promptly to the circuit clerk together with a list of the documents correspondingly numbered and reasonably identified. Unless directed to do so by a party or the circuit clerk, the clerk will not send to the court of appeals documents of unusual bulk or weight, physical exhibits other than documents, or other parts of the record designated for omission by local rule of the court of appeals. If the exhibits are unusually bulky or heavy, a party must arrange with the clerks in advance for their transportation and receipt.

(ii) All parties must do whatever else is necessary to enable the clerk to assemble and forward the record. The court of appeals may provide by rule or order that a certified copy of the docket entries be sent in place of the redesignated record, but any party may request at any time during the pendency of the appeal that the redesignated record be sent.

(D) **Filing the record.** Upon receiving the record—or a certified copy of the docket entries sent in place of the redesignated record—the circuit clerk must file it and immediately notify all parties of the filing date.

Rule 7.   Bond for Costs on Appeal in a Civil Case

In a civil case, the district court may require an appellant to file a bond or provide other security in any form and amount necessary to ensure payment of costs on appeal. Rule 8(b) applies to a surety on a bond given under this rule.

Rule 8.   Stay or Injunction Pending Appeal

(a) Motion for Stay.

(1) **Initial Motion in the District Court.** A party must ordinarily move first in the district court for the following relief:

(A) a stay of the judgment or order of a district court pending appeal;

(B) approval of a bond or other security provided to obtain a stay or judgment; or

(C) an order suspending, modifying, restoring, or granting an injunction while an appeal is pending.

(2) **Motion in the Court of Appeals; Conditions on Relief.** A motion for the relief mentioned in Rule 8(a)(1) may be made to the court of appeals or to one of its judges.

(A) The motion must:

(i) show that moving first in the district court would be impracticable; or

(ii) state that, a motion having been made, the district court denied the motion or failed to afford the relief requested and state any reasons given by the district court for its action.

(B) The motion must also include:

(i) the reasons for granting the relief requested and the facts relied on;

(ii) originals or copies of affidavits or other sworn statements supporting facts subject to dispute; and

(iii) relevant parts of the record.

(C) The moving party must give reasonable notice of the motion to all parties.

(D) A motion under this Rule 8(a)(2) must be filed with the circuit clerk and normally will be considered by a panel of the court. But in an exceptional case in which time requirements make that procedure impracticable, the motion may be made to and considered by a single judge.

(E) The court may condition relief on a party's filing a bond or other security in the district court.

(b) **Proceeding Against a Surety.** If a party gives security with one or more security providers, each provider submits to the jurisdiction of the district court and irrevocably appoints the district clerk as its agent on whom any papers affecting its liability on the security may be served. On motion, a security provider's liability may be enforced in the district court without the necessity of an independent action. The motion and any notice that the district court prescribes may be served on the district clerk, who must promptly send a copy to each security provider whose address is known.

(c) **Stay in a Criminal Case.** Rule 38 of the Federal Rules of Criminal Procedure governs a stay in a criminal case.

Rule 9.   Release in a Criminal Case

(a) **Release Before Judgment of Conviction.**

(1) The district court must state in writing, or orally on the record, the reasons for an order regarding the release or detention of a defendant in a criminal case. A party appealing from the order must file with the court of appeals a copy of the district court's order and the court's statement of reasons as soon as practicable after filing the notice of appeal. An appellant who questions the factual basis

for the district court's order must file a transcript of the release proceedings or an explanation of why a transcript was not obtained.

(2) After reasonable notice to the appellee, the court of appeals must promptly determine the appeal on the basis of the papers, affidavits, and parts of the record that the parties present or the court requires. Unless the court so orders, briefs need not be filed.

(3) The court of appeals or one of its judges may order the defendant's release pending the disposition of the appeal.

(b) Release After Judgment of Conviction. A party entitled to do so may obtain review of a district-court order regarding release after a judgment of conviction by filing a notice of appeal from that order in the district court, or by filing a motion in the court of appeals if the party has already filed a notice of appeal from the judgment of conviction. Both the order and the review are subject to Rule 9(a). The papers filed by the party seeking review must include a copy of the judgment of conviction.

(c) Criteria for Release. The court must make its decision regarding release in accordance with the applicable provisions of 18 U.S.C. §§3142, 3143, and 3145(c).

Rule 10.   The Record on Appeal

(a) Composition of the Record on Appeal. The following items constitute the record on appeal:

(1) the original papers and exhibits filed in the district court;

(2) the transcript of proceedings, if any; and

(3) a certified copy of the docket entries prepared by the district clerk.

(b) The Transcript of Proceedings.

(1) **Appellant's Duty to Order.** Within 14 days after filing the notice of appeal or entry of an order disposing of the last timely remaining motion of a type specified in Rule 4(a)(4)(A), whichever is later, the appellant must do either of the following:

(A) order from the reporter a transcript of such parts of the proceedings not already on file as the appellant considers necessary, subject to a local rule of the court of appeals and with the following qualifications:

(i) the order must be in writing;

(ii) if the cost of the transcript is to be paid by the United States under the Criminal Justice Act, the order must so state; and

(iii) the appellant must, within the same period, file a copy of the order with the district clerk; or

(B) file a certificate stating that no transcript will be ordered.

(2) **Unsupported Finding or Conclusion.** If the appellant intends to urge on appeal that a finding or conclusion is unsupported by the evidence or is

contrary to the evidence, the appellant must include in the record a transcript of all evidence relevant to that finding or conclusion.

(3) **Partial Transcript.** Unless the entire transcript is ordered:

(A) the appellant must—within the 14 days provided in Rule 10(b)(1)—file a statement of the issues that the appellant intends to present on the appeal and must serve on the appellee a copy of both the order or certificate and the statement;

(B) if the appellee considers it necessary to have a transcript of other parts of the proceedings, the appellee must, within 14 days after the service of the order or certificate and the statement of the issues, file and serve on the appellant a designation of additional parts to be ordered; and

(C) unless within 14 days after service of that designation the appellant has ordered all such parts, and has so notified the appellee, the appellee may within the following 14 days either order the parts or move in the district court for an order requiring the appellant to do so.

(4) **Payment.** At the time of ordering, a party must make satisfactory arrangements with the reporter for paying the cost of the transcript.

(c) **Statement of the Evidence When the Proceedings Were Not Recorded or When a Transcript Is Unavailable.** If the transcript of a hearing or trial is unavailable, the appellant may prepare a statement of the evidence or proceedings from the best available means, including the appellant's recollection. The statement must be served on the appellee, who may serve objections or proposed amendments within 14 days after being served. The statement and any objections or proposed amendments must then be submitted to the district court for settlement and approval. As settled and approved, the statement must be included by the district clerk in the record on appeal.

(d) **Agreed Statement as the Record on Appeal.** In place of the record on appeal as defined in Rule 10(a), the parties may prepare, sign, and submit to the district court a statement of the case showing how the issues presented by the appeal arose and were decided in the district court. The statement must set forth only those facts averred and proved or sought to be proved that are essential to the courts resolution of the issues. If the statement is truthful, it—together with any additions that the district court may consider necessary to a full presentation of the issues on appeal—must be approved by the district court and must then be certified to the court of appeals as the record on appeal. The district clerk must then send it to the circuit clerk within the time provided by Rule 11. A copy of the agreed statement may be filed in place of the appendix required by Rule 30.

(e) **Correction or Modification of the Record.**

(1) If any difference arises about whether the record truly discloses what occurred in the district court, the difference must be submitted to and settled by that court and the record conformed accordingly.

(2) If anything material to either party is omitted from or misstated in the record by error or accident, the omission or misstatement may be corrected and a supplemental record may be certified and forwarded:

(A) on stipulation of the parties;

(B) by the district court before or after the record has been forwarded; or

(C) by the court of appeals.

(3) All other questions as to the form and content of the record must be presented to the court of appeals.

Rule 11. Forwarding the Record

(a) **Appellant's Duty.** An appellant filing a notice of appeal must comply with Rule 10(b) and must do whatever else is necessary to enable the clerk to assemble and forward the record. If there are multiple appeals from a judgment or order, the clerk must forward a single record.

(b) **Duties of Reporter and District Clerk.**

(1) **Reporter's Duty to Prepare and File a Transcript.** The reporter must prepare and file a transcript as follows:

(A) Upon receiving an order for a transcript, the reporter must enter at the foot of the order the date of its receipt and the expected completion date and send a copy, so endorsed, to the circuit clerk.

(B) If the transcript cannot be completed within 30 days of the reporters receipt of the order, the reporter may request the circuit clerk to grant additional time to complete it. The clerk must note on the docket the action taken and notify the parties.

(C) When a transcript is complete, the reporter must file it with the district clerk and notify the circuit clerk of the filing.

(D) If the reporter fails to file the transcript on time, the circuit clerk must notify the district judge and do whatever else the court of appeals directs.

(2) **District Clerk's Duty to Forward.** When the record is complete, the district clerk must number the documents constituting the record and send them promptly to the circuit clerk together with a list of the documents correspondingly numbered and reasonably identified. Unless directed to do so by a party or the circuit clerk, the district clerk will not send to the court of appeals documents of unusual bulk or weight, physical exhibits other than documents, or other parts of the record designated for omission by local rule of the court of appeals. If the exhibits are unusually bulky or heavy, a party must arrange with the clerks in advance for their transportation and receipt.

(c) **Retaining the Record Temporarily in the District Court for Use in Preparing the Appeal.** The parties may stipulate, or the district court on motion may order, that the district clerk retain the record temporarily for the parties to use in preparing the papers on appeal. In that event the district clerk must certify to the circuit clerk that the record on appeal is complete. Upon receipt of the appellee's brief, or earlier if the court orders or the parties agree, the appellant must request the district clerk to forward the record.

(d) [Abrogated.]

(e) **Retaining the Record by Court Order.**
(1) The court of appeals may, by order or local rule, provide that a certified copy of the docket entries be forwarded instead of the entire record. But a party may at any time during the appeal request that designated parts of the record be forwarded.
(2) The district court may order the record or some part of it retained if the court needs it while the appeal is pending, subject, however, to call by the court of appeals.
(3) If part or all of the record is ordered retained, the district clerk must send to the court of appeals a copy of the order and the docket entries together with the parts of the original record allowed by the district court and copies of any parts of the record designated by the parties.

(f) **Retaining Parts of the Record in the District Court by Stipulation of the Parties.** The parties may agree by written stipulation filed in the district court that designated parts of the record be retained in the district court subject to call by the court of appeals or request by a party. The parts of the record so designated remain a part of the record on appeal.

(g) **Record for a Preliminary Motion in the Court of Appeals.** If, before the record is forwarded, a party makes any of the following motions in the court of appeals:

- for dismissal;
- for release;
- for a stay pending appeal;
- for additional security on the bond on appeal or on a bond or other security provided to obtain a stay of judgment; or
- for any other intermediate order
- the district clerk must send the court of appeals any parts of the record designated by any party.

Rule 12.   Docketing the Appeal; Filing a Representation
               Statement; Filing the Record

(a) **Docketing the Appeal.** Upon receiving the copy of the notice of appeal and the docket entries from the district clerk under Rule 3(d), the circuit clerk must docket the appeal under the title of the district-court action and must identify the appellant, adding the appellant's name if necessary.

(b) **Filing a Representation Statement.** Unless the court of appeals designates another time, the attorney who filed the notice of appeal must, within 14 days after filing the notice, file a statement with the circuit clerk naming the parties that the attorney represents on appeal.

(c) **Filing the Record, Partial Record, or Certificate.** Upon receiving the record, partial record, or district clerk's certificate as provided in Rule 11, the circuit clerk must file it and immediately notify all parties of the filing date.

Rule 12.1. Remand After an Indicative Ruling by the District Court on a Motion for Relief That Is Barred by a Pending Appeal

(a) **Notice to the Court of Appeals.** If a timely motion is made in the district court for relief that it lacks authority to grant because of an appeal that has been docketed and is pending, the movant must promptly notify the circuit clerk if the district court states either that it would grant the motion or that the motion raises a substantial issue.

(b) **Remand After an Indicative Ruling.** If the district court states that it would grant the motion or that the motion raises a substantial issue, the court of appeals may remand for further proceedings but retains jurisdiction unless it expressly dismisses the appeal. If the court of appeals remands but retains jurisdiction, the parties must promptly notify the circuit clerk when the district court has decided the motion on remand.

Title III.   Appeals from the United States Tax Court

Rule 13.   Appeals from the Tax Court

(a) **Appeal as of Right**
(1) **How Obtained; Time for Filing Notice of Appeal.**
    (A) An appeal as of right from the United States Tax Court is commenced by filing a notice of appeal with the Tax Court clerk within 90 days after the entry of the Tax Court's decision. At the time of filing, the appellant must furnish the clerk with enough copies of the notice to enable the clerk to comply with Rule 3(d). If one party files a timely notice of appeal, any other party may file a notice of appeal within 120 days after the Tax Court's decision is entered.

(B) If, under Tax Court rules, a party makes a timely motion to vacate or revise the Tax Court's decision, the time to file a notice of appeal runs from the entry of the order disposing of the motion or from the entry of a new decision, whichever is later.

(2) **Notice of Appeal; How Filed.** The notice of appeal may be filed either at the Tax Court clerk's office in the District of Columbia or by sending it to the clerk. If sent by mail the notice is considered filed on the postmark date, subject to § 7502 of the Internal Revenue Code, as amended, and the applicable regulations.

(3) **Contents of the Notice of Appeal; Service; Effect of Filing and Service.** Rule 3 prescribes the contents of a notice of appeal, the manner of service, and the effect of its filing and service. Form 2 in the Appendix of Forms is a suggested form of a notice of appeal.

(4) **The Record on Appeal; Forwarding; Filing.**

(A) Except as otherwise provided under Tax Court rules for the transcript of proceedings, the appeal is governed by the parts of Rules 10, 11, and 12 regarding the record on appeal from a district court, the time and manner of forwarding and filing, and the docketing in the court of appeals.

(B) If an appeal is taken to more than one court of appeals, the original record must be sent to the court named in the first notice of appeal filed. In an appeal to any other court of appeals, the appellant must apply to that other court to make provision for the record.

(b) **Appeal by Permission.** An appeal by permission is governed by Rule 5.

Rule 14.   Applicability of Other Rules to Appeals from the Tax Court

All provisions of these rules, except Rules 4, 15-20, and 22-23, apply to appeals from the Tax Court. References in any applicable rule (other than Rule 24(a)) to the district court and district clerk are to be read as referring to the Tax Court and its clerk.

Title IV.   Review or Enforcement of an Order of an Administrative Agency, Board, Commission, or Officer

Rule 15.   Review or Enforcement of an Agency Order—How Obtained; Intervention

(a) **Petition for Review; Joint Petition.**

(1) Review of an agency order is commenced by filing, within the time prescribed by law, a petition for review with the clerk of a court of appeals authorized

to review the agency order. If their interests make joinder practicable, two or more persons may join in a petition to the same court to review the same order.

(2) The petition must:

(A) name each party seeking review either in the caption or the body of the petition—using such terms as "et al.," "petitioners," or "respondents" does not effectively name the parties;

(B) name the agency as a respondent (even though not named in the petition, the United States is a respondent if required by statute); and

(C) specify the order or part thereof to be reviewed.

(3) Form 3 in the Appendix of Forms is a suggested form of a petition for review.

(4) In this rule "agency" includes an agency, board, commission, or officer; "petition for review" includes a petition to enjoin, suspend, modify, or otherwise review, or a notice of appeal, whichever form is indicated by the applicable statute.

(b) Application or Cross-Application to Enforce an Order; Answer; Default.

(1) An application to enforce an agency order must be filed with the clerk of a court of appeals authorized to enforce the order. If a petition is filed to review an agency order that the court may enforce, a party opposing the petition may file a cross-application for enforcement.

(2) Within 21 days after the application for enforcement is filed, the respondent must serve on the applicant an answer to the application and file it with the clerk. If the respondent fails to answer in time, the court will enter judgment for the relief requested.

(3) The application must contain a concise statement of the proceedings in which the order was entered, the facts upon which venue is based, and the relief requested.

(c) Service of the Petition or Application. The circuit clerk must serve a copy of the petition for review, or an application or cross-application to enforce an agency order, on each respondent as prescribed by Rule 3(d), unless a different manner of service is prescribed by statute. At the time of filing, the petitioner must:

(1) serve, or have served, a copy on each party admitted to participate in the agency proceedings, except for the respondents;

(2) file with the clerk a list of those so served; and

(3) give the clerk enough copies of the petition or application to serve each respondent.

(d) Intervention. Unless a statute provides another method, a person who wants to intervene in a proceeding under this rule must file a motion for leave to intervene with the circuit clerk and serve a copy on all parties. The motion—or other notice of intervention authorized by statute—must be filed within 30 days after the petition for review is filed and must contain a concise statement of the interest of the moving party and the grounds for intervention.

(e) Payment of Fees. When filing any separate or joint petition for review in a court of appeals, the petitioner must pay the circuit clerk all required fees.

Rule 15.1.   Briefs and Oral Argument in a National Labor Relations Board Proceeding

In either an enforcement or a review proceeding, a party adverse to the National Labor Relations Board proceeds first on briefing and at oral argument, unless the court orders otherwise.

Rule 16.   The Record on Review or Enforcement

(a) Composition of the Record. The record on review or enforcement of an agency order consists of:
(1) the order involved;
(2) any findings or report on which it is based; and
(3) the pleadings, evidence, and other parts of the proceedings before the agency.

(b) Omissions from or Misstatements in the Record. The parties may at any time, by stipulation, supply any omission from the record or correct a misstatement, or the court may so direct. If necessary, the court may direct that a supplemental record be prepared and filed.

Rule 17.   Filing the Record

(a) Agency to File; Time for Filing; Notice of Filing. The agency must file the record with the circuit clerk within 40 days after being served with a petition for review, unless the statute authorizing review provides otherwise, or within 40 days after it files an application for enforcement unless the respondent fails to answer or the court orders otherwise. The court may shorten or extend the time to file the record. The clerk must notify all parties of the date when the record is filed.

(b) Filing—What Constitutes.
(1) The agency must file:
(A) the original or a certified copy of the entire record or parts designated by the parties; or
(B) a certified list adequately describing all documents, transcripts of testimony, exhibits, and other material constituting the record, or describing those parts designated by the parties.

(2) The parties may stipulate in writing that no record or certified list be filed. The date when the stipulation is filed with the circuit clerk is treated as the date when the record is filed.

(3) The agency must retain any portion of the record not filed with the clerk. All parts of the record retained by the agency are a part of the record on review for all purposes and, if the court or a party so requests, must be sent to the court regardless of any prior stipulation.

Rule 18.   Stay Pending Review

(a) Motion for a Stay.

(1) **Initial Motion Before the Agency.** A petitioner must ordinarily move first before the agency for a stay pending review of its decision or order.

(2) **Motion in the Court of Appeals.** A motion for a stay may be made to the court of appeals or one of its judges.

(A) The motion must:

(i) show that moving first before the agency would be impracticable; or

(ii) state that, a motion having been made, the agency denied the motion or failed to afford the relief requested and state any reasons given by the agency for its action.

(B) The motion must also include:

(i) the reasons for granting the relief requested and the facts relied on;

(ii) originals or copies of affidavits or other sworn statements supporting facts subject to dispute; and

(iii) relevant parts of the record.

(C) The moving panty must give reasonable notice of the motion to all parties.

(D) The motion must be filed with the circuit clerk and normally will be considered by a panel of the court. But in an exceptional case in which time requirements make that procedure impracticable, the motion may be made to and considered by a single judge.

(b) Bond. The court may condition relief on the filing of a bond or other appropriate security.

Rule 19.   Settlement of a Judgment Enforcing an Agency Order in Part

When the court files an opinion directing entry of judgment enforcing the agency's order in part, the agency must within 14 days file with the clerk and serve on each other party a proposed judgment conforming to the opinion. A party who disagrees with the agency's proposed judgment must within 10 days file with the clerk and serve the agency with a proposed judgment that the party believes conforms to the opinion. The court will settle the judgment and direct entry without further hearing or argument.

Rule 20. Applicability of Rules to the Review or Enforcement of an Agency Order

All provisions of these rules, except Rules 3-14 and 22-23, apply to the review or enforcement of an agency order. In these rules, "appellant" includes a petitioner or applicant, and "appellee" includes a respondent.

Title V.   Extraordinary Writs

Rule 21.   Writs of Mandamus and Prohibition, and Other Extraordinary Writs

(a) Mandamus or Prohibition to a Court: Petition, Filing, Service, and Docketing.

(1) A party petitioning for a writ of mandamus or prohibition directed to a court must file the petition with the circuit clerk and serve it on all parties to the proceeding in the trial court. The party must also provide a copy to the trial-court judge. All parties to the proceeding in the trial court other than the petitioner are respondents for all purposes.

(2)(A) The petition must be titled "In re [name of petitioner]."

(B) The petition must state:

(i) the relief sought;

(ii) the issues presented;

(iii) the facts necessary to understand the issue presented by the petition; and

(iv) the reasons why the writ should issue.

(C) The petition must include a copy of any order or opinion or parts of the record that may be essential to understand the matters set forth in the petition.

(3) Upon receiving the prescribed docket fee, the clerk must docket the petition and submit it to the court.

(b) Denial; Order Directing Answer; Briefs; Precedence.

(1) The court may deny the petition without an answer. Otherwise, it must order the respondent, if any, to answer within a fixed time.

(2) The clerk must serve the order to respond on all persons directed to respond.

(3) Two or more respondents may answer jointly.

(4) The court of appeals may invite or order the trial-court judge to address the petition or may invite an amicus curiae to do so. The trial-court judge may request permission to address the petition but may not do so unless invited or ordered to do so by the court of appeals.

(5) If briefing or oral argument is required, the clerk must advise the parties, and when appropriate, the trial-court judge or amicus curiae.

(6) The proceeding must be given preference over ordinary civil cases.

(7) The circuit clerk must send a copy of the final disposition to the trial court judge.

(c) Other Extraordinary Writs. An application for an extraordinary writ other than one provided for in Rule 21(a) must be made by filing a petition with the circuit clerk and serving it on the respondents. Proceedings on the application must conform, so far as is practicable, to the procedures prescribed in Rule 21(a) and (b).

(d) Form of Papers; Number of Copies; Length Limits. All papers must conform to Rule 32(c)(2). An original and 3 copies must be filed unless the court requires the filing of a different number by local rule or by order in a particular case. Except by the court's permission, and excluding the accompanying documents required by Rule 21(a)(2)(C):

(1) a paper produced using a computer must not exceed 7,800 words; and

(2) a handwritten or typewritten paper must not exceed 30 pages.

Title VI.   Habeas Corpus; Proceedings in Forma Pauperis

Rule 22.   Habeas Corpus and Section 2255 Proceedings

(a) Application for the Original Writ. An application for a writ of habeas corpus must be made to the appropriate district court. If made to a circuit judge, the application must be transferred to the appropriate district court. If a district court denies an application made or transferred to it, renewal of the application before a circuit judge is not permitted. The applicant may, under 28 U.S.C. §2253, appeal to the court of appeals from the district court's order denying the application.

(b) Certificate of Appealability.

(1) In a habeas corpus proceeding in which the detention complained of arises from process issued by a state court, or in a 28 U.S.C. §2255 proceeding, the applicant cannot take an appeal unless a circuit justice or a circuit or district judge issues a certificate of appealability under 28 U.S.C. §2253(c). If an applicant files a notice of appeal, the district clerk must send to the court of appeals

the certificate (if any) and the statement described in Rule 11(a) of the Rules Governing Proceedings Under 28 U.S.C. §2254 or §2255 (if any), along with the notice of appeal and the file of the district-court proceedings. If the district judge has denied the certificate, the applicant may request a circuit judge to issue it.

(2) A request addressed to the court of appeals may be considered by a circuit judge or judges, as the court prescribes. If no express request for a certificate is filed, the notice of appeal constitutes a request addressed to the judges of the court of appeals.

(3) A certificate of appealability is not required when a state or its representative or the United States or its representative appeals.

Rule 23. Custody or Release of a Prisoner in a Habeas Corpus Proceeding

(a) **Transfer of Custody Pending Review.** Pending review of a decision in a habeas corpus proceeding commenced before a court, justice, or judge of the United States for the release of a prisoner, the person having custody of the prisoner must not transfer custody to another unless a transfer is directed in accordance with this rule. When, upon application, a custodian shows the need for a transfer, the court, justice, or judge rendering the decision under review may authorize the transfer and substitute the successor custodian as a party.

(b) **Detention or Release Pending Review of Decision Not to Release.** While a decision not to release a prisoner is under review, the court or judge rendering the decision, or the court of appeals, or the Supreme Court, or a judge or justice of either court, may order that the prisoner be:
(1) detained in the custody from which release is sought;
(2) detained in other appropriate custody; or
(3) released on personal recognizance, with or without surety.

(c) **Release Pending Review of Decision Ordering Release.** While a decision ordering the release of a prisoner is under review, the prisoner must—unless the court or judge rendering the decision, or the court of appeals, or the Supreme Court, or a judge or justice of either court orders otherwise—be released on personal recognizance, with or without surety.

(d) **Modification of the Initial Order on Custody.** An initial order governing the prisoner's custody or release, including any recognizance or surety, continues in effect pending review unless for special reasons shown to the court of appeals or the Supreme Court, or to a judge or justice of either court, the order is modified or an independent order regarding custody, release, or surety is issued.

Rule 24.   Proceeding in Forma Pauperis

(a) Leave to Proceed in Forma Pauperis.

(1) **Motion in the District Court.** Except as stated in Rule 24(a)(3), a party to a district-court action who desires to appeal in forma pauperis must file a motion in the district court. The party must attach an affidavit that:

(A) shows in the detail prescribed by Form 4 of the Appendix of Forms the party's inability to pay or to give security for fees and costs;

(B) claims an entitlement to redress; and

(C) states the issues that the party intends to present on appeal.

(2) **Action on the Motion.** If the district court grants the motion, the party may proceed on appeal without prepaying or giving security for fees and costs, unless a statute provides otherwise. If the district court denies the motion, it must state its reasons in writing.

(3) **Prior Approval.** A party who was permitted to proceed in forma pauperis in the district-court action, or who was determined to be financially unable to obtain an adequate defense in a criminal case, may proceed on appeal in forma pauperis without further authorization, unless:

(A) the district court—before or after the notice of appeal is filed—certifies that the appeal is not taken in good faith or finds that the party is not otherwise entitled to proceed in forma pauperis and states in writing its reasons for the certification or finding; or

(B) a statute provides otherwise.

(4) **Notice of District Court's Denial.** The district clerk must immediately notify the parties and the court of appeals when the district court does any of the following:

(A) denies a motion to proceed on appeal in forma pauperis;

(B) certifies that the appeal is not taken in good faith; or

(C) finds that the party is not otherwise entitled to proceed in forma pauperis.

(5) **Motion in the Court of Appeals.** A party may file a motion to proceed on appeal in forma pauperis in the court of appeals within 30 days after service of the notice prescribed in Rule 24(a)(4). The motion must include a copy of the affidavit filed in the district court and the district court's statement of reasons for its action. If no affidavit was filed in the district court, the party must include the affidavit prescribed by Rule 24(a)(1).

(b) Leave to Proceed in Forma Pauperis on Appeal from the United States Tax Court or on Appeal or Review of an Administrative-Agency Proceeding. A party may file in the court of appeals a motion for leave to proceed on appeal in forma pauperis with an affidavit prescribed by Rule 24(a)(1):

(1) in an appeal from the United States Tax Court; and

(2) when an appeal or review of a proceeding before an administrative agency, board, commission, or officer proceeds directly in the court of appeals.

(c) **Leave to Use Original Record.** A party allowed to proceed on appeal in forma pauperis may request that the appeal be heard on the original record without reproducing any part.

Title VII.   General Provisions

Rule 25.   Filing and Service

(a) **Filing.**
(1) **Filing with the Clerk.** A paper required or permitted to be filed in a court of appeals must be filed with the clerk.
(2) **Filing: Method and Timeliness.**
  (A) **Nonelectronic Filing.**
    (i) **In General.** For a paper not filed electronically, filing may be accomplished by mail addressed to the clerk, but filing is not timely unless the clerk receives the papers within the time fixed for filing.
    (ii) **A Brief or Appendix.** A brief or appendix not filed electronically is timely filed, however, if on or before the last day for filing, it is:

- mailed to the clerk by first-class mail, or other class of mail that is at least as expeditious, postage prepaid; or

- dispatched to a third-party commercial carrier for delivery to the clerk within 3 days.

    (iii) **Inmate Filing.** If an institution has a system designed for legal mail, an inmate confined there must use that system to receive the benefit of this Rule 25(a)(2)(A)(iii). A paper not filed electronically by an inmate is timely if it is deposited in the institution's internal mail system on or before the last day for filing and:

- it is accompanied by: a declaration in compliance with 28 U.S.C. §1746—or a notarized statement—setting out the date of deposit and stating that first-class postage is being prepaid; or evidence (such as a postmark or date stamp) showing that the paper was so deposited and that postage was prepaid; or

- the court of appeals exercises its discretion to permit the later filing of a declaration or notarized statement that satisfies Rule 25(a)(2)(A)(iii).

  (B) **Electronic Filing and Signing.**
    (i) **By a Represented Person—Generally Required; Exceptions.** A person represented by an attorney must file electronically, unless nonelectronic

filing is allowed by the court for good cause or is allowed or required by local rule.

(ii) **By an Unrepresented Person—When Allowed or Required.** A person not represented by an attorney:

- may file electronically only if allowed by court order or by local rule; and

- may be required to file electronically only by court order, or by a local rule that includes reasonable exceptions.

(iii) **Signing.** A filing made through a person's electronic-filing account and authorized by that person, together with that person's name on a signature block, constitutes the person's signature.

(iv) **Same as a Written Paper.** A paper filed electronically is a written paper for purposes of these rules.

(3) **Filing a Motion with a Judge.** If a motion requests relief that may be granted by a single judge, the judge may permit the motion to be filed with the judge; the judge must note the filing date on the motion and give it to the clerk.

(4) **Clerk's Refusal of Documents.** The clerk must not refuse to accept for filing any paper presented for that purpose solely because it is not presented in proper form as required by these rules or by any local rule or practice.

(5) **Privacy Protection.** An appeal in a case whose privacy protection was governed by Federal Rule of Bankruptcy Procedure 9037, Federal Rule of Civil Procedure 5.2, or Federal Rule of Criminal Procedure 49.1 is governed by the same rule on appeal. In all other proceedings, privacy protection is governed by Federal Rule of Civil Procedure 5.2, except that Federal Rule of Criminal Procedure 49.1 governs when an extraordinary writ is sought in a criminal case.

(b) Service of All Papers Required. Unless a rule requires service by the clerk, a party must, at or before the time of filing a paper, serve a copy on the other parties to the appeal or review. Service on a party represented by counsel must be made on the party's counsel.

(c) Manner of Service.

(1) Nonelectronic service may be any of the following:

(A) personal, including delivery to a responsible person at the office of counsel;

(B) by mail; or

(C) by third-party commercial carrier for delivery within 3 days.

(2) Electronic service of a paper may be made (A) by sending it to a registered user by filing it with the court's electronic-filing system or (B) by sending it by other electronic means that the person to be served consented to in writing.

(3) When reasonable considering such factors as the immediacy of the relief sought, distance, and cost, service on a party must be by a manner at least as expeditious as the manner used to file the paper with the court.

(4) Service by mail or by commercial carrier is complete on mailing or delivery to the carrier. Service by electronic means is complete on filing or sending, unless the party making service is notified that the paper was not received by the party served.

(d) Proof of Service.

(1) A paper presented for filing must contain either of the following if it was served other than through the court's electronic-filing system:

(A) an acknowledgment of service by the person served; or

(B) proof of service consisting of a statement by the person who made service certifying:

(i) the date and manner of service;

(ii) the names of the persons served; and

(iii) their mail or electronic addresses, facsimile numbers, or the addresses of the places of delivery, as appropriate for the manner of service.

(2) When a brief or appendix is filed by mailing or dispatch in accordance with Rule 25(a)(2)(A)(ii), the proof of service must also state the date and manner by which the document was mailed or dispatched to the clerk.

(3) Proof of service may appear on or be affixed to the papers filed.

(e) Number of Copies. When these rules require the filing or furnishing of a number of copies, a court may require a different number by local rule or by order in a particular case.

Rule 26.   Computing and Extending Time

(a) Computing Time. The following rules apply in computing any time period specified in these rules, in any local rule or court order, or in any statute that does not specify a method of computing time.

(1) **Period Stated in Days or a Longer Unit.** When the period is stated in days or a longer unit of time:

(A) exclude the day of the event that triggers the period;

(B) count every day, including intermediate Saturdays, Sundays, and legal holidays; and

(C) include the last day of the period, but if the last day is a Saturday, Sunday, or legal holiday, the period continues to run until the end of the next day that is not a Saturday, Sunday, or legal holiday.

(2) **Period Stated in Hours.** When the period is stated in hours:

(A) begin counting immediately on the occurrence of the event that triggers the period;

(B) count every hour, including hours during intermediate Saturdays, Sundays, and legal holidays; and

(C) if the period would end on a Saturday, Sunday, or legal holiday, the period continues to run until the same time on the next day that is not a Saturday, Sunday, or legal holiday.

(3) **Inaccessibility of the Clerk's Office.** Unless the court orders otherwise, if the clerk's office is inaccessible:

(A) on the last day for filing under Rule 26(a)(1), then the time for filing is extended to the first accessible day that is not a Saturday, Sunday, or legal holiday; or

(B) during the last hour for filing under Rule 26(a)(2), then the time for filing is extended to the same time on the first accessible day that is not a Saturday, Sunday, or legal holiday.

(4) **"Last Day" Defined.** Unless a different time is set by a statute, local rule, or court order, the last day ends:

(A) for electronic filing in the district court, at midnight in the court's time zone;

(B) for electronic filing in the court of appeals, at midnight in the time zone of the circuit clerk's principal office;

(C) for filing under Rules 4(c)(1), 25(a)(2)(A)(ii), and 25(a)(2)(A)(iii) — and filing by mail under Rule 13(a)(2) — at the latest time for the method chosen for delivery to the post office, third-party commercial carrier, or prison mailing system; and

(D) for filing by other means, when the clerk's office is scheduled to close.

(5) **"Next Day" Defined.** The "next day" is determined by continuing to count forward when the period is measured after an event and backward when measured before an event.

(6) **"Legal Holiday" Defined.** "Legal holiday" means:

(A) the day set aside by statute for observing New Year's Day, Martin Luther King Jr.'s Birthday, Washington's Birthday, Memorial Day, Independence Day, Labor Day, Columbus Day, Veterans' Day, Thanksgiving Day, or Christmas Day;

(B) any day declared a holiday by the President or Congress; and

(C) for periods that are measured after an event, any other day declared a holiday by the state where either of the following is located: the district court that rendered the challenged judgment or order, or the circuit clerk's principal office.

(b) **Extending Time.** For good cause, the court may extend the time prescribed by these rules or by its order to perform any act, or may permit an act to be done after that time expires. But the court may not extend the time to file:

(1) a notice of appeal (except as authorized in Rule 4) or a petition for permission to appeal; or

(2) a notice of appeal from or a petition to enjoin, set aside, suspend, modify, enforce, or otherwise review an order of an administrative agency, board, commission, or officer of the United States, unless specifically authorized by law.

(c) **Additional Time after Certain Kinds of Service.** When a party may or must act within a specified time after being served, and the paper is not served electronically on the party or delivered to the party on the date stated in the proof of service, 3 days are added after the period would otherwise expire under Rule 26(a).

Rule 26.1.   Corporate Disclosure Statement

(a) **Nongovernmental Corporations.** Any nongovernmental corporation that is a party to a proceeding in a court of appeals must file a statement that identifies any parent corporation and any publicly held corporation that owns 10% or more of its stock or states that there is no such corporation. The same requirement applies to a nongovernmental corporation that seeks to intervene.

(b) **Organizational Victims in Criminal Cases.** In a criminal case, unless the government shows good cause, it must file a statement that identifies any organizational victim of the alleged criminal activity. If the organizational victim is a corporation, the statement must also disclose the information required by Rule 26.1(a) to the extent it can be obtained through due diligence.

(c) **Bankruptcy Cases.** In a bankruptcy case, the debtor, the trustee, or, if neither is a party, the appellant must file a statement that:
(1) identifies each debtor not named in the caption; and
(2) for each debtor that is a corporation, discloses the information required by Rule 26.1(a).

(d) **Time for Filing; Supplemental Filing.** The Rule 26.1 statement must:
(1) be filed with the principal brief or upon filing a motion, response, petition, or answer in the court of appeals, whichever occurs first, unless a local rule requires earlier filing;
(2) be included before the table of contents in the principal brief; and
(3) be supplemented whenever the information required under Rule 26.1 changes.

(e) **Number of Copies.** If the Rule 26.1 statement is filed before the principal brief, or if a supplemental statement is filed, an original and 3 copies must be filed unless the court requires a different number by local rule or by order in a particular case.

Rule 27.   Motions

(a) **In General.**
(1) **Application for Relief.** An application for an order or other relief is made by motion unless these rules prescribe another form. A motion must be in writing unless the court permits otherwise.

(2) **Contents of a Motion.**

(A) **Grounds and relief sought.** A motion must state with particularity the grounds for the motion, the relief sought, and the legal argument necessary to support it.

(B) **Accompanying documents.**

(i) Any affidavit or other paper necessary to support a motion must be served and filed with the motion.

(ii) An affidavit must contain only factual information, not legal argument.

(iii) A motion seeking substantive relief must include a copy of the trial court's opinion or agency's decision as a separate exhibit.

(C) **Documents barred or not required.**

(i) A separate brief supporting or responding to a motion must not be filed.

(ii) A notice of motion is not required.

(iii) A proposed order is not required.

(3) **Response.**

(A) **Time to file.** Any party may file a response to a motion; Rule 27(a)(2) governs its contents. The response must be filed within 10 days after service of the motion unless the court shortens or extends the time. A motion authorized by Rules 8, 9, 18, or 41 may be granted before the 10-day period runs only if the court gives reasonable notice to the parties that it intends to act sooner.

(B) **Request for affirmative relief.** A response may include a motion for affirmative relief. The time to respond to the new motion, and to reply to that response, are governed by Rule 27(a)(3)(A) and (a)(4). The title of the response must alert the court to the request for relief.

(4) **Reply to Response.** Any reply to a response must be filed within 7 days after service of the response. A reply must not present matters that do not relate to the response.

(b) Disposition of a Motion for a Procedural Order. The court may act on a motion for a procedural order—including a motion under Rule 26(b)—at any time without awaiting a response, and may, by rule or by order in a particular case, authorize its clerk to act on specified types of procedural motions. A party adversely affected by the court's, or the clerk's, action may file a motion to reconsider, vacate, or modify that action. Timely opposition filed after the motion is granted in whole or in part does not constitute a request to reconsider, vacate, or modify the disposition; a motion requesting that relief must be filed.

(c) Power of a Single Judge to Entertain a Motion. A circuit judge may act alone on any motion, but may not dismiss or otherwise determine an appeal or other proceeding. A court of appeals may provide by rule or by order in a particular case that only the court may act on any motion or class of motions. The court may review the action of a single judge.

(d) Form of Papers; Length Limits; Number of Copies.

(1) **Format.**

(A) **Reproduction.** A motion, response, or reply may be reproduced by any process that yields a clear black image on light paper. The paper must be opaque and unglazed. Only one side of the paper may be used.

(B) **Cover.** A cover is not required, but there must be a caption that includes the case number, the name of the court, the title of the case, and a brief descriptive title indicating the purpose of the motion and identifying the party or parties for whom it is filed. If a cover is used, it must be white.

(C) **Binding.** The document must be bound in any manner that is secure, does not obscure the text, and permits the document to lie reasonably flat when open.

(D) **Paper size, line spacing, and margins.** The document must be on 8½ by 11 inch paper. The text must be double-spaced, but quotations more than two lines long may be indented and single-spaced. Headings and footnotes may be single-spaced. Margins must be at least one inch on all four sides. Page numbers may be placed in the margins, but no text may appear there.

(E) **Typeface and type styles.** The document must comply with the typeface requirements of Rule 32(a)(5) and the type-style requirements of Rule 32(a)(6).

(2) **Length Limits.** Except by the court's permission, and excluding the accompanying documents authorized by Rule 27(a)(2)(B):

(A) a motion or response to a motion produced using a computer must not exceed 5,200 words;

(B) a handwritten or typewritten motion or response to a motion must not exceed 20 pages;

(C) a reply produced using a computer must not exceed 2,600 words; and

(D) a handwritten or typewritten reply to a response must not exceed 10 pages.

(3) **Number of Copies.** An original and 3 copies must be filed unless the court requires a different number by local rule or by order in a particular case.

(e) Oral Argument. A motion will be decided without oral argument unless the court orders otherwise.

Rule 28.   Briefs

(a) Appellant's Brief. The appellant's brief must contain, under appropriate headings and in the order indicated:

(1) a disclosure statement if required by Rule 26.1;

(2) a table of contents, with page references;

(3) a table of authorities—cases (alphabetically arranged), statutes, and other authorities—with references to the pages of the brief where they are cited;

(4) a jurisdictional statement, including:

(A) the basis for the district court's or agency's subject-matter jurisdiction, with citations to applicable statutory provisions and stating relevant facts establishing jurisdiction;

(B) the basis for the court of appeals' jurisdiction, with citations to applicable statutory provisions and stating relevant facts establishing jurisdiction;

(C) the filing dates establishing the timeliness of the appeal or petition for review; and

(D) an assertion that the appeal is from a final order or judgment that disposes of all parties' claims, or information establishing the court of appeals' jurisdiction on some other basis;

(5) a statement of the issues presented for review;

(6) a concise statement of the case setting out the facts relevant to the issues submitted for review, describing the relevant procedural history, and identifying the rulings presented for review, with appropriate references to the record (see Rule 28(e));

(7) a summary of the argument, which must contain a succinct, clear, and accurate statement of the arguments made in the body of the brief, and which must not merely repeat the argument headings;

(8) the argument, which must contain:

(A) appellant's contentions and the reasons for them, with citations to the authorities and parts of the record on which the appellant relies; and

(B) for each issue, a concise statement of the applicable standard of review (which may appear in the discussion of the issue or under a separate heading placed before the discussion of the issues);

(9) a short conclusion stating the precise relief sought; and

(10) the certificate of compliance, if required by Rule 32(g)(1).

(b) **Appellee's Brief.** The appellee's brief must conform to the requirements of Rule 28(a)(1)-(8) and (10), except that none of the following need appear unless the appellee is dissatisfied with the appellant's statement:

(1) the jurisdictional statement;

(2) the statement of the issues;

(3) the statement of the case; and

(4) the statement of the standard of review.

(c) **Reply Brief.** The appellant may file a brief in reply to the appellee's brief. Unless the court permits, no further briefs may be filed. A reply brief must contain a table of contents, with page references, and a table of authorities — cases (alphabetically arranged), statutes, and other authorities — with references to the pages of the reply brief where they are cited.

(d) **References to Parties.** In briefs and at oral argument, counsel should minimize use of the terms "appellant" and "appellee." To make briefs clear, counsel should use the parties' actual names or the designations used in the lower court or agency proceeding, or such descriptive terms as "the employee," "the injured person," "the taxpayer," "the ship," "the stevedore."

(e) **References to the Record.** References to the parts of the record contained in the appendix filed with the appellant's brief must be to the pages of the appendix. If the appendix is prepared after the briefs are filed, a party referring to the record must follow one of the methods detailed in Rule 30(c). If the original record is used under Rule 30(f) and is not consecutively paginated, or if the brief refers to an unreproduced part of the record, any reference must be to the page of the original document. For example:

- Answer p. 7;
- Motion for Judgment p. 2;
- Transcript p. 231.

Only clear abbreviations may be used. A party referring to evidence whose admissibility is in controversy must cite the pages of the appendix or of the transcript at which the evidence was identified, offered, and received or rejected.

(f) **Reproduction of Statutes, Rules, Regulations, etc.** If the court's determination of the issues presented requires the study of statutes, rules, regulations, etc., the relevant parts must be set out in the brief or in an addendum at the end, or may be supplied to the court in pamphlet form.

(g) **[Reserved]**

(h) **[Reserved]**

(i) **Briefs in a Case Involving Multiple Appellants or Appellees.** In a case involving more than one appellant or appellee, including consolidated cases, any number of appellants or appellees may join in a brief, and any party may adopt by reference a part of another's brief. Parties may also join in reply briefs.

(j) **Citation of Supplemental Authorities.** If pertinent and significant authorities come to a party's attention after the party's brief has been filed—or after oral argument but before decision—a party may promptly advise the circuit clerk by letter, with a copy to all other parties, setting forth the citations. The letter must state the reasons for the supplemental citations, referring either to the page of the brief or to a point argued orally. The body of the letter must not exceed 350 words. Any response must be made promptly and must be similarly limited.

Rule 28.1. Cross-Appeals

(a) **Applicability.** This rule applies to a case in which a cross-appeal is filed. Rules 28(a)-(c), 31(a)(1), 32(a)(2), and 32(a)(7)(A)-(B) do not apply to such a case, except as otherwise provided in this rule.

(b) **Designation of Appellant.** The party who files a notice of appeal first is the appellant for the purposes of this rule and Rules 30 and 34. If notices are filed on the same day, the plaintiff in the proceeding below is the appellant. These designations may be modified by the parties' agreement or by court order.

(c) **Briefs.** In a case involving a cross-appeal:

(1) **Appellant's Principal Brief.** The appellant must file a principal brief in the appeal. That brief must comply with Rule 28(a).

(2) **Appellee's Principal and Response Brief.** The appellee must file a principal brief in the cross-appeal and must, in the same brief, respond to the principal brief in the appeal. That appellee's brief must comply with Rule 28(a), except that the brief need not include a statement of the case unless the appellee is dissatisfied with the appellant's statement.

(3) **Appellant's Response and Reply Brief.** The appellant must file a brief that responds to the principal brief in the cross-appeal and may, in the same brief, reply to the response in the appeal. That brief must comply with Rule 28(a)(2)-(8) and (10), except that none of the following need appear unless the appellant is dissatisfied with the appellee's statement in the cross-appeal:

    (A) the jurisdictional statement;

    (B) the statement of the issues;

    (C) the statement of the case; and

    (D) the statement of the standard of review.

(4) **Appellee's Reply Brief.** The appellee may file a brief in reply to the response in the cross-appeal. That brief must comply with Rule 28(a)(2)-(3) and (10) and must be limited to the issues presented by the cross-appeal.

(5) **No Further Briefs.** Unless the court permits, no further briefs may be filed in a case involving a cross-appeal.

(d) **Cover.** Except for filings by unrepresented parties, the cover of the appellant's principal brief must be blue; the appellee's principal and response brief, red; the appellant's response and reply brief, yellow; the appellee's reply brief, gray; and intervenor's or amicus curiae's brief, green; and any supplemental brief, tan. The front cover of a brief must contain the information required by Rule 32(a)(2).

(e) **Length.**

(1) **Page Limitation.** Unless it complies with Rule 28.1(e)(2), the appellant's principal brief must not exceed 30 pages; the appellee's principal and response

brief, 35 pages; the appellant's response and reply brief, 30 pages; and the appellee's reply brief, 15 pages.

(2) **Type-Volume Limitation.**

(A) The appellant's principal brief or the appellant's response and reply brief is acceptable if it:

(i) it contains no more than 13,000 words; or

(ii) uses a monospaced face and contains no more than 1,300 lines of text.

(B) The appellee's principal and response brief is acceptable if it:

(i) it contains no more than 15,300 words; or

(ii) uses a monospaced face and contains no more than 1,500 lines of text.

(C) The appellee's reply brief is acceptable if it contains no more than half of the type volume specified in Rule 28.1(e)(2)(A).

(f) **Time to Serve and File a Brief.** Briefs must be served and filed as follows:

(1) the appellant's principal brief, within 40 days after the record is filed;

(2) the appellee's principal and response brief, within 30 days after the appellant's principal brief is served;

(3) the appellant's response and reply brief, within 30 days after the appellee's principal and response brief is served; and

(4) the appellee's reply brief, within 21 days after the appellant's response and reply brief is served, but at least 7 days before argument unless the court, for good cause, allows a later filing.

Rule 29.   Brief of an Amicus Curiae

(a) **During Initial Consideration of a Case on the Merits.**

(1) **Applicability.** This Rule 29(a) governs amicus filings during a court's initial consideration of a case on the merits.

(2) **When Permitted.** The United States or its officer or agency or a state may file an amicus brief without the consent of the parties or leave of court. Any other amicus curiae may file a brief only by leave of court or if the brief states that all parties have consented to its filing, but a court of appeals may prohibit the filing of or may strike an amicus brief that would result in a judge's disqualification.

(3) **Motion for Leave to File.** The motion must be accompanied by the proposed brief and state:

(A) the movant's interest; and

(B) the reason why an amicus brief is desirable and why the matters asserted are relevant to the disposition of the case.

(4) **Contents and Form.** An amicus brief must comply with Rule 32. In addition to the requirements of Rule 32, the cover must identify the party or parties supported and indicate whether the brief supports affirmance or reversal. An amicus brief need not comply with Rule 28, but must include the following:

(A) if the amicus curiae is a corporation, a disclosure statement like that required of parties by Rule 26.1;

(B) a table of contents, with page references;

(C) a table of authorities—cases (alphabetically arranged), statutes, and other authorities—with references to the pages of the brief where they are cited;

(D) a concise statement of the identity of the amicus curiae, its interest in the case, and the source of its authority to file;

(E) unless the amicus curiae is one listed in the first sentence of Rule 29(a), a statement that indicates whether:

(i) a party's counsel authored the brief in whole or in part;

(ii) a party or a party's counsel contributed money that was intended to fund preparing or submitting the brief; and

(iii) a person—other than the amicus curiae, its members, or its counsel—contributed money that was intended to fund preparing or submitting the brief and, if so, identifies each such person;

(F) an argument, which may be preceded by a summary and which need not include a statement of the applicable standard of review; and

(G) a certificate of compliance, if required by Rule 32(a)(7).

(5) **Length.** Except by the court's permission, an amicus brief may be no more than one-half the maximum length authorized by these rules for a party's principal brief. If the court grants a party permission to file a longer brief, that extension does not affect the length of an amicus brief.

(6) **Time for Filing.** An amicus curiae must file its brief, accompanied by a motion for filing when necessary, no later than 7 days after the principal brief of the party being supported is filed. An amicus curiae that does not support either party must file its brief no later than 7 days after the appellant's or petitioner's principal brief is filed. A court may grant leave for later filing, specifying the time within which an opposing party may answer.

(7) **Reply Brief.** Except by the court's permission, an amicus curiae may not file a reply brief.

(8) **Oral Argument.** An amicus curiae may participate in oral argument only with the court's permission.

(b) During Consideration of Whether to Grant Rehearing.

(1) **Applicability.** This Rule 29(b) governs amicus filings during a court's consideration of whether to grant panel rehearing or rehearing en banc, unless a local rule or order in a case provides otherwise.

(2) **When Permitted.** The United States or its officer or agency or a state may file an amicus brief without the consent of the parties or leave of court. Any other amicus curiae may file a brief only by leave of court.

(3) **Motion for Leave to File.** Rule 29(a)(3) applies to a motion for leave.

(4) **Contents, Form, and Length.** Rule 29(a)(4) applies to the amicus brief. The brief must not exceed 2,600 words.

(5) **Time for Filing.** An amicus curiae supporting the petition for rehearing or supporting neither party must file its brief, accompanied by a motion for filing when necessary, no later than 7 days after the petition is filed. An amicus curiae opposing the petition must file its brief, accompanied by a motion for filing when necessary, no later than the date set by the court for the response.

Rule 30.   Appendix to the Briefs

(a) Appellant's Responsibility.
(1) **Contents of the Appendix.** The appellant must prepare and file an appendix to the briefs containing:

    (A) the relevant docket entries in the proceeding below;
    (B) the relevant portions of the pleadings, charge, findings, or opinion;
    (C) the judgment, order, or decision in question; and
    (D) other parts of the record to which the parties wish to direct the court's attention.

(2) **Excluded Material.** Memoranda of law in the district court should not be included in the appendix unless they have independent relevance. Parts of the record may be relied on by the court or the parties even though not included in the appendix.

(3) **Time to File; Number of Copies.** Unless filing is deferred under Rule 30(c), the appellant must file 10 copies of the appendix with the brief and must serve one copy on counsel for each party separately represented. An unrepresented party proceeding in forma pauperis must file 4 legible copies with the clerk, and one copy must be served on counsel for each separately represented party. The court may by local rule or by order in a particular case require the filing or service of a different number.

(b) All Parties' Responsibilities.
(1) **Determining the Contents of the Appendix.** The parties are encouraged to agree on the contents of the appendix. In the absence of an agreement, the appellant must, within 14 days after the record is filed, serve on the appellee a designation of the parts of the record the appellant intends to include in the appendix and a statement of the issues the appellant intends to present for review. The appellee may, within 14 days after receiving the designation, serve on the appellant a designation of additional parts to which it wishes to direct the court's attention. The appellant must include the designated parts in the appendix. The parties must not engage in unnecessary designation of parts of the record, because the entire record is available to the court. This paragraph applies also to a cross-appellant and a cross-appellee.

(2) **Costs of Appendix.** Unless the parties agree otherwise, the appellant must pay the cost of the appendix. If the appellant considers parts of the record designated by the appellee to be unnecessary, the appellant may advise the

appellee, who must then advance the cost of including those parts. The cost of the appendix is a taxable cost. But if any party causes unnecessary parts of the record to be included in the appendix, the court may impose the cost of those parts on that party. Each circuit must, by local rule, provide for sanctions against attorneys who unreasonably and vexatiously increase litigation costs by including unnecessary material in the appendix.

(c) Deferred Appendix.

(1) **Deferral Until After Briefs Are Filed.** The court may provide by rule for classes of cases or by order in a particular case that preparation of the appendix may be deferred until after the briefs have been filed and that the appendix may be filed 21 days after the appellee's brief is served. Even though the filing of the appendix may be deferred, Rule 30(b) applies; except that a party must designate the parts of the record it wants included in the appendix when it serves its brief, and need not include a statement of the issues presented.

(2) **References to the Record.**

(A) If the deferred appendix is used, the parties may cite in their briefs the pertinent pages of the record. When the appendix is prepared, the record pages cited in the briefs must be indicated by inserting record page numbers, in brackets, at places in the appendix where those pages of the record appear.

(B) A party who wants to refer directly to pages of the appendix may serve and file copies of the brief within the time required by Rule 31(a), containing appropriate references to pertinent pages of the record. In that event, within 14 days after the appendix is filed, the party must serve and file copies of the brief, containing references to the pages of the appendix in place of or in addition to the references to the pertinent pages of the record. Except for the correction of typographical errors, no other changes may be made to the brief.

(d) Format of the Appendix. The appendix must begin with a table of contents identifying the page at which each part begins. The relevant docket entries must follow the table of contents. Other parts of the record must follow chronologically. When pages from the transcript of proceedings are placed in the appendix, the transcript page numbers must be shown in brackets immediately before the included pages. Omissions in the text of papers or of the transcript must be indicated by asterisks. Immaterial formal matters (captions, subscriptions, acknowledgments, etc.) should be omitted.

(e) Reproduction of Exhibits. Exhibits designated for inclusion in the appendix may be reproduced in a separate volume, or volumes, suitably indexed. Four copies must be filed with the appendix, and one copy must be served on counsel for each separately represented party. If a transcript of a proceeding before an administrative agency, board, commission, or officer was used in a district-court action and has been designated for inclusion in the appendix, the transcript must be placed in the appendix as an exhibit.

(f) Appeal on the Original Record Without an Appendix. The court may, either by rule for all cases or classes of cases or by order in a particular case, dispense with the appendix and permit an appeal to proceed on the original record with any copies of the record, or relevant parts, that the court may order the parties to file.

Rule 31. Serving and Filing Briefs

(a) Time to Serve and File a Brief.

(1) The appellant must serve and file a brief within 40 days after the record is filed. The appellee must serve and file a brief within 30 days after the appellant's brief is served. The appellant may serve and file a reply brief within 21 days after service of the appellee's brief but a reply brief must be filed at least 7 days before argument, unless the court, for good cause, allows a later filing.

(2) A court of appeals that routinely considers cases on the merits promptly after the briefs are filed may shorten the time to serve and file briefs, either by local rule or by order in a particular case.

(b) Number of Copies. Twenty-five copies of each brief must be filed with the clerk and 2 copies must be served on each unrepresented party and on counsel for each separately represented party. An unrepresented party proceeding in forma pauperis must file 4 legible copies with the clerk, and one copy must be served on each unrepresented party and on counsel for each separately represented party. The court may by local rule or by order in a particular case require the filing or service of a different number.

(c) Consequence of Failure to File. If an appellant fails to file a brief within the time provided by this rule, or within an extended time, an appellee may move to dismiss the appeal. An appellee who fails to file a brief will not be heard at oral argument unless the court grants permission.

Rule 32. Form of Briefs, Appendices, and Other Papers

(a) Form of a Brief.

(1) **Reproduction.**

(A) A brief may be reproduced by any process that yields a clear black image on light paper. The paper must be opaque and unglazed. Only one side of the paper may be used.

(B) Text must be reproduced with a clarity that equals or exceeds the output of a laser printer.

(C) Photographs, illustrations, and tables may be reproduced by any method that results in a good copy of the original; a glossy finish is acceptable if the original is glossy.

(2) **Cover.** Except for filings by unrepresented parties, the cover of the appellant's brief must be blue; the appellee's, red; an intervenor's or amicus curiae's, green; any reply brief, gray and any supplemental brief, tan. The front cover of a brief must contain:

(A) the number of the case centered at the top;

(B) the name of the court;

(C) the title of the case (see Rule 12(a));

(D) the nature of the proceeding (e.g., Appeal, Petition for Review) and the name of the court, agency, or board below;

(E) the title of the brief, identifying the party or parties for whom the brief is filed; and

(F) the name, office address, and telephone number of counsel representing the party for whom the brief is filed.

(3) **Binding.** The brief must be bound in any manner that is secure, does not obscure the text, and permits the brief to lie reasonably flat when open.

(4) **Paper Size, Line Spacing, and Margins.** The brief must be on 8½ by 11 inch paper. The text must be double-spaced, but quotations more than two lines long may be indented and single-spaced. Headings and footnotes may be single-spaced. Margins must be at least one inch on all four sides. Page numbers may be placed in the margins, but no text may appear there.

(5) **Typeface.** Either a proportionally spaced or a monospaced face may be used.

(A) A proportionally spaced face must include serifs, but sans-serif type may be used in headings and captions. A proportionally spaced face must be 14-point or larger.

(B) A monospaced face may not contain more than 10½ characters per inch.

(6) **Type Styles.** A brief must be set in a plain, roman style, although italics or boldface may be used for emphasis. Case names must be italicized or underlined.

(7) **Length.**

(A) **Page limitation.** A principal brief may not exceed 30 pages, or a reply brief 15 pages, unless it complies with Rule 32(a)(7)(B).

(B) **Type-volume limitation.**

(i) A principal brief is acceptable if it:

- contains no more than 13,000 words; or

- it uses a monospaced face and contains no more than 1,300 lines of text.

(ii) A reply brief is acceptable if it contains no more than half of the type volume specified in Rule 32(a)(7)(B)(i).

(b) Form of an Appendix. An appendix must comply with Rule 32(a)(1), (2), (3), and (4), with the following exceptions:

(1) The cover of a separately bound appendix must be white.

(2) An appendix may include a legible photocopy of any document found in the record or of a printed judicial or agency decision.

(3) When necessary to facilitate inclusion of odd-sized documents such as technical drawings, an appendix may be a size other than 8 by 11 inches, and need not lie reasonably flat when opened.

(c) Form of Other Papers.

(1) **Motion.** The form of a motion is governed by Rule 27(d).

(2) **Other Papers.** Any other paper, including a petition for panel rehearing and a petition for hearing or rehearing en banc, and any response to such a petition, must be reproduced in the manner prescribed by Rule 32(a), with the following exceptions:

(A) A cover is not necessary if the caption and signature page of the paper together contain the information required by Rule 32(a)(2). If a cover is used, it must be white.

(B) Rule 32(a)(7) does not apply.

(d) Signature. Every brief, motion, or other paper filed with the court must be signed by the party filing the paper or, if the party is represented, by one of the party's attorneys.

(e) Local Variation. Every court of appeals must accept documents that comply with the form requirements of this rule and the length limits set by these rules. By local rule or order in a particular case a court of appeals may accept documents that do not meet all of the form requirements of this rule or the length limits set by these rules.

(f) Items Excluded from Length. In computing any length limit, headings, footnotes, and quotations count toward the limit but the following items do not:

- the cover page;
- disclosure statement;
- table of contents;
- table of citations;
- statement regarding oral argument;
- addendum containing statues, rules, or regulations;
- certificate of counsel;
- signature block;
- proof of service; and
- any item specifically excluded by these rules or by local rule.

(g) Certificate of Compliance.
(1) Briefs and Papers that Require a Certificate.

A brief submitted under Rules 28.1(e)(2), 29(b)(4), or 32(a)(7)(B)—and a paper submitted under rules 5(c)(1), 21(d)(1), 27(d)(2)(A), 27(d)(2)(C), 35(b)(2)(A), or 40(b)(1)—must include a certificate by the attorney, or an unrepresented part, that the document complies with the type-volume limitation. The person preparing the certificate may rely on the word or line count of the word-processing system used to prepare the document. The certificate must state the number of words—or the number of lines of monospaced type—in the document.

(2) Acceptable Form. Form 6 in the Appendix of Forms meets the requirements for a certificate of compliances.

Rule 32.1.   Citing Judicial Dispositions

(a) Citation Permitted. A court may not prohibit or restrict the citation of federal judicial opinions, orders, judgments, or other written dispositions that have been:

> (i) designated as "unpublished," "not for publication," "nonprecedential," "not precedent," or the like; and
>
> (ii) issued on or after January 1, 2007.

(b) Copies Required. If a party cites a federal judicial opinion, order, judgment, or other written disposition that is not available in a publicly accessible electronic database, the party must file and serve a copy of that opinion, order, judgment, or disposition with the brief or other paper in which it is cited.

Rule 33.   Appeal Conferences

The court may direct the attorneys—and, when appropriate, the parties—to participate in one or more conferences to address any matter that may aid in disposing of the proceedings, including simplifying the issues and discussing settlement. A judge or other person designated by the court may preside over the conference, which may be conducted in person or by telephone. Before a settlement conference, the attorneys must consult with their clients and obtain as much authority as feasible to settle the case. The court may, as a result of the conference, enter an order controlling the course of the proceedings or implementing any settlement agreement.

Rule 34.   Oral Argument

(a) In General.
(1) Party's Statement. Any party may file, or a court may require by local rule, a statement explaining why oral argument should, or need not, be permitted.

(2) **Standards.** Oral argument must be allowed in every case unless a panel of three judges who have examined the briefs and record unanimously agrees that oral argument is unnecessary for any of the following reasons:

 (A) the appeal is frivolous;

 (B) the dispositive issue or issues have been authoritatively decided; or

 (C) the facts and legal arguments are adequately presented in the briefs and record, and the decisional process would not be significantly aided by oral argument.

(b) Notice of Argument; Postponement. The clerk must advise all parties whether oral argument will be scheduled, and, if so, the date, time, and place for it, and the time allowed for each side. A motion to postpone the argument or to allow longer argument must be filed reasonably in advance of the hearing date.

(c) Order and Contents of Argument. The appellant opens and concludes the argument. Counsel must not read at length from briefs, records, or authorities.

(d) Cross-Appeals and Separate Appeals. If there is a cross-appeal, Rule 28.1(b) determines which party is the appellant and which is the appellee for purposes of oral argument. Unless the court directs otherwise, a cross-appeal or separate appeal must be argued when the initial appeal is argued. Separate parties should avoid duplicative argument.

(e) Nonappearance of a Party. If the appellee fails to appear for argument, the court must hear appellant's argument. If the appellant fails to appear for argument, the court may hear the appellee's argument. If neither party appears, the case will be decided on the briefs, unless the court orders otherwise.

(f) Submission on Briefs. The parties may agree to submit a case for decision on the briefs, but the court may direct that the case be argued.

(g) Use of Physical Exhibits at Argument; Removal. Counsel intending to use physical exhibits other than documents at the argument must arrange to place them in the courtroom on the day of the argument before the court convenes. After the argument, counsel must remove the exhibits from the courtroom, unless the court directs otherwise. The clerk may destroy or dispose of the exhibits if counsel does not reclaim them within a reasonable time after the clerk gives notice to remove them.

Rule 35.   En Banc Determination

(a) When Hearing or Rehearing En Banc May Be Ordered. A majority of the circuit judges who are in regular active service and who are not disqualified may order that an appeal or other proceeding be heard or reheard by the court of appeals en banc. An en banc hearing or rehearing is not favored and ordinarily will not be ordered unless:

(1) en banc consideration is necessary to secure or maintain uniformity of the court's decisions; or

(2) the proceeding involves a question of exceptional importance.

(b) Petition for Hearing or Rehearing En Banc. A party may petition for a hearing or rehearing en banc.

(1) The petition must begin with a statement that either:

(A) the panel decision conflicts with a decision of the United States Supreme Court or of the court to which the petition is addressed (with citation to the conflicting case or cases) and consideration by the full court is therefore necessary to secure and maintain uniformity of the court's decisions; or

(B) the proceeding involves one or more questions of exceptional importance, each of which must be concisely stated; for example, a petition may assert that a proceeding presents a question of exceptional importance if it involves an issue on which the panel decision conflicts with the authoritative decisions of other United States Courts of Appeals that have addressed the issue.

(2) Except by the court's permission:

(A) a petition for an en banc hearing or rehearing produced using a computer must not exceed 3,900 words, and

(B) a handwritten or typewritten petition for an en banc hearing or rehearing must not exceed 15 pages.

(3) For purposes of the limits in Rule 35(b)(2), if a party files both a petition for panel rehearing and a petition for rehearing en banc, they are considered a single document even if they are filed separately, unless separate filing is required by local rule.

(c) Time for Petition for Hearing or Rehearing En Banc. A petition that an appeal be heard initially en banc must be filed by the date when the appellee's brief is due. A petition for a rehearing en banc must be filed within the time prescribed by Rule 40 for filing a petition for rehearing.

(d) Number of Copies. The number of copies to be filed must be prescribed by local rule and may be altered by order in a particular case.

(e) Response. No response may be filed to a petition for an en banc consideration unless the court orders a response. The length limits in Rule 35(b)(2) apply to a response.

(f) Call for a Vote. A vote need not be taken to determine whether the case will be heard or reheard en banc unless a judge calls for a vote.

Rule 36.   Entry of Judgment; Notice

(a) **Entry.** A judgment is entered when it is noted on the docket. The clerk must prepare, sign, and enter the judgment:

(1) after receiving the court's opinion—but if settlement of the judgment's form is required, after final settlement; or

(2) if a judgment is rendered without an opinion, as the court instructs.

(b) **Notice.** On the date when judgment is entered, the clerk must serve on all parties a copy of the opinion—or the judgment, if no opinion was written— and a notice of the date when the judgment was entered.

Rule 37.   Interest on Judgment

(a) **When the Court Affirms.** Unless the law provides otherwise, if a money judgment in a civil case is affirmed, whatever interest is allowed by law is payable from the date when the district court's judgment was entered.

(b) **When the Court Reverses.** If the court modifies or reverses a judgment with a direction that a money judgment be entered in the district court, the mandate must contain instructions about the allowance of interest.

Rule 38.   Frivolous Appeal—Damages and Costs

If a court of appeals determines that an appeal is frivolous, it may, after a separately filed motion or notice from the court and reasonable opportunity to respond, award just damages and single or double costs to the appellee.

Rule 39.   Costs

(a) **Against Whom Assessed.** The following rules apply unless the law provides or the court orders otherwise:

(1) if an appeal is dismissed, costs are taxed against the appellant, unless the parties agree otherwise;

(2) if a judgment is affirmed, costs are taxed against the appellant;

(3) if a judgment is reversed, costs are taxed against the appellee;

(4) if a judgment is affirmed in part, reversed in part, modified, or vacated, costs are taxed only as the court orders.

(b) Costs For and Against the United States. Costs for or against the United States, its agency, or officer will be assessed under Rule 39(a) only if authorized by law.

(c) Costs of Copies. Each court of appeals must, by local rule, fix the maximum rate for taxing the cost of producing necessary copies of a brief or appendix, or copies of records authorized by Rule 30(f). The rate must not exceed that generally charged for such work in the area where the clerk's office is located and should encourage economical methods of copying.

(d) Bill of Costs: Objections; Insertion in Mandate.
A party who wants costs taxed must—within 14 days after entry of judgment—file with the circuit clerk and serve an itemized and verified bill of costs.

(2) Objections must be filed within 14 days after service of the bill of costs, unless the court extends the time.

(3) The clerk must prepare and certify an itemized statement of costs for insertion in the mandate, but issuance of the mandate must not be delayed for taxing costs. If the mandate issues before costs are finally determined, the district clerk must—upon the circuit clerk's request—add the statement of costs, or any amendment of it, to the mandate.

(e) Costs on Appeal Taxable in the District Court. The following costs on appeal are taxable in the district court for the benefit of the party entitled to costs under this rule:

(1) the preparation and transmission of the record;

(2) the reporter's transcript, if needed to determine the appeal;

(3) premiums paid for a bond or other security to preserve rights pending appeal; and

(4) the fee for filing the notice of appeal.

Rule 40.   Petition for Panel Rehearing

(a) Time to File; Contents; Answer; Action by the Court if Granted.
(1) **Time.** Unless the time is shortened or extended by order or local rule, a petition for panel rehearing may be filed within 14 days after entry of judgment. But in a civil case, unless an order shortens or extends the time, the petition may be filed by any party within 45 days after entry of judgment if one of the parties is:

(A) the United States;

(B) a United States agency;

(C) a United States officer or employee sued in an official capacity; or

(D) a current or former United States officer or employee sued in an individual capacity for an act or omission occurring in connection with duties performed on the United States' behalf—including all instances in which the United States represents that person when the court of appeals' judgment is entered or files the petition for that person.

(2) **Contents.** The petition must state with particularity each point of law or fact that the petitioner believes the court has overlooked or misapprehended and must argue in support of the petition. Oral argument is not permitted.

(3) **Response.** Unless the court requests, no response to a petition for panel rehearing is permitted. Ordinarily, rehearing will not be granted in the absence of such a request. If a response is requested, the requirements of Rule 40(b) apply to the response.

(4) **Action by the Court.** If a petition for panel rehearing is granted, the court may do any of the following:

(A) make a final disposition of the case without reargument;

(B) restore the case to the calendar for reargument or resubmission; or

(C) issue any other appropriate order.

(b) **Form of Petition; Length.** The petition must comply in form with Rule 32. Copies must be served and filed as Rule 31 prescribes. Except by the court's permission:

(1) a petition for panel rehearing produced using a computer must not exceed 3,900 words; and

(2) a handwritten or typewritten petition for panel rehearing must not exceed 15 pages.

Rule 41.   Mandate: Contents; Issuance and Effective Date; Stay

(a) **Contents.** Unless the court directs that a formal mandate issue, the mandate consists of a certified copy of the judgment, a copy of the court's opinion, if any, and any direction about costs.

(b) **When Issued.** The court's mandate must issue 7 days after the time to file a petition for rehearing expires, or 7 days after entry of an order denying a timely petition for panel rehearing, petition for rehearing en banc, or motion for stay of mandate, whichever is later. The court may shorten or extend the time by order.

(c) **Effective Date.** The mandate is effective when issued.

(d) **Staying the Mandate Pending a Petition for Certiorari.**

(1) **Motion to Stay.** A party may move to stay the mandate pending the filing of a petition for a writ of certiorari in the Supreme Court. The motion must be served on all parties and must show that the petition would present a substantial question and that there is good cause for a stay.

(2) **Duration of Stay; Extensions.** The stay must not exceed 90 days, unless:

    (A) the period is extended for good cause; or

    (B) the party who obtained the stay notifies the circuit clerk in writing within the period of the stay:

        (i) that the time for filing a petition has been extended, in which case the stay continues for the extended period; or

        (ii) that the petition has been filed, in which case the stay continues until the Supreme Court's final disposition.

(3) **Security.** The court may require a bond or other security as a condition to granting or continuing a stay of the mandate.

(4) **Issuance of Mandate.** The court of appeals must issue the mandate immediately on receiving a copy of a Supreme Court order denying the petition, unless extraordinary circumstances exist.

Rule 42.   Voluntary Dismissal

(a) **Dismissal in the District Court.** Before an appeal has been docketed by the circuit clerk, the district court may dismiss the appeal on the filing of a stipulation signed by all parties or on the appellant's motion with notice to all parties.

(b) **Dismissal in the Court of Appeals.** The circuit clerk may dismiss a docketed appeal if the parties file a signed dismissal agreement specifying how costs are to be paid and pay any fees that are due. But no mandate or other process may issue without a court order. An appeal may be dismissed on the appellant's motion on terms agreed to by the parties or fixed by the court.

Rule 43.   Substitution of Parties

(a) **Death of a Party.**

(1) **After Notice of Appeal Is Filed.** If a party dies after a notice of appeal has been filed or while a proceeding is pending in the court of appeals, the decedent's personal representative may be substituted as a party on motion filed with the circuit clerk by the representative or by any party. A party's motion must be served on the representative in accordance with Rule 25. If the decedent has no representative, any party may suggest the death on the record, and the court of appeals may then direct appropriate proceedings.

(2) **Before Notice of Appeal Is Filed—Potential Appellant.** If a party entitled to appeal dies before filing a notice of appeal, the decedent's personal representative—or, if there is no personal representative, the decedent's attorney of record—may file a notice of appeal within the time prescribed by these rules. After the notice of appeal is filed, substitution must be in accordance with Rule 43(a)(1).

(3) **Before Notice of Appeal Is Filed—Potential Appellee.** If a party against whom an appeal may be taken dies after entry of a judgment or order in the district court, but before a notice of appeal is filed, an appellant may proceed as if the death had not occurred. After the notice of appeal is filed, substitution must be in accordance with Rule 43(a)(1).

(b) **Substitution for a Reason Other Than Death.** If a party needs to be substituted for any reason other than death, the procedure prescribed in Rule 43(a) applies.

(c) **Public Officer: Identification; Substitution.**
(1) **Identification of Party.** A public officer who is a party to an appeal or other proceeding in an official capacity may be described as a party by the public officer's official title rather than by name. But the court may require the public officer's name to be added.
(2) **Automatic Substitution of Officeholder.** When a public officer who is a party to an appeal or other proceeding in an official capacity dies, resigns, or otherwise ceases to hold office, the action does not abate. The public officer's successor is automatically substituted as a party. Proceedings following the substitution are to be in the name of the substituted party, but any misnomer that does not affect the substantial rights of the parties may be disregarded. An order of substitution may be entered at any time, but failure to enter an order does not affect the substitution.

Rule 44. Case Involving a Constitutional Question When the United States or the Relevant State Is Not a Party

(a) **Constitutional Challenge to Federal Statute.** If a party questions the constitutionality of an Act of Congress in a proceeding in which the United States or its agency, officer, or employee is not a party in an official capacity, the questioning party must give written notice to the circuit clerk immediately upon the filing of the record or as soon as the question is raised in the court of appeals. The clerk must then certify that fact to the Attorney General.

(b) **Constitutional Challenge to State Statute.** If a party questions the constitutionality of a statute of a State in a proceeding in which that State or its agency, officer, or employee is not a party in an official capacity, the questioning party must give written notice to the circuit clerk immediately upon the filing of the record or as soon as the question is raised in the court of appeals. The clerk must then certify that fact to the attorney general of the State.

Rule 45.   Clerk's Duties

(a) General Provisions.

(1) **Qualifications.** The circuit clerk must take the oath and post any bond required by law. Neither the clerk nor any deputy clerk may practice as an attorney or counselor in any court while in office.

(2) **When Court Is Open.** The court of appeals is always open for filing any paper, issuing and returning process, making a motion, and entering an order. The clerk's office with the clerk or a deputy in attendance must be open during business hours on all days except Saturdays, Sundays, and legal holidays. A court may provide by local rule or by order that the clerk's office be open for specified hours on Saturdays or on legal holidays other than New Year's Day, Martin Luther King, Jr.'s Birthday, Washington's Birthday, Memorial Day, Independence Day, Labor Day, Columbus Day, Veterans' Day, Thanksgiving Day, and Christmas Day.

(b) Records.

(1) **The Docket.** The circuit clerk must maintain a docket and an index of all docketed cases in the manner prescribed by the Director of the Administrative Office of the United States Courts. The clerk must record all papers filed with the clerk and all process, orders, and judgments.

(2) **Calendar.** Under the court's direction, the clerk must prepare a calendar of cases awaiting argument. In placing cases on the calendar for argument, the clerk must give preference to appeals in criminal cases and to other proceedings and appeals entitled to preference by law.

(3) **Other Records.** The clerk must keep other books and records required by the Director of the Administrative Office of the United States Courts, with the approval of the Judicial Conference of the United States, or by the court.

(c) Notice of an Order or Judgment. Upon the entry of an order or judgment, the circuit clerk must immediately serve a notice of entry on each party, with a copy of any opinion, and must note the date of service on the docket. Service on a party represented by counsel must be made on counsel.

(d) Custody of Records and Papers. The circuit clerk has custody of the court's records and papers. Unless the court orders or instructs otherwise, the clerk must not permit an original record or paper to be taken from the clerk's office. Upon disposition of the case, original papers constituting the record on appeal or review must be returned to the court or agency from which they were received. The clerk must preserve a copy of any brief, appendix, or other paper that has been filed.

Rule 46.   Attorneys

(a) Admission to the Bar.

(1) **Eligibility.** An attorney is eligible for admission to the bar of a court of appeals if that attorney is of good moral and professional character and is admitted to practice before the Supreme Court of the United States, the highest court of a state, another United States court of appeals, or a United States district court (including the district courts for Guam, the Northern Mariana Islands, and the Virgin Islands).

(2) **Application.** An applicant must file an application for admission, on a form approved by the court that contains the applicant's personal statement showing eligibility for membership. The applicant must subscribe to the following oath or affirmation:

"I, _____, do solemnly swear [or affirm] that I will conduct myself as an attorney and counselor of this court, uprightly and according to law; and that I will support the Constitution of the United States."

(3) **Admission Procedures.** On written or oral motion of a member of the court's bar, the court will act on the application. An applicant may be admitted by oral motion in open court. But, unless the court orders otherwise, an applicant need not appear before the court to be admitted. Upon admission, an applicant must pay the clerk the fee prescribed by local rule or court order.

(b) Suspension or Disbarment.

(1) **Standard.** A member of the court's bar is subject to suspension or disbarment by the court if the member:

(A) has been suspended or disbarred from practice in any other court; or

(B) is guilty of conduct unbecoming a member of the court's bar.

(2) **Procedure.** The member must be given an opportunity to show good cause, within the time prescribed by the court, why the member should not be suspended or disbarred.

(3) **Order.** The court must enter an appropriate order after the member responds and a hearing is held, if requested, or after the time prescribed for a response expires, if no response is made.

(c) Discipline. A court of appeals may discipline an attorney who practices before it for conduct unbecoming a member of the bar or for failure to comply with any court rule. First, however, the court must afford the attorney reasonable notice, an opportunity to show cause to the contrary, and, if requested, a hearing.

Rule 47.   Local Rules by Courts of Appeals

(a) Local Rules.

(1) Each court of appeals acting by a majority of its judges in regular active service may, after giving appropriate public notice and opportunity for comment, make and amend rules governing its practice. A generally applicable direction to parties or lawyers regarding practice before a court must be in a local rule rather than an internal operating procedure or standing order. A local rule must be consistent with—but not duplicative of—Acts of Congress and rules adopted under 28 U.S.C. §2072 and must conform to any uniform numbering system prescribed by the Judicial Conference of the United States. Each circuit clerk must send the Administrative Office of the United States Courts a copy of each local rule and internal operating procedure when it is promulgated or amended.

(2) A local rule imposing a requirement of form must not be enforced in a manner that causes a party to lose rights because of a nonwillful failure to comply with the requirement.

(b) Procedure When There Is No Controlling Law. A court of appeals may regulate practice in a particular case in any manner consistent with federal law, these rules, and local rules of the circuit. No sanction or other disadvantage may be imposed for noncompliance with any requirement not in federal law, federal rules, or the local circuit rules unless the alleged violator has been furnished in the particular case with actual notice of the requirement.

Rule 48.   Masters

(a) Appointment; Powers. A court of appeals may appoint a special master to hold hearings, if necessary, and to recommend factual findings and disposition in matters ancillary to proceedings in the court. Unless the order referring a matter to a master specifies or limits the master's powers, those powers include, but are not limited to, the following:

(1) regulating all aspects of a hearing;

(2) taking all appropriate action for the efficient performance of the master's duties under the order;

(3) requiring the production of evidence on all matters embraced in the reference; and

(4) administering oaths and examining witnesses and parties.

(b) Compensation. If the master is not a judge or court employee, the court must determine the master's compensation and whether the cost is to be charged to any party.

Form lA
Notice of Appeal to a Court of Appeals From a
Judgment of a District Court

United States District Court for the _____
District of _____
Docket Number _____

A.B., Plaintiff	
v.	Notice of Appeal
C.D., Defendant	

_____ _____(name all parties taking the appeal)* appeal to the United States Court of Appeals for the __ Circuit from the final judgment entered on ___ (state the date the judgment was entered)

(s) _____
Attorney for _____
Address: _____

[**Note to inmate filers:** *If you are an inmate confined in an institution and you seek the timing benefit of Fed. R. App. P. 4(c)(J), complete Form 7 (Declaration of Inmate Filing) and file that declaration with this Notice of Appeal.*]

* See Rule 3(c) for permissible ways of identifying appellants.

* * * * *

Form lB
Notice of Appeal to a Court of Appeals From an
Appealable Order of a District Court

United States District Court for the _____
District of _____
Docket Number _____

A.B., Plaintiff v. C.D., Defendant	Notice of Appeal

_____(name all parties taking the appeal)* appeal to the United States Court of Appeals for the __ Circuit from the order entered on __ (state the date the judgment was entered)

(s) _____
Attorney for _____
Address: _____

[**Note to inmate filers:** *If you are an inmate confined in an institution and you seek the timing benefit of Fed. R. App. P. 4(c)(J), complete Form 7 (Declaration of Inmate Filing) and file that declaration with this Notice of Appeal.*]

* See Rule 3(c) for permissible ways of identifying appellants.

PART II

SUPPLEMENTAL MATERIALS

PLEADINGS AND RELATED MOTIONS

I

Page 30. Insert after Problem 1-2.

PROBLEM

1-2a. In 1993, Foster was convicted of various serious offenses relating to a carjacking and was sentenced to a term of life with the possibility of parole plus 12 years. To serve that sentence, Foster was assigned to Corcoran State Prison. On August 17, 2017, Foster and approximately 150 other prisoners were involved in what he describes as a racial incident in the Corcoran recreational yard. During the incident, Foster was injured and transported from Corcoran to the Kaweah Delta Medical Center in Visalia for treatment of his injuries. While Foster was there, prison officials took possession of his personal property, including legal papers, tennis shoes, a watch, sunglasses, shorts, toiletries, canteen food, and orthopedic boots. On his return to Corcoran, Foster requested the return of his personal property, but prison officials were unable to locate it. In response, Foster sued the appropriate prison officials for conversion. The essential elements of conversion are: (a) plaintiff's ownership or right to possession of personal property, (b) defendant's disposition of property in a manner inconsistent with plaintiff's property rights, and (c) resulting damages. Foster's complaint alleges that prior to his transfer he lawfully owned and possessed the above specified property, that prison officials took custody of that property during his stay at the Medical Center, that those officials failed to inventory and safely secure that property, leaving it instead in a supply room to which unsupervised inmates had access, and that prison officials have, in response to a proper demand, failed to return that property. In accord with *Doe v. City of Los Angeles*, has Foster pleaded facts sufficient to state a cause of action? More specifically, would Foster's allegations constitute conclusions of law or ultimate facts? Would he be required to describe the evidence on which he premised his allegations? What role might the doctrine of less particularity play in your assessment of the adequacy of the above allegations? *See Foster v. Sexton*, 61 Cal. App. 5th 998 (2021).

Page 70. Insert before subsection d.

PROBLEM

1-8(a). Whitaker, a quadriplegic who must use a wheelchair, sued Tesla Motors, Inc., in a United States District Court for violations of Title III of the Americans with Disabilities Act (ADA). The ADA provides that "no individual shall be discriminated against on the basis of disability in the full and equal enjoyment of the goods, services, facilities, privileges, advantages, or accommodations of any place of public accommodation." Thus, the ADA requires plaintiffs suing under it to allege and prove that they are disabled within the meaning of the ADA; that the defendant owns, leases, or operates a place of public accommodation—a business open to the public; and that defendant denied the plaintiff access to that place of public accommodation due to plaintiff's disability. Thus, a university that failed to provide wheelchair ramps to classrooms would likely be in violation of the ADA. Essentially, the ADA requires covered businesses to make reasonable accommodations for the disabled.

According to his complaint, Whitaker visited a Tesla dealership in Sherman Oaks, California ("the Dealership"), in July of 2019 and encountered inaccessible service counters that denied him full and equal access to the Dealership and "created difficulty and discomfort." The complaint further alleges that Tesla's continued failure to provide accessible service counters deters him from returning to the Dealership. Whitaker alleges "on information and belief, that there are other violations and barriers on the site that relate to his disability." More specifically, the complaint alleges:

- Whitaker is a quadriplegic and disabled within the meaning of the ADA;
- Tesla owns the Dealership, which is a "place of public accommodation" under the ADA;
- The Dealership contains an easily removed barrier to the service counter, which Tesla has failed to remove;
- Whitaker encountered this barrier on his visit to the Dealership; and
- The barrier continues to impact him because either he will return and face it again or he is being deterred from returning because of his knowledge of the barrier.

Tesla has filed a Rule 12(b)(6) motion to dismiss. Given the decision in *Ashcroft v. Iqbal*, how should the District Court rule? In answering this question consider whether any of these allegations are conclusory and whether collectively the factual allegations state a plausible claim for relief. See *Whitaker v. Tesla Motors, Inc.*, 985 F.3d 1173 (9th Cir. 2021).

PERSONAL JURISDICTION

II

Page 180. Insert below Note 1 in NOTES AND QUESTIONS.

World-Wide Volkswagen Corp. v. Woodson
444 U.S. 286 (1980)

Mr. Justice WHITE delivered the opinion of the Court.

The issue before us is whether, consistently with the Due Process Clause of the Fourteenth Amendment, an Oklahoma court may exercise *in personam* jurisdiction over a nonresident automobile retailer and its wholesale distributor in a products-liability action, when the defendants' only connection with Oklahoma is the fact that an automobile sold in New York to New York residents became involved in an accident in Oklahoma.

I

Respondents Harry and Kay Robinson purchased a new Audi automobile from petitioner Seaway Volkswagen, Inc. (Seaway), in Massena, N. Y., in 1976. The following year the Robinson family, who resided in New York, left that State for a new home in Arizona. As they passed through the State of Oklahoma, another car struck their Audi in the rear, causing a fire which severely burned Kay Robinson and her two children.

The Robinsons subsequently brought a products-liability action in the District Court for Creek County, Okla., claiming that their injuries resulted from defective design and placement of the Audi's gas tank and fuel system. They joined as defendants the automobile's manufacturer, Audi NSU Auto Union Aktiengesellschaft (Audi); its importer Volkswagen of America, Inc. (Volkswagen); its regional distributor, petitioner World-Wide Volkswagen Corp. (World-Wide); and its retail dealer, petitioner Seaway. Seaway and World-Wide entered special appearances, claiming that Oklahoma's exercise of jurisdiction over them would offend the limitations on the State's jurisdiction imposed by the Due Process Clause of the Fourteenth Amendment.

The facts presented to the District Court showed that World-Wide is incorporated and has its business office in New York. It distributes vehicles, parts, and accessories, under contract with Volkswagen, to retail dealers in New York, New Jersey, and Connecticut. Seaway, one of these retail dealers, is incorporated and has its place of business in New York. Insofar as the record reveals, Seaway and World-Wide are fully independent corporations whose relations with each other and with Volkswagen and Audi are contractual only. Respondents adduced no evidence that either World-Wide or Seaway does any business in Oklahoma, ships or sells any products to or in that State, has an agent to receive process there, or purchases advertisements in any media calculated to reach Oklahoma. In fact, as respondents' counsel conceded at oral argument, Tr. of Oral Arg. 32, there was no showing that any automobile sold by World-Wide or Seaway has ever entered Oklahoma with the single exception of the vehicle involved in the present case.

Despite the apparent paucity of contacts between petitioners and Oklahoma, the District Court rejected their constitutional claim and reaffirmed that ruling in denying petitioners' motion for reconsideration.[5] Petitioners then sought a writ of prohibition in the Supreme Court of Oklahoma to restrain the District Judge, respondent Charles S. Woodson, from exercising *in personam* jurisdiction over them. They renewed their contention that, because they had no "minimal contacts," App. 32, with the State of Oklahoma, the actions of the District Judge were in violation of their rights under the Due Process Clause.

The Supreme Court of Oklahoma denied the writ, holding that personal jurisdiction over petitioners was authorized by Oklahoma's "long-arm" statute. Although the court noted that the proper approach was to test jurisdiction against both statutory and constitutional standards, its analysis did not distinguish these questions, probably because has been interpreted as conferring jurisdiction to the limits permitted by the United States Constitution. The court's rationale was contained in the following paragraph,

> "In the case before us, the product being sold and distributed by the petitioners is by its very design and purpose so mobile that petitioners can foresee its possible use in Oklahoma. This is especially true of the distributor, who has the exclusive right to distribute such automobile in New York, New Jersey and Connecticut. The evidence presented below demonstrated that goods sold and distributed by the petitioners were used in the State of Oklahoma, and under the facts we believe it reasonable to infer, given the retail value of the automobile, that the petitioners derive substantial income from automobiles which from time to time are used in the State of Oklahoma. This being the case, we hold that under the facts presented, the trial court was justified in concluding that the petitioners derive substantial revenue from goods used or consumed in this State."

We granted certiorari to consider an important constitutional question with respect to state-court jurisdiction and to resolve a conflict between the Supreme Court of Oklahoma and the highest courts of at least four other States. We reverse.

II

The Due Process Clause of the Fourteenth Amendment limits the power of a state court to render a valid personal judgment against a nonresident defendant.

Personal Jurisdiction

A judgment rendered in violation of due process is void in the rendering State and is not entitled to full faith and credit elsewhere. Due process requires that the defendant be given adequate notice of the suit and be subject to the personal jurisdiction of the court, *International Shoe Co. v. Washington*, 326 U.S. 310 (1945). In the present case, it is not contended that notice was inadequate; the only question is whether these particular petitioners were subject to the jurisdiction of the Oklahoma courts.

As has long been settled, and as we reaffirm today, a state court may exercise personal jurisdiction over a nonresident defendant only so long as there exist "minimum contacts" between the defendant and the forum. The concept of minimum contacts, in turn, can be seen to perform two related, but distinguishable, functions. It protects the defendant against the burdens of litigating in a distant or inconvenient forum. And it acts to ensure that the States through their courts, do not reach out beyond the limits imposed on them by their status as coequal sovereigns in a federal system.

The protection against inconvenient litigation is typically described in terms of "reasonableness" or "fairness." We have said that the defendant's contacts with the forum State must be such that maintenance of the suit "does not offend 'traditional notions of fair play and substantial justice.' " *International Shoe Co. v. Washington, supra,* at 316. The relationship between the defendant and the forum must be such that it is "reasonable . . . to require the corporation to defend the particular suit which is brought there." 326 U.S., at 317. Implicit in this emphasis on reasonableness is the understanding that the burden on the defendant, while always a primary concern, will in an appropriate case be considered in light of other relevant factors, including the forum State's interest in adjudicating the dispute; the plaintiff's interest in obtaining convenient and effective relief, at least when that interest is not adequately protected by the plaintiff's power to choose the forum; the interstate judicial system's interest in obtaining the most efficient resolution of controversies; and the shared interest of the several States in furthering fundamental substantive social policies.

The limits imposed on state jurisdiction by the Due Process Clause, in its role as a guarantor against inconvenient litigation, have been substantially relaxed over the years. As we noted in *McGee v. International Life Ins. Co., supra,* 355 U.S., at 222-223, this trend is largely attributable to a fundamental transformation in the American economy:

> "Today many commercial transactions touch two or more States and may involve parties separated by the full continent. With this increasing nationalization of commerce has come a great increase in the amount of business conducted by mail across state lines. At the same time modern transportation and communication have made it much less burdensome for a party sued to defend himself in a State where he engages in economic activity."

The historical developments noted in *McGee*, of course, have only accelerated in the generation since that case was decided.

Nevertheless, we have never accepted the proposition that state lines are irrelevant for jurisdictional purposes, nor could we, and remain faithful to the principles of interstate federalism embodied in the Constitution. The economic interdependence of the States was foreseen and desired by the Framers. In the Commerce Clause, they provided that the Nation was to be a common market, a "free trade unit" in which the States are debarred from acting as separable economic entities. But the Framers also intended that the States retain many essential attributes of sovereignty, including, in particular, the sovereign power to try causes in their courts. The sovereignty of each State, in turn, implied a limitation on the sovereignty of all of its sister States—a limitation express or implicit in both the original scheme of the Constitution and the Fourteenth Amendment.

Hence, even while abandoning the shibboleth that "[t]he authority of every tribunal is necessarily restricted by the territorial limits of the State in which it is established," we emphasized that the reasonableness of asserting jurisdiction over the defendant must be assessed "in the context of our federal system of government," *International Shoe Co. v. Washington*, 326 U.S., at 317, and stressed that the Due Process Clause ensures not only fairness, but also the "orderly administration of the laws," *id.*, at 319. As we noted in *Hanson v. Denckla*, 357 U.S. 235, 250-251 (1958):

> "As technological progress has increased the flow of commerce between the States, the need for jurisdiction over nonresidents has undergone a similar increase. At the same time, progress in communications and transportation has made the defense of a suit in a foreign tribunal less burdensome. In response to these changes, the requirements for personal jurisdiction over nonresidents have evolved from the rigid rule of *Pennoyer v. Neff*, to the flexible standard of *International Shoe Co. v. Washington*. But it is a mistake to assume that this trend heralds the eventual demise of all restrictions on the personal jurisdiction of state courts. [Citation omitted.] Those restrictions are more than a guarantee of immunity from inconvenient or distant litigation. They are a consequence of territorial limitations on the power of the respective States."

Thus, the Due Process Clause "does not contemplate that a state may make binding a judgment *in personam* against an individual or corporate defendant with which the state has no contacts, ties, or relations." Even if the defendant would suffer minimal or no inconvenience from being forced to litigate before the tribunals of another State; even if the forum State has a strong interest in applying its law to the controversy; even if the forum State is the most convenient location for litigation, the Due Process Clause, acting as an instrument of interstate federalism, may sometimes act to divest the State of its power to render a valid judgment.

III

Applying these principles to the case at hand, we find in the record before us a total absence of those affiliating circumstances that are a necessary predicate to any exercise of state-court jurisdiction. Petitioners carry on no activity whatsoever in Oklahoma. They close no sales and perform no services there. They avail themselves of none of the privileges and benefits of Oklahoma law. They solicit no business there either through salespersons or through advertising reasonably calculated to reach the State. Nor does the record show that they regularly sell cars at wholesale or retail to Oklahoma customers or residents or that they indirectly, through others, serve or seek to serve the Oklahoma market. In short, respondents seek to base jurisdiction on one, isolated occurrence and whatever inferences can be drawn therefrom: the fortuitous circumstance that a single Audi automobile, sold in New York to New York residents, happened to suffer an accident while passing through Oklahoma.

It is argued, however, that because an automobile is mobile by its very design and purpose it was "foreseeable" that the Robinsons' Audi would cause injury in Oklahoma. Yet "foreseeability" alone has never been a sufficient benchmark for personal jurisdiction under the Due Process Clause. In *Hanson v. Denckla, supra,* it was no doubt foreseeable that the settlor of a Delaware trust would subsequently move to Florida and seek to exercise a power of appointment there; yet we held that Florida courts could not constitutionally exercise jurisdiction over a Delaware trustee that had no other contacts with the forum State. In *Kulko v. California Superior Court,* 436 U.S. 84 (1978), it was surely "foreseeable" that a divorced wife would move to California from New York, the domicile of the marriage, and that a minor daughter would live with the mother. Yet we held that California could not exercise jurisdiction in a child-support action over the former husband who had remained in New York.

If foreseeability were the criterion, a local California tire retailer could be forced to defend in Pennsylvania when a blowout occurs there; a Wisconsin seller of a defective automobile jack could be haled before a distant court for damage caused in New Jersey; or a Florida soft-drink concessionaire could be summoned to Alaska to account for injuries happening there. Every seller of chattels would in effect appoint the chattel his agent for service of process. His amenability to suit would travel with the chattel. We recently abandoned the outworn rule of *Harris v. Balk,* 198 U.S. 215 (1905), that the interest of a creditor in a debt could be extinguished or otherwise affected by any State having transitory jurisdiction over the debtor. *Shaffer v. Heitner,* 433 U.S. 186 (1977). Having inferred the mechanical rule that a creditor's amenability to a *quasi in rem* action travels with his debtor, we are unwilling to endorse an analogous principle in the present case.

This is not to say, of course, that foreseeability is wholly irrelevant. But the foreseeability that is critical to due process analysis is not the mere likelihood that a product will find its way into the forum State. Rather, it is that the defendant's conduct and connection with the forum State are such that he should reasonably anticipate being haled into court there. The Due Process Clause, by ensuring the "orderly administration of the laws," gives a degree of predictability to the legal system that allows potential defendants to structure their primary conduct with some minimum assurance as to where that conduct will and will not render them liable to suit.

When a corporation "purposefully avails itself of the privilege of conducting activities within the forum State," it has clear notice that it is subject to suit there, and can act to alleviate the risk of burdensome litigation by procuring insurance, passing the expected costs on to customers, or, if the risks are too great, severing its connection with the State. Hence if the sale of a product of a manufacturer or distributor such as Audi or Volkswagen is not simply an isolated occurrence, but arises from the efforts of the manufacturer or distributor to serve directly or indirectly, the market for its product in other States, it is not unreasonable to subject it to suit in one of those States if its allegedly defective merchandise has there been the source of injury to its owner or to others. The forum State does not exceed its powers under the Due Process Clause if it asserts personal jurisdiction over a corporation that delivers its products into the stream of commerce with the expectation that they will be purchased by consumers in the forum State.

But there is no such or similar basis for Oklahoma jurisdiction over World-Wide or Seaway in this case. Seaway's sales are made in Massena, N. Y. World-Wide's market, although substantially larger, is limited to dealers in New York, New Jersey, and Connecticut. There is no evidence of record that any automobiles distributed by World-Wide are sold to retail customers outside this tristate area. It is foreseeable that the purchasers of automobiles sold by World-Wide and Seaway may take them to Oklahoma. But the mere "unilateral activity of those who claim some relationship with a nonresident defendant cannot satisfy the requirement of contact with the forum State."

In a variant on the previous argument, it is contended that jurisdiction can be supported by the fact that petitioners earn substantial revenue from goods used in Oklahoma. The Oklahoma Supreme Court so found, drawing the inference that because one automobile sold by petitioners had been used in Oklahoma, others might have been used there also. While this inference seems less than compelling on the facts of the instant case, we need not question the court's factual findings in order to reject its reasoning.

This argument seems to make the point that the purchase of automobiles in New York, from which the petitioners earn substantial revenue, would not occur *but for* the fact that the automobiles are capable of use in distant States like Oklahoma. Respondents observe that the very purpose of an automobile is to travel, and that travel of automobiles sold by petitioners is facilitated by an extensive chain of Volkswagen service centers throughout the country, including some in Oklahoma. However, financial benefits accruing to the defendant from a collateral relation to the forum State will not support jurisdiction if they do not stem from a constitutionally cognizable contact with that State. In our view, whatever marginal revenues petitioners may receive by virtue of the fact that their products are capable of use in Oklahoma is far too attenuated a contact to justify that State's exercise of *in personam* jurisdiction over them.

Personal Jurisdiction

Because we find that petitioners have no "contacts, ties, or relations" with the State of Oklahoma, the judgment of the Supreme Court of Oklahoma is *Reversed.*

Mr. Justice BRENNAN, dissenting. . . .

[T]he interest of the forum State and its connection to the litigation is strong. The automobile accident underlying the litigation occurred in Oklahoma. The plaintiffs were hospitalized in Oklahoma when they brought suit. Essential witnesses and evidence were in Oklahoma. The State has a legitimate interest in enforcing its laws designed to keep its highway system safe, and the trial can proceed at least as efficiently in Oklahoma as anywhere else.

The petitioners are not unconnected with the forum. Although both sell automobiles within limited sales territories, each sold the automobile which in fact was driven to Oklahoma where it was involved in an accident. It may be true, as the Court suggests, that each sincerely intended to limit its commercial impact to the limited territory, and that each intended to accept the benefits and protection of the laws only of those States within the territory. But obviously these were unrealistic hopes that cannot be treated as an automatic constitutional shield.

An automobile simply is not a stationary item or one designed to be used in one place. An automobile is *intended* to be moved around. Someone in the business of selling large numbers of automobiles can hardly plead ignorance of their mobility or pretend that the automobiles stay put after they are sold. It is not merely that a dealer in automobiles foresees that they will move. The dealer actually intends that the purchasers will use the automobiles to travel to distant States where the dealer does not directly "do business." The sale of an automobile does *purposefully* inject the vehicle into the stream of interstate commerce so that it can travel to distant States. . . .

Mr. Justice MARSHALL, with whom Mr. Justice BLACKMUN joins, dissenting. . . .

This is a difficult case, and reasonable minds may differ as to whether respondents have alleged a sufficient "relationship among the defendant[s], the forum, and the litigation," to satisfy the requirements of *International Shoe*. I am concerned, however, that the majority has reached its result by taking an unnecessarily narrow view of petitioners' forum-related conduct. The majority asserts that "respondents seek to base jurisdiction on one, isolated occurrence and whatever inferences can be drawn therefrom: the fortuitous circumstance that a single Audi automobile, sold in New York to New York residents, happened to suffer an accident while passing through Oklahoma." If that were the case, I would readily agree that the minimum contacts necessary to sustain jurisdiction are not present. But the basis for the assertion of jurisdiction is not the happenstance that an individual over whom petitioner had no control made a unilateral decision to take a chattel with him to a distant State. Rather, jurisdiction is premised on the deliberate and purposeful actions of the defendants themselves in choosing to become part of a nationwide, indeed a global, network for marketing and servicing automobiles. . . .

Mr. Justice BLACKMUN, dissenting. . . .

For me, a critical factor in the disposition of the litigation is the nature of the instrumentality under consideration. It has been said that we are a nation on wheels. What we are concerned with here is the automobile and its peripatetic character. One need only examine our national network of interstate highways, or make an appearance on one of them, or observe the variety of license plates present not only on those highways but in any metropolitan area, to realize that any automobile is likely to wander far from its place of licensure or from its place of distribution and retail sale. Miles per gallon on the highway (as well as in the city) and mileage per tankful are familiar allegations in manufacturers' advertisements today. To expect that any new automobile will remain in the vicinity of its retail sale—like the 1914 electric driven car by the proverbial "little old lady"—is to blink at reality. The automobile is intended for distance as well as for transportation within a limited area. . . .

Page 212. Insert before Problem 2-15.

Bristol-Myers Squibb Co. v. Superior Court
137 S. Ct. 1773 (2017)

JUSTICE ALITO delivered the opinion of the Court.

More than 600 plaintiffs, most of whom are not California residents, filed this civil action in a California state court against Bristol-Myers Squibb Company (BMS), asserting a variety of state-law claims based on injuries allegedly caused by a BMS drug called Plavix. The California Supreme Court held that the California courts have specific jurisdiction to entertain the nonresidents' claims. We now reverse.

I

A

BMS, a large pharmaceutical company, is incorporated in Delaware and headquartered in New York, and it maintains substantial operations in both New York and New Jersey. Over 50 percent of BMS's work force in the United States is employed in those two States.

BMS also engages in business activities in other jurisdictions, including California. Five of the company's research and laboratory facilities, which employ a total of around 160 employees, are located there. BMS also employs about 250 sales representatives in California and maintains a small state-government advocacy office in Sacramento.

One of the pharmaceuticals that BMS manufactures and sells is Plavix, a prescription drug that thins the blood and inhibits blood clotting. BMS did not develop Plavix in California, did not create a marketing strategy for Plavix in California, and did not manufacture, label, package, or work on the regulatory approval of the product in California. BMS instead engaged in all of these activities in either New York or New Jersey. *Ibid.* But BMS does sell Plavix in California. Between 2006 and 2012, it sold almost 187 million Plavix pills in the State and took in more than $900 million from those sales. This amounts to a little over one percent of the company's nationwide sales revenue.

B

A group of plaintiffs—consisting of 86 California residents and 592 residents from 33 other States—filed eight separate complaints in California Superior Court, alleging that Plavix had damaged their health. All the complaints asserted 13 claims under California law, including products liability, negligent misrepresentation, and misleading advertising claims. The nonresident plaintiffs did not allege that they obtained Plavix through California physicians or from any other California source; nor did they claim that they were injured by Plavix or were treated for their injuries in California.

Asserting lack of personal jurisdiction, BMS moved to quash service of summons on the nonresidents' claims, but the California Superior Court denied this motion, finding that the California courts had general jurisdiction over BMS "[b]ecause [it] engages in extensive activities in California." App. to Pet. for Cert. 150. BMS unsuccessfully petitioned the State Court of Appeal for a writ of mandate, but after our decision on general jurisdiction in *Daimler Ag v. Bauman*, 134 S. Ct. 746 (2014), the California Supreme Court instructed the Court of Appeal "to vacate its order denying mandate and to issue an order to show cause why relief sought in the petition should not be granted."

The Court of Appeal then changed its decision on the question of general jurisdiction. Under *Daimler*, it held, general jurisdiction was clearly lacking, but it went on to find that the California courts had specific jurisdiction over the nonresidents' claims against BMS.

The California Supreme Court affirmed. The court unanimously agreed with the Court of Appeal on the issue of general jurisdiction, but the court was divided on the question of specific jurisdiction. The majority applied a "sliding scale approach to specific jurisdiction." Under this approach, "the more wide ranging the defendant's forum contacts, the more readily is shown a connection between the forum contacts and the claim." *Ibid.* (internal quotation marks omitted). Applying this test, the majority concluded that "BMS's extensive contacts with California" permitted the exercise of specific jurisdiction "based on a less direct connection between BMS's forum activities and plaintiffs' claims than might otherwise be required." This attenuated requirement was met, the majority found, because the claims of the nonresidents were similar in several ways to the claims of the California residents (as to which specific jurisdiction was uncontested). The court noted that "[b]oth the resident and nonresident plaintiffs' claims are based on the same allegedly defective product and the assertedly misleading marketing and promotion of that product.". And while acknowledging that "there is no claim that Plavix itself was designed and developed in [BMS's California research facilities]," the court thought it significant that other research was done in the State.

Three justices dissented. "The claims of . . . nonresidents injured by their use of Plavix they purchased and used in other states," they wrote, "in no sense arise from BMS's marketing and sales of Plavix in California," and they found that the "mere similarity" of the residents' and nonresidents' claims was not enough. The dissent accused the majority of "expand[ing] specific jurisdiction to the point that, for a large category of defendants, it becomes indistinguishable from general jurisdiction."

We granted certiorari to decide whether the California courts' exercise of jurisdiction in this case violates the Due Process Clause of the Fourteenth Amendment.

II

A

It has long been established that the Fourteenth Amendment limits the personal jurisdiction of state courts. Because "[a] state court's assertion of jurisdiction exposes defendants to the State's coercive power," it is "subject to review for compatibility with the Fourteenth Amendment's Due Process Clause," *Goodyear Dunlop Tires Operations, S.A. v. Brown*, 564 U.S. 915, 918 (2011), which "limits the power of a state court to render a valid personal judgment against a nonresident defendant," *World-Wide Volkswagen v. Woodson*, 444 U.S. 286, 291 (1980). The primary focus of our personal jurisdiction inquiry is the defendant's relationship to the forum State.

Since our seminal decision in *International Shoe*, our decisions have recognized two types of personal jurisdiction: "general" (sometimes called "all purpose") jurisdiction and "specific" (sometimes called "case-linked") jurisdiction. "For an individual, the paradigm forum for the exercise of general jurisdiction is the individual's domicile; for a corporation, it is an equivalent place, one in which the corporation is fairly regarded as at home." A court with general jurisdiction may hear *any* claim against that defendant, even if all the incidents underlying the claim occurred in a different State. But "only a limited set of affiliations with a forum will render a defendant amenable to" general jurisdiction in that State.

Personal Jurisdiction

Specific jurisdiction is very different. In order for a state court to exercise specific jurisdiction, "the *suit*" must "aris[e] out of or relat[e] to the defendant's contacts with the *forum*." In other words, there must be "an affiliation between the forum and the underlying controversy, principally, [an] activity or an occurrence that takes place in the forum State and is therefore subject to the State's regulation." For this reason, "specific jurisdiction is confined to adjudication of issues deriving from, or connected with, the very controversy that establishes jurisdiction."

B

In determining whether personal jurisdiction is present, a court must consider a variety of interests. These include "the interests of the forum State and of the plaintiff in proceeding with the cause in the plaintiff's forum of choice." But the "primary concern" is "the burden on the defendant." Assessing this burden obviously requires a court to consider the practical problems resulting from litigating in the forum, but it also encompasses the more abstract matter of submitting to the coercive power of a State that may have little legitimate interest in the claims in question. As we have put it, restrictions on personal jurisdiction "are more than a guarantee of immunity from inconvenient or distant litigation. They are a consequence of territorial limitations on the power of the respective States." *Hanson v. Denckla*, 357 U.S. 235, 251 (1958). "[T]he States retain many essential attributes of sovereignty, including, in particular, the sovereign power to try causes in their courts. The sovereignty of each State . . . implie[s] a limitation on the sovereignty of all its sister States." *World-Wide Volkswagen*, 444 U.S., at 293. And at times, this federalism interest may be decisive. As we explained in *World-Wide Volkswagen*, "[e]ven if the defendant would suffer minimal or no inconvenience from being forced to litigate before the tribunals of another State; even if the forum State has a strong interest in applying its law to the controversy; even if the forum State is the most convenient location for litigation, the Due Process Clause, acting as an instrument of interstate federalism, may sometimes act to divest the State of its power to render a valid judgment." *Id.* at 294.

III

A

Our settled principles regarding specific jurisdiction control this case. In order for a court to exercise specific jurisdiction over a claim, there must be an "affiliation between the forum and the underlying controversy, principally, [an] activity or an occurrence that takes place in the forum State." When there is no such connection, specific jurisdiction is lacking regardless of the extent of a defendant's unconnected activities in the State.

For this reason, the California Supreme Court's "sliding scale approach" is difficult to square with our precedents. Under the California approach, the strength of the requisite connection between the forum and the specific claims at issue is relaxed if the defendant has extensive forum contacts that are unrelated to those claims. Our cases provide no support for this approach, which resembles a loose and spurious form of general jurisdiction. For specific jurisdiction, a defendant's general connections with the forum are not enough. As we have said, "[a] corporation's 'continuous activity of some sorts within a state . . . is not enough to support the demand that the corporation be amenable to suits unrelated to that activity.'"

The present case illustrates the danger of the California approach. The State Supreme Court found that specific jurisdiction was present without identifying any adequate link between the State and the nonresidents' claims. As noted, the nonresidents were not prescribed Plavix in California, did not purchase Plavix in California, did not ingest Plavix in California, and were not injured by Plavix in California. The mere fact that *other* plaintiffs were prescribed, obtained, and ingested Plavix in California—and allegedly sustained the same injuries as did the nonresidents—does not allow the State to assert specific jurisdiction over the nonresidents' claims. As we have explained, "a defendant's relationship with a . . . third party, standing alone, is an insufficient basis for jurisdiction." This remains true even when third parties (here, the plaintiffs who reside in California) can bring claims similar to those brought by the nonresidents. Nor is it sufficient—or even relevant—that BMS conducted research in California on matters unrelated to Plavix. What is needed—and what is missing here—is a connection between the forum and the specific claims at issue.

Our decision in *Walden v. Fiore*, 134 S. Ct. 1115 (2014), illustrates this requirement. In that case, Nevada plaintiffs sued an out-of-state defendant for conducting an allegedly unlawful search of the plaintiffs while they were in Georgia preparing to board a plane bound for Nevada. We held that the Nevada courts lacked specific jurisdiction even though the plaintiffs were Nevada residents and "suffered foreseeable harm in Nevada." Because the *"relevant* conduct occurred entirely in Georgi[a] . . . the mere fact that [this] conduct affected plaintiffs with connections to the forum State d[id] not suffice to authorize jurisdiction."

In today's case, the connection between the nonresidents' claims and the forum is even weaker. The relevant plaintiffs are not California residents and do not claim to have suffered harm in that State. In addition, as in *Walden*, all the conduct giving rise to the nonresidents' claims occurred elsewhere. It follows that the California courts cannot claim specific jurisdiction. See *World-Wide Volkswagen, supra* (finding no personal jurisdiction in Oklahoma because the defendant "carr[ied] on no activity whatsoever in Oklahoma" and dismissing "the fortuitous circumstance that a single Audi automobile, sold [by defendants] in New York to New York residents, happened to suffer an accident while passing through Oklahoma" as an "isolated occurrence").

B

The nonresidents maintain that two of our cases support the decision below, but they misinterpret those precedents.

In *Keeton v. Hustler Magazine, Inc.*, 465 U.S. 770 (1984), a New York resident sued Hustler in New Hampshire, claiming that she had been libeled in five issues of the magazine, which was distributed throughout the country, including in New Hampshire, where it sold 10,000 to 15,000 copies per month. Concluding that specific jurisdiction was present, we relied principally on the connection between the circulation of the magazine in New Hampshire and damage allegedly caused within the State. We noted that "[f]alse statements of fact harm both the subject of the falsehood and the readers of the statement." This factor amply distinguishes *Keeton* from the present case, for here the nonresidents' claims involve no harm in California and no harm to California residents.

The nonresident plaintiffs in this case point to our holding in *Keeton* that there was jurisdiction in New Hampshire to entertain the plaintiff's request for damages suffered outside the State, but that holding concerned jurisdiction to determine *the scope of a claim* involving in-state injury and injury to residents of the State, not, as in this case, jurisdiction to entertain claims involving no in-state injury and no injury to residents of the forum State. *Keeton* held that there was jurisdiction in New Hampshire to consider the full measure of the plaintiff's claim, but whether she could actually recover out-of-state damages was a merits question governed by New Hampshire libel law.

The Court's decision in *Phillips Petroleum Co. v. Shutts*, 472 U.S. 797 (1985), which involved a class action filed in Kansas, is even less relevant. The Kansas court exercised personal jurisdiction over the claims of nonresident class members, and the defendant, Phillips Petroleum, argued that this violated the due process rights of these class members because they lacked minimum contacts with the State. According to the defendant, the out-of-state class members should not have been kept in the case unless they affirmatively opted in, instead of merely failing to opt out after receiving notice.

Holding that there had been no due process violation, the Court explained that the authority of a State to entertain the claims of nonresident class members is entirely different from its authority to exercise jurisdiction over an out-of-state defendant. Since *Shutts* concerned the due process rights of *plaintiffs*, it has no bearing on the question presented here.

Respondents nevertheless contend that *Shutts* supports their position because, in their words, it would be "absurd to believe that [this Court] would have reached the exact opposite result if the petitioner [Phillips] had only invoked its own due-process rights, rather than those of the non-resident plaintiffs." Brief for Respondents 28-29, n.6 (emphasis deleted). But the fact remains that Phillips did not assert that Kansas improperly exercised personal jurisdiction over it, and the Court did not address that issue. Indeed, the Court stated specifically that its "discussion of personal jurisdiction [did not] address class actions where the jurisdiction is asserted against a *defendant* class." *Shutts, supra,* at 812 n.3.

C

In a last ditch contention, respondents contend that BMS's "decision to contract with a California company [McKesson] to distribute [Plavix] nationally" provides a sufficient basis for personal jurisdiction. Tr. of Oral Arg. 32. But as we have explained, "[t]he requirements of *International Shoe* . . . must be met as to each defendant over whom a state court exercises jurisdiction." In this case, it is not alleged that BMS engaged in relevant acts together with McKesson in California. Nor is it alleged that BMS is derivatively liable for McKesson's conduct in California. And the nonresidents "have adduced no evidence to show how or by whom the Plavix they took was distributed to the pharmacies that dispensed it to them." The bare fact that BMS contracted with a California distributor is not enough to establish personal jurisdiction in the State.

IV

Our straightforward application in this case of settled principles of personal jurisdiction will not result in the parade of horribles that respondents conjure up. Our decision does not prevent the California and out-of-state plaintiffs from joining together in a consolidated action in the States that have general jurisdiction over BMS. BMS concedes that such suits could be brought in either New York or Delaware. See Brief for Petitioner 13. Alternatively, the plaintiffs who are residents of a particular State—for example, the 92 plaintiffs from Texas and the 71 from Ohio—could probably sue together in their home States. In addition, since our decision concerns the due process limits on the exercise of specific jurisdiction by a State, we leave open the question whether the Fifth Amendment imposes the same restrictions on the exercise of personal jurisdiction by a federal court.

The judgment of the California Supreme Court is reversed, and the case is remanded for further proceedings not inconsistent with this opinion.

It is so ordered.

JUSTICE SOTOMAYOR, dissenting.

Three years ago, the Court imposed substantial curbs on the exercise of general jurisdiction in its decision in *Daimler AG v. Bauman.* Today, the Court takes its first step toward a similar contraction of specific jurisdiction by holding that a corporation that engages in a nationwide course of conduct cannot be held accountable in a state court by a group of injured people unless all of those people were injured in the forum State.

Personal Jurisdiction

I fear the consequences of the Court's decision today will be substantial. The majority's rule will make it difficult to aggregate the claims of plaintiffs across the country whose claims may be worth little alone. It will make it impossible to bring a nationwide mass action in state court against defendants who are "at home" in different States. And it will result in piecemeal litigation and the bifurcation of claims. None of this is necessary. A core concern in this Court's personal jurisdiction cases is fairness. And there is nothing unfair about subjecting a massive corporation to suit in a State for a nationwide course of conduct that injures both forum residents and nonresidents alike. . . .

[T]he California courts appropriately exercised specific jurisdiction over respondents' claims.

First, there is no dispute that Bristol-Myers "purposefully avail[ed] itself," of California and its substantial pharmaceutical market. Bristol-Myers employs over 400 people in California and maintains half a dozen facilities in the State engaged in research, development, and policymaking. It contracts with a California-based distributor, McKesson, whose sales account for a significant portion of its revenue. And it markets and sells its drugs, including Plavix, in California, resulting in total Plavix sales in that State of nearly $1 billion during the period relevant to this suit.

Second, respondents' claims "relate to" Bristol-Myers' in-state conduct. A claim "relates to" a defendant's forum conduct if it has a "connect[ion] with" that conduct. So respondents could not, for instance, hale Bristol-Myers into court in California for negligently maintaining the sidewalk outside its New York headquarters—a claim that has no connection to acts Bristol-Myers took in California. But respondents' claims against Bristol-Myers look nothing like such a claim. Respondents' claims against Bristol-Myers concern conduct materially identical to acts the company took in California: its marketing and distribution of Plavix, which it undertook on a nationwide basis in all 50 States. That respondents were allegedly injured by this nationwide course of conduct in Indiana, Oklahoma, and Texas, and not California, does not mean that their claims do not "relate to" the advertising and distribution efforts that Bristol-Myers undertook in that State. All of the plaintiffs—residents and nonresidents alike—allege that they were injured by the same essential acts. Our cases require no connection more direct than that.

Finally, and importantly, there is no serious doubt that the exercise of jurisdiction over the nonresidents' claims is reasonable. Because Bristol-Myers already faces claims that are identical to the nonresidents' claims in this suit, it will not be harmed by having to defend against respondents' claims: Indeed, the alternative approach—litigating those claims in separate suits in as many as 34 different States—would prove far more burdensome. By contrast, the plaintiffs' "interest in obtaining convenient and effective relief," is obviously furthered by participating in a consolidated proceeding in one State under shared counsel, which allows them to minimize costs, share discovery, and maximize recoveries on claims that may be too small to bring on their own. California, too, has an interest in providing a forum for mass actions like this one: Permitting the nonresidents to bring suit in California alongside the residents facilitates the efficient adjudication of the residents' claims and allows it to regulate more effectively the conduct of both nonresident corporations like Bristol-Myers and resident ones like McKesson.

Nothing in the Due Process Clause prohibits a California court from hearing respondents' claims—at least not in a case where they are joined to identical claims brought by California residents.

III

Bristol-Myers does not dispute that it has purposefully availed itself of California's markets, nor—remarkably—did it argue below that it would be "unreasonable" for a California court to hear respondents' claims. Instead, Bristol-Myers contends that respondents' claims do not "arise out of or relate to" its California conduct. The majority agrees, explaining that no "adequate link" exists "between the State and the nonresidents' claims,"—a result that it says follows from "settled principles [of] specific jurisdiction." But our precedents do not require this result, and common sense says that it cannot be correct.

A

The majority casts its decision today as compelled by precedent. *Ibid.* But our cases point in the other direction.

The majority argues at length that the exercise of specific jurisdiction in this case would conflict with our decision in *Walden v. Fiore.* That is plainly not true. *Walden* concerned the requirement that a defendant "purposefully avail" himself of a forum State or "purposefully direc[t]" his conduct toward that State, not the separate requirement that a plaintiff's claim "arise out of or relate to" a defendant's forum contacts. The lower court understood the case that way. The parties understood the case that way. See Brief for Petitioner 17-31, Brief for Respondent 20-44, Brief for United States as *Amicus Curiae* 12-18, in *Walden v. Fiore,* O.T. 2013, No. 12-574. And courts and commentators have understood the case that way. *Walden* teaches only that a defendant must have purposefully availed itself of the forum, and that a plaintiff cannot rely solely on a defendant's contacts with a forum resident to establish the necessary relationship. But that holding has nothing to do with the dispute between the parties: Bristol-Myers has purposefully availed itself of California—to the tune of millions of dollars in annual revenue. Only if its language is taken out of context, can *Walden* be made to seem relevant to the case at hand.

By contrast, our decision in *Keeton v. Hustler Magazine, Inc.,* suggests that there should be no such barrier to the exercise of jurisdiction here. In *Keeton,* a New York resident brought suit against an Ohio corporation, a magazine, in New Hampshire for libel. She alleged that the magazine's nationwide course of conduct—its publication of defamatory statements—had injured her in every

State, including New Hampshire. This Court unanimously rejected the defendant's argument that it should not be subject to "nationwide damages" when only a small portion of those damages arose in the forum State; exposure to such liability, the Court explained, was the consequence of having "continuously and deliberately exploited the New Hampshire market." The majority today dismisses *Keeton* on the ground that the defendant there faced one plaintiff's claim arising out of its nationwide course of conduct, whereas Bristol-Myers faces many more plaintiffs' claims. But this is a distinction without a difference: In either case, a defendant will face liability in a single State for a single course of conduct that has impact in many States. *Keeton* informs us that there is no unfairness in such a result.

The majority's animating concern, in the end, appears to be federalism: "[T]erritorial limitations on the power of the respective States," we are informed, may—and today do—trump even concerns about fairness to the parties. Indeed, the majority appears to concede that this is not, at bottom, a case about fairness but instead a case about power: one in which "'the defendant would suffer minimal or no inconvenience from being forced to litigate before the tribunals of another State; . . . the forum State has a strong interest in applying its law to the controversy; [and] the forum State is the most convenient location for litigation'" but personal jurisdiction still will not lie. But I see little reason to apply such a principle in a case brought against a large corporate defendant arising out of its nationwide conduct. What interest could any single State have in adjudicating respondents' claims that the other States do not share? I would measure jurisdiction first and foremost by the yardstick set out in *International Shoe*—"fair play and substantial justice." The majority's opinion casts that settled principle aside.

B

I fear the consequences of the majority's decision today will be substantial. Even absent a rigid requirement that a defendant's in-state conduct must actually cause a plaintiff's claim,[3] the upshot of today's opinion is that plaintiffs cannot join their claims together and sue a defendant in a State in which only some of them have been injured. That rule is likely to have consequences far beyond this case.

First, and most prominently, the Court's opinion in this case will make it profoundly difficult for plaintiffs who are injured in different States by a defendant's nationwide course of conduct to sue that defendant in a single, consolidated action. The holding of today's opinion is that such an action cannot be brought in a State in which only some plaintiffs were injured. Not to worry, says the majority: The plaintiffs here could have sued Bristol-Myers in New York or Delaware; could "probably" have subdivided their separate claims into 34 lawsuits in the States in which they were injured; and might have been able to bring a single suit in federal court (an "open . . . question"). Even setting aside the majority's caveats, what is the purpose of such limitations? What interests are served by preventing the consolidation of claims and limiting the forums in which they can be consolidated? The effect of the Court's opinion today is to eliminate nationwide mass actions in any State other than those in which a defendant is "'essentially at home.'"[4] Such a rule hands one more tool to corporate defendants determined to prevent the aggregation of individual claims, and forces injured plaintiffs to bear the burden of bringing suit in what will often be far flung jurisdictions.

Second, the Court's opinion today may make it impossible to bring certain mass actions at all. After this case, it is difficult to imagine where it might be possible to bring a nationwide mass action against two or more defendants headquartered and incorporated in different States. There will be no State where both defendants are "at home," and so no State in which the suit can proceed. What about a nationwide mass action brought against a defendant not headquartered or incorporated in the United States? Such a defendant is not "at home" in any State. Especially in a world in which defendants are subject to general jurisdiction in only a handful of States, the effect of today's opinion will be to curtail—and in some cases eliminate—plaintiffs' ability to hold corporations fully accountable for their nationwide conduct.

The majority chides respondents for conjuring a "parade of horribles," but says nothing about how suits like those described here will survive its opinion in this case. The answer is simple: They will not.

It "does not offend 'traditional notions of fair play and substantial justice,'" *International Shoe*, 326 U.S., at 316, to permit plaintiffs to aggregate claims arising out of a single nationwide course of conduct in a single suit in a single State where some, but not all, were injured. But that is exactly what the Court holds today is barred by the Due Process Clause.

This is not a rule the Constitution has required before. I respectfully dissent.

Ford Motor Co. v. Montana Eighth Judicial District Court
141 S. Ct. 1017 (2021)

Justice KAGAN delivered the opinion of the Court.

In each of these two cases, a state court held that it had jurisdiction over Ford Motor Company in a products-liability suit stemming from a car accident. The accident happened in the State where suit was brought. The victim was one of the State's residents. And Ford did substantial business in the State—among other things, advertising, selling, and servicing the model of vehicle the suit claims is defective. Still, Ford contends that jurisdiction is improper because the particular

---

4. The Court today does not confront the question whether its opinion here would also apply to a class action in which a plaintiff injured in the forum State seeks to represent a nationwide class of plaintiffs, not all of whom were injured there. Cf. *Devlin v. Scardelletti*, 536 U.S. 1, 9-10, 122 S. Ct. 2005, 153 L. Ed. 2d 27 (2002) ("Nonnamed class members . . . may be parties for some purposes and not for others"); see also Wood, Adjudicatory Jurisdiction and Class Actions, 62 Ind. L.J. 597, 616-617 (1987).

car involved in the crash was not first sold in the forum State, nor was it designed or manufactured there. We reject that argument. When a company like Ford serves a market for a product in a State and that product causes injury in the State to one of its residents, the State's courts may entertain the resulting suit.

I

Ford is a global auto company. It is incorporated in Delaware and head-quartered in Michigan. But its business is everywhere. Ford markets, sells, and services its products across the United States and overseas. In this country alone, the company annually distributes over 2.5 million new cars, trucks, and SUVs to over 3,200 licensed dealerships. Ford also encourages a resale market for its products: Almost all its dealerships buy and sell used Fords, as well as selling new ones. To enhance its brand and increase its sales, Ford engages in wide-ranging promotional activities, including television, print, online, and direct-mail adver-tisements. No matter where you live, you've seen them: "Have you driven a Ford lately?" or "Built Ford Tough." Ford also ensures that consumers can keep their vehicles running long past the date of sale. The company provides original parts to auto supply stores and repair shops across the country. (Goes another slogan: "Keep your Ford a Ford.") And Ford's own network of dealers offers an array of maintenance and repair services, thus fostering an ongoing relationship between Ford and its customers.

Accidents involving two of Ford's vehicles—a 1996 Explorer and a 1994 Crown Victoria—are at the heart of the suits before us. One case comes from Montana. Markkaya Gullett was driving her Explorer near her home in the State when the tread separated from a rear tire. The vehicle spun out, rolled into a ditch, and came to rest upside down. Gullett died at the scene of the crash. The representative of her estate sued Ford in Montana state court, bringing claims for a design defect, failure to warn, and negligence. The second case comes from Minnesota. Adam Bandemer was a passenger in his friend's Crown Victoria, trav-eling on a rural road in the State to a favorite ice-fishing spot. When his friend rear-ended a snowplow, this car too landed in a ditch. Bandemer's air bag failed to deploy, and he suffered serious brain damage. He sued Ford in Minnesota state court, asserting products-liability, negligence, and breach-of-warranty claims.

Ford moved to dismiss the two suits for lack of personal jurisdiction, on basi-cally identical grounds. According to Ford, the state court (whether in Montana or Minnesota) had jurisdiction only if the company's conduct in the State had given rise to the plaintiff's claims. And that causal link existed, Ford continued, only if the company had designed, manufactured, or—most likely—sold in the State the particular vehicle involved in the accident. In neither suit could the plaintiff make that showing. Ford had designed the Explorer and Crown Victoria in Michigan, and it had manufactured the cars in (respectively) Kentucky and Canada. Still more, the company had originally sold the cars at issue outside the forum States—the Explorer in Washington, the Crown Victoria in North

Dakota. Only later resales and relocations by consumers had brought the vehicles to Montana and Minnesota. That meant, in Ford's view, that the courts of those States could not decide the suits.

Both the Montana and the Minnesota Supreme Courts (affirming lower court decisions) rejected Ford's argument. . . .

We granted certiorari to consider if Ford is subject to jurisdiction in these cases. We hold that it is.

II

A

The Fourteenth Amendment's Due Process Clause limits a state court's power to exercise jurisdiction over a defendant. The canonical decision in this area remains *International Shoe Co. v. Washington,* 326 U.S. 310 (1945). There, the Court held that a tribunal's authority depends on the defendant's having such "contacts" with the forum State that "the maintenance of the suit" is "reasonable, in the context of our federal system of government," and "does not offend traditional notions of fair play and substantial justice." In giving content to that formulation, the Court has long focused on the nature and extent of "the defendant's relationship to the forum State." *Bristol-Myers Squibb Co. v. Superior Court,* 137 S. Ct. 1773, 1779 (2017). That focus led to our recognizing two kinds of personal jurisdiction: general (sometimes called all-purpose) jurisdiction and specific (sometimes called case-linked) jurisdiction. See *Goodyear Dunlop Tires Operations, S.A. v. Brown,* 564 U.S. 915, 919 (2011).

A state court may exercise general jurisdiction only when a defendant is "essentially at home" in the State. General jurisdiction, as its name implies, extends to "any and all claims" brought against a defendant. Those claims need not relate to the forum State or the defendant's activity there; they may concern events and conduct anywhere in the world. But that breadth imposes a correlative limit: Only a select "set of affiliations with a forum" will expose a defendant to such sweeping jurisdiction. *Daimler AG v. Bauman,* 571 U.S. 117, 137 (2014). In what we have called the "paradigm" case, an individual is subject to general jurisdiction in her place of domicile. And the "equivalent" forums for a corporation are its place of incorporation and principal place of business. *Ibid.* (internal quotation marks omitted); see *id.,* at 139, n. 19 (leaving open "the possibility that in an exceptional case" a corporation might also be "at home" elsewhere). So general jurisdiction over Ford (as all parties agree) attaches in Delaware and Michigan—not in Montana and Minnesota.

Specific jurisdiction is different: It covers defendants less intimately connected with a State, but only as to a narrower class of claims. The contacts needed for this kind of jurisdiction often go by the name "purposeful availment." *Burger King Corp. Rudzewicz,* 471 U.S. 462, 475 (1985). The defendant, we have said, must take "some act by which [it] purposefully avails itself of the privilege of conducting activities within the forum State." The contacts must be the defendant's own choice and not "random, isolated, or fortuitous." They must show that the defendant deliberately "reached out beyond" its home—by, for example, "exploi[ting] a market" in the forum State or entering a contractual relationship centered there. Yet even then—because the defendant is not "at home"—the forum State may exercise jurisdiction in only certain cases. The plaintiff's claims, we have often stated, "must arise out of or relate to the defendant's contacts" with the forum. *Bristol-Myers*, 137 S. Ct., 1780. Or put just a bit differently, "there must be 'an affiliation between the forum and the underlying controversy, principally, [an] activity or an occurrence that takes place in the forum State and is therefore subject to the State's regulation.'" *Walden v. Fiore*, 571 U.S. 277, 285 (2014).

These rules derive from and reflect two sets of values—treating defendants fairly and protecting "interstate federalism." Our decision in *International Shoe* founded specific jurisdiction on an idea of reciprocity between a defendant and a State: When (but only when) a company "exercises the privilege of conducting activities within a state"—thus "enjoy[ing] the benefits and protection of [its] laws"—the State may hold the company to account for related misconduct. Later decisions have added that our doctrine similarly provides defendants with "fair warning"—knowledge that "a particular activity may subject [it] to the jurisdiction of a foreign sovereign." A defendant can thus "structure [its] primary conduct" to lessen or avoid exposure to a given State's courts. And this Court has considered alongside defendants' interests those of the States in relation to each other. One State's "sovereign power to try" a suit, we have recognized, may prevent "sister States" from exercising their like authority. The law of specific jurisdiction thus seeks to ensure that States with "little legitimate interest" in a suit do not encroach on States more affected by the controversy.

B

Ford contends that our jurisdictional rules prevent Montana's and Minnesota's courts from deciding these two suits. In making that argument, Ford does not contest that it does substantial business in Montana and Minnesota—that it actively seeks to serve the market for automobiles and related products in those States. Or to put that concession in more doctrinal terms, Ford agrees that it has "purposefully avail[ed] itself of the privilege of conducting activities" in both places. Ford's claim is instead that those activities do not sufficiently connect to the suits, even though the resident-plaintiffs allege that Ford cars malfunctioned in the forum States. In Ford's view, the needed link must be causal in nature: Jurisdiction attaches "only if the defendant's forum conduct *gave rise* to the plaintiff's claims." Brief for Petitioner 13 (emphasis in original). And that rule reduces, Ford thinks, to locating specific jurisdiction in the State where Ford sold the car in question, or else the States where Ford designed and manufactured the vehicle. On that view, the place of accident and injury is immaterial. So (Ford says) Montana's and Minnesota's courts have no power over these cases.

But Ford's causation-only approach finds no support in this Court's requirement of a "connection" between a plaintiff's suit and a defendant's activities. That rule indeed serves to narrow the class of claims over which a state court may exercise specific jurisdiction. But not quite so far as Ford wants. None of our precedents has suggested that only a strict causal relationship between the defendant's in-state activity and the litigation will do. As just noted, our most common formulation of the rule demands that the suit "arise out of *or relate to* the defendant's contacts with the forum." The first half of that standard asks about causation; but the back half, after the "or," contemplates that some relationships will support jurisdiction without a causal showing. That does not mean anything goes. In the sphere of specific jurisdiction, the phrase "relate to" incorporates real limits, as it must to adequately protect defendants foreign to a forum. But again, we have never framed the specific jurisdiction inquiry as always requiring proof of causation—*i.e.*, proof that the plaintiff's claim came about because of the defendant's in-state conduct. So the case is not over even if, as Ford argues, a causal test would put jurisdiction in only the States of first sale, manufacture, and design. A different State's courts may yet have jurisdiction, because of another "activity [or] occurrence" involving the defendant that takes place in the State.

And indeed, this Court has stated that specific jurisdiction attaches in cases identical to the ones here—when a company like Ford serves a market for a product in the forum State and the product malfunctions there. In *World-Wide Volkswagen v. Woodson*, the Court held that an Oklahoma court could not assert jurisdiction over a New York car dealer just because a car it sold later caught fire in Oklahoma. 444 U.S., at 295. But in so doing, we contrasted the dealer's position to that of two other defendants—Audi, the car's manufacturer, and Volkswagen, the car's nationwide importer (neither of which contested jurisdiction):

> "[I]f the sale of a product of a manufacturer or distributor such as Audi or Volkswagen is not simply an isolated occurrence, but arises from the efforts of the manufacturer or distributor to serve, directly or indirectly, the market for its product in [several or all] other States, it is not unreasonable to subject it to suit in one of those States if its allegedly defective merchandise has there been the source of injury to its owner or to others." *Id.*, at 297.

Or said another way, if Audi and Volkswagen's business deliberately extended into Oklahoma (among other States), then Oklahoma's courts could hold the companies accountable for a car's catching fire there—even though the vehicle had been designed and made overseas and sold in New York. For, the Court explained, a company thus "purposefully avail[ing] itself" of the Oklahoma auto market "has clear notice" of its exposure in that State to suits arising from local accidents involving its cars. And the company could do something about that exposure: It could "act to alleviate the risk of burdensome litigation by procuring insurance, passing the expected costs on to customers, or, if the risks are [still] too great, severing its connection with the State."

Our conclusion in *World-Wide Volkswagen*—though, as Ford notes, technically "dicta," has appeared and reappeared in many cases since. . . . On two other occasions, we reaffirmed that rule by reciting the above block-quoted language verbatim. See *Goodyear*, 564 U.S., at 927; *Asahi Metal Industry Co. v. Superior Court*, 480 U.S. 102, 110 (1987)..). And in *Daimler*, we used the Audi/Volkswagen scenario as a paradigm case of specific jurisdiction (though now naming Daimler, the maker of Mercedes Benzes). Said the Court, to "illustrate[ ]" specific jurisdiction's "province[ ]": A California court would exercise specific jurisdiction "if a California plaintiff, injured in a California accident involving a Daimler-manufactured vehicle, sued Daimler [in that court] alleging that the vehicle was defectively designed." As in *World-Wide Volkswagen*, the Court did not limit jurisdiction to where the car was designed, manufactured, or first sold. Substitute Ford for Daimler, Montana and Minnesota for California, and the Court's "illustrat[ive]" case becomes . . . the two cases before us.

To see why Ford is subject to jurisdiction in these cases (as Audi, Volkswagen, and Daimler were in their analogues), consider first the business that the company regularly conducts in Montana and Minnesota. Small wonder that Ford has here conceded "purposeful availment" of the two States' markets. By every means imaginable—among them, billboards, TV and radio spots, print ads, and direct mail—Ford urges Montanans and Minnesotans to buy its vehicles, including (at all relevant times) Explorers and Crown Victorias. Ford cars—again including those two models—are available for sale, whether new or used, throughout the States, at 36 dealerships in Montana and 84 in Minnesota. And apart from sales, Ford works hard to foster ongoing connections to its cars' owners. The company's dealers in Montana and Minnesota (as elsewhere) regularly maintain and repair Ford cars, including those whose warranties have long since expired. And the company distributes replacement parts both to its own dealers and to independent auto shops in the two States. Those activities, too, make Ford money. And by making it easier to own a Ford, they encourage Montanans and Minnesotans to become lifelong Ford drivers.

Now turn to how all this Montana- and Minnesota-based conduct relates to the claims in these cases, brought by state residents in Montana's and Minnesota's courts. Each plaintiff's suit, of course, arises from a car accident in one of those States. In each complaint, the resident-plaintiff alleges that a defective Ford vehicle—an Explorer in one, a Crown Victoria in the other—caused the crash and resulting harm. And as just described, Ford had advertised, sold, and serviced those two car models in both States for many years. (Contrast a case, which we do not address, in which Ford marketed the models in only a different State or region.) In other words, Ford had systematically served a market in Montana and Minnesota for the very vehicles that the plaintiffs allege malfunctioned and injured them in those States. So there is a strong "relationship among the defendant, the forum, and the litigation"—the "essential foundation" of specific jurisdiction. That is why this Court has used this exact fact pattern (a resident-plaintiff sues a global car company, extensively serving the state market in a vehicle, for an in-state accident) as an illustration—even a paradigm example—of how specific jurisdiction works.[4]

The only complication here, pressed by Ford, is that the company sold the specific cars involved in these crashes outside the forum States, with consumers later selling them to the States' residents. Because that is so, Ford argues, the plaintiffs' claims "would be precisely the same if Ford had never done anything in Montana and Minnesota." Of course, that argument merely restates Ford's demand for an exclusively causal test of connection—which we have already shown is inconsistent with our caselaw. And indeed, a similar assertion could have been made in *World-Wide Volkswagen*—yet the Court made clear that systematic contacts in Oklahoma rendered Audi accountable there for an in-state accident, even though it involved a car sold in New York. So too here, and for the same reasons, even supposing (as Ford does) that without the company's Montana or Minnesota contacts the plaintiffs' claims would be just the same.

But in any event, that assumption is far from clear. For the owners of these cars might never have bought them, and so these suits might never have arisen, except for Ford's contacts with their home States. Those contacts might turn any resident of Montana or Minnesota into a Ford owner—even when he buys his car from out of state. He may make that purchase because he saw ads for the car in local media. And he may take into account a raft of Ford's in-state activities designed to make driving a Ford convenient there: that Ford dealers stand ready to service the car; that other auto shops have ample supplies of Ford parts; and that Ford fosters an active resale market for its old models. The plaintiffs here did not in fact establish, or even allege, such causal links. Nor should jurisdiction in cases like these ride on the exact reasons for an individual plaintiff's purchase, or on his ability to present persuasive evidence about them. But the possibilities listed above—created by the reach of Ford's Montana and Minnesota contacts—underscore the aptness of finding jurisdiction here, even though the cars at issue were first sold out of state.

For related reasons, allowing jurisdiction in these cases treats Ford fairly, as this Court's precedents explain. In conducting so much business in Montana and Minnesota, Ford "enjoys the benefits and protection of [their] laws"—the enforcement of contracts, the defense of property, the resulting formation of effective markets. All that assistance to Ford's in-state business creates reciprocal obligations—most relevant here, that the car models Ford so extensively markets

---

4. None of this is to say that any person using any means to sell any good in a State is subject to jurisdiction there if the product malfunctions after arrival. We have long treated isolated or sporadic transactions differently from continuous ones. And we do not here consider internet transactions, which may raise doctrinal questions of their own. So consider, for example, a hypothetical offered at oral argument. "[A] retired guy in a small town" in Maine "carves decoys" and uses "a site on the Internet" to sell them. "Can he be sued in any state if some harm arises from the decoy?" *Ibid.* The differences between that case and the ones before us virtually list themselves. (Just consider all our descriptions of Ford's activities outside its home bases.) So we agree with the plaintiffs' counsel that resolving these cases does not also resolve the hypothetical.

in Montana and Minnesota be safe for their citizens to use there. Thus our repeated conclusion: A state court's enforcement of that commitment, enmeshed as it is with Ford's government-protected in-state business, can "hardly be said to be undue." And as *World-Wide Volkswagen* described, it cannot be thought surprising either. An automaker regularly marketing a vehicle in a State, the Court said, has "clear notice" that it will be subject to jurisdiction in the State's courts when the product malfunctions there (regardless where it was first sold). Precisely because that exercise of jurisdiction is so reasonable, it is also predictable—and thus allows Ford to "structure [its] primary conduct" to lessen or even avoid the costs of state-court litigation.

Finally, principles of "interstate federalism" support jurisdiction over these suits in Montana and Minnesota. Those States have significant interests at stake— "providing [their] residents with a convenient forum for redressing injuries inflicted by out-of-state actors," as well as enforcing their own safety regulations. *Burger King*, 471 U.S., at 473. Consider, next to those, the interests of the States of first sale (Washington and North Dakota)—which Ford's proposed rule would make the most likely forums. For each of those States, the suit involves all out-of-state parties, an out-of-state accident, and out-of-state injuries; the suit's only connection with the State is that a former owner once (many years earlier) bought the car there. In other words, there is a less significant "relationship among the defendant, the forum, and the litigation." So by channeling these suits to Washington and North Dakota, Ford's regime would undermine, rather than promote, what the company calls the Due Process Clause's "jurisdiction-allocating function."

C

Ford mainly relies for its rule on two of our recent decisions—*Bristol-Myers* and *Walden*. But those precedents stand for nothing like the principle Ford derives from them. If anything, they reinforce all we have said about why Montana's and Minnesota's courts can decide these cases.

Ford says of *Bristol-Myers* that it "squarely foreclose[s]" jurisdiction. In that case, non-resident plaintiffs brought claims in California state court against Bristol-Myers Squibb, the manufacturer of a nationally marketed prescription drug called Plavix. The plaintiffs had not bought Plavix in California; neither had they used or suffered any harm from the drug there. Still, the California Supreme Court thought it could exercise jurisdiction because Bristol-Myers Squibb sold Plavix in California and was defending there against identical claims brought by the State's residents. This Court disagreed, holding that the exercise of jurisdiction violated the Fourteenth Amendment. In Ford's view, the same must be true here. Each of these plaintiffs, like the plaintiffs in *Bristol-Myers*, alleged injury from a particular item (a car, a pill) that the defendant had sold outside the forum State. Ford reads *Bristol-Myers* to preclude jurisdiction when that is true, even if the defendant regularly sold "the same *kind* of product" in the State. Reply Brief 2 (emphasis in original).

But that reading misses the point of our decision. We found jurisdiction improper in *Bristol-Myers* because the forum State, and the defendant's activities there, lacked any connection to the plaintiffs' claims. The plaintiffs, the Court explained, were not residents of California. They had not been prescribed Plavix in California. They had not ingested Plavix in California. And they had not sustained their injuries in California. In short, the plaintiffs were engaged in forum-shopping—suing in California because it was thought plaintiff-friendly, even though their cases had no tie to the State. That is not at all true of the cases before us. Yes, Ford sold the specific products in other States, as Bristol-Myers Squibb had. But here, the plaintiffs are residents of the forum States. They used the allegedly defective products in the forum States. And they suffered injuries when those products malfunctioned in the forum States. In sum, each of the plaintiffs brought suit in the most natural State—based on an "affiliation between the forum and the underlying controversy, principally, [an] activity or an occurrence that t[ook] place" there. So *Bristol-Myers* does not bar jurisdiction.

Ford falls back on *Walden* as its last resort. In that case, a Georgia police officer working at an Atlanta airport searched, and seized money from, two Nevada residents before they embarked on a flight to Las Vegas. The victims of the search sued the officer in Nevada, arguing that their alleged injury (their inability to use the seized money) occurred in the State in which they lived. This Court held the exercise of jurisdiction in Nevada improper even though "the plaintiff[s] experienced [the] effect[s]" of the officer's conduct there. According to Ford, our ruling shows that a plaintiff's residence and place of injury can never support jurisdiction. See Brief for Petitioner 32. And without those facts, Ford concludes, the basis for jurisdiction crumbles here as well.

But *Walden* has precious little to do with the cases before us. In *Walden*, only the plaintiffs had any contacts with the State of Nevada; the defendant-officer had never taken any act to "form[ ] a contact" of his own. The officer had "never traveled to, conducted activities within, contacted anyone in, or sent anything or anyone to Nevada." So to use the language of our doctrinal test: He had not "purposefully avail[ed himself] of the privilege of conducting activities" in the forum State. Because that was true, the Court had no occasion to address the necessary connection between a defendant's in-state activity and the plaintiff's claims. But here, Ford has a veritable truckload of contacts with Montana and Minnesota, as it admits. The only issue is whether those contacts are related enough to the plaintiffs' suits. As to that issue, so what if (as *Walden* held) the place of a plaintiff's injury and residence cannot create a defendant's contact with the forum State? Those places still may be relevant in assessing the link between the defendant's forum contacts and the plaintiff's suit—including its assertions of who was injured where. And indeed, that relevance is a key part of *Bristol-Myers'* reasoning. One of Ford's own favorite cases thus refutes its appeal to the other.

* * *

Personal Jurisdiction

Here, resident-plaintiffs allege that they suffered in-state injury because of defective products that Ford extensively promoted, sold, and serviced in Montana and Minnesota. For all the reasons we have given, the connection between the plaintiffs' claims and Ford's activities in those States—or otherwise said, the "relationship among the defendant, the forum[s], and the litigation"—is close enough to support specific jurisdiction. The judgments of the Montana and Minnesota Supreme Courts are therefore affirmed.

It is so ordered.

Justice BARRETT took no part in the consideration or decision of these cases.

Justice ALITO, concurring in the judgment. . . .

Justice GORSUCH, with whom Justice THOMAS joins, concurring in the judgment. . . .

Today's case tests the old boundaries from another direction. Until now, many lower courts have proceeded on the premise that specific jurisdiction requires two things. First, the defendant must "purposefully avail" itself of the chance to do business in a State. Second, the plaintiff's suit must "arise out of or relate to" the defendant's in-state activities. Typically, courts have read this second phrase as a unit requiring at least a but-for causal link between the defendant's local activities and the plaintiff's injuries. As every first year law student learns, a but-for causation test isn't the most demanding. At a high level of abstraction, one might say any event in the world would not have happened "but for" events far and long removed.

Now, though, the Court pivots away from this understanding. Focusing on the phrase "arise out of or relate to" that so often appears in our cases, the majority asks us to parse those words "as though we were dealing with language of a statute." In particular, the majority zeros in on the disjunctive conjunction "or," and proceeds to build its entire opinion around that linguistic feature. The majority admits that "arise out of " may connote causation. But, it argues, "relate to" is an independent clause that does not.

Where this leaves us is far from clear. For a case to "relate to" the defendant's forum contacts, the majority says, it is enough if an "affiliation" or "relationship" or "connection" exists between them. But what does this assortment of nouns *mean*? Loosed from any causation standard, we are left to guess. The majority promises that its new test "does not mean anything goes," but that hardly tells us what does. In some cases, the new test may prove more forgiving than the old causation rule. But it's hard not to wonder whether it may also sometimes turn out to be more demanding. Unclear too is whether, in cases like that, the majority would treat causation and "affiliation" as alternative routes to specific jurisdiction, or whether it would deny jurisdiction outright. . . .

None of this is to cast doubt on the outcome of these cases. The parties have not pointed to anything in the Constitution's original meaning or its history that might allow Ford to evade answering the plaintiffs' claims in Montana or Minnesota courts. No one seriously questions that the company, seeking to do business, entered those jurisdictions through the front door. And I cannot see why, when faced with the process server, it should be allowed to escape out the back. The real struggle here isn't with settling on the right outcome in these cases, but with making sense of our personal jurisdiction jurisprudence and *International Shoe*'s increasingly doubtful dichotomy. On those scores, I readily admit that I finish these cases with even more questions than I had at the start. Hopefully, future litigants and lower courts will help us face these tangles and sort out a responsible way to address the challenges posed by our changing economy in light of the Constitution's text and the lessons of history.

NOTES AND QUESTIONS

1. *On relatedness as a bridge.* What distinction does the Court draw between the "arising-out-of" standard and the "relatedness" standard? Do the precedents cited by the Court support that distinction? Is the distinction a workable one or is it hopelessly ambiguous? Might we see it as embracing a transitional area between classic "substantive relevance" and the increasingly narrow realm of general jurisdiction? In other words, does it fill a gap between these two categories? Or, better, does it suggest that rather than two categories of personal jurisdiction, specific and general, there is a single due-process category premised on a spectrum of possibilities that ranges from hard-edged specific jurisdiction (e.g., proximate cause) and the distinct and narrow realm of "at home" general jurisdiction? What does the Court's decision in *International Shoe* have to say about this?

SERVICE OF PROCESS AND NOTICE

III

Page 249. Insert after Problem 3-2.

PROBLEM

3.2(a). Greene sued Huggett, the manager of the Sugar Mill West Apartment complex, for various violations of his rights under federal law. Service on Huggett was purportedly accomplished by delivering a copy of the summons and complaint to Czernia, a 30-year-old administrative assistant to Huggett, who was working in the office located on the premises of the apartment complex at the time of the attempted service. Huggett also works out of that same office. Huggett has filed a timely Rule 12(b)(5) motion to dismiss. Focusing solely on federal service standards, how should the District Court rule on Huggett's motion? Would it make any difference if Huggett did or did not reside in the apartment complex? See *Greene v. 1st Lake Properties, Inc.*, 2018 WL 5631420 (E.D. Louisiana Oct. 31, 2018).

Page 254. Insert above subsection "c."

PROBLEM

3-2(b). Nature's First, Inc. ("Plaintiff") sued Nature's First Law, Inc. ("Defendant"), in a United States District Court, alleging trademark infringement. Plaintiff arranged for service of the summons and complaint on August 12, 2004. The proof of service signed by the process server asserts that on that day, the process server left a copy of the summons and complaint with Marni, who identified herself as a "Sales Executive" in Defendant's employ and as the "manager" of Defendant's principal place of business. When the process server handed Marni the summons and complaint and identified them as such, Marni acknowledged their receipt. A copy of the documents was thereafter mailed via first-class, addressed to "Nature's First Law, Inc.," at the address of its principal place of business. Defendant did not answer or respond. Thereafter Plaintiff successfully moved for entry of default and a default judgment. Defendant, denying that it was served, has filed a timely Rule 60(b)(4) motion to set aside the default and default judgment. According to an accompanying affidavit signed by Marni, she was not "in charge" of Defendant's office at any time prior to or after August 2004, she was not served with any legal papers in August 2004 or any time thereafter, and, to her knowledge, no one came into Defendant's office on or about August 12, 2004 to serve any such papers. In addition, the motion included an affidavit of Thor, Defendant's Chief Financial Officer and co-founder, in which he states that (1) Marni, although employed by Defendant at its principal place of business, never held an officer position there and was never designated or authorized by Defendant to accept service on behalf of it; (2) is not and was not a "sales executive," nor were her job responsibilities such that she was authorized to accept service on behalf of Defendant; and (3) she never advised Thor or any other of Defendant's officers that she was served with legal papers on August 12, 2004 or anytime thereafter. Focusing solely on Fed. R. Civ. P. 4(h), how should the District Court rule on Defendant's motion? See *Nature's First Inc. v. Nature's First Law, Inc.*, 436 F.Supp. 2d 368 (D. Conn. 2006).

Page 280. Insert before heading C.

Despite the need for prior court approval, service under Rule 4(f)(3) stands on an equal footing with the methods outlined in 4(f)(1) and 4(f)(2). A plaintiff seeking to invoke 4(f)(3) thus need not show that they first "attempt[ed] service by other means" to serve an individual in a foreign country. *Rio Properties, supra,* 284 F.3d at 1015. However, if plaintiff has not first tried these alternatives, a court may deny the Rule 4(f)(3) motion, without prejudice to plaintiff's renewing it later if the alternatives failed. And since due process must also be satisfied – including its requirement that notice be reasonable *under the circumstances –* use of 4(f)(3) is more likely to pass muster if more reliable means of notice were at least attempted.

Federal courts "have authorized a wide variety of alternative methods of service including publication, ordinary mail, mail to the defendant's last known address, delivery to the defendant's attorney, telex, and . . . email" under Rule 4(f)(3) – where these means were not prohibited by international agreement. *Id.* at 1016. Some of the more recent cases authorizing service under Rule 4(f)(3) are: *Fabian v. LeMahieu*, 2020 WL 3402800 (N.D. Calif. June 19, 2020) (approving service on Italian defendants by mail, email, and social media, to their bankruptcy trustee and legal counsel in Italy); *Securities and Exchange Comm'n v. de Nicholas Guiterrez*, 2020 WL 1307143 (S.D. Calif. March 19, 2020) (authorizing service on Mexican defendants by email, and by serving their U.S. based counsel who were not authorized to accept process, after numerous other efforts at service failed); *NOCO Co. v. Liu Chang*, 2020 WL 533021 (N.D. Ohio Feb. 3, 2020) (authorizing service on Chinese defendants by using Amazon messaging center, after using Hague Convention processes under 4(f)(1) failed); *Newmont USA Ltd. v. Imatech Systems Cyprus Pty Ltd.*, 2019 WL 3219144 (D.

Nev. July 17, 2019) (authorizing service on Cypriot defendant by email to defendant's U.S. counsel, after repeated attempts to have defendant waive service and to use Hague Convention processes failed); *Assef v. Does 1-10*, 2016 WL 1191683 (N.D. Calif. March 28, 2016) (authorizing service on unknown Singapore and/or Australian defendants by email and by posting on defendants' internet blog, where repeated efforts to obtain more information about defendants' names and addresses through Google and other means had failed).

PROBLEM

3-6(a). Plaintiff TV Ears, Inc. sued several business entities ("the Defendants") on federal trademark claims in a United States District Court located in California. Each of the Defendants maintains a business addresses located in either the People's Republic of China or Hong Kong. All the Defendants do business exclusively over the Internet and none of the Defendants has appointed an agent for service of process in the United States. After the District Court entered an order to show cause for failure to serve, Plaintiff filed a motion seeking an order authorizing service of process on Defendants via email. Plaintiff contends that "alternate service by email is appropriate and necessary in this case because Defendants (1) operate via the Internet, (2) rely on electronic communications to operate their businesses, and (3) can be contacted via specific email addresses, which Plaintiff has established are valid working emails." Plaintiff further asserts that while "Defendants maintain addresses in the People's Republic of China ('China') and the Hong Kong Special Administrative Region of the People's Republic of China ('Hong Kong'), "none of the addresses provided by Defendants on their websites and other public information show as an address in Google map search." As to the email addresses, Plaintiff asserts that "the emails and related online contact forms for all named Defendants are working, with no emails failing to send, being bounced back or returned undeliverable." Some of the Defendants did, in fact, receive emails sent to them. What should the District Court do? More specifically, would service by email be permitted under the Federal Rules and, if so, would service by email satisfy the standards of Due Process? See *TV Ears, Inc. v. Joyshiya Development Ltd.*, 2021 WL 165013 (S.D. Calif. Jan. 19, 2021).

Page 284. Insert after Note 2.

3. *Direct vs. collateral attack.* The *Gardiner* case at the end of Note 2 allowed a confession of judgment clause to be challenged "collaterally" in the courts of sister state North Carolina, rather than being challenged "directly" in the courts of Ohio, the state where the judgment was entered. In *Leidholm*, by contrast, the attack on the confessed judgment was direct, for the defendant asked a North

Dakota state court to vacate its own prior judgment. In allowing a collateral attack, *Gardiner* found the clause's *facial* invalidity to be so apparent – due to failure to comply with Ohio's law as to type size and distinctiveness – as to strip the Ohio court of subject matter jurisdiction. And as we will see in Chapter 4, part B.2, *infra*, a state court's lack of subject matter jurisdiction can sometimes be challenged collaterally. However, in most confession of judgment cases, the defendant is (like Leidholm) challenging the clause not on the basis that it is facially invalid, but rather on the ground that any waiver of the right to be heard was not knowing, voluntary or intelligent. This is a much more fact-specific inquiry that must normally be raised in the court that rendered the original judgment, rather than collaterally. *See AKF, Inc. v. Upcountry Services of Sharon, Inc.*, 2020 WL 1172156, at *4 (Conn. Super. Ct. Feb. 5, 2020) (claim that N.Y. confessed judgment was fraudulently obtained must be raised in N.Y. courts); *Watts v. R.E. Michel, LLC*, 2019 WL 2167381, at *5 (W. Va. May 20, 2019) (validity of Md. judgment pursuant to confession of judgment clause must be challenged in Md. courts); *Funding Metrics LLC v. Owens*, 2018 W.L. 6252436, at *2 (Ariz. Ct. App. Nov. 22, 2018) (challenge to validity of N.Y. confessed judgment must be made in N.Y. courts).

Page 285. Insert after last paragraph.

Where a plaintiff uses trickery or fraud to lure a defendant into the forum state in order to effect service of process, courts sometimes merely quash service, rather than dismiss the action, particularly where it is clear that plaintiff can properly re-serve the defendant before the statute of limitations has run. But if a statute is tolled only by proper service, dismissal for improper service may prove fatal if in the interim the statute has run. Rather than making such statute of limitations inquiries in these cases, many courts simply dismiss the action, thereby forcing plaintiff to refile. In *Esebag v. Whaley*, 2018 WL 8131221 (C.D. Calif. Dec. 10, 2018), for example, the court dismissed the action under Federal Rule 12(b) (5) ("insufficient service of process") where trickery and fraud were used to lure defendants from Arkansas to California in order to effect service of process one week before the extended deadline for service was to run, even though their presence was not necessary for acquiring personal jurisdiction. Courts are particularly "chary of trickery used to induce a defendant to enter a foreign jurisdiction . . . when such trickery impedes the orderly settlement of disputes before they reach the courts." *Coyne v. Grupo Indus. Trieme, S.A. de C.V.*, 105 F.R.D. 627, 629 (D.D.C. 1985). This element was also present in *Esebag*, for defendants were told that their presence was desired to discuss settlement of the underlying dispute. 2018 WL 8131221 at *1.

Service of Process and Notice

Page 299. Insert new Problem 3-11(a) before Problem 3-12.

3-11(a). The District of Columbia participates in the federal Medicaid program which, among other things, provides free prescription drug coverage to needy individuals. Because private pharmacies work with the District in making drugs available to Medicaid recipients, the pharmacies engage in governmental action that is subject to the same Due Process constraints as apply to the District itself. Under District law, if a pharmacy denies a Medicaid recipient's claim for prescription drug coverage, it is not obligated to inform the recipient as to why coverage was denied (to the extent the pharmacist knows), or to inform the recipient that they may request a hearing before the District to challenge the denial. If the pharmacist denies a Medicaid claim, the individual may still obtain the drug by paying out-out-pocket. If they later prevail at an administrative hearing, they will recover their out-of-pocket costs for the drug. The District has been sued by a group of Medicaid recipients who claim that under the Due Process Clause, they are entitled to: (1) written on-the-spot notice from the local pharmacist explaining why Medicaid coverage was denied to the extent the pharmacist knows; (2) written on-the-spot notice from the local pharmacist of their right to request a hearing; (3) detailed notice from the District as to why coverage was denied; and (4) immediate reinstatement of drug coverage from the date a hearing is requested until a hearing decision is rendered. How should the court rule on plaintiffs' claims, and why? *See NB ex rel. Peacock v. District of Columbia*, 682 F.3d 77 (D.C. Cir. 2012); *NB v. District of Columbia*, 34 F. Supp. 3d 146 (D.D.C. 2014); *NB ex rel. Peacock v. District of Columbia*, 794 F.3d 31 (D.C. Cir. 2015); *N.B. v. District of Columbia*, 244 F. Supp. 3d 176 (D.D.C. 2017); *Maldonado v. District of Columbia*, 2019 W.L. 6877913 (D.D.C. Dec. 16, 2019).

SUBJECT MATTER JURISDICTION

IV

Page 321. Insert after Note 2.

3. *Other statutory grounds of jurisdiction.* Our focus is on the scope of statutory "arising under" jurisdiction, *i.e.*, on those jurisdictional statutes that include an express arising-under component. Some jurisdictional statutes, however, use different language to confer federal question jurisdiction. For example, the statutory basis for jurisdiction in *Osborn v. United States*, discussed *supra*, at 306-308, provided that the second Bank of the United States could "'sue and be sued, plead and be impleaded, answer and be answered, defend and be defended, in . . . any Circuit Court of the United States.'" 22 U.S. (9 Wheat.), at 817. The Court held that this language conferred federal question jurisdiction over any suit brought by or against the Bank. But such "sue and be sued" language will confer subject matter jurisdiction only if the statutory text specifically references federal courts (as in *Osborn*) and does not include any language that qualifies that reference. *See Lightfoot v. Cendant Mortgage Corp.*, 137 S. Ct. 553, 560-561 (2017) (statutory text allowing a specific entity to "sue and be sued . . . in any court of competent jurisdiction, State or Federal" does not itself confer federal question jurisdiction over suits against that entity, as the phrase "competent jurisdiction" implies an existing basis of subject matter jurisdiction).

Page 343. Insert at the end of "A Note on the Citizenship of Artificial Entities":

Consistently with the above, in *Americold Realty Trust v. Conagra Foods, Inc.*, 577 U.S. 378 (2016), the Supreme Court held that the citizenship of an unincorporated real estate investment trust was to be measured by the citizenship of each of its member shareholders.

Page 366. Insert at end of Note 4.

In deciding whether a statute suffices to overcome the presumption that each party, win or lose, must pay their own attorneys' fees, "Congress must provide a sufficiently 'specific and explicit' indication of its intent to overcome the American Rule's presumption against fee shifting." *Peter v. Nantkwest, Inc.*, 140 S. Ct. 365, 372 (2019). While the lack of an express reference to "attorneys' fees" is not necessarily fatal, it is likely to be dispositive. A statute that simply allows recovery of "costs" or "expenses" – or even of "all expenses" – is not by itself enough to "authorize recovery of attorney's fees." *Id.* at 372-373. It is thus only in very clear cases that attorneys' fees may be taken into account in determining the amount in controversy.

Page 366. Insert after Note 5.

PROBLEM

4-13(a). Bucksar was a guest at The Cape Cod Guest House in Provincetown, Massachusetts, owned by Mayo. On August 8, 2008, while on the landing at the rear entrance to the Guest House, and while opening the storm door to allow her sister to enter, Bucksar fell off the landing and injured herself. The accident was alleged to have been caused by the size of the landing relative to how wide the door opens, the lack of a railing on the landing, defendant's failure to "properly inspect, maintain, repair and/or warn the plaintiff about the hazardous condition of the landing," and violations of applicable Massachusetts Building Codes. As a result of the accident, Bucksar sustained various physical injuries. She has sued Mayo in a United States District Court, invoking that court's diversity jurisdiction and seeking $150,000 in damages. As to the damages, she alleged medical bills more than $13,000 and loss of wages and earning capacity of at least $9,000. She based the balance of her demand for damages on pain and suffering and on the allegation that she will never experience the level of mobility she enjoyed prior to the accident, a fact that has caused a demoralizing effect on her mental well-being. More specifically, Bucksar's complaint alleges, in addition to the initial pain and suffering, that she suffers continuing "significant, constant, and daily pain," inability "to raise her left arm above the shoulder level," and "permanent partial spinal impairment of 25% of the whole body." The complaint includes supporting medical opinions from several doctors who diagnosed and treated her. Mayo has filed a motion to dismiss pursuant to Fed. R. Civ. P. 12(b)(1), arguing Bucksar has failed to satisfy the amount in controversy requirement. How should the District Court rule on that motion? Stated somewhat differently, under what standard should the District Court assess the monetary value of her alleged injuries? See *Bucksar v. Mayo*, 2011 WL 13254244 (October 24, 2011); see also *Torres v. Doctors Center Hospital Manati*, 2012 WL 1952833 (May 30, 2012) (applying legal certainty test to a claim asserting emotional distress).

Page 391. Insert at the end of the first partial paragraph.

That privilege does not extend to a defendant brought into the case on a counterclaim. *Home Depot U.S.A. Inc. v. Jackson*, 139 S. Ct. 1743 (2019). In other words, under § 1441, only the defendants on the claim asserted by the plaintiff are entitled to the privilege of removal.

Page 394. Insert at end of first full paragraph, and before section e.

If a state court ignores the command of § 1446(d) and continues to act in a removed case while it is still pending before the federal court, any such state court proceedings are null and void. The Supreme Court recently confronted such a case in *Roman Catholic Arch. of San Juan, Puerto Rico v. Acevedo Feliciano*, 140 S. Ct. 365 (2020) (per curiam). There, a suit was removed from a Puerto Rico court to the federal district court where it remained until remanded five months later. During that five-month period, the Puerto Rico court continued to issue orders in the case. The Supreme Court, noting that the federal removal statutes apply to the courts of Puerto Rico in the same way that they apply to state courts, went on to explain:

> Once a notice of removal is filed . . . [t]he state court "los[es] all jurisdiction over the case, and, being without jurisdiction, its subsequent proceedings and judgment [are] not . . . simply erroneous, but absolutely void." *Kern v. Huidekoper*, 103 U.S. 485, 493 (1881). "Every order thereafter made in that court [is] *coram non judice*," meaning "not before a judge." *Steamship Co. v. Tugman*, 106 U.S. 118, 122 (1882); Black's Law Dictionary 426 (11th ed. 2019). See also 14C C. Wright, A. Miller, E. Cooper, J. Steinman, & M. Kane, Federal Practice and Procedure § 3736, pp. 727–729 (2018).

140 S. Ct. at 700. Because the Puerto Rico court "issued its . . . orders after the proceeding was removed . . . but before the federal court remanded the proceeding back to the Puerto Rico court," the latter "[a]t that time . . . had no jurisdiction over the proceeding. The orders are therefore void." *Id.*

Page 406. Insert after Problem 4-27.

4-28. Brown, formerly employed as a mortgage underwriter by People's United Bank ("PUB"), a Connecticut corporation, filed a suit against PUB in a Connecticut Superior Court asserting state-law claims for unjust enrichment, negligent infliction of emotional distress, wrongful termination, and breach of the covenant of good faith and fair dealing. In his complaint, Brown cited the Fair

Labor Standards Act, a federal statute, as an example of "numerous important public policies embodied in statutory provisions concerning payment of wages." PUB removed the case to federal court and then filed a Rule 12(b)(6) motion to dismiss the complaint for failure to state a claim, arguing that FLSA preempted all of the plaintiff's state law claims. May the district court rule on PUB's Rule 12(b)(6) motion? *See Fracasse v. People's United Bank*, 747 F.3d 141 (2d Cir. 2014).

VENUE, TRANSFER, AND FORUM NON CONVENIENS

V

*Page 419. Insert as an additional paragraph at the end of the text before
PROBLEMS.*

The patent venue statute, 28 U.S.C. §1400(b), which provides the exclusive
means for establishing venue in patent infringement cases, provides that "[a]ny
civil action for patent infringement may be brought in the judicial district where
the defendant resides, or where the defendant has committed acts of infringement and has a regular and established place of business." In *TC Heartland LLC
v. Kraft Foods Group Brands LLC*, 137 S. Ct. 1514 (2017), the Supreme Court
held, in the context of a domestic corporation, that the definition of corporate
residence found in §1391(c) did not apply to §1400(b). Instead, for purposes of
§1400(b), a domestic corporation resides only in its place of incorporation, which
had been the rule prior to the adoption of §1391(c).

JOINDER OF CLAIMS AND PARTIES

VIII

Pages 643-645. Replace Burlington Northern Railroad Co. v. Strong *and Note 1.*

PROBLEMS

8-2(a). MGD is a corporation organized and existing under the laws of the State of Delaware, with its principal place of business in Illinois. A & A is a corporation organized and existing under the laws of, and has its principal place of business in, the Commonwealth of Pennsylvania. MGD sued A & A in a United States District Court, invoking that court's diversity jurisdiction. The complaint asserted two similar but factually distinct rights of action. Count I of the complaint alleged that in August 2015, MGD entered a contract by which MGD agreed to sell and A & A agreed to buy certain equipment; that A & A executed an installment note to cover the cost of the equipment under which it agreed to pay to MGD the amount of $222,103 in monthly installments; and that A & A has defaulted on that obligation, for which MGD seeks $45,000 in arrears. Count II of the complaint alleges a similar pattern premised on a contract for the sale of additional goods entered in March 2018, under which A & A executed a second installment note obligating it to pay MGD the sum of $93,390 in monthly installments. MGD alleges that A & A has defaulted on that note with an arrearage of $47,250. In short, MGD demands judgment against A & A in the aggregate sum of $92,250 plus interest and costs. Do the federal rules permit MGD to file these factually distinct claims in a single proceeding? If so, would MGD be permitted to aggregate its claims against A & A for purposes of establishing subject matter jurisdiction? See *MGD Graphic Systems, Inc. v. A & A Bindery, Inc.*, 76 F.R.D. 66 (E.D. PA 1977) (similar facts under a lower amount in controversy requirement).

8-2(b). Rossi was indicted by a grand jury in the Southern District of New York in June of 2000. The indictment alleged that Rossi conspired with others to sell shares of a publicly traded company to union pension funds by bribing union officials, thereby committing securities fraud, wire fraud, and violations of the RICO statute. Shortly after his indictment, Rossi hired the Firm to represent him in the criminal case. Rossi and The Firm entered into a retainer agreement under which Rossi agreed to pay the Firm's customary hourly rate and any expenses incurred using experts on his behalf. Rossi was acquitted of all charges. Thereafter he refused to pay the Firm's fees and expenses. The Firm, joined by the experts who had not been paid, sued Rossi in a United States District Court to recover the unpaid fees and expenses. In that proceeding, the Firm represented itself and the experts. The district court granted summary judgment for the plaintiffs on all claims and the circuit court affirmed. Rossi has now sued the Firm, seeking to recover substantial damages for breach of fiduciary duty and fraud, claiming he was harmed by the Firm entering into agreements with experts on his behalf, by The Firm's failure to forward the experts' invoices to him for his approval, and by representing the experts against him in the fee-collection proceeding. The Firm has filed a Rule 12(b)(6) motion to dismiss pursuant to Rule 13(a). How should the court rule? *See Rossi v. Wohl*, 633 F.Supp.2d 270 (N.D. Tex. 2009)

Pace v. Timmermann's Ranch and Saddle Shop Inc.
795 F.3d 748 (7th Cir. 2015)

RIPPLE, Circuit Judge.

In 2011, Timmermann's Ranch and Saddle Shop ("Timmermann's") brought an action against its former employee, Jeanne Pace, for conversion, breach of fiduciary duty, fraud, and unjust enrichment. It alleged that Ms. Pace had stolen merchandise and money from the company. Ms. Pace filed her answer and a counterclaim in early 2011.

In 2013, Ms. Pace and Dan Pace, her husband, filed a separate action against Timmermann's and four of its employees, Dale Timmermann, Carol Timmermann, Dawn Manley, and Tammy Rigsby (collectively "the individual defendants"). They alleged that these defendants had conspired to facilitate Ms. Pace's false arrest. Ms. Pace alleged that, as a result of their actions, she had suffered severe and extreme emotional distress. Mr. Pace claimed a loss of consortium.

Ms. Pace filed a motion to consolidate these two actions. The court granted the motion with respect to discovery, but denied the motion with respect to trial and instructed Ms. Pace that she should request consolidation for trial after the close of discovery. In the midst of discovery, however, the district court dismissed Ms. Pace's 2013 action after concluding that her claims were actually compulsory counterclaims that should have been filed with her answer to the company's 2011 complaint. Ms. Pace appeals the dismissal of her 2013 action and the court's denial of her motion to consolidate.

We hold that Ms. Pace's claims against parties other than Timmermann's were not compulsory counterclaims because Federal Rules of Civil Procedure 13 and 20, in combination, do not compel a litigant to join additional parties to bring what would otherwise be a compulsory counterclaim. We also hold that because Ms. Pace's claim for abuse of process against Timmermann's arose prior to the filing of her counterclaim, it was a mandatory counterclaim. We therefore affirm in part and reverse in part the judgment of the district court and remand the case for further proceedings.

Joinder of Claims and Parties

I. BACKGROUND

A.

The issues in this case present a somewhat complex procedural situation. For ease of reading, we first will set forth the substantive allegations of each party. Then, we will set forth the procedural history of this litigation in the district court.

1.

Timmermann's boards, buys, and sells horses, as well as operates both a ranch and a "saddle shop," in which it sells merchandise for owners and riders of horses. When this dispute arose, Carol and Dale Timmermann managed Timmermann's. Dawn Manley and Tammy Rigsby were employees of Timmermann's.

In its 2011 complaint, Timmermann's alleged that, while employed as a bookkeeper at Timmermann's, Ms. Pace had embezzled funds and stolen merchandise. According to the complaint, beginning at an unknown time, Ms. Pace regularly began removing merchandise from Timmermann's without paying; she would then sell those articles on eBay for her personal benefit. Timmermann's further alleged that it discovered that Ms. Pace was selling items on eBay through a private sting operation.

According to the complaint, in February 2011, a Timmermann's employee discovered some of the company's merchandise in Ms. Pace's car. At this point, Timmermann's fired Ms. Pace. Thereafter, during a review of its records, including the checking account maintained by Ms. Pace, Timmermann's discovered that a check that Ms. Pace had represented as being payable to a hay vendor actually had been made payable to cash. Timmermann's also discovered that, on at least eight occasions, Ms. Pace had utilized the company's business credit card to make personal purchases.

2.

In her 2013 complaint, Ms. Pace alleged that her conduct while working at Timmermann's was consistent with its usual course of business. She stated that Timmermann's had a practice of allowing employees to use cash to purchase merchandise at cost or, alternatively, by deducting the merchandise's value from the employee's pay. She maintains that she had purchased the company's merchandise under that established practice. She also alleged that Carol Timmermann, her supervisor, knew that she had sold the company's merchandise at flea markets and never had objected.

Ms. Pace also maintained that she was instructed to write corporate checks out to cash and to note the payee in the check records. Pursuant to those instructions, Ms. Pace had written checks to cash and recorded the payee and purpose of the check in the check records. Ms. Pace further alleged that Carol Timmermann had instructed her to use Carol's credit card, which was used as the corporate credit card, for personal purchases and to reimburse Carol, and not Timmermann's, for those purchases.

According to Ms. Pace's complaint, on February 14, 2011, Dale Timmermann called the Lake County, Illinois, Sheriff's Office and accused Ms. Pace of stealing over $100,000 in merchandise from Timmermann's. On February 14 and 15, Dale Timmermann took affirmative steps to convince the Sheriff's Office to arrest Ms. Pace by stating that Ms. Pace had stolen approximately $100,000 in merchandise and that Ms. Pace had been changing inventory on the computer. Ms. Pace was taken into custody by the Lake County Sheriff's Office on February 15, 2011, and released on February 16.

Following her release from custody, the individual defendants continued to provide the Sherriff's Office with information about Ms. Pace's allegedly unlawful conduct. On March 13, 2012, the State's Attorney brought charges against Ms. Pace premised on the information provided by the company's employees. Ms. Pace was charged with theft, forgery, and unlawful use of a credit card.

B.

We turn now to the procedural history of this litigation in the district court, a history that produced the situation before us today.

On March 3, 2011, Timmermann's filed its civil complaint against Ms. Pace, alleging conversion, breach of fiduciary duty, fraud, and unjust enrichment. It sought to recover the value of the merchandise and money that Ms. Pace allegedly had stolen. Ms. Pace filed her answer and counterclaims on April 5, 2011.

On February 1, 2013, Ms. Pace and Mr. Pace (collectively "the Paces") filed a complaint against Timmermann's and the individual defendants, alleging that they had conspired to facilitate Ms. Pace's false arrest. Ms. Pace alleged that she had suffered severe and extreme emotional distress; Mr. Pace claimed a loss of consortium. Specifically, the Paces' complaint included seven counts: "false arrest/false imprisonment/in concert liability" (Count I); "abuse of process" (Count II); "intentional infliction of emotional distress" (Count III); "conspiracy to commit abuse of process and intentional infliction of emotional distress" (Count IV); "in concert activity" (Count V); "aiding and abetting abuse of process and intentional infliction of emotional distress" (Count VI); and "loss of consortium" (Count VII). Only four counts, Counts I-III and Count VII, listed Timmermann's as a defendant. The remaining counts were directed at Dale and Carol Timmermann or the other individual defendants.

On March 15, 2013, Ms. Pace filed a motion to consolidate the two cases. On April 2, 2013, the district court consolidated the cases for the purpose of discovery and pretrial practice. The court denied without prejudice the motion to consolidate the cases for trial; it stated that it would rule on a motion to consolidate for trial after discovery.

Joinder of Claims and Parties

On May 2, 2013, Timmermann's and the individual defendants moved to dismiss Ms. Pace's action under Federal Rules of Civil Procedure 12(b)(6) and 13(a). They contended that her allegations should have been filed as compulsory counterclaims in the 2011 action. Thereafter, Ms. Pace moved to amend her 2011 counterclaim and to consolidate the cases for trial. The district court set a briefing schedule for the company's motion to dismiss and held Ms. Pace's motion to consolidate in abeyance.

In December 2013, the district court granted the company's motion to dismiss. The court concluded that Ms. Pace's separate claims were barred because they were compulsory counterclaims that should have been brought in the 2011 action because the claims arose out of the same transaction or occurrence. Noting that her 2013 complaint had indicated that the fear of being indicted caused her emotional distress, the court held that Ms. Pace's claims were in existence when the 2011 action was filed; it therefore rejected Ms. Pace's argument that her abuse-of-process claim was not in existence until she was charged. In the district court's view, the absence of Mr. Pace and the individual defendants from the 2011 action did not preclude the court's conclusion that Ms. Pace's claims were compulsory counterclaims because Mr. Pace and the individual defendants could have been joined in the 2011 action under Federal Rule of Civil Procedure 20.

II. DISCUSSION

The Paces now appeal the dismissal of the 2013 action. They concede that Ms. Pace's false arrest and emotional distress claims against Timmermann's were compulsory counterclaims and therefore properly dismissed. They contend, however, that Ms. Pace's claims against the individual defendants and Mr. Pace's claims for loss of consortium were not compulsory counterclaims. They also submit that Ms. Pace's abuse of process claim against Timmermann's did not "exist" when the 2011 action was filed and therefore could not have been a compulsory counterclaim. . . .

A.

Federal Rule of Civil Procedure governs compulsory counterclaims. Rule 13(a)(1) provides:

> *In General.* A pleading must state as a counterclaim any claim that—at the time of its service—the pleader has against an opposing party if the claim:
> (A) arises out of the transaction or occurrence that is the subject matter of the opposing party's claim; and
> (B) does not require adding another party over whom the court cannot acquire jurisdiction.

The text of this subsection limits the definition of compulsory counterclaim to those claims that the pleader has against *an opposing party*; it does *not* provide for the joinder of parties. Instead, in a later subsection, it expressly incorporates the standards set out for the required joinder of parties under Rule 19 and the permissive joinder of parties under Rule 20. Specifically, subsection 13(h) provides: "Rules 19 and 20 govern the addition of a person as a party to a counterclaim or crossclaim."

Rule 19 *requires* that a party be joined if, "in that person's absence, the court cannot accord complete relief among existing parties," or if proceeding in the party's absence may "impair or impede the person's ability to protect [his] interest" or "leave an existing party subject to a substantial risk of incurring double, multiple, or otherwise inconsistent obligations." Fed.R.Civ.P. 19(a)(1). In contrast, Rule 20 *allows* for parties to be joined if "any right to relief is asserted against them jointly, severally, or in the alternative with respect to or arising out of the same transaction, occurrence, or series of transactions or occurrences; and . . . any question of law or fact common to all defendants will arise in the action."

The district court did *not* hold, and Timmermann's does *not* contend, that the individual defendants named in Ms. Pace's complaint were opposing parties under Rule 13(a) in the 2011 action. Nor does the company's claim that the individual defendants were required parties under Rule 19. Instead, Timmermann's submits that, because the district court *could* have acquired jurisdiction over the individual defendants and *could* have joined them under Rule 20, it was appropriate to treat Ms. Pace's claims as compulsory counterclaims. In essence, Timmermann's combines the permissive joinder rule under Rule 20 with the compulsory counterclaim requirement in Rule 13 to create a rule for compulsory joinder.

The text of the rules, however, do not permit such an arrangement. Timmermann's relies on the text of Rule 13(a)(1)(B), which provides that a claim is not a compulsory counterclaim if it "require[s] adding another party over whom the court cannot acquire jurisdiction." From this statement, Timmermann's devises that, because the district court could have exercised jurisdiction over the individual defendants, the claims against them must be brought as compulsory counterclaims. Rule 13, however, does not *require* the joinder of parties. Its scope is limited to the filing of counterclaims. Although Rule 13(a)(1(B), like Rule 19, encourages that all claims be resolved in one action with all the interested parties before the court, Rule 13 fulfills this objective by allowing, not mandating, that a defendant bring counterclaims that require additional parties. Whether a *party must* be joined in an action continues to be governed only by Rule 19. Rule 13(a)(1)(B) does not transform Rule 20 into a mandatory joinder rule. . . .

Requiring Ms. Pace to bring the claims against the individual defendants as a counterclaim in the initial action might well serve judicial economy, but the Federal Rules of Civil Procedure do not require such a result. The Rules strike a delicate balance between (1) a plaintiff's interest in structuring litigation, (2) a defendant's "wish to avoid multiple litigation, or inconsistent relief," (3) an outsider's interest in joining the litigation, and (4) "the interest of the courts and the public in complete, consistent, and efficient settlement of controversies." The rules generally allow for a plaintiff to decide who to join in an action. A plaintiff's interest in structuring litigation is overridden only when the prejudice to the defendant or an absent party is substantial and cannot be avoided. Otherwise, the threat of duplicative litigation generally is insufficient to override a plaintiff's interest in this regard.

Indeed, if Ms. Pace had brought her claim before Timmermann's filed suit, she could have chosen to file separate actions against Timmermann's and the individual defendants. It makes little sense to *require* Ms. Pace to join the individual defendants under Rule 20 in order to bring all of her claims in the same action when, if she initially had been the plaintiff, she would not have been required to join those same parties.

. . . . Therefore, because a party is not *required* to join additional parties under Rule 13 or 20, the district court erred by barring Ms. Pace's claims against the individual defendants and Mr. Pace's claims for failing to join them when she brought her counterclaim.

B.

We turn now to whether the district court appropriately characterized Ms. Pace's claim against Timmermann's for abuse of process as a compulsory counterclaim. Ms. Pace submits that her abuse of process claim did not exist until there was "process" in the form of an information or indictment. She contends that the facts alleged in the 2013 complaint that occurred before she was charged only demonstrated one element of the claim, the defendants' mens rea. "In order to be a compulsory counterclaim, Rule 13(a) requires that a claim . . . exist at the time of pleading. . . ." Thus, "a party need not assert . . . a compulsory counterclaim if it has not matured when the party serves his answer."

Under Illinois law, "[t]he *only* elements necessary to plead a cause of action for abuse of process are: (1) the existence of an ulterior purpose or motive and (2) some act in the use of legal process not proper in the regular prosecution of the proceedings." Although neither an indictment nor an arrest is a necessary element to bring an abuse of process claim under Illinois law, a plaintiff is required to plead some improper use of legal process. To satisfy this requirement, a plaintiff must plead facts that "show that the process was used to accomplish some result that is beyond the purview of the process." In most circumstances, this requirement is met through an arrest or physical seizure of property.

Ms. Pace was arrested on February 15, 2011. The company's 2011 complaint was filed on March 3, 2011, and Ms. Pace filed her answer and counterclaim on April 5, 2011. Consequently, the only fact not in Ms. Pace's possession at the time she filed her answer was the March 13, 2012 information. Illinois courts are clear, however, that an arrest is sufficient to bring an abuse of process claim. Ms. Pace's abuse of process claim therefore matured when she was arrested, which occurred before she filed her responsive pleading. Her failure to raise the abuse of process claim as a counterclaim along with her answer therefore contravenes Rule 13.

Indeed, in alleging an abuse of process, Ms. Pace primarily relies on her 2011 arrest, and not on the fact that she was charged. The complaint alleges that the defendants intentionally injured and caused injury to Ms. Pace by giving "false information to law enforcement and explicitly or implicitly urg[ing] the arrest and/or the indictment of [Ms. Pace]." The complaint makes it clear that Ms. Pace could have brought her claim following her 2011 arrest, and thus, her abuse of process claim matured at that time.

Because we conclude that the district court erred in dismissing both Ms. Pace's claims against the individual defendants and Mr. Pace's claims, we need not address the party's arguments about Ms. Pace's motion to consolidate. The district court will have the opportunity to consider the motion to consolidate on remand.

CONCLUSION

We conclude that the district court erred in dismissing the Paces' 2013 complaint in its entirety. Because neither Rule 13 nor Rule 20 provide for compulsory joinder, Ms. Pace's claims against the individual defendants and Mr. Pace's claims for loss of consortium were not compulsory counterclaims. Ms. Pace's abuse of process claim against Timmermann's was in existence when Ms. Pace filed her 2011 answer and counterclaim, and therefore the district court was correct to bar her subsequent abuse of process claim against Timmermann's. The judgment of the district court is therefore affirmed in part and reversed in part and the case is remanded for proceedings consistent with this opinion. Ms. Pace may recover her costs in this appeal.

NOTES AND QUESTIONS

1. *Distinguishing* Jerris Leonard. There were two separate Rule 13 issues presented in *Timmermann's*. What were those issues and how did they differ from the Rule 13 issues presented and resolved in *Jerris Leonard*? With respect to the Paces' claims against Timmermann's (the entity), was the logical relationship test satisfied? Would it have been satisfied with respect to her claims against the individual defendants? If so, why weren't those claims deemed compulsory?

* * *

Page 651. Insert after Problem 8-3.

8-3(a). On October 1, 1971, Montgomery Ward and Juster, owners of contiguous parcels of land, entered a contract providing for an enclosed shopping mall to be built on this land. The contract if Juster would maintain the common areas and in turn Montgomery Ward would make periodic payments to Juster as compensation for the maintenance. Several years later, Juster's accountant determined that Montgomery Ward was not paying the amount required by the contract. Juster sued Montgomery Ward in a United States District Court, properly invoking that court's diversity jurisdiction and claiming that Montgomery Ward owed more than it had been paying. The plain language of the contract would sustain Juster's claim, but Montgomery Ward argued that the language of the contract was inconsistent with the parties' intent. Nonetheless, the District Court entered judgment for Juster. Montgomery Ward then filed its own diversity suit against Juster in federal court, seeking a reformation of the contract to the original intent of the parties, the subject clause being a drafting error that was inconsistent with the parties' intent. Under the Federal Rules, should Montgomery Ward be permitted to proceed with this lawsuit? See *Montgomery Ward Development Corp. v. Juster*, 932 F.2d 1378 (1991).

Page 651. Insert after the introductory paragraph on Crossclaims.

PROBLEM

8-3(b). Blair was employed by the Railroad Company as an electric lineman. He was injured while working on the steel work of a catenary bridge, when a high-speed drill he was operating burst and a fragment struck his eye causing permanent partial loss of vision. He sued the Railroad Company and the Drill Company that provided the drill. He charged negligence on the part of the Railroad Company in the operation and control of the drilling machine and catenary bridge, in the furnishing of a defective drill, in failing to exercise ordinary care to provide a safe place to work, in failing to provide a mask or goggles for his use, and in adopting an unsafe and dangerous method for performing the work on which he was engaged. He charged negligence on the part of the Drill Company in manufacturing and supplying a drill which was defective and unsafe when used for the purpose for which it was intended, with knowledge of such purpose; failing to temper and inspect the drill; and selling a drill not reasonably fit for the purpose for which it was intended, thereby breaching its statutory warranty of fitness. The Railroad Company filed an answer admitting employment of plaintiff but denying all allegations of negligence on its part. It also filed a crossclaim against the Drill Company alleging that the drill involved was a new one, purchased from the Drill Company in reliance on its skill and judgment in the manufacture of such devices, and repeating plaintiff's allegations of negligence on the part of the cross-defendant. The Drill Company filed an answer denying all allegations of negligence on its part. It also filed a motion to strike the crossclaim on the ground the crossclaim was premature in that no liability had yet been established against the Railroad Company. How should the District Court rule on the Drill Company's motion to strike? In answering this question, read Fed. R. Civ. P. 13(g) carefully to determine if the claim filed by the Railroad Company falls within the terms of that rule. See *Blair v. Cleveland Twist Drill Co.*, 197 F.2d 842 (7th Cir. 1952).

Page 658. Insert as the last sentence in Note 2.

Other courts following *Harrison* have been equally oblivious to the subject matter jurisdiction ramifications of joinder. See *Pierre v. T&K Express, Inc.*, 2017 WL 4102119 (E.D. La. Sept. 15, 2017). You, of course, will not be.

Page 660. Insert before Exxon Mobil Corp. v. Allapattah Services, Inc.

PROBLEM

8-4(a). Plaintiff Courthouse News Service specializes in reporting news about ongoing civil litigation. Defendant Shaeffer is the Clerk for the Circuit Court for the City of Norfolk, Virginia, and Defendant Smith is the Clerk for the Circuit Court for Prince William County, Virginia. Plaintiff contends that Defendants employ common "policies and practices . . . of withholding complaints from the press and the public until after administrative processing" and that such a delay violates Plaintiff's rights under the First Amendment freedom of the press. Plaintiff alleges that only sixteen percent (16%) of civil complaints filed in Norfolk Circuit Court are made available on the same day that they are filed, with fifty percent (50%) being delayed three (3) days or longer. Plaintiff goes on to allege that only twenty-seven percent (27%) of complaints filed in Prince William County Circuit Court are made available on the same day that they are filed, with forty percent (40%) being delayed three (3) days or longer. These delays, argues Plaintiff, deprive the media and public of First Amendment rights to contemporaneous access to civil filings. Defendants have filed a motion to dismiss the claim against Smith on a theory that her joinder as a co-defendant was improper under Fed. R. Civ. P. 20. How should the District Court rule on this motion? To answer that question, you must attend carefully to the text of Rule 20. See *Courthouse News Service v. Schaeffer*, 429 F. Supp. 3d 196 (E.D. Va. 2019).

Page 673. Insert after Problem 8-8.

8-8(a). Isabel, a resident of Oklahoma, was driving a rented Phoenix SUV on Interstate 10, along with her brother Juan, a resident of Arizona. She lost control of the vehicle, resulting in a rollover and in the deaths of both Isabel and Juan.

Maria, the mother of Isabel and Juan and the guardian of Isabel's children, has filed a wrongful death action on behalf of the children against Phoenix, Inc., the manufacturer of the vehicle, and Haul Y'all, Inc., the rental agency. Isabel's children reside with Maria in Oklahoma. Phoenix is an Arizona corporation; Haul Y'all is a Delaware corporation with its headquarters in Ohio. Would joinder of these defendants be proper under Rule 20? Assuming it would, Maria has now filed a joint motion with Ruby, Juan's wife, to allow Maria to amend her complaint to join Ruby as a co-plaintiff seeking to vindicate Juan's rights pursuant to Rule 20. Would Ruby's joinder be proper under Rule 20? If so, would the court have subject matter jurisdiction over Ruby's claim? Would you reach a different conclusion if Maria had sued only Phoenix? See *Barragan v. General Motors LLC*, 112 F. Supp. 3d 544 (W.D. Tex. 2015).

Page 674. Insert after the final paragraph on page 674.

PROBLEM

8-8(b). Norfolk Southern Railway Company ("NSR") filed a diversity suit against Smoker Craft, Inc., alleging that a Smoker Craft employee caused a collision with an NSR train. More specifically, Norfolk alleged that the driver of a Smoker Craft semi-tractor was towing a "Lowboy" trailer loaded with three pontoon boats and three outboard motors. While on route to his intended destination, the driver was diverted due to construction by the Indiana Department of Transportation (INDOT). He didn't follow the INDOT-recommended detour. Instead, he drove his truck over the Van Buren Street railroad crossing and bottomed out the trailer. While stuck on the tracks, the driver exited the vehicle and called 911. He allegedly didn't call Norfolk's direct emergency telephone number posted on the crossing's gate mechanisms. Several minutes later, a southbound Norfolk train (two locomotives and 64 railcars) struck the trailer. In response to NSR's complaint, Smoker Craft filed a counterclaim against NSR, charging the latter with negligence in the maintenance of the railroad crossing. Smoker Craft joined the Town of Leesburg to that claim on the theory that the Town was jointly and severally liable for the negligent maintenance of the railroad crossing. The Town has filed a motion to dismiss, arguing that it was improperly joined in the case since Smoker Craft was not seeking indemnity from it. How should the District Court rule on that motion? See *Norfolk Southern Railway Co. v. Smock, Inc.*, 2020 WL 306532 (N.D. Ind. June 6, 2020).

Page 687. Insert after Note 4.

5. *Crossclaims between a defendant and a third-party defendant.* Courts are split on whether a third-party defendant joined under Rule 14 is a co-party

within the meaning of Rule 13(g) (crossclaims between co-parties). *See Luyster v. Textron, Inc.*, 266 F.R.D. 54 (S.D.N.Y. 2010) (answering the question in the affirmative); *Nye v. Hilo Medical Center*, 2010 WL 931926 (D. Hawaii March 11, 2010) (answering the question in the negative).

Page 687. Insert after Problem 8-11.

8-11(a). On October 27, 2010, Punko was driving a tractor trailer and was making a delivery to TAM. Pursuant to his delivery instructions, Punko was required to pull into TAM's parking lot, turn around in the rear of the building, and pull out of the parking lot in a forward-facing position. But, at the time of delivery, Punko was unable to pull into TAM's lot because there was no room for his trailer. As a result, Punko was forced to back his tractor trailer into the lot in order to make the delivery. While backing the trailer into the lot, Punko blocked the center lane of State Route 29. A car traveling northbound on Route 29 struck the trailer and the driver was seriously injured. The injured driver filed a tort action against various defendants, including Punko and TAM. The action settled for $6,900,000 which was paid in its entirety by National Specialty Insurance ("NSI"). NSI has now filed a diversity suit against TAM seeking TAM's proportionate share of the settlement. In response, TAM has filed a Rule 14 claim against Punko for contribution as a joint tortfeasor. Under the applicable state law, TAM is entitled to contribution only if Punko is a joint-tortfeasor and if TAM has paid (or will be required to pay) more than its pro-rata share of the claim at issue. Punko has filed a motion to dismiss TAM's Rule 14 claim. How should the district court rule on Punko's motion? Assume that subject matter jurisdiction is satisfied as to all claims. *See National Specialty Ins. Co. v. Tunkhannock Auto Mart, Inc.*, 2017 WL 6405737 (M.D. Pa. Dec. 15, 2017).

Page 697. Insert as an additional paragraph to Note 3.

In *Town of Chester, New York v. Laroe Estates, Inc.*, 137 S. Ct. 1645 (2017), the Supreme Court held that "an intervenor of right must have Article III standing in order to pursue relief that is different from that which is sought by a party with standing." *Id.* at 1651. This means that a proposed intervenor seeking such additional relief must allege, with respect to that relief, that a party to the litigation has caused it to suffer a legally recognized and redressable injury. Was the relief sought by the Group in *Great Atlantic* identical to that sought by the Town or was all or some of that relief additional? To the extent that the relief was additional, do you think that the Group would have satisfied the requirements of Article III standing?

Page 698. Insert as new paragraph at the end of Note 5.

A person or entity that did not initially seek to intervene in a district court proceeding, perhaps because it was clear their interests were then being adequately represented, may seek to intervene for the first time under Rule 24(a)(2) if the party representing their interests loses the case and decides they don't want to appeal. *See Food Marketing Inst. v. Argus Leader Media*, 139 S. Ct. 2356, 2362 (2019) (appellant properly allowed to intervene as defendant in district court after the original defendant lost and decided not to appeal, where intervenor appellant met Article III standing requirements).

Page 703. Insert after Problem 8-15.

8-15(a). Recall the facts of Problem 8-8a: Isabel and her brother Juan were killed when the rented vehicle in which they were riding rolled over. Maria, the mother of Isabel and Juan and the guardian of Isabel's children, filed a wrongful death action on behalf of the children against the manufacturer of the vehicle and the rental agency. Complete diversity was satisfied. Problem 8-8a asked you to consider the potential joinder of Ruby, Juan's spouse, under Rule 20. Suppose instead that Ruby, seeking to file a wrongful death action on her husband's behalf, filed a timely motion to intervene under Rule 24. Would Rule 24 require or permit Ruby's joinder? If so, would the court have subject matter jurisdiction over her claim? *See Barragan v. General Motors LLC*, 112 F. Supp. 3d 544 (W.D. Tex. 2015). Can you distinguish this scenario from that in *Mattel?*

Page 707. Insert before Indianapolis Colts v. Mayor and City Council of Baltimore.

PROBLEM

8-15(b). This case arises from a dispute over the proceeds of a $400,000 Servicemembers' Group Life Insurance (SGLI) plan issued by Prudential Insurance, a Connecticut corporation, and held by decedent Robert. Robert, a member of the U.S. Navy, met Shelly while he was stationed in Florida. They married shortly thereafter and purchased a home in Florida. Robert was then posted to Hawaii, but before leaving he completed an SGLI Election Form in which he designated his mother, Barbara, a resident of Lexington, Kentucky, and Sally, a resident of Florida, as equal, co-beneficiaries of a $400,000 life insurance policy. Sally followed Robert to Hawaii, but the couple soon separated, and she returned to their home in Florida. Robert then obtained a copy of the SGLI Election Form, and in the section titled "Beneficiaries and Payment Options," drew a line through Sally's name, her relationship to him (wife), and her designated share. He initialed the alteration, signed at the bottom of the form, and dated it. He did not alter the writing designating Barbara a 50% beneficiary of the life insurance policy. One year later, Robert died. In determining entitlement to the proceeds under the policy, Prudential concluded that the designation of beneficiaries on Robert's SGLI was an "unclear designation," and by letter so notified Barbara and Sally. The letters offered them release forms, by which they could simultaneously propose and authorize distribution of the proceeds. But Barbara, who claimed entitlement to the entire $400,000, and Sally, who claimed entitlement to $200,000, were unable to agree on the appropriate distribution. Prudential then filed an interpleader action in the United States District Court for the Eastern District of Kentucky, which embraces Lexington, Kentucky, naming Barbara and Sally as adverse claimants to the policy proceeds. It deposited the proceeds of the policy with the court. Is this a proper interpleader action? Think in terms of stake, stake holder and adverse claimants. Are the subject matter jurisdiction standards of rule interpleader satisfied? If the action proceeds under rule interpleader, would venue be proper in the Eastern District of Kentucky, and would the claimants both be subject to personal jurisdiction there (assuming no waiver)? Would the subject matter standards of statutory interpleader be satisfied? Would venue be proper in the Eastern District of Kentucky, and would the claimants both be subject to personal jurisdiction there (assuming no waiver)? See *Mudd v. Yarbrough*, 786 F. Supp 2d 1236 (E.D. Ky. 2011) (upholding interpleader on slightly different procedural posture).

Page 712. Insert after Problem 8-16.

8-16(a). In 2008, the Prudent Insurance, Inc. ("PI"), a Connecticut corporation, issued a $500,000 life insurance policy to John. John designated his adult daughter Kara as the primary beneficiary. At the time, John resided with his daughter in New York. John subsequently married Sheryl and moved with her to Florida. Shortly thereafter, he submitted a form to PI designating Sheryl as the primary beneficiary under the policy. In 2013, John and Sheryl were divorced but remained domestic partners. John passed away the next year. Sheryl then filed a claim with PI for the death benefit due under the policy. Kara notified PI that the second form was completed either without John's consent or while John was incompetent and asserted her right to the death benefit. When PI refused to accede to Sheryl's claim, she instituted a diversity action against PI in a United States District Court seeking to enforce her rights under the policy. PI responded with a counterclaim in interpleader naming Kara as a defendant on the counterclaim. Sheryl has filed a motion to dismiss the interpleader. How should the court rule? *See Jacques v. Prudential Ins. Co. of Am.*, 2016 WL 3746538 (M.D. Fla. July 12, 2016).

Page 730. Insert at the end of the NOTES AND QUESTIONS.

Maldonado-Viñas v. National Western Life Ins. Co.
862 F.3d 118 (1st Cir. 2017)

TORRUELLA, Circuit Judge.

Defendant-appellant National Western Life Insurance Co. ("National Western") appeals from a judgment in favor of Plaintiffs Damaris Maldonado-Viñas ("Maldonado"), Juan Carlos Iglesias Maldonado, and José Carlos Iglesias Maldonado (collectively, "Plaintiffs") that invalidated two life insurance annuity policies. National Western argues that: (1) the beneficiary of the two annuities was a necessary party under Fed. R. Civ. P. 19, even though National Western had already paid him; (2) one annuity policy was not void even though the application was not executed in accordance with National Western's internal policies; and (3) the second annuity policy was not void under Puerto Rico law solely because it was processed by an insurance agent who was not licensed by the Office of the Commissioner of Insurance of the Commonwealth of Puerto Rico.

We vacate the judgment and remand for further findings concerning the necessity of joining the beneficiary under Rule 19.

I. BACKGROUND

A. Factual Background

At the time of his death on November 2, 2011, Carlos Iglesias-Álvarez ("Carlos" or "the decedent") had been married to Maldonado for about twenty-two years. Plaintiffs Juan Carlos Iglesias Maldonado and José Carlos Iglesias Maldonado are the children of Maldonado and Carlos. Plaintiffs are Carlos's legal heirs.

This case primarily concerns defects in the execution of two life insurance annuity policies which Carlos purchased through National Western. On April 30, 2011, Carlos purchased a life insurance policy through National Western ("Annuity No. 1"). Two days later, on May 2, 2011, Carlos purchased a second policy. Due to issues with the execution of that policy, it was cancelled by National Western and reissued ("Annuity No. 2"). Under both policies, Carlos named his brother, Francisco Iglesias-Álvarez ("Francisco") as the sole beneficiary.

Carlos paid $1,467,500 each, a total of $2,935,000, for the annuities. Both policies contained defects in their execution. The agent who issued Annuity No. 1 on National Western's behalf was not licensed by Puerto Rico Office of the

Commissioner of Insurance. Annuity No. 2 was not executed in accordance with National Western's internal policies. Despite these defects, National Western issued the two policies on April 30, 2011 and June 7, 2011.

After Carlos's death on November 2, 2011, Francisco mailed a claim form to National Western seeking benefits from Annuity No. 2. National Western informed Francisco that he was also the beneficiary of Annuity No. 1 and that he needed to submit a second claim form and some additional information. Francisco mailed the requested information on February 9, 2012. National Western paid Francisco the benefits from the annuities on February 23, 2012 and March 13, 2012.

On April 24, 2015, three years after National Western had paid Francisco the benefits from the annuities and more than a year after Plaintiffs sued National Western, Francisco submitted a document in which he claimed to be "Francisco J. Iglesias," the owner of Annuity No. 2, and attempted to ratify the policy. All communications were between Francisco's residence in Spain and Western National's office in Texas.

B.   Procedural History

Plaintiffs sued National Western in the U.S. District Court for the District of Puerto Rico on March 11, 2014, seeking a declaration that the policies were void and a return of the premiums paid by Carlos. On May 12, 2014, National Western filed a motion to dismiss because Plaintiffs failed to join a necessary party, Francisco. The district court issued an Opinion and Order denying that motion on November 10, 2014. Shortly after, National Western answered the complaint and filed a motion for reconsideration, which the district court also denied.

On December 16, 2015, the parties filed motions for summary judgment. On March 31, 2016, a magistrate judge granted Plaintiffs' motion for summary judgment and denied National Western's motion. National Western's motion for reconsideration was denied on May 5, 2016. National Western timely appealed.

II.   ANALYSIS

. . . .

Relying on Delgado v. Plaza Las Americas, Inc., 139 F.3d 1 (1st Cir. 1998), the district court ruled that even though National Western "would certainly have paid out double on the annuities" if two different courts reached different conclusions about whether the policies were void, that would not subject it to double obligations. In Delgado, a woman sued a shopping center in state court after she was raped on the shopping center's premises. Id. at 2. Separately, her father brought a diversity action in federal court seeking damages for the emotional pain he suffered as a result of his daughter's rape. Id. The district court ruled that the daughter must be joined if feasible under Rule 19(a) because otherwise the shopping center might face inconsistent obligations. Id. It reasoned that the shopping center might be found liable to the father in the federal action, but not to the daughter in the state action, or vice versa, even though the father's claims were derivative of the daughter's. Id. at 3. We reversed, reasoning that:

> where two suits arising from the same incident involve different causes of action, defendants are not faced with the potential for double liability because separate suits have different consequences and different measures of damages . . . [and] the mere possibility of inconsistent results in separate actions does not make the plaintiff in each action a necessary party to the other.

Id.

Rule 19(a)(1)(B)(ii) requires the joinder of a person if feasible where that unjoined person's interest creates a substantial risk that an existing party will be subject to double or multiple obligations. There was no such risk in Delgado for a very simple reason: even if the absent daughter had been joined, the shopping center may well have been liable to both the father and the daughter. The shopping center's complaint was that it might be liable to one or the other, when logically it should only be liable to both or neither. The fact that the case was divided, however, could never result in it owing obligations to more parties than it ever would in a single action. Thus, the absent daughter's interest could not increase the shopping center's potential liability from the incident as a whole.

Here, however, Francisco's interest might do just that. In a single action, the policies could never be void as to Plaintiffs—thus obliging National Western to return the premiums—but not void as to Francisco—thus obliging National Western to pay him benefits. But where, as here, Francisco is not a party, National Western may well be subject to both obligations. The issue is not that two courts may reach inconsistent conclusions, it is that by reaching those conclusions, National Western may be subject to double obligations.

The district court, however, reasoned that National Western might be unable to recover from Francisco even if the policies were void because Francisco "could possibly assert a defense that but for National Western's negligence, the annuities would have remained valid." If National Western could never obtain a return of the benefits it paid to Francisco even if the policies are void, then it would not, in fact, be subject to double obligations. Rather, it would owe an obligation to Plaintiffs because the policies were void, but it would be unable to collect from Francisco because of its own negligence, an entirely different theory, and one that could apply in either a consolidated or a separate case.

Neither the district court nor Plaintiffs, however, cite any authority to support the district court's assertion. We have not found any Puerto Rico case directly on point, but "[a]s a general rule, if an insurer pays a loss as a result of fraud or a mistake as to facts which would have been a sufficient defense in an action by the insured upon the policy, the money so paid may be recovered." Francisco's alternative defenses are therefore no sure thing, and he would almost certainly argue that the policies are not void in any separate action. In addition, although the district court found that the policies were void, there remains a "substantial risk" that a different court would decide otherwise, and so subject National Western to "double . . . obligations."

"[I]t is the object of courts to prevent the payment of any debt twice over." Harris v. Balk, 198 U.S. 215, 226 (1905). Rule 19(a)(1)(B)(ii)'s preference for the joinder of parties in order to avoid double or multiple obligations furthers that purpose. Because, as the district court recognized, National Western might have to "pa[y] out double on the annuities," and there is a substantial risk that this would occur if Francisco was not joined, Francisco was a person required to be joined if feasible under Rule 19(a).

Because Francisco was a person required to be joined if feasible under Rule 19(a), and the parties agree that he could not feasibly be joined because the district court lacked personal jurisdiction over him, the district court should have "determine[d] whether, in equity and good conscience, the action should [have] proceed[ed] among the existing parties or should [have been] dismissed." Fed. R. Civ. P. 19(b). The district court, however, never reached this step.

The parties' briefs contain some discussion of the Rule 19(b) analysis. We grant deference to a district court's Rule 19(b) determinations, however, and the decision is ultimately an equitable one, "steeped in pragmatic considerations." Here, the district court has not exercised its discretion. Nor has it made findings on important issues such as whether another court in Texas, Spain, or elsewhere could obtain jurisdiction over both National Western and Francisco, and so provide Plaintiffs with an adequate remedy in another forum. We therefore decline to reach the Rule 19(b) issue in the first instance.

III.   CONCLUSION

Because Francisco was a person required to be joined if feasible under Rule 19(a), we **vacate** the district court's judgment and **remand** to the district court to determine whether it is nevertheless equitable for the case to proceed without him. Each party is to bear its own costs.

NOTES AND QUESTIONS

1. *Two Courts, Two Conclusions.* Which of the two courts—the District Court or the Court of Appeals—got it right? Is the Court of Appeals' solution a pragmatic one or is it based on equitable principles?

Page 745. Insert after Problem 8-23.

8-23(a). Boone, a resident of Louisiana, purchased a new Eldorado Cadillac from Duplessis Cadillac, Inc., a Louisiana corporation. After the car suffered several engine problems and had been repeatedly serviced by Duplessis without success, Boone brought a diversity suit in a United States District Court against General Motors Corp., a Michigan corporation, the manufacturer of the vehicle. Boone's complaint alleged "design defect and internal vices," rendering the vehicle unfit for its intended purpose. General Motors moved to dismiss for Boone's failure to join Duplessis Cadillac, allegedly an indispensable party whose joinder would destroy the District Court's diversity jurisdiction. In making this motion, General Motors asserted that the so-called design defects could have been a product of the poor servicing by Duplessis, and that Duplessis might well be liable to it for any damages awarded to Boone. How should the District Court rule on this motion? *See Boone v. General Motors Acceptance Corp.*, 682 F.2d 552 (5th Cir. 1982).

CLASS ACTIONS

IX

Page 783. Insert as an additional paragraph at the end of "A Note on Class Actions and the Statute of Limitations."

In *China Agritech, Inc. v. Resh*, 138 S. Ct. 1800 (2018), the Supreme Court held that the tolling principle established in *American Pipe* would not apply to subsequently filed class actions filed by members of a putative class that was denied certification:

> The question presented in the case now before us: Upon denial of class certification, may a putative class member, in lieu of promptly joining an existing suit or promptly filing an individual action, commence a class action anew beyond the time allowed by the applicable statute of limitations? Our answer is no. *American Pipe* tolls the statute of limitations during the pendency of a putative class action, allowing unnamed class members to join the action individually or file individual claims if the class fails. But *American Pipe* does not permit the maintenance of a follow-on class action past expiration of the statute of limitations.

138 S. Ct. at 1804.

Page 805. Insert after Note 4:

5. *Employee collective actions.* The decision in *Wal-Mart* does not foreclose collective actions by employees who assert that their employer has engaged in an illegal employment practice. For example, in *Tyson Foods, Inc. v. Bouaphakeo*, 136 S. Ct. 1036 (2016), employees at a specific meat-processing plant operated by Tyson Foods brought a class action against Tyson, claiming that its refusal to compensate them for time spent "donning and doffing" protective gear violated the overtime-pay provisions of the Fair Labor Standards Act ("FLSA"). Note that the plaintiffs' suit challenged a specific practice at a specific facility—quite unlike the nationwide Title VII claim at issue in *Wal-Mart*. The primary common question that pervaded the collective action against Tyson was "whether time spent donning and doffing the required protective gear is compensable work under the FLSA." *Id.* at 1046. Based on that common question, which would necessarily have a common answer, the district court certified the class. At trial, the district court allowed the employees to rely on statistical or representative evidence to

establish the amount of time each had spent donning and doffing protective gear. At the Supreme Court, Tyson argued that reliance on statistical or representative evidence defeated the commonality requirement. The Supreme Court disagreed. Whether such evidence could be used in a collective action depended on the nature of the issue presented and the relevance of the evidence to that issue. More generally, the Court explained, if an individual suing the employer could use such evidence under similar circumstances, then a class representative could do the same. In concluding that an individual could rely on statistical or representative evidence under the circumstances presented, the Court emphasized that Tyson had unlawfully failed to keep records of the time spent by each employee donning and doffing. *Id*. at 1047. There was, therefore, no other way the employees could prove their case. *Tyson Foods* certainly does not undermine the ruling in *Wal-Mart*; it does, however, suggest a modest window of opportunity for more narrowly circumscribed employee-based collective actions.

APPELLATE REVIEW

XII

Page 1046. Insert at the end of first paragraph in Section B. 1.

See *Hall v. Hall*, 138 S. Ct. 1118 (2018) (in the context of cases consoli-dated under FED. R. CIV. P.42(a), a judgment in one case that is otherwise final is appealable and does not lose that status by virtue of the non-finality of the case with which it was consolidated).

Page 1050. Insert as a new paragraph at the end of Note 5.

Without seeking an extension of time under Rule 4(a)(5), a party can in effect obtain an extension of time to appeal by filing a motion to alter or amend the court's judgment under FED. R. CIV. P. 59(e). This motion, which must be filed in the district court within 28 days after entry of judgment, gives the district court a chance to rectify its own mistakes, thereby perhaps avoiding the need for an appeal. The effect of filing a timely Rule 59(e) motion is to suspend the finality of the original judgment, so that the 30-day clock for filing an appeal does not then begin to run until the district court has disposed of the motion. *See Banister v. Davis*, 140 S. Ct. 1698, 1703 (2020) (explaining purpose and effect of Rule 59(e)).

Page 1058. Insert a new Problem 12-1(a).

12-1(a). Morton Eisen sued several brokerage houses in federal district court on behalf of a nationwide class of 3,750,000 people who had purchased and sold "odd lots" on the New York Stock Exchange, alleging that defendants violated federal antitrust and securities laws. The cost of giving individual notice to each of the 2,250,000 class members whose names and addresses were ascertainable would have been $225,000, a prohibitive amount for Eisen who stood to recover only $70 in damages. The district court therefore approved a notice scheme that would cost only $21,720, and ordered that defendants pay 90 percent of that amount, leaving Eisen with an affordable notice cost of $2,172. Defendants appealed the notice order under 28 U.S.C. § 1291, arguing that individual notice had to be given to each of the 2,250,000 class members. Eisen has moved to dismiss the appeal. Does the appeal satisfy all three components of the collateral order doctrine? *See Eisen v. Carlisle & Jacquelin*, 417 U.S. 156 (1974) (discussed in Chapter IX ("Class Actions"), at part C.2, *supra*).

Page 1062. Insert a new Problems 12-4(a).

12-4(a). Carol, a former attorney employee of New York's Office of the Attorney General (OAG), suffers from Chronic Fatigue Syndrome. Her position with OAG was terminated while she was on unpaid medical leave. She sued OAG in federal court claiming that OAG failed to reasonably accommodate her employment because of her disability, in violation of the federal Rehabilitation Act. OAG moved to dismiss the complaint for lack of subject matter jurisdiction, arguing that Carol was employed by OAG at a policymaking level, and was therefore subject to the Government Employee Rights Act (GERA) which required her to pursue her claim initially through state or federal administrative agencies, with a right of review in a federal court of appeals, rather than initiating suit in the federal district court. The district court denied OAG's motion, ruling that GERA did not apply because Carol's position was not on a policymaking level. OAG has appealed that ruling, invoking the collateral order doctrine. Carol has moved to dismiss the appeal.

    A. Is this case controlled by *Quackenbush v. Allstate Insurance Co.* (p. 1058), where defendant likewise moved to dismiss the federal case on abstention grounds, arguing that plaintiff was required to first pursue its claim in another forum?

    B. Whether or not *Quakenbush* is controlling, can OAG satisfy each of the three requirements for invoking the collateral order doctrine?

See Fisher v. New York State Dep't of Law, 812 F.3d 268 (2d Cir. 2016).

Page 1073. Insert as an additional paragraph to Note 2.

In *Microsoft Corp. v. Baker*, 137 S. Ct. 1702 (2017), the Supreme Court held that the discretionary standards of Rule 23(f) could not be avoided by voluntarily dismissing a class action after the denial of class certification. Such a tactic would, in the Court's estimation, undermine the goals of efficiency and the careful calibration of costs and benefits reflected in Rule 23(f). The Court has also held that Rule 26(f)'s 14-day limitation on filing a petition for permission to appeal a grant or denial of certification is not subject to equitable tolling. *Nutraceutical Corp. v. Lambert*, 139 S. Ct. 710 (2019).

Page 1086. Insert after "Notes and Questions".

Williams v. County of Dakota, Nebraska
687 F.3d 1064 (8th Cir. 2012)

SHEPHERD, Circuit Judge.

Charvette Williams sued the County of Dakota, Nebraska, and former sheriff's deputy Rodney Herron (Defendants), alleging Title VII violations, sexual harassment by both the employer and individual supervisors, and violation of the Equal Pay Act. The County advanced a limited offer of judgment to settle the Title VII and Equal Pay Act claims in the amount of $2,439.20 plus interest, which Williams accepted. Williams then sought an award of attorney's fees on the partial judgment, and the district court ultimately awarded $24,500 in attorney's fees to Williams in two separate orders. The district court certified its orders as final judgments under Federal Rule of Civil Procedure 54(b) so as to allow for an interlocutory appeal. Defendants now appeal, arguing that the court abused its discretion in failing to reduce the amount of the fee awards. We conclude that the district court abused its discretion by entering final judgment under Rule 54(b), and we dismiss this appeal for lack of jurisdiction.

I.

. . .

On June 12, 2009, Williams filed a complaint in state court. . . . The case was subsequently removed to federal court. . . . The second amended complaint . . . alleged claims in four separate counts: (1) the County violated Title VII by discriminating against Williams on the basis of her race and gender with respect to the terms and conditions of her employment, including pay; (2) the County, including Herron in his official capacity, violated Williams's equal protection rights by maintaining a work environment that was sexually hostile to women; (3) Herron acted in his individual capacity to violate Williams's equal protection rights by maintaining a sexually hostile work environment; and (4) the County violated the Equal Pay Act by paying female employees less than their male counterparts for similar work performed under similar conditions.

On June 29, 2010, Defendants advanced a limited offer of judgment under Federal Rule of Civil Procedure 68(a) to settle the discriminatory pay claims in Counts 1 and 4. Defendants offered $2,439.20 plus interest and "reasonable costs . . . including attorneys fees." Williams accepted the offer, and the parties agreed that Counts 2 and 3, which consisted of the sexual harassment and hostile work environment claims, would continue to be litigated. Shortly thereafter, Williams filed a motion seeking $30,940 in attorney's fees based on 88.4 hours of work at the rate of $350 per hour. Defendants filed an opposing brief, supported by an affidavit from Defendants' attorney, which argued that the rate and amount sought by Williams was excessive. The court ultimately determined that counsel for Williams performed 88 hours of work and found $250 to be a more reasonable hourly rate than $350 under the circumstances. Two days later, the court, on its own motion, awarded Williams an additional $2,500 in attorney's fees for the time spent by Williams's counsel in responding to Defendants' objection to the original motion for attorney's fees.

Defendants subsequently moved to alter or amend the two orders awarding attorney's fees, requesting that they be certified as final judgments under Federal Rule of Civil Procedure 54(b) because there was "no just reason for delay." In her response, Williams agreed that the orders should be made immediately appealable and cited the hardship to Williams's counsel if payment of the attorney's fees were delayed. The court granted the motion and amended the orders awarding attorney's fees "to include a certification that there is 'no reason for delay' pursuant to Fed. R. Civ. P. 54(b)." Defendants now appeal.

II.

Defendants argue that the district court abused its discretion by failing to limit the amount of attorney's fees. However, as an initial matter, we must determine whether we have jurisdiction to address Defendants' arguments at this time. Although both Williams and Defendants agree that Rule 54(b) certification was properly granted so as to litigate the issue of attorney's fees on appeal, the parties "may not create jurisdiction 'by waiver or consent.'" "We are obligated to consider *sua sponte* our jurisdiction to entertain a case where, as here, we believe that jurisdiction may be lacking."

"[W]e generally consider only orders that dispose of all claims as final and appealable under [28 U.S.C.] § 1291." "Rule 54(b) creates a well-established exception to this rule by allowing a district court to enter a final judgment on some but not all of the claims in a lawsuit." However, the district court may enter final judgment under this rule "only if the court expressly determines that there is no just reason for delay." Fed. R. Civ. P. 54(b). We review the court's decision to grant Rule 54(b) certification for an abuse of discretion, noting that such interlocutory appeals are "generally disfavored" and that "it is only the special case that warrants an immediate appeal from a partial resolution of the lawsuit."

When deciding whether to grant Rule 54(b) certification, the district court must undertake a two-step analysis. The court "'must first determine that it is dealing with a final judgment . . . . in the sense that it is an ultimate disposition of an individual claim.'" Second, "[i]n determining that there is no just reason for delay, the district court must consider both the equities of the situation and judicial administrative interests, particularly the interest in preventing piecemeal appeals." "Certification should be granted only if there exists 'some danger of hardship or injustice through delay which would be alleviated by immediate appeal.'" *Hayden v. McDonald*, 719 F.2d 266, 268 (8th Cir.1983) (per curiam) (citation omitted).

Appellate Review

Generally, we give substantial deference to the district court's decision to certify orders under Rule 54(b) as the district court is "'most likely to be familiar with the case and with any justifiable reasons for delay.'" However, this deference "rests on the assumption that the district court undertook to weigh and examine the competing interests involved in a certification decision." Here, the district court's analysis of the motion for Rule 54(b) certification was limited to the following sentences:

> Defendants request that the judgments be altered or amended to include a certification that there is "no reason for delay" pursuant to Fed. R. Civ. P. 54(b). Plaintiff has filed a response agreeing that this court should so amend its judgments, so that the parties can litigate the attorney fee issue on appeal. The remainder of the case will proceed to trial. The court has reviewed the request and response and finds the motion should be granted.

A detailed statement of reasons why there is "no just reason for delay" need not accompany a Rule 54(b) entry of judgment, but "where the district court gives no specific reasons, our review of that court's decision is necessarily more speculative and less circumscribed than would be the case had the court explained its actions more fully." "If, as here, a district court's decision does not reflect an evaluation of such factors as the interrelationship of the claims so as to prevent piecemeal appeals or show a familiar[ity] with the case and with any justifiable reasons for delay, we scrutinize its decision carefully."

... Because of the failure by the district court and Defendants to provide any justification for Rule 54(b) certification, we are left to draw one of two conclusions: (1) the court abused its discretion by granting certification "as a routine matter or as an accommodation to counsel," or (2) the court relied on the reasons provided in Williams's response to Defendants' motion for Rule 54(b) certification, which is the only document in the record that gives any reason why an interlocutory appeal might be warranted. Assuming that the court took the latter approach, and further assuming that we may consider Williams's response when determining our jurisdiction, we nevertheless find that the certification was in error.

In her response to Defendants' motion for Rule 54(b) certification, Williams asserted that the orders awarding attorney's fees were final because they were "ancillary to the claims for which there ha[d] been an Order and Judgment ha[d] been entered." Williams also stated that "given the length and complexity of this action," delaying payment of the fees "will create great hardship to Plaintiff's counsel." We find these reasons insufficient to justify Rule 54(b) certification. Even if we accept that each of the orders awarding attorney's fees constituted a final judgment in the sense that they were ultimate dispositions of individual claims, we cannot find any authority to support the contention that a delay in the payment of attorney's fees rises to the level of a "hardship or injustice" that is properly alleviated by interlocutory appeal. We have also found no authority suggesting that hardship experienced by counsel as opposed to a party herself is or ought to be a legitimate consideration in the Rule 54(b) analysis.

More importantly, had the court adequately considered judicial administrative interests when considering whether to grant Rule 54(b) certification, it should have determined that such interests weigh against allowing an interlocutory appeal in this case. For example, one of the major issues in the present appeal is whether the district court improperly compensated Williams for legal work that was performed on the remaining claims in Counts 2 and 3. This issue arguably turns on the extent of Williams's success in the litigation to this point and whether the settled claims and the remaining claims are related under *Hensley v. Eckerhart*, 461 U.S. 424 (1983). If Williams is ultimately successful in her remaining claims, the issue will become moot. And even if Williams is unsuccessful, the court will have the benefit of further litigation of the claims to reconsider whether Williams's remaining claims involved "a common core of facts" and were not "distinct in all respects" from her settled ones. *See Hensley*, 461 U.S. at 435, 440, 103 S. Ct. 1933.

The district court's decision also conflicts with the interest in preventing piecemeal appeals. This case has already generated two interlocutory appeals, including this one. If we were to find jurisdiction and reach the merits of this appeal, it is possible we would face yet another appeal after Williams's remaining claims are finally resolved. A future appeal might well involve the issue of attorney's fees; indeed, the district court's original order awarding attorney's fees tacitly acknowledged that the issue could reappear with regard to Williams's remaining claims when it noted that "[t]o the extent that an ultimate resolution of the case requires it, any overlap in fees [between the settled and remaining claims] can be deducted from a subsequent award." Thus, the interest in judicial economy counsels that we wait until all possible claims can be resolved in a single appeal.

The district court did not offer an adequate explanation for why there was "no just reason for delay" in entering final judgment, and as the foregoing analysis demonstrates, "this is not a case where sufficient reason for Rule 54(b) certification is evident from the record." We conclude that the district court abused its discretion in granting Rule 54(b) certification to its orders awarding attorney's fees. Accordingly, we lack jurisdiction to reach the merits of this appeal.

III.

For the foregoing reasons, we dismiss this appeal for lack of jurisdiction.

NOTES AND QUESTIONS

1. *Deference to the district court.* In *Olympia Hotels Corp.*, *supra*, Judge Posner noted that it won't always be clear how a district judge should rule on a

Rule 54(b) motion, particularly when "there is some but not complete factual overlap between nominally separate claims. . . ." In such cases, he said, an appellate court should give considerable deference to the district court's ruling, even if the appellate court might have resolved the issue differently. Did the *Williams* court give the same level of deference to the district court, or did it in effect decide the question *de novo*? Was the *Williams* court's deference at all affected by the district court's failure to explain why there was "no just reason for delay"? Who made that case in the court of appeals? Apart from the question of appellate deference, was the likelihood of there actually being an overlap in the issues raised by successive appeals the same in the two cases?

2. *No just reason for delay.* Is it enough under Rule 54(b) to show that the certified claim is separate from the remaining claims and "that there is no just reason for delay of the appeal"? The language suggests that certification is proper *unless* good reason can be shown to *disallow it.* Yet the court in *Williams* said, "Certification should be granted only if there exists 'some danger of hardship or injustice through delay which would be alleviated by immediate appeal.' *Hayden v. McDonald,* 719 F.2d 266, 268 (8th Cir.1983)." Does this suggest the opposite presumption, *i.e.,* that certification should be rejected unless good reason can be shown to *allow it*? Did the reasons that appellant's counsel gave in *Williams* meet this standard? Might the result have been different had the hardship involved appellant herself, rather than that of her lawyer? Under the approach taken in *Williams,* might the decision in *Olympia Hotels Corp.* have come out differently?

A NOTE ON PENDENT APPELLATE JURISDICTION

Under the doctrine of "pendent appellate jurisdiction," a federal court of appeals may sometimes be able to review, on interlocutory appeal, a ruling that by itself would not have been appealable, if the issue is raised in conjunction with other issues properly before the court. The doctrine's concept has been recognized by all of the federal circuits, even though the Supreme Court has so far declined to "definitively" settle "whether or when it may be proper for a court of appeals, with jurisdiction over one ruling, to review, conjunctively, related rulings that are not themselves independently appealable." *Swint v. Chambers County Comm'n,* 514 U.S. 35, 44 n.2, 50-51 (1995). The Court's concern was that "a rule loosely allowing pendent appellate jurisdiction would encourage parties to parlay . . . collateral orders into multi-issue interlocutory appeal tickets. . . ." *Id.* at 49-50.

Based upon the Court's language in *Swint,* federal circuits will "exercise pendent jurisdiction over an otherwise non-appealable issue only in two 'narrow' circumstances: (1) if it is 'inextricably intertwined' with or (2) 'necessary to ensure meaningful review of' the order properly before [the court] on interlocutory appeal." *K.W. v. Armstrong,* 789 F.3d 962, 975 (9th Cir. 2015) (quoting

Swint). For these purposes, "[a] nonappealable order is 'inextricably intertwined' with an appealable order only if determination of the pendent issue is 'essential to the resolution of properly appealed collateral orders.'" *Martin v. Howard*, 799 Fed. Appx. 815, 821 (11th Cir. 2020) (quoting *Swint*). Otherwise, the would-be pendent ruling must await a final decision in the district court before it may be reviewed on appeal.

Pendent appellate jurisdiction was exercised in *Hudson v. Hall*, 231 F.3d 1289 (11th Cir. 2000). There, a driver and two passengers brought a 42 U.S.C. § 1983 action against a police officer, alleging that he violated their 4th Amendment rights in stopping their car for failing to signal a turn. The officer moved for summary judgment on qualified immunity grounds. The district court granted the motion as it pertained to the initial traffic stop but denied it with respect to the subsequent search of plaintiffs' persons (which included looking into their pants). The officer appealed the denial of qualified immunity claim with respect to his search of the driver and passengers, while plaintiffs cross-appealed the grant of qualified immunity with respect to the initial traffic stop. The officer's appeal was proper under 28 U.S.C. § 1291, for an order denying qualified immunity is a well-recognized final decision under the collateral-order doctrine. (*See* p. 1057 n.3, *supra*.) Can you explain why plaintiffs' cross-appeal probably did not satisfy any of the interlocutory appeal standards? However, "[f]or the sake of judicial economy," the court elected to take pendent appellate jurisdiction over that claim, concluding that it was "inextricably intertwined" with the officer's appeal. As the court explained, "to decide whether every reasonable officer in Hall's position would have known that Plaintiffs had not consented voluntarily to a search of their persons, we must consider . . . whether Plaintiffs' consent (if any) was tainted by an illegal traffic stop and, more important, whether every reasonable officer would have been aware of such taint." 231 F.3d at 1294 & n.4.

PROBLEM

12-7(a). Mario, an event promoter, scheduled a performance by a well-known rapper at the Bill Harris Arena in Birmingham, Alabama, but a last-minute change forced him to change the venue to the Club Atlantis. When the rapper then failed to show up and the crowd grew angry, Mario sought to leave the Club to see what had happened to the rapper. However, he was prevented from doing so by several off-duty Birmingham police officers who had been hired to provide security at the event. They told Mario that he, rather than the Club, was responsible for paying them, and that unless he did so they would have him criminally charged with theft of services. The officers refused to let Mario leave until they were paid, but Mario could come up with only $600 in cash. At this point, Sgt. Howard of the Birmingham Police Department showed up. He threatened Mario with arrest unless he paid the officers. After it was agreed that Mario would give the officers an additional $575, his share of the event's bar sales, he was finally allowed to leave.

Mario sued the City of Birmingham, Sgt. Howard, and the Club in an Alabama federal district court. He also sued the participating police officers, whose identity he did not know, as Fictitious Defendant Officers John Doe and Jane Doe #1-10, hoping to later replace them by their names. The complaint asserted 42 U.S.C. § 1983 damages claims against the city, Sgt. Howard, and the unknown officers, alleging that they had violated his 4th Amendment right to be free from unreasonable searches. Against the Club he asserted state law claims for unjust enrichment and negligence. Eighteen months after the complaint was filed, Mario sought to amend his complaint under Rule 15(a)(2) to formally name the fictitious defendant officers, but the motion was denied. The court later granted summary judgment for defendants on all of Mario's claims, except on his § 1983 claim against Howard, who had asserted common law immunity, and on his state law claims against the Club.

Howard appealed the court's refusal to dismiss the § 1983 damages claim against him, arguing he was entitled to qualified immunity because the 4th Amendment rights he violated were not clearly established at the time.

Martin cross-appealed the court's grant of summary judgment for the city on his § 1983 damages claim, and the court's denial of his motion to amend the complaint. The court's ruling for the city was based on its finding that Howard's actions did not involve the execution of any city custom or policy. The denial of leave to amend to insert the names of the fictitious defendants was based on a variety of factors, including the fact that leave wasn't sought until 18 months after the complaint was filed.

A. On what basis will Howard argue that he has a right to immediately appeal the district court's refusal to dismiss the § 1983 claim against him?

B. Might Mario's cross-appeal qualify for immediate review under Rule 54(b)? What must Mario do to take advantage of this route? Assuming he was able to take the necessary steps, should the court of appeals find this to be a proper invocation of Rule 54(b) with respect to either: (1) the dismissal of his § 1983 claim against the city; or (2) the denial of leave to amend his complaint to replace the fictitious defendants with their actual names?

C. If Mario did not proceed under Rule 54(b), is there any other basis on which he might seek immediate review of the district court's dismissal of the § 1983 claim or its refusal to let him amend his complaint? How likely would he be to succeed here, and why?

See Martin v. Howard, 799 Fed. Appx. 815 (11th Cir. 2020).

Page 1107. Insert at end of Problem 12-9 and Before Section D.

A NOTE ON THE PROPER ROLE OF APPELLATE COURTS IN OUR ADVERSARIAL SYSTEM

We have been discussing the standard of review to be applied by a federal court of appeals in reviewing a federal district court decision. In all the material we have considered, it was assumed that in performing its appellate function, the court of appeals would review and evaluate the case based upon the evidence and arguments presented in the court below. However, there are times when an appellate court may be tempted to play a more aggressive role, one in which it may displace or considerably supplement the work of counsel. In our adversarial system, there is some legitimate room for an appellate tribunal to help shape a case or strengthen the arguments that are made. But there may come a point where the appellate court has crossed the line that distinguishes an adversarial system from one that is judicially controlled in a way that relegates counsel to a secondary role.

A recent case where that line was crossed is *United States v. Sineneng-Smith*, 140 S. Ct. 1575 (2020). While *Sineneng-Smith* involved a criminal action, the principles that the Court invoked there in setting limits on an appellate court's role apply equally in civil and criminal cases. In that case, Evelyn, the defendant, operated an immigration consulting firm. She was convicted under 8 U.S.C. § 1324, which makes it a federal crime to encourage or induce an alien to come into this country knowing their entry would be in violation of the law. Evelyn induced clients to pay her substantial fees even though she knew that their applications would be filed after the applicable federal deadline. In the district court, Evelyn argued that the statute in question did not cover her conduct, and that even if it did, it violated the Petition and Free Speech Clauses of the First Amendment as applied to the facts in her case.

On appeal to the Ninth Circuit, Evelyn repeated the arguments she made in the district court. After oral argument by the parties, the court of appeals, instead of deciding the case as presented by the parties, named three *amici* and invited them to brief and argue three issues framed by the appellate court panel, including a question Evelyn herself never raised earlier: "[W]hether the statute of conviction is overbroad . . . under the First Amendment." In the ensuing do over of the appeal, counsel for the parties were assigned a secondary role. They were allowed to file supplemental briefs, but only in response to points raised in the *amici*'s briefs, and Evelyn counsel was given only 10 of the 30 minutes allocated for oral argument to her client's side. After this second round of briefing and arguments, the Ninth Circuit issued a decision which held in accord with the invited *amici*'s arguments that § 1324 was unconstitutionally overbroad.

The Supreme Court granted cert and reversed, concluding that "the appeals panel departed so drastically from the principle of party presentation as to constitute an abuse of discretion." *Id.* at 1578. In her opinion for the Court, Justice Ginsburg explained as follows:

> In our adversarial system of adjudication, we follow the principle of party presentation. As this Court stated in *Greenlaw v. United States*, 554 U.S. 237, 243 (2008), "in both civil and criminal cases, in the first instance and on appeal . . ., we rely on the parties to frame the issues for decision and assign to courts the role of neutral arbiter of matters the parties present." In criminal cases, departures from the party presentation principle have usually occurred "to protect a *pro se* litigant's rights." *Id.*, at 244; . . . But as a general rule, our system "is designed around the premise that [parties represented by competent counsel] know what is best for them, and are responsible for advancing the facts and argument entitling them to relief." *Castro v. United States*, 540 U.S. 375, 386 (2003) (Scalia, J., concurring in part and concurring in judgment).
>
> In short: "[C]ourts are essentially passive instruments of government." *United States v. Samuels*, 808 F.2d 1298, 1301 (CA8 1987) (Arnold, J., concurring in denial of reh'g en banc). They "do not, or should not, sally forth each day looking for wrongs to right. [They] wait for cases to come to [them], and when [cases arise, courts] normally decide only questions presented by the parties." *Ibid.*

140 S. Ct. at 1579-1580.

The Court recognized that the "party presentation principle is supple, not ironclad. There are no doubt circumstances in which a modest initiating role for a court is appropriate," such as correcting a party's "evident miscalculation of the elapsed time" under a statute of limitations. *Id.* at 1579. "But this case," said the Court, "scarcely fits that bill," for "the Ninth Circuit's radical transformation of this case goes well beyond the pale." *Id.* at 1581-1582. The Court noted that while Evelyn's counsel then adopted *amici*'s overbreadth argument, "[h]ow could she do otherwise? Understandably, she rode with an argument suggested by the panel. In the panel's adjudication, her own arguments, differently directed, fell by the wayside, for they did not mesh with the panel's overbreadth theory of the case." *Id.* at 1581. The Court vacated the Ninth Circuit's judgment and remanded the case "for an adjudication of the appeal attuned to the case shaped by the parties rather than the case designed by the appeals panel." *Id.* at 1578.

Page 1108. Insert, as additional paragraphs, before the paragraph that begins "The two key statutes . . ."

In recent years, the Supreme Court's docket has shrunk a bit. During the period 2014-2018, the Court received between 7,400 and 8,000 petitions for review a year, roughly three-quarters of them in forma pauperis. The Court granted about 1 percent of the petitions, and issued full or per curiam opinions in 69 to 82 cases a year. *See* JUDICIAL BUSINESS OF THE UNITED STATES COURTS, 2020, ANNUAL REPORT, at tbl. A-1.

The Supreme Court, like all federal courts, is constrained by Article III, § 2's limitation of the federal judicial power to specifically enumerated categories of "cases" or "controversies," *e.g.*, those arising under federal law, and those between parties of diverse citizenship. *See* Chapter IV, *supra*. However, within these subject matter categories, federal courts may only decide live cases or controversies, as "distinguished from a difference or dispute of a hypothetical or abstract character; from one that is academic or moot." *Aetna Life Ins. Co. v. Haworth*, 300 U.S. 227, 240 (1937). A federal court's resolution of academic or moot matters would entail its issuing purely "advisory opinions," something implicitly prohibited by the "case" or "controversy" limitation of Article III, § 2. Because of this constraint, it may happen that after a case has reached the Supreme Court, developments occur that would render any opinion by the court purely advisory in nature. As a result, the case has become moot and must be dismissed since it no longer falls within the federal judicial power.

The Supreme Court recently addressed this situation in *New York Rifle & Pistol Association v. City of New York*, 140 S. Ct. 1525 (2020), a case challenging the constitutionality of a state gun control law. After the Supreme Court had granted cert, the state amended its law in a way that met plaintiffs' objections, thus mooting their claim for declaratory and injunctive relief. Had plaintiffs also sought monetary damages there would still have been a live "case" or "controversy," but as things stood, the case was moot. The Court therefore vacated the appellate court judgment and remanded the case, leaving open the possibility that plaintiffs could amend their complaint to add a claim for damages, thereby saving the case from having to be dismissed on mootness grounds.

Page 1109. Insert at end of 2nd to last paragraph.

The Supreme Court has accepted only four certified questions since 1946 and has accepted none since 1981. *See United States v. St. Hurbert*, 918 F.3d 1174, 1198 n.4 (11th Cir. 2019) (Wilson, J., et al., dissenting).

Page 1124. Insert a new Problem 12-13(a).

12-13(a). Atlantic Richfield is the current owner of a former copper smelting site in Montana that severely contaminated the surrounding area with arsenic and lead. The federal Environmental Protection Agency (EPA), which is charged with enforcing CERCLA, a federal environmental cleanup act, has also been working for years to restore the site. A group of neighboring property owners sued Atlantic Richfield in a Montana state court, asserting state law claims for nuisance, trespass, and strict liability, as well as a claim for restoration damages that would allow them to rehabilitate their properties. The EPA intervened and moved for summary judgment on the claim for restoration damages, arguing that it is preempted by CERCLA which allows the EPA to consider restoration measures. The trial court denied the motion, concluding that the state law damages remedy will not impair the EPA's own efforts to clean up the site in accord with CERCLA. The Montana Supreme Court affirmed and remanded the case to the trial court for further proceedings. Atlantic Richfield has petitioned the U.S. Supreme Court for review under § 1257. Is the Montana Supreme Court decision a "final judgment" within the meaning of § 1257?

A. Does the case fall within any of the *Cox Broadcasting* categories: (1) Will the state court's no-preemption ruling be conclusive or pre-ordain the outcome of further proceedings in state court? (2) Will the preemption issue survive and necessarily require decision no matter how the case proceeds on remand? (3) Is this a case where unless the Supreme Court addresses the issue now, there is no way the Court could review it later? (4) Is this a situation where the federal issue has been finally decided in the state courts and where further proceedings on remand could render Supreme Court review of the issue unnecessary, but where immediate review of the issue could be preclusive of any further litigation of the claims involved?

B. Would your § 1257 reasoning change if under Montana law, a dissatisfied party, rather than having to take an interlocutory appeal from a trial court order, can instead initiate a new, self-contained action in the Montana Supreme Court asking it to address the specific question presented? Under the latter approach, which involves a so-called petition for "writ of supervisory control," would a state high court ruling be a "final judgment" under § 1257? Why might that be so?

See Atlantic Richfield Co. v. Christian, 140 S. Ct. 1335 (2020).

Page 1125. Insert at bottom of page.

NOTES AND QUESTIONS

1. *An ironclad rule?* Based on the language of *Cardinale*, is it ever permissible under § 1257 for the Court to address and decide a question not raised, preserved, or passed upon by the state courts below? Despite the seemingly ironclad nature of the rule recited in that case, the Court has not always honored this principle. As the Court later acknowledged in *Illinois v. Gates*, 462 U.S. 213, 219 (1983):

several of our more recent cases have treated the so-called "not pressed or passed upon below" rule as merely a prudential restriction. In *Terminiello v. Chicago*, 337 U.S. 1 (1949), the Court reversed a state criminal conviction on a ground not urged in state court, nor even in this Court. Likewise, in *Vachon v. New Hampshire*, 414 U.S. 478 (1974), the Court summarily reversed a state criminal conviction on [a] ground, not raised in state court, or here. . . . The Court indicated in a footnote that it possessed discretion to ignore the failure to raise in state court the question on which it decided the case.

The *Gates* Court left open the question of "[w]hether the 'not pressed or passed upon below' rule is jurisdictional, as our earlier decisions indicate, or prudential, as several of our later decisions assume," 462 U.S. at 222, but made it clear that any exceptions to the rule—if they are ever to be allowed—would be invoked sparingly.

THE BINDING EFFECT OF
A FINAL JUDGMENT

XIII

Page 1162. Insert after Problem 13-5.

13-5(a). Adolf was shot and killed by police officers in an incident in Anaheim, California. Adolf's mother and minor child sued the city and the officers in a California federal court. Their complaint sought relief under federal civil rights laws and state tort law, both claims being premised on a theory of excessive force. The federal district court granted summary judgment in favor of the defendants on the federal claim, concluding that the police officers had not used excessive force nor acted unreasonably. It then declined to exercise supplemental jurisdiction over the state-tort claims and dismissed them without prejudice. The plaintiffs appealed the summary judgment to the Ninth Circuit and immediately filed the state claims in a California Superior Court. While the federal appeal was pending, defendants demurred in the state court proceeding on grounds of issue preclusion. The Superior Court sustained the demurrer without leave to amend and plaintiffs appealed. In the meantime, a panel of the Ninth Circuit affirmed the grant of summary judgment. The California Court of Appeal, relying on that judgment, affirmed the judgment of the Superior Court. Nine months later, after the state-court decision was no longer reviewable or subject to reconsideration, the Ninth Circuit, sitting en banc, reversed the decision of the panel and vacated the decision of the federal district court. Plaintiffs then filed a new complaint in state court reasserting their previously foreclosed state-law claims. Defendants again demurred, but this time on claim preclusion grounds. What should the trial court do? *See F.E.V. v. City of Anaheim*, 15 Cal. App. 5th 462 (Cal. Ct. App. 2016).

Page 1188. Insert after Note 4.

5. *An alternate approach to an intervening change in the law.* An intervening change in the law is sometimes treated as an equitable exception to the otherwise applicable doctrine of issue preclusion. *See Herrera v. Wyoming*, 139 S. Ct. 1686, 1697 (2019) (intervening change in the law operates as an exception to the application of issue preclusion). In other words, despite the change in the law, the issues are presumed to be the same. Nonetheless equity will prevent enforcement

of the prior determination. We think the cleaner approach is to interpret the elements of preclusion doctrine as including equitable considerations. In the immediate context, that requires a determination of whether the issues ought to be treated as the same given the change in the law. But regardless of which approach you adopt, the result should be the same: a significant change in the law will render the prior determination non-preclusive.

Page 1205. Insert before Aldrich v. State of New York.

Samara v. Matar
6 Cal.5th 322 (2018)

Cantil-Sakauye, C. J.

When a trial court judgment rests on more than one ground, it may be impossible for a losing party to obtain appellate review of all of the court's determinations. In a breach of contract action, for example, a trial court might grant a defense motion for summary judgment because no contract was formed, and because in any event there was no breach. On direct review, an appellate court could affirm if either of those conclusions was correct, without resolving or even considering the other one. Thus, a plaintiff who argues on appeal that there was a contract (and that the contract was breached) might lose based on a lack of breach without appellate review of whether a contract existed in the first place.

This case concerns the claim- and issue-preclusive significance, in future litigation, of a conclusion relied on by the trial court and challenged on appeal, but not addressed by the appellate court. We hold that the preclusive effect of the judgment should be evaluated as though the trial court had not relied on the unreviewed ground. . . .

I. BACKGROUND

A. Claim and Issue Preclusion

The law of preclusion helps to ensure that a dispute resolved in one case is not relitigated in a later case. Although the doctrine has ancient roots, its contours and associated terminology have evolved over time. We now refer to "claim preclusion" rather than "res judicata" and use "issue preclusion" in place of "direct or collateral estoppel"

Claim and issue preclusion have different requirements and effects. Claim preclusion prevents relitigation of entire causes of action. Claim preclusion applies only when "a second suit involves (1) the same cause of action (2) between the same parties [or their privies] (3) after a final judgment on the merits in the first suit." Issue preclusion, by contrast, prevents "relitigation of previously decided issues," rather than causes of action as a whole. It applies only "(1) after final adjudication (2) of an identical issue (3) actually litigated and necessarily decided in the first suit and (4) asserted against one who was a party in the first suit or one in privity with that party." Courts have understood the " 'necessarily decided' " prong to "require[ ] only that the issue not have been 'entirely unnecessary' to the judgment in the initial proceeding"—leaving room for a decision based on two grounds to be preclusive as to both.

B.   Facts and Procedural History

Plaintiff Rana Samara was missing a tooth. Dr. Haitham Matar recommended that she receive a dental implant, and Dr. Stephen Nahigian performed the implantation surgery. Samara later sued them both for professional negligence. Our focus is Samara's contention that defendant Matar is vicariously liable for former defendant Nahigian's alleged tort.

1.   First judgment, in favor of Nahigian

Nahigian moved for summary judgment. He argued, in pertinent part, that the suit against him was untimely and that he did not cause Samara's alleged injuries. The trial court agreed that the suit was untimely with respect to Nahigian (unlike Matar) and further agreed that no material factual dispute prevented judgment in Nahigian's favor on the issue of causation. The court entered judgment on both grounds.

Samara appealed. She conceded that the judgment against her could be affirmed based on the statute of limitations. Concerned about the potential preclusive effect of the trial court's determination regarding a lack of causation, however, she urged the Court of Appeal to reverse that portion of the trial court's decision. The Court of Appeal declined to do so in an unpublished opinion, stating, "We need not, and do not, reach the court's alternative ground for granting summary judgment." It added, "Because the question is not before us, we also do not address whether collateral estoppel may be used with regard to an alternative ground for judgment not reviewed by the appellate court."

2.   Second judgment, in favor of Matar

Around the time Samara noticed an appeal from the first judgment, Matar moved for summary judgment in the trial court. As relevant here, Matar argued that the court's earlier no-causation determination precluded holding him liable for Nahigian's conduct. After the remittitur issued in the first appeal, the trial court agreed, granting Matar's motion for summary judgment. Although the particulars of the trial court's reasoning are not entirely clear, the core of its rationale was that because Nahigian was not liable to Samara for his conduct, Matar could not be liable for that conduct vicariously.

The Court of Appeal, in an opinion issued by the same panel that decided the first appeal, reversed and remanded the matter. It concluded that preclusion provided no basis for the trial court's decision. The court's analysis of claim preclusion focused on whether there had been "a final judgment on the merits in the first suit." The court observed that the prior judgment was affirmed solely because of the statute of limitations, which the court believed to be a "purely procedural ground" rather than a decision on the merits. Nevertheless, the court acknowledged that under our decision in *People v. Skidmore*, 27 Cal. 287 (1865), a judgment on the merits affirmed on purely procedural grounds might qualify as a judgment on the merits in the relevant sense. Noting that "the Supreme Court [of California] might want to address" the continuing vitality of the "Civil War-era" the *Skidmore* decision, the Court of Appeal instead ruled that claim preclusion was unavailable because Samara sued Nahigian and Matar in a single lawsuit, rather than two successive suits. The court further held that *Skidmore* was inapplicable to issue preclusion, concluding that "an affirmance on an alternative ground operates as collateral estoppel/issue preclusion only on the ground reached by the appellate court."

We granted Matar's petition for review. He contends that the Court of Appeal's claim- and issue-preclusion analysis is inconsistent with *Skidmore* and asks us to "address the viability of" that 1865 decision. Because we conclude that *Skidmore* must be overruled, we agree with the Court of Appeal that Matar is not entitled to summary judgment on preclusion grounds.

II. *SKIDMORE'S* VIABILITY

A. The *Skidmore* Decision

To contextualize *Skidmore's* analysis of the preclusive effect of a particular judgment, we begin by describing the litigation resulting in that judgment.

Walter Skidmore was charged with murder. To secure his appearance to answer the charge, Skidmore and his sureties entered into a recognizance, something roughly akin to a bail bond. Skidmore also created a trust for his sureties' financial protection, pledging property toward the payment and extinguishment of the recognizance should he fail to appear. After he failed to appear, the People sued. The suit sought equitable relief against the trustee, urging that the property held in trust "be applied to the debt due by the recognizance." The trial court entered judgment against the People, and the People appealed.

We affirmed. Our opinion addressed a demurrer based on "a misjoinder of causes of action, among other [objections]." Declining to reach those other objections, we agreed that there had been a misjoinder: "It may be that the sureties will not be held liable at all; or it may be, if they are, that they are ready and willing to pay whenever their liability is declared; and in that case, there would be no necessity of coming upon this fund. If, after judgment, the defendants are insolvent, another question might arise, or the question might arise of a right to sell or subject this property as the property of Skidmore. But it is not necessary to pass upon this matter in advance of the proper stage of the inquiry." "The effect of the judgment and of this affirmance," we added, "will not be to preclude the plaintiff from suing again when the cause of action can be more formally set out."

A second suit followed. In the decision at the core of this case, we held that the People's claim was barred. In determining whether the decision in the first case barred the second suit, we treated as dictum our earlier statement that the first suit would not preclude a second one and deemed the dispositive issue whether the judgment in the first suit was "based upon the merits". We concluded that it was. The judgment entered by the trial court, we reasoned, was "based upon the merits of the claim, and not upon the dilatory matters raised by the demurrer nor any other mere technical defect." And although our affirmance had been limited to the misjoinder problem—a non-merits issue—we noted that we had not reversed or modified the trial court's judgment. As we explained, "in examining the judgment in connection with the errors assigned, [we] found that there was at least one ground upon which the judgment could be justified, and therefore very properly refrained from considering it in connection with the other errors. But the affirmance, still, was an affirmance to the whole extent of the legal effect of the judgment at the time when it was entered in the court below. [We] found no error in the record, and therefore not only allowed it to stand, but affirmed it as an entirety, and by direct expression." Treating "the judgment rendered in the first action . . . now as it was in the beginning," we held that the People's claim was barred. In doing so, we allowed a trial court's ruling to determine the preclusive effect of the judgment, without regard for whether that ruling was addressed on appeal.

Courts considering have disagreed about whether its precedential force extends to issue preclusion. It might be argued that *Skidmore* addressed only claim preclusion and that requirements unique to issue preclusion make *Skidmore* inapplicable in that context. *Skidmore* however, cannot be so easily limited. It is not enough to observe, for example, that issue preclusion applies only to issues "actually litigated and necessarily decided in the first suit", because it matters which court's decision is the focus of the inquiry. If, as in *Skidmore*, the focus of the preclusion inquiry is the trial court's decision, then an issue might have been "actually litigated and necessarily decided" whether or not an appellate court agreed with the trial court's disposition of the issue.

We need not decide exactly what *Skidmore* means for the law of issue preclusion. For present purposes, it is enough to say that *Skidmore*'s focus on the trial court's decision, without regard for the basis of the appellate court's affirmance, could reasonably be understood to bear on the issue preclusion inquiry.

B. *Skidmore's* Aftermath

Although *Skidmore* has not been widely cited, there was once broad support for the view that the preclusive effect of an affirmed judgment should be determined without regard for the basis of the affirmance.

However, courts' understanding of preclusion has evolved in the more than 150 years since *Skidmore* was decided. Although no precise turning point can or must be identified, one influential development occurred in 1942, when the Restatement First of Judgments diverged from *Skidmore*'s reasoning. The Restatement, concerning claim preclusion, conveyed that "[w]here the trial court bases the judgment for the defendant upon two alternative grounds, one on the merits and the other not on the merits, and an appellate court affirms the judgment solely on the ground which is not on the merits, the judgment does not bar a subsequent action by the plaintiff based upon the same cause of action." (Rest., Judgments (1942) § 49, com. c., p. 196. The Restatement similarly opined, in passages addressing issue preclusion, that a judgment affirmed on one of two alternative grounds "is not conclusive in a subsequent action in which the other ground is in issue" (Rest., Judgments, *supra*, § 68, com. n, p. 308), and that "[i]f the appellate court determines that one of these grounds is sufficient and refuses to consider whether or not the other ground is sufficient, and accordingly affirms the judgment, the judgment is conclusive only as to the first ground" (*id.*, § 69, com. b, p. 316). In short, the Restatement would evaluate the claim- and issue-preclusive effect of the judgment without regard for a determination relied upon by the trial court but not embraced on appeal.

The Restatement Second of Judgments, published in 1982, echoes the position of the Restatement First of Judgments with respect to issue preclusion. (See Rest.2d Judgments (1982) § 27, com. o, p. 263.) The second Restatement does not appear to take an explicit position on the claim preclusive effect of a judgment affirmed on a non-merits ground, perhaps reflecting aversion to the terminology " 'on the merits[,]' " which has "possibly misleading connotations." (*Id.*, § 19, com. a, p. 161.) Regardless, the second Restatement conveys that in the absence of an appeal, a trial court "dismissal . . . based on two or more determinations, at least one of which, standing alone, would not render the judgment a bar to another action on the same claim . . . should not operate as a bar." (*Id.*, § 20, com. e, p. 172.) Nothing in the second Restatement suggests that if such a judgment is affirmed solely on grounds that would not trigger claim preclusion, the judgment should be imbued with claim preclusive effect.

The weight of more recent authority is in accord with these Restatements, at least with respect to cases in which an appeal has been taken. (See 18 Wright et al., Fed. Practice and Procedure: Jurisdiction & Related Matters (3d ed. 2016) § 4421, p. 619 ["The federal decisions agree with the Restatement view that once an appellate court has affirmed on one ground and passed over another, preclusion does not attach to the ground omitted from its decision"]; 18A Wright et al., *supra*, § 4432, p. 60 ["the nature of the ultimate final judgment in a case ordinarily is controlled by the actual appellate disposition"]. Although most of these authorities concern issue rather than claim preclusion, their refusal to afford preclusive significance to a trial court determination that evades appellate review is informative.

C. *Skidmore's* Continuing Vitality

1. *Skidmore reflects a flawed view of preclusion*

We agree with the weight of modern authority that *Skidmore's* approach to preclusion is flawed.

Rules of claim and issue preclusion are, or at least should be, inextricably intertwined with rules of procedure. (See Rest.2d Judgments, *supra*, Introduction, pp. 5-13.) The law of preclusion reflects a view "that at some point arguable questions of right and wrong for practical purposes simply cannot be argued any more. It compels repose. In substituting compulsion for persuasion, the law of [preclusion] trenches upon freedom to petition about grievances and autonomy of action, very serious concerns in an open society." (*Id.*, at p. 11.) This finality "has to be accepted if the idea of law is to be accepted, certainly if there is to be practical meaning to the idea that legal disputes can be resolved by judicial process." (*Ibid.*) But that does not mean finality should be embraced reflexively, nor attached to every decision rendered. "The 'chance' to litigate is not simply some unspecified opportunity for disputation over legal rights; it is the opportunity to submit a dispute over legal rights to a tribunal legally empowered to decide it according to definite procedural rules." (*Id.*, at pp. 6-7.) The less robust the process involved in resolving litigation the first time, the stronger the argument for permitting litigation once more.

The availability of a direct appeal reflects a sensible determination that the process culminating in a trial court's disputed decision is not sufficient to resolve litigation conclusively. Of course, a litigant's ability to secure appellate review may be waived or forfeited, as when a litigant fails to file a timely notice of appeal or fails to make an objection in the trial court. But when a litigant properly seeks appellate review of a ground underlying a trial court's determination, the fortuity that the judgment may be sustained on some other ground should not imbue the challenged ground with final and conclusive effect. The challenged ground is no more reliable—no more deserving of finality—merely because it need not be evaluated to resolve the appeal.

Recall, for example, the hypothetical breach of contract action in which the trial court concludes that no contract existed, and that even if a contract existed, the contract was not breached. (See *ante*, 234 Cal.Rptr.3d at p. 448, 419 P.3d at p. 925.) If an appellate court agrees that any existing contract was not breached—but does not consider whether any contract existed in the first place—it would be harsh indeed to bind the plaintiff to the trial court's "no contract" determination, preventing the plaintiff from suing the defendant on the contract even for subsequent conduct that clearly would constitute a material breach. Perhaps there was a contract, perhaps not. But the trial court's answer to that question should not be final merely because the judgment could be affirmed on another ground. *Skidmore's* focus on the trial court's reasoning, however, is in tension with this conclusion.

Skidmore also is in tension with some of our other preclusion case law. We have repeatedly underscored the important role that the availability of appellate review plays in ensuring that a determination is sufficiently reliable to be conclusive in future litigation. We have, for example:

- Refused to give preclusive effect to a trial court's legal ruling on child custody issues presented by writ of habeas corpus, acknowledging that, "[s]ince an order denying an application for writ of habeas corpus is not appealable," finding preclusion would "wrongfully deprive[ ]" "the unsuccessful petitioner" "of custody until such time as he could allege a change in circumstances";
- Held that a finding made in connection with a cause of action should not have preclusive effect when the finding was adverse to the party that prevailed on that cause of action, in part because the party could not appeal;
- Embraced a rule that an entity cannot be bound by a judgment as a privy, based on alleged control over the underlying litigation, if the entity lacks control over whether to take an appeal;
- Held that at least a certain type of issue preclusion might not attach to the decision of a private arbitrator, in part because "the arbitrator's errors must be accepted without opportunity for review"; and
- Explained that, when evaluating the preclusive effect of an administrative determination, " '[t]he opportunity for judicial review of adverse rulings' is an important procedural protection against a potentially erroneous determination and is a factor to consider in determining whether collateral estoppel [(that is, issue preclusion)] applies.

The fundamental problem with *Skidmore*, then, is that it improperly gave effect to a trial court determination that evaded appellate review. Our opinion in the appeal preceding *Skidmore* considered only whether there had been a misjoinder of causes of action. We nevertheless held in *Skidmore* that the judgment at issue in the first case was "upon the merits," because of a trial court determination that we did not embrace on appeal. More than a century later, and consistent with the modern approach to preclusion described above, we now conclude that a ground reached by the trial court and properly challenged on appeal, but not embraced by the appellate court's decision, should not affect the judgment's preclusive effect. This approach aligns far better with the recognition that although trial court decisions are often thorough, thoughtful, and correct, litigants should be afforded more procedural fairness before being bound by all aspects of a trial court's challenged determination.

Matar contends, however, that *Skidmore* properly reflects the principle that a trial court's judgment is presumptively correct. This argument confuses two concepts. It is true that a trial court's judgment is presumed correct, and so ordinarily will not be set aside on appeal absent an affirmative showing of reversible error. But that principle governs how appellate courts should review trial court determinations; it does not speak to the preclusive effect, in future litigation, of a challenged trial court determination that evaded appellate review. The distinction is particularly clear under California law: Although the presumption of correctness applies while direct review is ongoing, under California law, an unsatisfied trial court judgment has no preclusive effect until the appellate process is complete.

Matar also argues that affording preclusive effect to a trial court's alternative (but ultimately unnecessary) determination would reduce litigation, thereby promoting judicial economy. We are not so sure. "While the rules of preclusion are supported in part by considerations of efficiency, affording the possibility of reconsideration is also a matter of efficiency, for it relaxes the requirements of procedural meticulousness in the first instance." (Rest.2d Judgments, *supra*, Introduction, p. 12.) To hold that an unreviewed alternative ground has preclusive effect "would put pressure on appellate courts to review alternative grounds as a matter of course . . . ." Thus, "[a]ny benefit that might result from precluding" relitigation in future cases—cases "which may or may not arise"—"would come at the cost of increasing the burden on the appellate court in the initial action."

Nor is it clear that affording preclusive effect to such an alternative ground would protect parties from the burdens of litigation, as Matar also argues. If all unreversed trial court determinations must be given preclusive effect, then nonparties, armed with the issue preclusive effect of the trial court's unreviewed determination, may be encouraged to engage in litigation with the party bound by the effectively unappealable determination.

In any event, our judicial system does not exist simply to resolve cases quickly, nor to prevent litigation from ever taking place. It is a serious matter whether a decision is correct in law and results from a fair process for all sides. Affording preclusive effect to a trial court determination that evades appellate review might speed up the resolution of controversies, but it would do so at the expense of fairness, accuracy, and the integrity of the judicial system. We decline to endorse that tradeoff.

We further observe that Matar's concerns about repetitive litigation are overstated. For one thing, if Matar had sought summary judgment on causation grounds when Nahigian did, Matar, too, would have had the benefit of the trial court's decision. Had Samara appealed, the judgment would not have been affirmed *with respect to Matar* simply because Samara's suit *against Nahigian* was untimely; the Court of Appeal would likely have confronted the merits of the trial court's no-causation ruling. In other words, Matar could have promoted judicial economy and protected himself from the burdens of further litigation simply by timely filing such a motion.

More generally, courts are not powerless to prevent a waste of judicial resources. Appellate courts can affirm on multiple grounds where appropriate. Trial courts can decline to reach issues that are unnecessary for judgment. And although, on remand, the trial court in this case should resolve Matar's motion for summary judgment without relying on the supposedly preclusive effect of the judgment in favor of Nahigian, the court need not forget or ignore the work it has already completed in this litigation. Declining to find preclusion does not require that a new judge be assigned and the case start afresh; it means only that a prior determination by itself does not necessarily, as a matter of law, bind the future one—and that the correctness of that future determination, if appealed, can be reviewed on its merits. . . .

III. NEITHER CLAIM NOR ISSUE PRECLUSION SUPPORTS THE SUMMARY JUDGMENT IN FAVOR OF MATAR

Whether the trial court erred by granting Matar's motion for summary judgment is a question of law we review de novo. We hold that it did. The critical point here is that the preclusive effect of the judgment in favor of Nahigian should be evaluated as though the trial court had not reached the causation issue. That premise implies that the causation issue was not "necessarily decided in the first suit," or even "decided" at all, rendering issue preclusion unavailable. Moreover, the Court of Appeal concluded, and Matar's briefing does not dispute, that a decision on timeliness grounds is not a decision "on the merits" in the relevant sense. Accepting that premise as undisputed (and without deciding its correctness), it follows that the ruling in favor of Nahigian was not a "final judgment on the merits," and that claim preclusion is likewise unavailable. Thus, neither claim nor issue preclusion can support the summary judgment entered in favor of Matar, and the trial court's ruling to the contrary was erroneous.

IV. DISPOSITION

We affirm the judgment of the Court of Appeal.

NOTES AND QUESTIONS

1. *Streamlining the standards.* Notice that the California Supreme Court not only overruled the decision in *Skidmore*, but more generally relied on the Restatement of Judgements in modernizing California's approach to issue preclusion. Might it eventually do the same with respect to claim preclusion? Should it?

Page 1230. Insert above Part C.

The Doctrine of Defense Preclusion

Lucky Brand Dungarees, Inc. v. Marcel Fashions Group, Inc.
140 S. Ct. 1589 (2020).

Justice SOTOMAYOR delivered the opinion of the Court.
This case arises from protracted litigation between petitioners Lucky Brand Dungarees, Inc., and others (collectively Lucky Brand) and respondent Marcel

The Binding Effect of a Final Judgment

Fashions Group, Inc. (Marcel). In the latest lawsuit between the two, Lucky Brand asserted a defense against Marcel that it had not pressed fully in a preceding suit between the parties. This Court is asked to determine whether Lucky Brand's failure to litigate the defense in the earlier suit barred Lucky Brand from invoking it in the later suit. Because the parties agree that, at a minimum, the preclusion of such a defense in this context requires that the two suits share the same claim to relief—and because we find that the two suits here did not—Lucky Brand was not barred from raising its defense in the later action.

I

Marcel and Lucky Brand both sell jeans and other apparel. Both entities also use the word "Lucky" as part of their marks on clothing. In 1986, Marcel received a federal trademark registration for "Get Lucky"; a few years later, in 1990, Lucky Brand began selling apparel using the registered trademark "Lucky Brand" and other marks that include the word "Lucky."

Three categories of marks are at issue in this case: Marcel's "Get Lucky" mark; Lucky Brand's "Lucky Brand" mark; and various other marks owned by Lucky Brand that contain the word "Lucky." These trademarks have led to nearly 20 years of litigation between the two companies, proceeding in three rounds.

A

In 2001—the first round—Marcel sued Lucky Brand, alleging that Lucky Brand's use of the phrase "Get Lucky" in advertisements infringed Marcel's trademark. In 2003, the parties signed a settlement agreement. As part of the deal, Lucky Brand agreed to stop using the phrase "Get Lucky." In exchange, Marcel agreed to release any claims regarding Lucky Brand's use of its own trademarks.

B

The ink was barely dry on the settlement agreement when, in 2005, the parties began a second round of litigation (2005 Action). Lucky Brand filed suit, alleging that Marcel and its licensee violated its trademarks by copying its designs and logos in a new clothing line. As relevant here, Marcel filed several counter-claims that all turned, in large part, on Lucky Brand's alleged continued use of "Get Lucky": One batch of allegations asserted that Lucky Brand had continued to use Marcel's "Get Lucky" mark in violation of the settlement agreement, while others alleged that Lucky Brand's use of the phrase "Get Lucky" and "Lucky Brand" together was "confusingly similar to"—and thus infringed—Marcel's "Get Lucky" mark. None of Marcel's counterclaims alleged that Lucky Brand's use of its own marks alone—*i.e.*, independent of any alleged use of "Get Lucky"—infringed Marcel's "Get Lucky" mark.

Lucky Brand moved to dismiss the counterclaims, alleging that they were barred by the release provision of the settlement agreement. After the District Court denied the motion without prejudice, Lucky Brand noted the release defense once more in its answer to Marcel's counterclaims. But as the 2005 Action proceeded, Lucky Brand never again invoked the release defense.

The 2005 Action concluded in two phases. First, as a sanction for misconduct during discovery, the District Court concluded that Lucky Brand violated the settlement agreement by continuing to use "Get Lucky" and permanently enjoined Lucky Brand from copying or imitating Marcel's "Get Lucky" mark. The injunction did not enjoin, or even mention, Lucky Brand's use of any other marks or phrases containing the word "Lucky." The case then proceeded to trial. The jury found against Lucky Brand on Marcel's remaining counterclaims — those that alleged infringement from Lucky Brand's continued use of the "Get Lucky" catchphrase alongside its own marks.

C

In April 2011, the third round of litigation began: Marcel filed an action against Lucky Brand (2011 Action), maintaining that Lucky Brand continued to infringe Marcel's "Get Lucky" mark and, in so doing, contravened the judgment issued in the 2005 Action.

This complaint did not reprise Marcel's earlier allegation (in the 2005 Action) that Lucky Brand continued to use the "Get Lucky" phrase. Marcel argued only that Lucky Brand's continued, post-2010 use of Lucky Brand's own marks — some of which used the word "Lucky" — infringed Marcel's "Get Lucky" mark in a manner that (according to Marcel) was previously found infringing.[1] Marcel requested that the District Court enjoin Lucky Brand from using any of Lucky Brand's marks containing the word "Lucky."

The District Court granted Lucky Brand summary judgment, concluding that Marcel's claims in the 2011 Action were essentially the same as its counterclaims in the 2005 Action.

But the Court of Appeals for the Second Circuit disagreed. The court concluded that Marcel's claims in the 2011 Action were distinct from those it had asserted in the 2005 Action, because the claims at issue in the 2005 Action were "for earlier infringements." As the court noted, "[w]inning a judgment . . . does not deprive the plaintiff of the right to sue" for the defendant's "subsequent similar violations."

The Second Circuit further rejected Marcel's request to hold Lucky Brand in contempt for violating the injunction issued in the 2005 Action. The court noted that the conduct at issue in the 2011 Action was Lucky Brand's use of its own marks — not the use of the phrase "Get Lucky." By contrast, the 2005 injunction prohibited Lucky Brand from using the "Get Lucky" mark — not Lucky Brand's own marks that happened to contain the word "Lucky." Moreover, the court reasoned that the jury in the 2005 Action had been "free to find infringement of Marcel's 'Get Lucky' mark based solely on Lucky Brand's use of [the phrase] 'Get Lucky.' " The court vacated and remanded for further proceedings.

On remand to the District Court, Lucky Brand moved to dismiss, arguing—for the first time since its motion to dismiss and answer in the 2005 Action—that Marcel had released its claims by entering the settlement agreement. Marcel countered that Lucky Brand was precluded from invoking the release defense, because it could have pursued the defense fully in the 2005 Action but had neglected to do so. The District Court granted Lucky Brand's motion to dismiss, holding that it could assert its release defense and that the settlement agreement indeed barred Marcel's claims.

The Second Circuit vacated and remanded, concluding that a doctrine it termed "defense preclusion" prohibited Lucky Brand from raising the release defense in the 2011 Action. Noting that a different category of preclusion—issue preclusion—may be wielded against a defendant, the court reasoned that the same should be true of claim preclusion: A defendant should be precluded from raising an unlitigated defense that it should have raised earlier. The panel then held that "defense preclusion" bars a party from raising a defense where: "(i) a previous action involved an adjudication on the merits"; "(ii) the previous action involved the same parties"; "(iii) the defense was either asserted or could have been asserted, in the prior action"; and "(iv) the district court, in its discretion, concludes that preclusion of the defense is appropriate." Finding each factor satisfied in this case, the panel vacated the District Court's judgment. We granted certiorari to resolve differences among the Circuits regarding when, if ever, claim preclusion applies to defenses raised in a later suit.

II

A

This case asks whether so-called "defense preclusion" is a valid application of res judicata: a term that now comprises two distinct doctrines regarding the preclusive effect of prior litigation. The first is issue preclusion (sometimes called collateral estoppel), which precludes a party from relitigating an issue actually decided in a prior case and necessary to the judgment.

The second doctrine is claim preclusion (sometimes itself called res judicata). Unlike issue preclusion, claim preclusion prevents parties from raising issues that could have been raised and decided in a prior action—even if they were not actually litigated. If a later suit advances the same claim as an earlier suit between the same parties, the earlier suit's judgment "prevents litigation of all grounds for, or defenses to, recovery that were previously available to the parties, regardless of whether they were asserted or determined in the prior proceeding. Suits involve the same claim (or "cause of action") when they " 'aris[e] from the same transaction,' or involve a "common nucleus of operative facts.". . .

As the Second Circuit itself seemed to recognize, this Court has never explicitly recognized "defense preclusion" as a standalone category of res judicata, unmoored from the two guideposts of issue preclusion and claim preclusion. Instead, our case law indicates that any such preclusion of defenses must, at a minimum, satisfy the strictures of issue preclusion or claim preclusion.[1] The parties thus agree that where, as here, issue preclusion does not apply, a defense can be barred only if the "causes of action are the same" in the two suits—that is, where they share a " 'common nucleus of operative fact[s].' "

B

Put simply, the two suits here were grounded on different conduct, involving different marks, occurring at different times. They thus did not share a "common nucleus of operative facts."

To start, claims to relief may be the same for the purposes of claim preclusion if, among other things, " 'a different judgment in the second action would impair or destroy rights or interests established by the judgment entered in the first action.' " Here, however, the 2011 Action did not imperil the judgment of the 2005 Action because the lawsuits involved both different conduct and different trademarks.

In the 2005 Action, Marcel alleged that Lucky Brand infringed Marcel's "Get Lucky" mark both by directly imitating its "Get Lucky" mark and by using the "Get Lucky" slogan alongside Lucky Brand's other marks in a way that created consumer confusion. . . .

By contrast, the 2011 Action did not involve any alleged use of the "Get Lucky" phrase. Indeed, Lucky Brand had been enjoined in the 2005 Action from using "Get Lucky," and in the 2011 Action, Lucky Brand was found not to have violated that injunction. The parties thus do not argue that Lucky Brand continued to use "Get Lucky" after the 2005 Action concluded, and at oral argument, counsel for Marcel appeared to confirm that Marcel's claims in the 2011 Action did not allege that Lucky Brand continued to use "Get Lucky." Instead, Marcel alleged in the 2011 Action that Lucky Brand committed infringement by using Lucky Brand's own marks containing the word "Lucky"—not the "Get Lucky" mark itself. Plainly, then, the 2011 Action challenged different conduct, involving different marks.

---

1. There may be good reasons to question any application of claim preclusion to defenses. It has been noted that in suits involving successive claims against the same defendant, courts often "assum[e] that the defendant may raise defenses in the second action that were not raised in the first, even though they were equally available and relevant in both actions." Wright & Miller § 4414. This is because "[v]arious considerations, other than actual merits, may govern" whether to bring a defense, "such as the smallness of the amount or the value of the property in controversy, the difficulty of obtaining the necessary evidence, the expense of the litigation, and [a party's] own situation." Here, however, this Court need not determine when (if ever) applying claim preclusion to defenses may be appropriate, because a necessary predicate—identity of claims—is lacking.

The Binding Effect of a Final Judgment

Not only that, but the complained-of conduct in the 2011 Action occurred after the conclusion of the 2005 Action. Claim preclusion generally "does not bar claims that are predicated on events that postdate the filing of the initial complaint." This is for good reason: Events that occur after the plaintiff files suit often give rise to new "[m]aterial operative facts" that "in themselves, or taken in conjunction with the antecedent facts," create a new claim to relief.

This principle takes on particular force in the trademark context, where the enforceability of a mark and likelihood of confusion between marks often turns on extrinsic facts that change over time. As Lucky Brand points out, liability for trademark infringement turns on marketplace realities that can change dramatically from year to year. Brief for Petitioners 42-45. It is no surprise, then, that the Second Circuit held that Marcel's 2011 Action claims were not barred by the 2005 Action. By the same token, the 2005 Action could not bar Lucky Brand's 2011 defenses.

At bottom, the 2011 Action involved different marks, different legal theories, and different conduct—occurring at different times. Because the two suits thus lacked a "common nucleus of operative facts," claim preclusion did not and could not bar Lucky Brand from asserting its settlement agreement defense in the 2011 Action. . . .

* * *

At bottom, Marcel's 2011 Action challenged different conduct—and raised different claims—from the 2005 Action. Under those circumstances, Marcel cannot preclude Lucky Brand from raising new defenses. The judgment of the Second Circuit is therefore reversed, and the case is remanded for proceedings consistent with this opinion.

It is so ordered.

NOTES AND QUESTIONS

1. *Defense preclusion endorsed?* Had the Court found that the 2005 Action and the 2011 Action arose from a common nucleus of operative facts, would the Court have held that Lucky Brands was precluded from raising the release defense in the 2011 Action? Read footnote 2 to the Court's opinion carefully. What message is the Court sending? Does *Lucky Brands* reflect a general reluctance to expand preclusion beyond its traditional boundaries? Do you see any similarity in attitude between this opinion and the Court's opinion in *Taylor v. Sturgell*, 553 U.S. 880 (2008) [Casebook, at 1165]?

Made in the USA
Las Vegas, NV
06 January 2023

65131039R00177